Y0-DKP-058

# Houghton Mifflin Mathematics

**Authors**

| | | |
|---|---|---|
| Lelon R. Capps | W.G. Quast | Mary Ann Haubner |
| William L. Cole | Leland Webb | Charles E. Allen |

**Coordinating Author**

Ernest R. Duncan

**Houghton Mifflin Company**   BOSTON

Atlanta     Dallas     Geneva, Ill.     Lawrenceville, N.J.     Palo Alto     Toronto

## Authors

**Lelon R. Capps**
University of Kansas
Lawrence, Kansas

**W. G. Quast**
Slippery Rock University
Slippery Rock, Pennsylvania

**Mary Ann Haubner**
Mount Saint Joseph College
Cincinnati, Ohio

**William L. Cole**
Michigan State University
East Lansing, Michigan

**Leland Webb**
California State College
Bakersfield, California

**Charles E. Allen**
Los Angeles Center for Enriched Studies
Los Angeles Unified School District
Los Angeles, California

## Coordinating Author

**Ernest R. Duncan**
Professor Emeritus
Rutgers University
New Brunswick, New Jersey

## Consultants

**Arlene Lyons**
Teacher
Westmeade Elementary School
Nashville, Tennessee

**Elvie Rhone**
Mathematics Resource Teacher
Coles School
Chicago, Illinois

Printed in U.S.A.

ISBN: 0-395-46214-2

CDEFGHIJ–D–9876543210

# CONTENTS

# 9 GEOMETRY, PERIMETER 249

# 10 MULTIPLICATION BY TWO-DIGIT NUMBERS 277

# 11 DIVISION WITH TWO-DIGIT DIVISORS 305

# 12 FRACTIONS 329

# 13 GEOMETRY, AREA AND VOLUME 367

1

Suppose you pick 1 hundred red tulips, 1 hundred yellow tulips, and 1 hundred pink tulips. How many tulips do you pick in all?

ADDITION AND SUBTRACTION FACTS, PLACE VALUE

# ADDITION FACTS THROUGH 18

The High Jumps are warming up for a basketball game. The team is using 6 basketballs. There are 9 basketballs still in the rack. How many basketballs are there in all?

You *add* 6 and 9 to find the total number of basketballs. You can write the addition fact in two ways.

**number sentence**
$6 + 9 = 15$

$$
\begin{array}{r}
6 \leftarrow \textbf{addend} \\
+\ 9 \leftarrow \textbf{addend} \\
\hline
15 \leftarrow \textbf{sum}
\end{array}
$$

You read *six plus nine equals fifteen.* There are 15 basketballs in all.

 **Think:** Knowing the sums of *doubles* can help you remember some facts. $7 + 7$ is a double. Its sum is 14. To find $7 + 8$, think: $7 + 8$ is 1 more than $7 + 7$, so $7 + 8 = 15$.

The **Zero Property** can help you remember some facts. The sum of zero and any number is that number.

$$0 + 8 = 8 \qquad 5 + 0 = 5$$
$$0 + 0 = 0$$

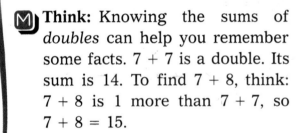

# CLASS EXERCISES

Which numbers are addends? Which number is the sum?

**1.** $9 + 4 = 13$   **2.** $3 + 6 = 9$   **3.** $6 + 6 = 12$   **4.** $5 + 2 = 7$   **5.** $4 + 6 = 10$

**6.**
$$
\begin{array}{r}
2 \\
+\ 3 \\
\hline
5
\end{array}
$$

**7.**
$$
\begin{array}{r}
0 \\
+\ 7 \\
\hline
7
\end{array}
$$

**8.**
$$
\begin{array}{r}
2 \\
+\ 9 \\
\hline
11
\end{array}
$$

**9.**
$$
\begin{array}{r}
1 \\
+\ 4 \\
\hline
5
\end{array}
$$

**10.**
$$
\begin{array}{r}
7 \\
+\ 5 \\
\hline
12
\end{array}
$$

# PRACTICE

Add.

**11.** $8 + 3$  **12.** $5 + 8$  **13.** $2 + 7$  **14.** $8 + 7$  **15.** $6 + 3$  **16.** $0 + 9$

**17.** $9 + 6$  **18.** $4 + 9$  **19.** $9 + 9$  **20.** $9 + 2$  **21.** $8 + 8$  **22.** $5 + 5$

**23.** $\begin{array}{r} 8 \\ + 5 \\ \hline \end{array}$  **24.** $\begin{array}{r} 7 \\ + 4 \\ \hline \end{array}$  **25.** $\begin{array}{r} 9 \\ + 3 \\ \hline \end{array}$  **26.** $\begin{array}{r} 6 \\ + 0 \\ \hline \end{array}$  **27.** $\begin{array}{r} 6 \\ + 8 \\ \hline \end{array}$  **28.** $\begin{array}{r} 5 \\ + 9 \\ \hline \end{array}$

**29.** $\begin{array}{r} 4 \\ + 7 \\ \hline \end{array}$  **30.** $\begin{array}{r} 3 \\ + 8 \\ \hline \end{array}$  **31.** $\begin{array}{r} 9 \\ + 7 \\ \hline \end{array}$  **32.** $\begin{array}{r} 4 \\ | \ 8 \\ \hline \end{array}$  **33.** $\begin{array}{r} 3 \\ + 7 \\ \hline \end{array}$  **34.** $\begin{array}{r} 4 \\ + 5 \\ \hline \end{array}$

Write the number sentence.

**35.** Eight plus six equals fourteen.   **36.** Seven plus nine is sixteen.

**37.** Zero plus three equals three.   ★ **38.** The sum of five and itself is ten.

★ **39.** The sum of eight and one more than eight is seventeen.

Complete.

★ **40.** $5 + \blacksquare = 8$   ★ **41.** $8 + \blacksquare = 15$   ★ **42.** $\blacksquare + 7 = 9 + 2$

Add using doubles. Write the double that helps you.

**43.** $5 + 6$   **44.** $6 + 7$   **45.** $9 + 8$   **46.** $6 + 5$   **47.** $8 + 9$

**48. Think:** How many doubles have addends less than 10?

**MENTAL MATH**

## PROBLEM SOLVING APPLICATIONS
### Using What You Know

Solve.

**49.** Robby made 7 baskets. Claire made 6 more baskets than Robby. How many baskets did Claire make?

**50.** Tammy's mother, aunt, and 3 cousins came to watch Tammy play in the game. How many people came to watch Tammy play?

★ **51.** Alfred has 4 tickets in his pocket. Brian has 5 more tickets than Alfred. How many tickets do Alfred and Brian have together?

★ **52.** Yoshi has scored 8 points. Kerry has scored 4 points. How many more points does Kerry need to score more points than Yoshi?

# ORDER AND GROUPING PROPERTIES

Here are two ideas that can help you with addition.

**Order Property of Addition**

Changing the order of the addends does not change the sum.

$$4 + 9 = 13 \qquad 9 + 4 = 13$$

**Grouping Property of Addition**

Changing the grouping of the addends does not change the sum.

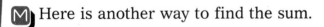

$$\boxed{\begin{array}{r} 3 \\ 2 \end{array}} \quad \begin{array}{r} 5 \\ +7 \\ \hline 12 \end{array} \qquad \begin{array}{r} 3 \\ \boxed{\begin{array}{r}2\\7\end{array}} \end{array} \quad \begin{array}{r} 3 \\ +9 \\ \hline 12 \end{array}$$

You can use parentheses to group numbers in addition. The parentheses show which numbers to add first.

$$\begin{array}{ll} (3 + 2) + 7 & 3 + (2 + 7) \\ \quad 5 \quad + 7 = 12 & 3 + \quad 9 \quad = 12 \end{array}$$

Here is another way to find the sum.

$$3 + 2 + 7$$
$$10 + 2 = 12$$

Looking for sums of 10 can help you add mentally.

## CLASS EXERCISES

Add.

| | | | | | |
|---|---|---|---|---|---|
| **1.** $7 + 5$ | **2.** $6 + 9$ | **3.** $8 + 9$ | **4.** $9 + 4$ | **5.** $8 + 3$ | **6.** $7 + 8$ |
| $5 + 7$ | $9 + 6$ | $9 + 8$ | $4 + 9$ | $3 + 8$ | $8 + 7$ |

**7.** $(2 + 3) + 1$          **8.** $(6 + 2) + 4$          **9.** $1 + (6 + 2)$
$2 + (3 + 1)$              $6 + (2 + 4)$             $(1 + 6) + 2$

# PRACTICE

Add.

| | | | | | | |
|---|---|---|---|---|---|---|
| **10.** $\begin{array}{r} 5 \\ +\,8 \\ \hline \end{array}$ | **11.** $\begin{array}{r} 8 \\ +\,2 \\ \hline \end{array}$ | **12.** $\begin{array}{r} 7 \\ +\,9 \\ \hline \end{array}$ | **13.** $\begin{array}{r} 3 \\ +\,9 \\ \hline \end{array}$ | **14.** $\begin{array}{r} 8 \\ +\,7 \\ \hline \end{array}$ | **15.** $\begin{array}{r} 7 \\ +\,6 \\ \hline \end{array}$ | **16.** $\begin{array}{r} 9 \\ +\,7 \\ \hline \end{array}$ |
| **17.** $\begin{array}{r} 6 \\ 3 \\ +\,5 \\ \hline \end{array}$ | **18.** $\begin{array}{r} 5 \\ 4 \\ +\,4 \\ \hline \end{array}$ | **19.** $\begin{array}{r} 5 \\ 1 \\ +\,8 \\ \hline \end{array}$ | **20.** $\begin{array}{r} 8 \\ 1 \\ +\,7 \\ \hline \end{array}$ | **21.** $\begin{array}{r} 7 \\ 2 \\ +\,6 \\ \hline \end{array}$ | **22.** $\begin{array}{r} 3 \\ 1 \\ +\,8 \\ \hline \end{array}$ | **23.** $\begin{array}{r} 4 \\ 5 \\ +\,2 \\ \hline \end{array}$ |

**24.** $2 + 6 + 3$    **25.** $4 + 2 + 5$    **26.** $7 + 1 + 5$    **27.** $9 + 0 + 6$

**28.** $4 + 3 + 5$    **29.** $7 + 2 + 4$    **30.** $8 + 0 + 9$    **31.** $4 + 3 + 6$

**32.** Using the numbers 5 and 8, write two number sentences to show the order property.

**33.** Using the numbers 5, 3, and 4, write two number sentences to show the grouping property.

★ **34.** Using the numbers 9 and 0, write number sentences with two addends to show two properties. Name the properties.

Add mentally. Look for sums of 10. Write only the total.

**MENTAL MATH**

**35.** $6 + 4 + 1$    **36.** $5 + 3 + 5$    **37.** $5 + 2 + 8$

**38.** $4 + 3 + 6$    **39.** $8 + 9 + 1$    **40.** $3 + 4 + 7$

**41. Think:** Is it easiest to use paper and pencil, a calculator, or mental math to solve Exercises 35–40?

## PROBLEM SOLVING APPLICATIONS
### Choosing the Operation

Solve.

**42.** Rita, her 3 brothers, and her 4 friends went to the store. How many children went to the store?

**43.** Joleen bought 5 robots at the toy store. Miguel bought 6 robots. Who bought more robots?

★ **44.** Lisa and Jay bought the same number of stuffed animals. Altogether, they bought 12 stuffed animals. How many stuffed animals did Lisa buy?

★ **45.** Erik bought 4 model cars. Cynthia bought 3 more model cars than Erik. Jacob bought 2 more model cars than Erik. How many model cars did they buy in all?

# MENTAL MATH, ONE ADDEND GREATER THAN TEN

Patterns can help you add numbers greater than 10 mentally.

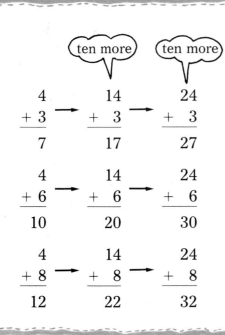

$$\begin{array}{ccc} & \text{ten more} & \text{ten more} \\ \begin{array}{r} 4 \\ +\ 3 \\ \hline 7 \end{array} \rightarrow & \begin{array}{r} 14 \\ +\ 3 \\ \hline 17 \end{array} \rightarrow & \begin{array}{r} 24 \\ +\ 3 \\ \hline 27 \end{array} \end{array}$$

$$\begin{array}{ccc} \begin{array}{r} 4 \\ +\ 6 \\ \hline 10 \end{array} \rightarrow & \begin{array}{r} 14 \\ +\ 6 \\ \hline 20 \end{array} \rightarrow & \begin{array}{r} 24 \\ +\ 6 \\ \hline 30 \end{array} \end{array}$$

$$\begin{array}{ccc} \begin{array}{r} 4 \\ +\ 8 \\ \hline 12 \end{array} \rightarrow & \begin{array}{r} 14 \\ +\ 8 \\ \hline 22 \end{array} \rightarrow & \begin{array}{r} 24 \\ +\ 8 \\ \hline 32 \end{array} \end{array}$$

You can use mental math in this way when you add 3 or more numbers.

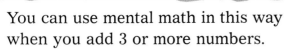

$$\begin{array}{r} \boxed{\begin{array}{r} 6 \\ 9 \end{array}} \\ +\ 8 \end{array} \quad \begin{array}{r} 15 \\ +\ 8 \\ \hline 23 \end{array}$$

$$\begin{array}{r} \boxed{\begin{array}{r} 6 \\ 9 \\ 8 \end{array}} \\ +\ 8 \end{array} \quad \begin{array}{r} \boxed{\begin{array}{r} 15 \\ 8 \end{array}} \\ +\ 8 \end{array} \quad \begin{array}{r} 23 \\ +\ 8 \\ \hline 31 \end{array}$$

# CLASS EXERCISES

Add.

**1.**
$$\begin{array}{r} 3 \\ +5 \\ \hline \end{array} \rightarrow \begin{array}{r} 13 \\ +\ 5 \\ \hline \end{array} \rightarrow \begin{array}{r} 23 \\ +\ 5 \\ \hline \end{array}$$

**2.**
$$\begin{array}{r} 7 \\ +5 \\ \hline \end{array} \rightarrow \begin{array}{r} 17 \\ +\ 5 \\ \hline \end{array} \rightarrow \begin{array}{r} 27 \\ +\ 5 \\ \hline \end{array}$$

**3.**
$$\begin{array}{r} 8 \\ +4 \\ \hline \end{array} \rightarrow \begin{array}{r} 18 \\ +\ 4 \\ \hline \end{array} \rightarrow \begin{array}{r} 28 \\ +\ 4 \\ \hline \end{array}$$

**4.** 6 + 2
26 + 2

**5.** 5 + 4
25 + 4

**6.** 7 + 3
27 + 3

**7.** 8 + 3
28 + 3

**8.** 7 + 6
27 + 6

# PRACTICE

Use mental math to add.

| | | | | | |
|---|---|---|---|---|---|
| **9.** 14 <br> + 7 | **10.** 13 <br> + 8 | **11.** 19 <br> + 7 | **12.** 18 <br> + 5 | **13.** 12 <br> + 8 | **14.** 16 <br> + 5 |
| **15.** 27 <br> + 3 | **16.** 25 <br> + 6 | **17.** 28 <br> + 7 | **18.** 24 <br> + 9 | **19.** 32 <br> + 9 | **20.** 35 <br> + 7 |
| **21.** 5 <br> 6 <br> + 7 | **22.** 8 <br> 3 <br> + 5 | **23.** 7 <br> 8 <br> + 4 | **24.** 9 <br> 5 <br> + 7 | **25.** 8 <br> 4 <br> + 6 | **26.** 6 <br> 7 <br> + 9 |
| **27.** 7 <br> 5 <br> 8 <br> + 3 | **28.** 5 <br> 7 <br> 5 <br> + 4 | **29.** 9 <br> 5 <br> 4 <br> + 2 | **30.** 7 <br> 6 <br> 2 <br> + 8 | **31.** 4 <br> 3 <br> 9 <br> + 2 | **32.** 8 <br> 5 <br> 3 <br> + 4 |

**33.** 7 + 4 + 8          **34.** 6 + 8 + 5          **35.** 7 + 5 + 9

**36.** 9 + 1 + 5 + 7      **37.** 2 + 9 + 3 + 8      **38.** 5 + 6 + 4 + 7

---

Write the answer.

| | | | | |
|---|---|---|---|---|
| **39.** 8 <br> + 2 | **40.** 4 <br> + 7 | **41.** 5 <br> + 9 | **42.** 3 <br> 6 <br> + 4 | **43.** 5 <br> 2 <br> + 7 |

**MIXED REVIEW**

---

# PROBLEM SOLVING APPLICATIONS
## Number Sentences

Write a number sentence for the problem. Then solve.

**44.** Eight chickens, four pigs, and three goats are in the barnyard. How many animals are in the barnyard?

**45.** Rena planted nine rows of peas, five rows of carrots, one row of lettuce, and two rows of beans. How many rows did she plant?

★ **46.** Thomas and Julio each run seven laps around the farm. Robin and Maria each run six laps. How many laps do they run in all?

# SUBTRACTION FACTS THROUGH 18

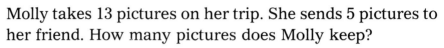

Molly takes 13 pictures on her trip. She sends 5 pictures to her friend. How many pictures does Molly keep?

*Subtract* to find how many pictures Molly keeps. Thirteen minus five equals eight.

$$13 - 5 = 8$$

difference →

$$\begin{array}{r} 13 \\ -\ 5 \\ \hline 8 \end{array}$$

Molly keeps 8 pictures.

 You know that Molly keeps fewer than 13 pictures because you are subtracting.

Subtracting zero is a special case.

### Zero Property

The difference of any number and zero is that number.

$$8 - 0 = 8$$

The difference of any number and itself is zero.

$$8 - 8 = 0$$

## CLASS EXERCISES

Write the difference.

| | | | | | |
|---|---|---|---|---|---|
| **1.** 8 − 6 | **2.** 10 − 3 | **3.** 7 − 4 | **4.** 9 − 8 | **5.** 11 − 6 | **6.** 8 − 5 |
| 8 − 2 | 10 − 7 | 7 − 3 | 9 − 1 | 11 − 5 | 8 − 3 |
| **7.** 12 − 4 | **8.** 5 − 0 | **9.** 7 − 2 | **10.** 8 − 5 | **11.** 14 − 6 | **12.** 6 − 4 |
| 12 − 8 | 5 − 5 | 7 − 5 | 8 − 3 | 14 − 8 | 6 − 2 |

## PRACTICE

Subtract.

| | | | | | |
|---|---|---|---|---|---|
| **13.** 9 − 5 | **14.** 10 − 4 | **15.** 5 − 3 | **16.** 9 − 2 | **17.** 12 − 7 | **18.** 12 − 9 |
| **19.** 8 − 7 | **20.** 11 − 7 | **21.** 8 − 1 | **22.** 8 − 4 | **23.** 10 − 6 | **24.** 13 − 4 |

| **25.** 18<br>− 9 | **26.** 11<br>− 2 | **27.** 15<br>− 7 | **28.** 12<br>− 6 | **29.** 12<br>− 3 | **30.** 14<br>− 9 |
|---|---|---|---|---|---|
| **31.** 15<br>− 6 | **32.** 12<br>− 5 | **33.** 6<br>− 0 | **34.** 10<br>− 5 | **35.** 11<br>− 8 | **36.** 9<br>− 4 |
| **37.** 14<br>− 5 | **38.** 11<br>− 4 | **39.** 10<br>− 1 | **40.** 11<br>− 9 | **41.** 14<br>− 7 | **42.** 15<br>− 9 |
| **43.** 17<br>− 9 | **44.** 11<br>− 3 | **45.** 16<br>− 8 | **46.** 13<br>− 5 | **47.** 15<br>− 8 | **48.** 13<br>− 9 |

**49.** What number can you subtract from another number more than once and still have the same answer?

Complete.

★ **50.** 16 − ▨ = 8  ★ **51.** 13 − ▨ = 5  ★ **52.** 9 − ▨ = 0  ★ **53.** ▨ − 7 = 5

Will the answer be *greater than, less than,* or the *same* as the number you start with?

| **54.** 13<br>− 4 | **55.** 8<br>+ 0 | **56.** 15<br>− 8 | **57.** 17<br>− 0 | **58.** 10<br>+ 4 |
|---|---|---|---|---|

ESTIMATE

## PROBLEM SOLVING APPLICATIONS
### Using Pictures

Use the pictures to answer.

**59.** Simon is using Clearview film. He has taken 9 pictures. How many more pictures can he take?

6 more pictures.

**60.** Lou has taken 13 pictures without changing the film in his camera. Is he using Starbrite or Clearview film?

Lou is useing clear view.

★ **61.** Mei-lin and Nora are sharing a roll of Starbrite film. Mei-lin has taken 6 pictures and Nora has taken 5 pictures. How many pictures are left?

1 more picture is left.

# FACT FAMILIES

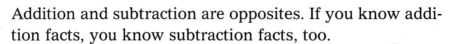

Addition and subtraction are opposites. If you know addition facts, you know subtraction facts, too.

$$7 + 5 = 12 \qquad 5 + 7 = 12$$
$$12 - 5 = 7 \qquad 12 - 7 = 5$$

These four facts make up a **fact family.**

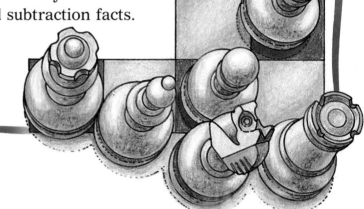

Ⓜ Fact families make it easy to memorize your addition and subtraction facts.

## CLASS EXERCISES

Add or subtract.

| | 1. | 2. | 3. | 4. | 5. |
|---|---|---|---|---|---|
| | 4 + 3 | 4 + 9 | 7 + 8 | 9 + 2 | 5 + 6 |
| | 7 − 3 | 13 − 9 | 15 − 8 | 11 − 2 | 11 − 6 |
| | 3 + 4 | 9 + 4 | 8 + 7 | 2 + 9 | 6 + 5 |
| | 7 − 4 | 13 − 4 | 15 − 7 | 11 − 9 | 11 − 5 |

6.
$$\begin{array}{r} 8 \\ + 3 \\ \hline \end{array} \quad \begin{array}{r} 11 \\ - 3 \\ \hline \end{array} \quad \begin{array}{r} 3 \\ + 8 \\ \hline \end{array} \quad \begin{array}{r} 11 \\ - 8 \\ \hline \end{array}$$

7.
$$\begin{array}{r} 9 \\ + 8 \\ \hline \end{array} \quad \begin{array}{r} 17 \\ - 8 \\ \hline \end{array} \quad \begin{array}{r} 8 \\ + 9 \\ \hline \end{array} \quad \begin{array}{r} 17 \\ - 9 \\ \hline \end{array}$$

## PRACTICE

Add or subtract.

8.
$$\begin{array}{r} 8 \\ + 5 \\ \hline \end{array}$$
9.
$$\begin{array}{r} 13 \\ - 7 \\ \hline \end{array}$$
10.
$$\begin{array}{r} 6 \\ + 7 \\ \hline \end{array}$$
11.
$$\begin{array}{r} 7 \\ + 4 \\ \hline \end{array}$$
12.
$$\begin{array}{r} 10 \\ - 2 \\ \hline \end{array}$$
13.
$$\begin{array}{r} 12 \\ - 9 \\ \hline \end{array}$$

14.
$$\begin{array}{r} 6 \\ + 4 \\ \hline \end{array}$$
15.
$$\begin{array}{r} 10 \\ - 9 \\ \hline \end{array}$$
16.
$$\begin{array}{r} 16 \\ - 9 \\ \hline \end{array}$$
17.
$$\begin{array}{r} 5 \\ + 7 \\ \hline \end{array}$$
18.
$$\begin{array}{r} 14 \\ - 7 \\ \hline \end{array}$$
19.
$$\begin{array}{r} 8 \\ + 6 \\ \hline \end{array}$$

20.
$$\begin{array}{r} 4 \\ + 7 \\ \hline \end{array}$$
21.
$$\begin{array}{r} 14 \\ - 8 \\ \hline \end{array}$$
22.
$$\begin{array}{r} 6 \\ + 9 \\ \hline \end{array}$$
23.
$$\begin{array}{r} 14 \\ - 5 \\ \hline \end{array}$$
24.
$$\begin{array}{r} 16 \\ - 8 \\ \hline \end{array}$$
25.
$$\begin{array}{r} 18 \\ - 9 \\ \hline \end{array}$$

| 26. 9 <br> + 3 | 27. 4 <br> + 5 | 28. 15 <br> − 9 | 29. 7 <br> + 9 | 30. 8 <br> − 3 | 31. 5 <br> + 9 |
|---|---|---|---|---|---|
| 32. 9 <br> + 9 | 33. 6 <br> + 6 | 34. 15 <br> − 6 | 35. 12 <br> − 8 | 36. 9 <br> + 5 | 37. 9 <br> + 7 |

Add or subtract. Write the other facts in the fact family.

**38.** 7 + 4 **39.** 6 + 8 **40.** 10 − 2 **41.** 15 − 6 ★ **42.** 8 + 0 ★ **43.** 14 − 7

★ **44.** How many fact families with sums of 18 or less have doubles in them? Which ones are they?

Think of a related subtraction fact. Write only the missing addend.

MENTAL MATH

**45.** 5 + ▦ = 12    **46.** 8 + ▦ = 12    **47.** 9 + ▦ = 15

**48.** ▦ + 6 = 13    **49.** ▦ + 9 = 17    **50.** 7 + ▦ = 14

## PROBLEM SOLVING APPLICATIONS
### Number Sentences

Complete the number sentence to solve the problem. Then write the other facts in the fact family.

**51.** Jan has 14 books. She read 6 books to her sister. How many books does Jan have left to read?

**52.** Rudy played 17 games of chess with Marta. Rudy won 8 games. How many games did Marta win?

▦ − ▦ = ▦

**53.** Philip swam 9 laps. Ella swam 3 more laps than Philip. How many laps did Ella swim?

Write your own word problem for the fact.

★ **54.** 11 − 8 = 3    ★ **55.** 9 + 7 = 16

★ **56.** 15 − 6 = 9    ★ **57.** 4 + 3 = 7

# PROBLEM SOLVING
## Strategy: Choosing The Operation

Steven is a gymnast. He plans to learn 14 new floor exercises this year. He already has learned 9 new exercises. How many more does he plan to learn?

The four steps below can help you solve the problem.

*1. Understand the problem.*

*2. Make a plan.*

*3. Use the plan to do the work.*

*4. Answer and check for sense.*

| | |
|---|---|
| **1.** What do you know? What do you want to know? | Wants to learn 14 exercises, already learned 9. How many more to learn? |
| **2.** What do you do to solve the problem? | To find how many more, you subtract 9 from 14. |
| **3.** Show your work. | $14 - 9 = 5$ |
| **4.** Check to be sure your answer makes sense. | 5 exercises $5 + 9 = 14$ ✓ |

## CLASS EXERCISES

Read the problem. Next state what you know and what you want to know. Then choose *a* or *b* for your plan.

1. Vilma practices on the trampoline for 18 minutes. Erin practices for 9 minutes. How much longer does Vilma practice than Erin?
   **a.** $18 + 9$     **b.** $18 - 9$

2. While 5 children are practicing on the ropes, 8 children are waiting their turns. How many children are there in all?
   **a.** $5 + 8$     **b.** $8 - 5$

3. There were 12 students on the team. This month 4 more students joined the team. How many students are on the team now?
   **a.** $12 + 4$     **b.** $12 - 4$

4. Jeff learned 7 new exercises last year. He learned 3 new exercises this year. How many more exercises did he learn last year?
   **a.** $7 + 3$     **b.** $7 - 3$

# PRACTICE

Write *add* or *subtract* for your plan. Then solve.

**5.** Diane practiced for 8 hours this week and for 5 hours last week. How many more hours did she practice this week?

**6.** Daniel won 8 ribbons last year. He won 16 ribbons this year. How many ribbons did Daniel win in all for both years?

**7.** Christine has 14 points, Ella has 9 points, and Sue has 6 points. Together how many points do they have?

**8.** Joey has 19 points. He needs 8 more to win a ribbon. How many points does Joey need in all to win a ribbon?

**9.** There are 8 more people in the first row of seats than there are in the second row. If there are 17 people in the first row, how many people are in the second row?

★ **10.** Frank and Della each won 5 ribbons, Paulo won 7 ribbons, and Karyn won 2 more ribbons than Paulo. How many ribbons did they win altogether?

★ **11.** Maryanne does 8 warm-up exercises each day. How many warm-up exercises does she do in 1 week?

# CHECKPOINT 1

**Add.** *(pages 2–7)*

| | | | | | |
|---|---|---|---|---|---|
| **1.** | 4 <br> + 8 | **2.** | 7 <br> + 7 | **3.** | 5 <br> + 7 |
| **4.** | 3 <br> 2 <br> + 7 | **5.** | 5 <br> 1 <br> + 4 | **6.** | 9 <br> 5 <br> + 6 |
| **7.** | 12 <br> + 6 | **8.** | 24 <br> + 7 | **9.** | 18 <br> + 9 |

**Subtract.** *(pages 8–11)*

| | | | | | |
|---|---|---|---|---|---|
| **10.** | 12 <br> − 6 | **11.** | 10 <br> − 4 | **12.** | 14 <br> − 5 |
| **13.** | 17 <br> − 9 | **14.** | 13 <br> − 8 | **15.** | 11 <br> − 7 |

**Solve.** *(pages 12–13)*

**16.** At the neighborhood pet show, there were 16 dogs and 9 cats. How many fewer cats than dogs were there?

*Extra practice on page 402*

# PLACE VALUE, HUNDREDS

You use the ten **digits** shown below to write any number.

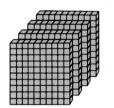

| hundreds | tens | ones |
|----------|------|------|
| 4 | 3 | 5 |

4 hundreds    3 tens    5 ones

The digit 4 is in the *hundreds' place.*
Its value is 400.

The digit 3 is in the *tens' place.*
Its value is 30.

The digit 5 is in the *ones' place.*
Its value is 5.

 The **standard form** is 435. On a calculator it looks like this:
435. You read 435 as *four hundred thirty-five.*
The **expanded form** is 400 + 30 + 5.

## CLASS EXERCISES

Write the standard form.

1.
| hundreds | tens | ones |
|----------|------|------|
| 6 | 5 | 2 |

2.
| hundreds | tens | ones |
|----------|------|------|
| 6 | 0 | 8 |

3.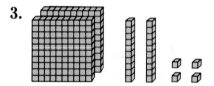

4.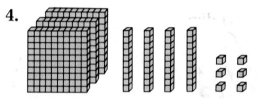

Read the number. What is the value of the digit 3
in the number?

**5.** 973    **6.** 534    **7.** 386    **8.** 731    **9.** 302    **10.** 213

# PRACTICE

Write the value of the underlined digit.

**11.** <u>7</u>21      **12.** 94<u>5</u>      **13.** 1<u>3</u>7      **14.** <u>6</u>04      **15.** 5<u>9</u>2      **16.** 14<u>0</u>

Write the standard form.

**17.** 3 tens

**18.** 1 hundred 3 tens

**19.** 7 tens 8 ones

**20.** 3 hundreds 9 tens 9 ones

**21.** 4 hundreds 1 ten

**22.** 8 hundreds 6 ones

**23.** two hundred twenty-eight

**24.** eighty-three

**25.** four hundred eight

**26.** nine hundred ninety-nine

Write the expanded form.

**27.** 524      **28.** 937      **29.** 888      **30.** 75      **31.** 208      **32.** 650

Which symbols and numbers would you press on a calculator to make this change?

CALCULATOR

**33.** Change 320 to 329

**34.** Change 24 to 324

**35.** Change 505 to 585

**36.** Change 400 to 460

# PROBLEM SOLVING APPLICATIONS
## Nonroutine Problems

Solve. Do not use a number cube more than once in any number.

**37.** Kim rolled three number cubes. The digits 3, 6, and 4 came up. How many different three-digit numbers can Kim make with these digits?

**38.** John rolled three number cubes. The digits 5, 5, and 1 came up. How many different three-digit numbers can he make with these digits?

★ **39.** I'm thinking of a three-digit number. The ones' digit is greater than 1. The hundreds' digit is 5 more than the ones' digit. The tens' digit is the sum of the hundreds' digit and the ones' digit. What is the number?

# PLACE VALUE, THOUSANDS

You can rename 10 ones as 1 ten and 10 tens as 1 hundred.
You can rename 10 hundreds as 1 thousand.

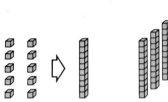 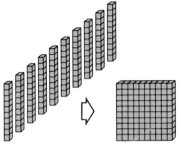 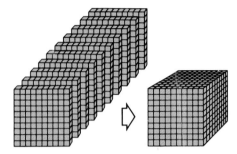

10 ones = 1 ten    10 tens = 1 hundred    10 hundreds = 1 thousand

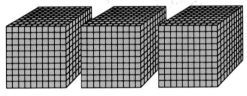

| thousands | hundreds | tens | ones |
|-----------|----------|------|------|
| 3 | 2 | 5 | 8 |

3 thousands    2 hundreds    5 tens    8 ones

The digit 3 is in the *thousands' place*. Its value is 3000. The standard form is 3258. You read 3258 as *three thousand two hundred fifty-eight*. You write 3258 in expanded form as 3000 + 200 + 50 + 8.

## CLASS EXERCISES

Write the standard form.

**1.** 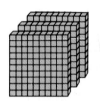     **2.**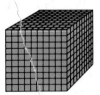

Read the number. What is the value of the underlined digit?

**3.** <u>4</u>821    **4.** 326<u>1</u>    **5.** 3<u>8</u>27    **6.** 56<u>3</u>7    **7.** 8<u>4</u>09    **8.** <u>2</u>064    **9.** 395<u>6</u>

# PRACTICE

Write the value of the underlined digit.

**10.** 8<u>2</u>91    **11.** 26<u>4</u>9    **12.** 304<u>2</u>    **13.** 80<u>5</u>0    **14.** <u>6</u>057    **15.** 7<u>3</u>01    **16.** <u>9</u>143

Write the standard form.

**17.** 7 thousands
5 hundreds
3 tens
4 ones

**18.** 2 thousands
5 hundreds
5 tens
6 ones

**19.** 1 thousand
9 hundreds
6 tens
4 ones

**20.** 4 thousands
0 hundreds
2 tens
3 ones

**21.** 6 thousands

**22.** 9 thousands 8 hundreds

**23.** 7 thousands 6 hundreds 4 ones

**24.** 5 thousands 3 hundreds 6 tens

**25.** one thousand four hundred

**26.** six thousand twelve

**27.** seven thousand fifty-two

**28.** two thousand one hundred six

**29.** nine thousand seven

**30.** three thousand ten

Write the number in words.

**31.** 785    **32.** 9584    **33.** 9999    **34.** 56    **35.** 1070    **36.** 6590    **37.** 3005

Write the number in expanded form.

**38.** 7823    **39.** 5216    **40.** 9999    **41.** 1212    **42.** 1070    **43.** 3005    **44.** 2000

# PROBLEM SOLVING APPLICATIONS
## Reasonable Answers

Choose the answer that makes sense. Write *a*, *b*, or *c*.

**45.** Lori spends about ▓ hours at school each day.
   **a.** 7    **b.** 70    **c.** 700

**46.** A giraffe can grow to ▓ feet tall.
   **a.** 18    **b.** 180    **c.** 1800

**47.** The shopping mall has 45 stores. When the parking lot is full, it holds about ▓ cars.
   **a.** 2    **b.** 20    **c.** 2000

# PLACE VALUE, MILLIONS

Let's look at some greater numbers.

| Thousands | | | Ones | | |
|---|---|---|---|---|---|
| hundreds | tens | ones | hundreds | tens | ones |
| 5 | 2 | 1 | 8 | 6 | 7 |

The value of the digit 1 is 1000. The value of the digit 2 is 20,000. The value of the digit 5 is 500,000. You read 521,867 as *five hundred twenty-one thousand, eight hundred sixty-seven.*

| Millions | | | Thousands | | | Ones | | |
|---|---|---|---|---|---|---|---|---|
| hundreds | tens | ones | hundreds | tens | ones | hundreds | tens | ones |
| 3 | 2 | 5 | 8 | 4 | 6 | 0 | 0 | 0 |

The value of the digit 5 is 5,000,000. The value of the digit 2 is 20,000,000. The value of the digit 3 is 300,000,000. You read 325,846,000 as *three hundred twenty-five million, eight hundred forty-six thousand.*

The moon is about 238,840 miles from Earth. You write this number with a comma. When you enter the number on a calculator, you do not enter the comma.

238840

## CLASS EXERCISES
Read the number. What is the value of the digit 8?

**1.** 85,423  **2.** 128,543  **3.** 801,372  **4.** 8,951,362

**5.** 84,773,259  **6.** 27,638,540  **7.** 826,547,137  **8.** 581,209,371

## PRACTICE

Write the value of the underlined digit.

9. 7̲6,510  10. 1̲54,326  11. 2̲45,955  12. 689̲,240

13. 1̲,486,005  14. 27,9̲84,332  15. 4̲32,664,589  16. 58̲3,019,748

Write the standard form.

17. 52 thousand  18. 600 thousand  19. 18 thousand, 784

20. 43 million  21. 9 million, 123 thousand  22. 78 million, 329

23. 518 million, 109 thousand, 234  24. 999 million, 999 thousand, 999

25. 77 million, 77 thousand, 77  26. 142 million, 700 thousand, 3

27. five hundred thousand, sixty  28. three hundred thousand, nine

29. six million, four hundred seventy  30. forty three million, six thousand

31. four hundred eleven thousand, two hundred twelve

32. two hundred million, six hundred fifty thousand, two

Without adding, how could you enter this on a calculator?

33. 5,000,000 + 300,000 + 90,000 + 6,000 + 400 + 20 + 5

34. 90,000,000 + 60,000 + 2000 + 40 + 9

35. 40,000,000 + 500,000 + 2000 + 1

CALCULATOR

 PROBLEM SOLVING APPLICATIONS
Reading Numbers

Choose the number that is different. Write *a*, *b*, or *c*. Name the places of the digits that are different.

36. a. 939,393  37. a. 487,687,887  38. a. 78,063,010
   b. 939,339      b. 487,687,887      b. 78,630,010
   c. 939,393      c. 487,678,887      c. 78,630,010

★ 39. a. 4 more than 5,826,532  ★ 40. a. 20 less than 23,986,538
   b. 7 more than 5,826,528       b. 30 less than 23,986,558
   c. 5 more than 5,826,530       c. 10 less than 23,986,528

# COMPARING AND ORDERING NUMBERS

When you compare numbers to find which is less and which is greater, you can use < or >.

45 *is less than* 49 — 45 < 49

49 *is greater than* 45 — 49 > 45

To compare numbers, begin with the greatest place value and compare the digits. Let's compare 3248 and 3529.

First compare the thousands.

| thousands | hundreds | tens | ones |
|---|---|---|---|
| 3 | 2 | 4 | 8 |
| 3 | 5 | 2 | 9 |

same

Then compare the hundreds.

| thousands | hundreds | tens | ones |
|---|---|---|---|
| 3 | 2 | 4 | 8 |
| 3 | 5 | 2 | 9 |

2 hundreds are less than 5 hundreds

2 hundreds < 5 hundreds

so 3248 < 3529

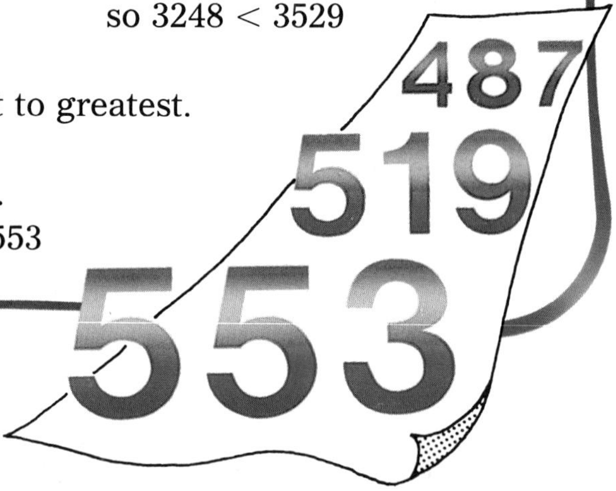


M These numbers are in order from least to greatest.

487 519 553

To check, compare the digits mentally.

487 < 519 and 519 < 553

## CLASS EXERCISES

Compare the numbers. Write < or >.

**1.**

| hundreds | tens | ones |
|---|---|---|
| 8 | 8 | 8 |
| 8 | 9 | 8 |

888 ▢ 898

**2.**

| thousands | hundreds | tens | ones |
|---|---|---|---|
| 2 | 4 | 7 | 8 |
| 2 | 4 | 7 | 6 |

2478 ▢ 2476

**3.** How would you compare 57,364 and 48,291?

Order the numbers from greatest to least.

**4.** 518 524 593

**5.** 3867 2115 4478

# PRACTICE

Compare the numbers. Write $<$ , $>$ , or $=$ .

**6.** 57 ▓ 94      **7.** 34 ▓ 43      **8.** 430 ▓ 429      **9.** 809 ▓ 817

**10.** 276 ▓ 2076      **11.** 1805 ▓ 185      **12.** 1643 ▓ 1634      **13.** 2452 ▓ 2459

**14.** 5677 ▓ 5577      **15.** 8412 ▓ 7598      **16.** 19,212 ▓ 20,536

**17.** 37,841 ▓ 37,841      **18.** 25,411 ▓ 24,511      **19.** 54,036 ▓ 54,360

**20.** 174,232 ▓ 174,240      **21.** 516,726 ▓ 516,726      **22.** 215,319 ▓ 213,591

★ **23.** 5,247,362 ▓ 5,227,584      ★ **24.** 22,591,308 ▓ 213,486,112

Write the numbers in order from greatest to least.

**25.** 544    516    527        **26.** 9001    9076    9700

**27.** 3794    3799    3953       **28.** 26,509    24,956    26,211

Use all the digits to write the least and the greatest numbers possible.

**29.** 4, 6, 3    **30.** 7, 1, 9, 8    **31.** 8, 9, 9, 1    **32.** 5, 4, 3, 8, 1

**MENTAL MATH**

★ **33. Think:** Using any digits from 1 to 9 as often as you wish, what is the least 6-digit number? the greatest?

## PROBLEM SOLVING APPLICATIONS
### Reasonable Answers

2794 VOTES FOR CLARISSA WILLIAMS

Solve and check. The answer is not a number.

**34.** Bernie and Petra are running for president of the fourth grade class. Bernie receives 76 votes and 67 students vote for Petra. Who receives the most votes?

**35.** Clarissa Williams is running against Henry Elkins for the school board. Clarissa receives 2794 votes and Henry receives 2789 votes. Who loses?

★ **36.** In 1860, Stephen A. Douglas received 1,375,157 votes. John Bell received 589,581 votes. John C. Breckinridge received 845,763 votes. Abraham Lincoln received 1,866,352 votes. List the candidates in order from the greatest to the least number of votes. Who was elected President in 1860?

# ROUNDING NUMBERS

Exactly 87 post cards are in the rack. If you do not need to know the exact number, you can **round** 87 to the nearest ten.

80 81 82 83 84 85 86 87 88 89 90

87 is between 80 and 90. It is nearer to 90. You can say about 90 post cards are in the rack.

Round 536 to the nearest hundred.

500   510   520   530   540   550   560   570   580   590   600

536 is nearer to 500 than to 600. To the nearest hundred, 536 is rounded to 500.

Round 6500 to the nearest thousand.

6000  6100  6200  6300  6400  6500  6600  6700  6800  6900  7000

6500 is in the middle between 6000 and 7000. When a number is in the middle, you round up. 6500 rounded to the nearest thousand is 7000.

## CLASS EXERCISES

Round to the place of the underlined digit.
Use the number lines above to help you.

1. 8̲2
2. 8̲8
3. 8̲4
4. 8̲5
5. 5̲80
6. 5̲19
7. 5̲42
8. 5̲50
9. 6̲700
10. 6̲160
11. 6̲656
12. 6̲328

## PRACTICE

Round to the nearest ten.

13. 51
14. 36
15. 82
16. 55
17. 94
18. 67

Round to the nearest hundred.

**19.** 482  **20.** 591  **21.** 833  **22.** 647  **23.** 754  **24.** 230

**25.** 249  **26.** 774  **27.** 105  **28.** 150  **29.** 606  ★ **30.** 994

Round to the nearest thousand.

**31.** 3781  **32.** 6293  **33.** 1713  **34.** 4472  **35.** 6900  **36.** 8500

**37.** 7029  **38.** 3089  **39.** 1299  **40.** 1985  **41.** 2543  ★ **42.** 9999

---

Write the answer.

**43.** 17 − 8  **44.** 8 + 6  **45.** 9 + 9  **46.** 15 − 6  **47.** 11 − 2

**48.** 9 + 7  **49.** 13 − 5  **50.** 12 − 8  **51.** 5 + 6  **52.** 15 + 6

**MIXED REVIEW**

---

## PROBLEM SOLVING APPLICATIONS
### Using a Table

| DISTANCE BETWEEN CITIES | |
|---|---|
| CITIES | DISTANCE IN MILES |
| Albany, NY, and San Francisco, CA | 3146 |
| Albuquerque, NM, and Boston, MA | 2220 |
| Boise, ID, and Chicago, IL | 1819 |
| Cleveland, OH, and Cheyenne, WY | 1326 |
| Hartford, CT, and St. Louis, MO | 1079 |
| Washington, D.C., and Portland, OR | 2946 |

Round the distances in the table to the nearest thousand to answer.

**53.** Which cities are about 1000 miles apart?

**54.** Which cities are about 2000 miles apart?

**55.** Name two cities that are about 1000 miles farther apart than Cleveland and Cheyenne.

★ **56.** Name the cities that have about the same distance between them.

# ROUNDING GREATER NUMBERS

To round to a certain place, look at the digit to the right of that place. Here are some examples.

| | | | |
|---|---|---|---|
| Round 864 to the nearest ten.<br>8<u>6</u>4 | The digit to the right of the tens is 4. | Is this digit 5 or more?<br>No. | Round 864 down to 860. |

| | | | |
|---|---|---|---|
| Round 5893 to the nearest hundred.<br>5<u>8</u>93 | The digit to the right of the hundreds is 9. | Is this digit 5 or more?<br>Yes. | Round 5893 up to 5900. |

| | | | |
|---|---|---|---|
| Round 83,571 to the nearest thousand.<br>8<u>3</u>,571 | The digit to the right of the thousands is 5. | Is this digit 5 or more?<br>Yes. | Round 83,571 up to 84,000. |

 Rounding to the greatest place value of a number can help you find an estimated answer. The number 6584 rounded to the greatest place value is 7000.

<u>6</u>584  The greatest place value is thousands. Look at the digit to the right.

## CLASS EXERCISES

What digit do you look at to round the number to this place? Do you round up or down?

1. 723 to the nearest ten

2. 465 to the nearest ten

3. 4328 to the nearest hundred

4. 5873 to the nearest hundred

5. 43,809 to the nearest thousand

6. 15,408 to the nearest thousand

Round to the place of the underlined digit.

7. <u>7</u>23      8. 7<u>2</u>3      9. <u>8</u>546      10. 8<u>5</u>46      11. <u>2</u>6,243      12. 2<u>6</u>,243

# PRACTICE

Round to the nearest ten.

**13.** 44 **14.** 38 **15.** 249 **16.** 561 **17.** 568

Round to the nearest hundred.

**18.** 238 **19.** 684 **20.** 4350 **21.** 6831 **22.** 5119

Round to the nearest thousand.

**23.** 5601 **24.** 6452 **25.** 52,347 **26.** 68,974 **27.** 56,719

Round to the place of the underlined digit.

**28.** 33$\underline{8}$ **29.** 5$\underline{8}$1 **30.** 7$\underline{4}$65 **31.** $\underline{2}$872 **32.** 1$\underline{5}$53

**33.** 49$\underline{2}$4 **34.** 8$\underline{9}$,545 **35.** 76,$\underline{3}$14 **36.** 188,3$\underline{6}$9 **37.** 94$\underline{4}$,827

Round to the greatest place value.

**38.** 239 **39.** 4554 **40.** 57 **41.** 5728 **42.** 761

**43.** 85,307 **44.** 11,786 **45.** 392,943 ★ **46.** 5,844,326 ★ **47.** 8,432,655

Do you think the number was counted exactly or estimated? Write *exact* or *estimated*.

ESTIMATE

**48.** 38 pears in the basket **49.** A bowl 3000 years old

**50.** 9000 people at the game **51.** 30 days in September

## PROBLEM SOLVING APPLICATIONS
### Using What You Know

Solve.

**52.** The Music Club mailed 1850 invitations to the concerts. To the nearest thousand, how many invitations did the club mail?

**53.** On Friday night, 2493 people attended the concert. There were 2528 seats. Were there enough seats for all the people?

★ **54.** Rounded to the nearest thousand, $9000 was collected for tickets. What could be the greatest and the least amounts collected?

# PROBLEM SOLVING
## Strategy: Using A Bar Graph

1. Understand
2. Plan
3. Work
4. Answer/ Check

Elena Fuentes keeps track of the number of computers sold each week at Creative Computing Center. She made a **bar graph** to show the sales for the first week in May.

The bar graph shows that sales were lowest for the Ideas! computers.

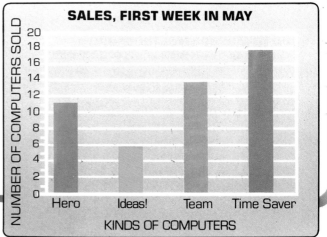

## CLASS EXERCISES

Use the graph above to answer the questions.

1. What is the title of the bar graph?

2. What do the numbers on the side of the graph mean?

3. What does each bar on the graph represent?

4. How many Hero computers were sold?

5. If 15 Team computers had been sold, where would Elena draw the end of the bar?

6. Which computer had the greatest sales?

## PRACTICE

Use the graph above to answer the questions.

7. How many more Time Saver computers than Ideas! computers were sold?

8. How many Team and Ideas! computers were sold in all?

9. How many computers were sold in all?

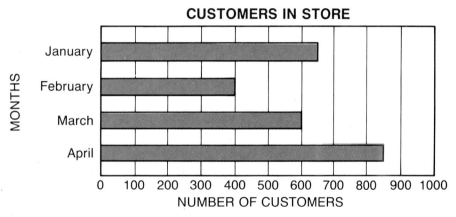

**CUSTOMERS IN STORE**

Use the graph to answer the question.

**10.** Were there more customers in January or in March?

**11.** During which month did the store have the fewest customers?

**12.** During which month was the number of customers greatest?

**13.** During which months were there more than 600 customers?

★ **14.** Jack Collins kept track of the number of demonstrations that he gave each week in April. Use the information to make a bar graph. Remember to include a title, labels, and numbers.

| NUMBER OF DEMONSTRATIONS | |
|---|---|
| First week | 40 |
| Second week | 20 |
| Third week | 35 |
| Fourth week | 60 |
| Fifth week | 15 |

# CHECKPOINT 2

Write the standard form.
*(pages 14–19)*

**1.** 5 hundreds 6 tens 3 ones

**2.** 605 thousand, 823

Write < , > , or = . *(pages 20–21)*

**3.** 6200 ▨ 6199

**4.** 267,385 ▨ 287,016

Round to the place of the underlined digit. *(pages 22–25)*

**5.** 6$\underline{7}$41    **6.** $\underline{5}$21    **7.** $\underline{3}$985

Use the graph above to solve.
*(pages 26–27)*

**8.** How many customers were in the store in February?

**9.** During which month were 850 customers in the store?

*Extra practice on page 402*

Write the answer. *(pages 2–7)*

**1.** 9
+ 7

**2.** 6
+ 6

**3.** 4
5
+ 3

**4.** 6
7
+ 4

Write the answer. *(pages 8–11)*

**5.** 15 − 8          **6.** 7 − 0          **7.** 12 − 3          **8.** 16 − 9

Write *add* or *subtract* for your plan. Then solve. *(pages 12–13)*

**9.** Vern has 13 tapes in his music collection. He received 5 more tapes for his birthday. How many tapes does Vern have now?

**10.** There are 15 books on the desk and 6 books on the table. How many more books are on the desk than are on the table?

Write the value of the underlined digit. *(pages 14–19)*

**11.** 1294          **12.** 43,066          **13.** 4,581,673          **14.** 762,306,421

Write the numbers in order from greatest to least. *(pages 20–21)*

**15.** 631     652     611          **16.** 37,483     37,519     35,901

Round to the place of the underlined digit. *(pages 22–25)*

**17.** 54          **18.** 793          **19.** 1601          **20.** 25,542

**DOGS IN A DOG SHOW**

NUMBER OF DOGS

20
18
16
14
12
10
8
6
4
2
0

Poodles   Boxers   Setters   Collies

BREEDS OF DOGS

Use the bar graph to answer the questions. *(pages 26–27)*

**21.** Which breed had 13 dogs in the show?

**22.** Which breed had the least number of dogs in the show?

*Extra Practice on page 403*

Maryland

Salisbury

Taconik

olk

5242
68
596
843
522

# MATHEMATICS and HISTORY

| CENSUS OF 1980 | |
|---|---|
| Alaska | 401,851 |
| Georgia | 5,463,105 |
| Idaho | 943,935 |
| Maryland | 4,216,975 |
| California | 23,667,902 |

A census is an official count of a population. The first census of the United States was given in 1790. The constitution states that a census of the population of the United States be given every ten years.

Kent
Torrington
Norfolk

147
573

# WHAT'S THE COUNT?

Use the table to answer the questions.

1. Which states have less than one million people?

2. Which state has more than ten million people?

Write the names of the states that are being compared.
Is the comparison correct? Write *yes* or *no*.

3. $401,851 < 4,216,975$  4. $23,667,902 > 5,463,105$  5. $943,935 < 401,851$

Write the population of the states. Then compare.

6. Georgia ▮ Maryland  7. Alaska ▮ Idaho  8. Idaho ▮ California

9. Write the name of each state. Then round each population to the nearest thousand.

★10. Which state has about one hundred thousand less than one million people?

# Enrichment

Have you ever seen symbols like those shown at the right? The symbols are called **Roman numerals.** They stand for numbers and were invented by the Romans long ago.

Instead of using place value, the Romans used three symbols and different combinations of the symbols to write the numbers up to 39.

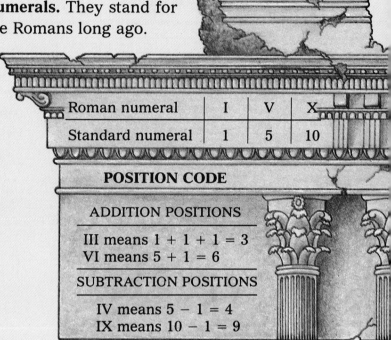

| Roman numeral | I | V | X |
|---|---|---|---|
| Standard numeral | 1 | 5 | 10 |

**POSITION CODE**

ADDITION POSITIONS

III means 1 + 1 + 1 = 3
VI means 5 + 1 = 6

SUBTRACTION POSITIONS

IV means 5 − 1 = 4
IX means 10 − 1 = 9

The position code shows how to read and write Roman numerals. Use the position code and the symbols at the right to write the missing numerals.

**1.**

| STANDARD NUMERAL | 1 | 2 | 3 | 4 | 5 | 6 | 7 | 8 | 9 | 10 |
|---|---|---|---|---|---|---|---|---|---|---|
| ROMAN NUMERAL | I | II | III | IV | V | VI | ? | ? | IX | X |

**2.**

| STANDARD NUMERAL | 11 | 12 | 13 | 14 | 15 | 16 | 17 | 18 | 19 | 20 |
|---|---|---|---|---|---|---|---|---|---|---|
| ROMAN NUMERAL | XI | ? | ? | XIV | ? | ? | ? | ? | XIX | ? |

The Romans used these symbols to write greater numbers.

| ROMAN NUMERAL | L | C | D | M |
|---|---|---|---|---|
| STANDARD NUMERAL | 50 | 100 | 500 | 1000 |

## ROMAN NUMERALS

You may have seen a date at the end of a movie written with these symbols.

MCMXLIII

1000 + 900 + 40 + 3 = 1943

Complete.

**3.**

| 241 | 242 | 243 | 244 |
|-----|-----|-----|-----|
| CCXLI | ? | ? | ? |

**4.**

| 1866 | 1876 | 1886 | 1896 |
|------|------|------|------|
| MDCCCLXVI | ? | ? | ? |

Write the standard form.

**5.** VII     **6.** XXI     **7.** LXIX     **8.** CCCV     **9.** DCCVII     **10.** CMV

Solve.

**11.** A book has opening pages numbered to IV, regular pages numbered from 1 to 10, and two blank pages. How many pages are there altogether?

**12.** In what year was a movie dated MCMXLIX made?

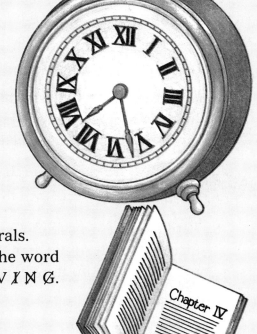

Write the standard form of the date.

**13.** MCDXCV      **14.** MDCCXXXIX

**15.** MCMLXXX      **16.** MDCLXI

Write the Roman numeral for the date.

**17.** 1556    **18.** 1849    **19.** 1965

**20.** 1483    **21.** 1675    **22.** 1776

There are brain teasers based on Roman numerals. For example, can you cross out four letters in the word LIVING and still leave four? Yes, like this: L̸ I V I̸ N̸ G̸

Solve the teaser.

**23.** Take ALL from a MALL but leave a thousand.

**24.** Take a BOAR from a BOXCAR and leave ninety.

**25.** Show that one letter in ELEVEN and one letter in SEVEN are equal to one letter in SIX.

# CUMULATIVE REVIEW

Choose the correct answer. Write *a, b, c,* or *d.*

Find the answer.

**1.** 6 + 7
  **a.** 12
  **b.** 14
  **c.** 13
  **d.** none of these

**2.** 3 + 9
  **a.** 12
  **b.** 13
  **c.** 10
  **d.** none of these

**3.** 8 + 6
  **a.** 13
  **b.** 14
  **c.** 11
  **d.** none of these

Find the answer.

**4.**   10
  −  0
  **a.** 0
  **b.** 10
  **c.** 9
  **d.** none of these

**5.**   15
  −  6
  **a.** 9
  **b.** 10
  **c.** 11
  **d.** none of these

**6.**   13
  −  8
  **a.** 8
  **b.** 6
  **c.** 5
  **d.** none of these

Read the problem. Choose the correct answer.

**7.** Tran has read 8 pages of his book. He wants to read a total of 17 pages before he goes to sleep. How many more pages does Tran have to read?

  **a.** $17 - 8 = 9$
  **b.** $8 - 17 = 9$
  **c.** $17 + 8 = 25$
  **d.** none of these

**8.** Pat has 6 pictures from the family vacation, Joe has 7 pictures, and Annie has 3 pictures. Together, how many pictures do they have?

  **a.** $7 - 3 = 4$
  **b.** $7 + 6 + 3 = 15$
  **c.** $6 + 7 + 3 = 16$
  **d.** none of these

**9.** Martha learned 14 songs this month. She learned 9 songs last month. How many songs did she learn?

  **a.** $14 - 9 = 5$
  **b.** $14 + 9 = 23$
  **c.** $14 + 9 + 9 = 42$
  **d.** none of these

Find the standard form.

**10.** 8000 + 500 + 20 + 1
   **a.** 800,521
   **b.** 8521
   **c.** 85,201
   **d.** none of these

**11.** 4000 + 20 + 7
   **a.** 4027
   **b.** 4,000,207
   **c.** 427
   **d.** none of these

Compare the numbers.

**12.** 385 ▨ 3085
   **a.** >
   **b.** <
   **c.** =
   **d.** none of these

**13.** 22,481 ▨ 22,184
   **a.** >
   **b.** <
   **c.** =
   **d.** none of these

**14.** 625,976 ▨ 625,976
   **a.** >
   **b.** <
   **c.** =
   **d.** none of these

Round to the greatest place value.

**15.** 37
   **a.** 30
   **b.** 70
   **c.** 40
   **d.** none of these

**16.** 633
   **a.** 600
   **b.** 630
   **c.** 700
   **d.** none of these

**17.** 7488
   **a.** 7000
   **b.** 7490
   **c.** 7500
   **d.** none of these

# LANGUAGE and VOCABULARY REVIEW

Read each sentence. On your paper, write *True* or *False*.

**1.** 7 + 10 = 17 is an example of a number sentence.

**2.** The answer in subtraction is called the difference.

**3.** The answer in addition is called an addend.

**4.**

| | |
|---|---|
| 7 + 5 = 12 | 5 + 7 = 12 |
| 12 − 5 = 7 | 12 − 7 = 5 |

The facts in the box are a fact family.

**5.** You can write "67 is less than 76" as 67 > 76.

**6.** Round a number only when you need to know the exact number.

# USES IN OUR LIVES: ROBOTS

**COMPUTER LITERACY**

Robots are machines that help people do jobs. They can be told to do jobs that are too difficult for people to do.

A robot can do a job over and over again. It never gets tired. A robot can work in places that are too hot or too cold for a person to work.

Sometimes robots are built with wheels. Then they can be used to move very heavy objects from one place to another.

A computer inside the robot gives the robot directions for a job. The computer must be given directions so the robot will do the job correctly.

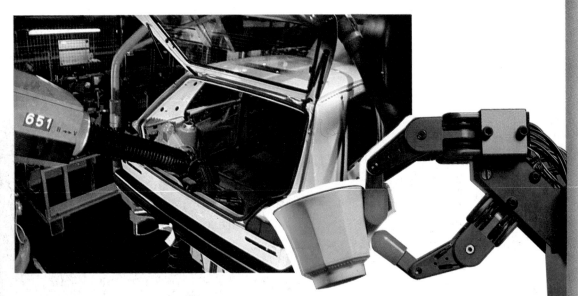

Tell if a person or a robot should do the job.

1. give a haircut

2. put car parts together

3. deliver mail

4. baby-sit

5. sharpen 1,000,000 pencils

6. work 24 hours without stopping

7. drive a bus

8. lift 2000 pounds

# 2

As the sun begins to set, 20 street lights blink on. Then 3 more blink on. How many street lights are shining altogether?

ADDITION AND SUBTRACTION
GREATER NUMBERS

# TWO-DIGIT ADDITION

When you add two-digit numbers, the sum of the ones may be greater than 9. You have to rename 10 ones as 1 ten.

To add 24 and 18, follow these steps.

Add the ones. Rename
12 ones as 1 ten 2 ones.

Add the tens.

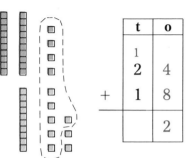

| | t | o |
|---|---|---|
| | 1 | |
| | 2 | 4 |
| + | 1 | 8 |
| | | 2 |

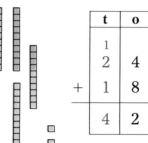

| | t | o |
|---|---|---|
| | 1 | |
| | 2 | 4 |
| + | 1 | 8 |
| | 4 | 2 |

Here are some other examples.

```
   1              1          2
  75      33     54        48
+ 27    + 24   +  9        17
----    ----   ----      + 26
 102      57     63         91
```

M You can use mental math to add some numbers.

```
  47     Think:   30 is 1 more than 29.
+ 29              47 + 30 = 77, so 47 + 29 = 76.
----
  76
```

LAKE TOURS

76 Seats Available

## CLASS EXERCISES

Complete.

1. 16 ones = ▨ ten ▨ ones     2. 19 ones = ▨ ten ▨ ones

3. 22 ones = ▨ tens ▨ ones     4. 17 ones = ▨ ten ▨ ones

Add. Do you need to rename? Explain why.

```
5.   63     6.   17     7.   14     8.   35     9.   68     10.   72
   + 25        + 44        + 26        + 62        +  7         + 27
```

# PRACTICE

Add.

| | | | | | |
|---|---|---|---|---|---|
| **11.** 41 <br> + 48 | **12.** 58 <br> + 33 | **13.** 64 <br> + 5 | **14.** 32 <br> + 78 | **15.** 56 <br> + 29 | **16.** 56 <br> + 8 |
| **17.** 57 <br> + 35 | **18.** 76 <br> + 6 | **19.** 79 <br> + 32 | **20.** 84 <br> + 9 | **21.** 22 <br> + 54 | **22.** 43 <br> + 18 |
| **23.** 26 <br> 31 <br> + 42 | **24.** 35 <br> 40 <br> + 13 | **25.** 16 <br> 45 <br> + 24 | **26.** 23 <br> 58 <br> + 19 | **27.** 53 <br> 86 <br> + 7 | **28.** 38 <br> 6 <br> + 29 |

**29.** 54 + 23     **30.** 16 + 35     **31.** 49 + 5     **32.** 64 + 47

**33.** 17 + 42 + 38     **34.** 3 + 24 + 52     **35.** 39 + 42 + 9

Add mentally. Write only the answer.

| | | | | |
|---|---|---|---|---|
| **36.** 36 <br> + 59 | **37.** 25 <br> + 19 | **38.** 49 <br> + 22 | **39.** 64 <br> + 18 | **40.** 28 <br> + 38 |

**MENTAL MATH**

## PROBLEM SOLVING APPLICATIONS
### Choosing the Operation

Solve.

**41.** The first car of a train traveling from Los Angeles to San Diego has 28 passengers. The second car has 47 passengers. Together how many passengers are in the first two cars?

**42.** Fifty-three tickets were sold at the station for the two o'clock train. On the train, one conductor sold 22 tickets and the other sold 16 tickets. How many tickets were sold in all?

**43.** Seventeen seats are empty on the train to Watertown. Nine seats are empty on the train to Easton. How many more seats are empty on the train to Watertown than on the train to Easton?

★ **44.** The last car of the train to Delray has 60 seats. Forty-six people are sitting in the car and 19 more people are waiting to go in. Are there enough seats in the car?

247

# ESTIMATING SUMS

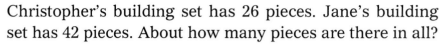

Christopher's building set has 26 pieces. Jane's building set has 42 pieces. About how many pieces are there in all?

To answer, you do not need to know exactly how many pieces there are. You can find an **estimate** to tell about how many.

For a quick mental estimate of a sum, round each addend to its greatest place value. Then add the rounded numbers.

$$
\begin{array}{rcr}
26 & \rightarrow & 30 \\
+\ 42 & \rightarrow & +\ 40 \\
\hline
& & 70
\end{array}
$$

There are about 70 pieces in all.

## CLASS EXERCISES

Round to the greatest place value.

**1.** 48     **2.** 39     **3.** 25     **4.** 51     **5.** 76     **6.** 94

Round each addend. Then estimate the sum.

| **7.** 12<br>+ 54 | **8.** 15<br>+ 54 | **9.** 15<br>+ 57 | **10.** 64<br>+ 34 | **11.** 64<br>+ 36 | **12.** 68<br>+ 36 |
|---|---|---|---|---|---|

## PRACTICE

Estimate the sum.

| **13.** 52<br>+ 32 | **14.** 35<br>+ 46 | **15.** 22<br>+ 65 | **16.** 33<br>+ 25 | **17.** 55<br>+ 43 | **18.** 31<br>+ 47 |
|---|---|---|---|---|---|
| **19.** 61<br>+ 28 | **20.** 14<br>+ 24 | **21.** 28<br>+ 15 | **22.** 34<br>+ 37 | **23.** 81<br>+ 29 | **24.** 39<br>+ 17 |

| 25. | 38 | 26. | 44 | 27. | 26 | 28. | 58 | 29. | 71 | 30. | 36 |
|---|---|---|---|---|---|---|---|---|---|---|---|
| | + 56 | | + 27 | | + 35 | | + 29 | | + 14 | | + 19 |

| 31. | 36 | 32. | 24 | 33. | 59 | 34. | 42 | 35. | 46 | 36. | 52 |
|---|---|---|---|---|---|---|---|---|---|---|---|
| | 23 | | 63 | | 16 | | 37 | | 24 | | 45 |
| | + 27 | | + 14 | | + 11 | | + 23 | | + 19 | | + 12 |

Write the numbers in order from least to greatest.

**37.** 35  86  71

**38.** 480  109  326

**39.** 511  115  155

**40.** 5914  5927  5923

**41.** 4237  3654  6523

**42.** 36,945  38,552  36,847

# PROBLEM SOLVING APPLICATIONS
## Estimate or Exact?

Should you estimate to find the answer? Write *exact* or *estimate* to tell whether you need an exact answer or an estimate. Then solve.

**43.** Mary Ellen decides to use two building sets. One has 37 pieces and the other has 48 pieces. Are there more than 100 pieces in the two sets together?

**44.** Anton has 28 space vehicles and Roy has 31. Who has more space vehicles?

**45.** Sally needs 47 more connecting blocks to finish her tower. She has 13 blue blocks, 15 green blocks, and 16 red blocks. Does she have enough blocks to finish the tower?

★ **46.** Miles has a building set with 42 yellow pieces, 28 orange pieces, and 13 more green pieces than orange pieces. About how many pieces are in the building set?

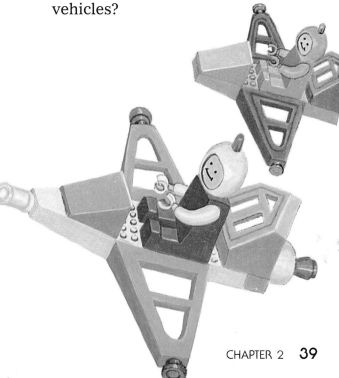

# THREE-DIGIT ADDITION

Sometimes when you add, you have to rename 10 tens as 1 hundred.

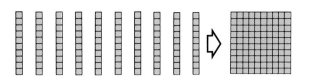

Let's add 194 and 283.

| Add the ones. | Add the tens. Rename 17 tens as 1 hundred 7 tens. | Add the hundreds. |
|---|---|---|

| h | t | o |
|---|---|---|
| 1 | 9 | 4 |
| + 2 | 8 | 3 |
|  |  | 7 |

| h | t | o |
|---|---|---|
| 1 |  |  |
| 1 | 9 | 4 |
| + 2 | 8 | 3 |
|  | 7 | 7 |

| h | t | o |
|---|---|---|
| 1 |  |  |
| 1 | 9 | 4 |
| + 2 | 8 | 3 |
| 4 | 7 | 7 |

To add 375 and 239, you must rename more than once.

$$\begin{array}{r} \overset{1}{375} \\ + 239 \\ \hline 4 \end{array}\qquad \begin{array}{r} \overset{1\phantom{0}1}{375} \\ + 239 \\ \hline 14 \end{array}\qquad \begin{array}{r} \overset{1\phantom{0}1}{375} \\ + 239 \\ \hline 614 \end{array}$$

 You can use mental math to find this sum.

$$\begin{array}{r} 424 \\ + 125 \\ \hline 549 \end{array}$$

**Think:** $424 + 100 = 524$
$524 + 20 = 544$
$544 + 5 = 549$

SITWELL PARK

549    CAME TO THE PARK LAST WEEK

## CLASS EXERCISES

Complete.

**1.** 13 tens = ▦ hundred ▦ tens      **2.** 18 tens = ▦ hundred ▦ tens

**3.** 17 tens = ▦ hundred ▦ tens      **4.** 25 tens = ▦ hundreds ▦ tens

Add. Build on what you know.

**5.**
$$\begin{array}{r} 33 \\ + 46 \\ \hline \end{array} \rightarrow \begin{array}{r} 133 \\ + 246 \\ \hline \end{array} \rightarrow \begin{array}{r} 136 \\ + 246 \\ \hline \end{array}$$

**6.**
$$\begin{array}{r} 62 \\ + 29 \\ \hline \end{array} \rightarrow \begin{array}{r} 262 \\ + 329 \\ \hline \end{array} \rightarrow \begin{array}{r} 262 \\ + 379 \\ \hline \end{array}$$

## PRACTICE

Add.

| | | | | | |
|---|---|---|---|---|---|
| **7.** 723 <br> + 168 | **8.** 238 <br> + 534 | **9.** 417 <br> + 520 | **10.** 602 <br> + 239 | **11.** 475 <br> + 315 | **12.** 335 <br> + 726 |
| **13.** 195 <br> + 564 | **14.** 773 <br> + 256 | **15.** 552 <br> + 285 | **16.** 327 <br> + 592 | **17.** 500 <br> + 825 | **18.** 287 <br> + 462 |
| **19.** 265 <br> 487 <br> + 123 | **20.** 157 <br> 148 <br> + 395 | **21.** 405 <br> 408 <br> + 169 | **22.** 317 <br> 59 <br> + 247 | **23.** 623 <br> 298 <br> + 87 | **24.** 985 <br> 132 <br> + 98 |

**25.** 628 + 272     **26.** 868 + 54     **27.** 255 + 275 + 309     **28.** 514 + 69 + 132

Complete.

★ **29.** 324 + 119 = 119 + ▨

★ **30.** ▨ + 214 = 214 + 87

★ **31.** 204 + ▨ = 204

★ **32.** 146 + (▨ + 67) = (146 + 35) + 67

Use mental math to find the sum. Write only the answer.

MENTAL MATH

| | | | | |
|---|---|---|---|---|
| **33.** 34 <br> + 23 | **34.** 77 <br> + 22 | **35.** 365 <br> + 623 | **36.** 162 <br> + 27 | **37.** 435 <br> + 302 |

**38. Think:** Can you solve Exercises 33–37 more quickly using mental math or paper and pencil?

## PROBLEM SOLVING APPLICATIONS
### Choosing the Operation

Solve.

**39.** In the park, 146 rose bushes are in bloom and 214 are not. How many rose bushes are there?

**40.** The bicycle path is 13 miles long. The hiking path is 7 miles long. Which path is longer?

**41.** The park director plans to buy 448 tulip bulbs and 520 daffodil bulbs to plant this fall. Does he plan to buy more tulip bulbs or more daffodil bulbs?

★ **42.** The park had 139 visitors last Saturday and 257 visitors last Sunday. This weekend twice as many visitors are expected. How many are expected this weekend?

# ADDING GREATER NUMBERS

To find the sum of 3526 and 1792, you need to rename twice. Remember, you can rename 10 hundreds as 1 thousand.

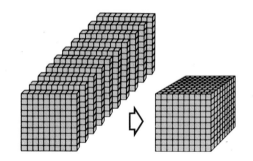

| Add the ones. | Add the tens. Rename 11 tens as 1 hundred 1 ten. | Add the hundreds. Rename 13 hundreds as 1 thousand 3 hundreds. | Add the thousands. |
|---|---|---|---|
| | 1 | 11 | 11 |
| 3526 | 3526 | 3526 | 3526 |
| + 1792 | + 1792 | + 1792 | + 1792 |
| 8 | 18 | 318 | 5318 |

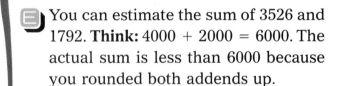 You can estimate the sum of 3526 and 1792. **Think:** 4000 + 2000 = 6000. The actual sum is less than 6000 because you rounded both addends up.

You may need to rename several times when you add greater numbers.

$$\begin{array}{r} {}^{1}\ \ {}^{11}\phantom{0} \\ 83{,}175 \\ +\ 29{,}346 \\ \hline 112{,}521 \end{array}$$

ALREADY ABOUT **6000** PEOPLE HAVE SEEN THIS FILM

**A**DVENTURE IN VAIL

## CLASS EXERCISES

Add. How many times do you need to rename?

| | | | | | | | | | |
|---|---|---|---|---|---|---|---|---|---|
| **1.** 5342 + 2235 | **2.** 5342 + 2835 | **3.** 5392 + 2835 | **4.** 53,926 + 28,353 | **5.** 53,926 + 28,357 |
| **6.** 4903 + 3615 | **7.** 4907 + 3615 | **8.** 49,074 + 36,158 | **9.** 49,074 + 36,958 | **10.** 49,074 + 46,958 |

# PRACTICE

Add.

| | | | | |
|---|---|---|---|---|
| **11.** 7142<br>+ 2094 | **12.** 6058<br>+ 2044 | **13.** 7644<br>+ 1595 | **14.** 9566<br>+ 4428 | **15.** 3940<br>+ 5980 |
| **16.** 5746<br>+ 4344 | **17.** 15,204<br>+ 34,791 | **18.** 27,882<br>+ 42,093 | **19.** 55,346<br>+ 12,780 | **20.** 79,386<br>+ 17,743 |
| **21.** 85,468<br>+ 29,391 | **22.** 64,821<br>+ 25,173 | **23.** 54,673<br>+ 83,798 | **24.** 10,955<br>+ 3,039 | **25.** 11,656<br>+ 2,238 |
| **26.** 26<br>45<br>+ 38 | **27.** 174<br>38<br>+ 9 | **28.** 984<br>329<br>+ 644 | **29.** 3507<br>469<br>+ 1852 | **30.** 4813<br>7659<br>+ 1999 |

**31.** 1538 + 7754    **32.** 9309 + 492    **33.** 20,399 + 19,799    **34.** 99,699 + 1,622

Round each addend to its greatest place value and estimate the sum. Then tell whether the actual sum will be less than or greater than the estimate.

ESTIMATE

| | | | |
|---|---|---|---|
| **35.** 3952<br>+ 4864 | **36.** 5169<br>+ 3205 | **37.** 42,309<br>+ 24,526 | **38.** 27,931<br>+ 16,540 |

## PROBLEM SOLVING APPLICATIONS
### Choosing the Operation

Solve.

**39.** So far at Cinema City, 13,842 tickets have been sold to *Journey to Saturn* and 10,987 tickets have been sold to *The Seven Stars*. How many tickets have been sold for both movies?

**40.** Five different movies are playing at Cinema City this week and 8 different movies are playing at The Movie Loft. How many more movies are playing at The Movie Loft than at Cinema City?

**41.** There are 368 seats in Theater 1. There are 290 seats in Theater 2. How many people can watch movies in these theaters at the same time?

★ **42.** When the movie begins, 147 people are seated. Then 23 people come in late. Before the movie ends, 20 people leave. How many people see the end of the movie?

# PROBLEM SOLVING
## Strategy: Reasonable Answers

The art classes are making decorations for the Crafts Festival. The morning class made 48 decorations and the afternoon class made 57 decorations. Marilee wants to find out how many decorations have been made so far. She adds to find the total.

$$\begin{array}{r} 48 \\ +57 \\ \hline 95 \end{array}$$

Is Marilee's answer reasonable? She uses estimation to check. She thinks $50 + 60 = 110$. Her estimate and her answer are not very close. Marilee tries the addition again and finds that she forgot to add the ten she got when she renamed. The answer should be 105 decorations.

$$\begin{array}{r} 48 \\ +57 \\ \hline \cancel{95} \\ 105 \end{array}$$

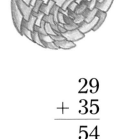

## CLASS EXERCISES

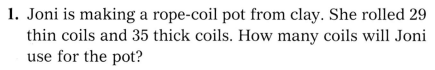
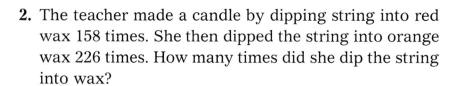

Is the answer reasonable? Use estimation to check. If the answer is not reasonable, what went wrong?

1. Joni is making a rope-coil pot from clay. She rolled 29 thin coils and 35 thick coils. How many coils will Joni use for the pot?

$$\begin{array}{r} 29 \\ + 35 \\ \hline 54 \end{array}$$

2. The teacher made a candle by dipping string into red wax 158 times. She then dipped the string into orange wax 226 times. How many times did she dip the string into wax?

$$\begin{array}{r} 158 \\ + 226 \\ \hline 384 \end{array}$$

3. Joseph made 17 stained glass pictures. He broke 9 of the pictures. How many stained glass pictures are left?

$$\begin{array}{r} 17 \\ - 9 \\ \hline 26 \end{array}$$

4. Luisa's art teacher brought in 12 boxes of crayons, 14 boxes of pastels, and 13 boxes of charcoal. How many boxes did Luisa's art teacher bring to class?

$$\begin{array}{r} 12 \\ 14 \\ + 13 \\ \hline 49 \end{array}$$

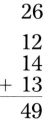

# PRACTICE

Estimate. If the answer is reasonable, write *reasonable*. If the answer is not reasonable, give the correct answer.

**5.** On Saturday morning, 17 people signed up for macrame lessons. That afternoon, 24 people signed up for lessons. How many people signed up Saturday for macrame lessons? *Answer:* 31 people

**6.** Last year Margaret Zimmer taught art for 1042 hours. This year she will teach art for 1968 hours. How many hours will Margaret Zimmer teach art in all? *Answer:* 2010 hours

**7.** Elise painted 36 oval signs, 52 rectangular signs, and 63 square signs. How many signs did Elise paint? *Answer:* 151 signs

**8.** Ken is making 15 invitations. He finished 8 of the invitations. How many more must Ken make? *Answer:* 23 invitations

★ **9.** A poster contest was held for third and fourth graders. For the contest, 617 third graders made posters. Twice as many fourth graders made posters. How many students entered the contest? *Answer:* 1234 students

★ **10.** Benito is making a beaded necklace. He has 8 solid beads, 7 spotted beads, and 9 striped beads. Unfortunately, 3 beads are cracked. How many beads can Benito use for the necklace? *Answer:* 31 beads

## CHECKPOINT 1

Estimate the sum. *(pages 38–39)*

**1.**   29
       + 36

**2.**   45
       + 18

**3.**   54
       + 33

Add. *(pages 36–37, 40–43)*

**4.**   23
       + 57

**5.**   584
       + 372

**6.**   6356
       + 2678

**7.**   43,466
       + 29,534

If the answer is reasonable, write *reasonable*. If it is not, give the correct answer. *(pages 44–45)*

**8.** Workout Sports Store had 296 baseball bats. A shipment arrived with 128 more. How many bats does Workout Sports Store have now? *Answer:* 314 baseball bats

*Extra practice on page 404*

# TWO-DIGIT SUBTRACTION

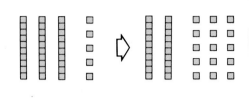

To subtract 18 from 35, you must first rename 3 tens 5 ones as 2 tens 15 ones.

| t | o |
|---|---|
| 2 | 15 |
| 3̶ | 5̶ |
| − 1 | 8 |

Now subtract the ones.

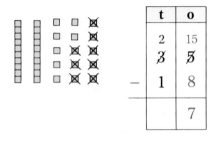

| t | o |
|---|---|
| 2 | 15 |
| 3̶ | 5̶ |
| − 1 | 8 |
| | 7 |

Then subtract the tens.

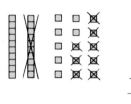

| t | o |
|---|---|
| 2 | 15 |
| 3̶ | 5̶ |
| − 1 | 8 |
| 1 | 7 |

Use addition to check the subtraction.

$$35 - 18 = 17 \qquad 17 + 18 = 35 \checkmark \text{ It checks.}$$

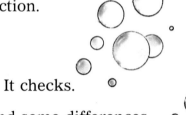

Mental math can help you find some differences.

$$\begin{array}{r} 37 \\ -18 \\ \hline 19 \end{array}$$

**Think:** 37 is 1 less than 38.
$38 - 18 = 20$, so $37 - 18 = 19$.

37 quarts

## CLASS EXERCISES

Complete.

1. 58 = 4 tens ⬚ ones
2. 43 = 3 tens ⬚ ones
3. 27 = 1 ten ⬚ ones
4. 74 = ⬚ tens 14 ones
5. 89 = ⬚ tens 19 ones
6. 62 = 5 tens ⬚ ones

Subtract. Do you need to rename? Explain why.

7. $\begin{array}{r} 57 \\ -36 \end{array}$
8. $\begin{array}{r} 84 \\ -14 \end{array}$
9. $\begin{array}{r} 65 \\ -37 \end{array}$
10. $\begin{array}{r} 38 \\ -25 \end{array}$
11. $\begin{array}{r} 72 \\ -49 \end{array}$
12. $\begin{array}{r} 43 \\ -28 \end{array}$

## PRACTICE

Subtract and check by adding.

| | | | | | | | | | | | |
|---|---|---|---|---|---|---|---|---|---|---|---|
| **13.** | 41<br>− 26 | **14.** | 69<br>− 39 | **15.** | 72<br>− 36 | **16.** | 22<br>− 19 | **17.** | 97<br>− 26 | **18.** | 53<br>− 38 |
| **19.** | 75<br>− 62 | **20.** | 42<br>− 18 | **21.** | 66<br>− 49 | **22.** | 83<br>− 8 | **23.** | 71<br>− 65 | **24.** | 92<br>− 6 |
| **25.** | 23<br>− 7 | **26.** | 55<br>− 48 | **27.** | 32<br>− 14 | **28.** | 63<br>− 29 | **29.** | 41<br>− 9 | **30.** | 56<br>− 38 |

**31.** 45 − 18    **32.** 37 − 24    **33.** 92 − 47    **34.** 35 − 6    **35.** 84 − 8

Complete.

★ **36.** 84 − ▢ = 61       ★ **37.** ▢ − 17 = 32       ★ **38.** 35 + ▢ = 81

Use mental math to subtract. Write only the difference.

| | | | | | | | | | |
|---|---|---|---|---|---|---|---|---|---|
| **39.** | 94<br>− 55 | **40.** | 22<br>− 13 | **41.** | 86<br>− 27 | **42.** | 68<br>− 39 | **43.** | 77<br>− 48 |

**MENTAL MATH**

## PROBLEM SOLVING APPLICATIONS
### Choosing the Operation

Solve.

**44.** At the beginning of the month, Pal's Pet Center had 97 leashes on hand. At the end of the month, 48 were left. How many were sold during the month?

**45.** Pal's Pet Center has 24 flea collars in stock now. The manager ordered 68 more. How many flea collars will the store have in all?

**46.** Bubbles shampoo is on sale. When the store opened, there were 54 bottles of Bubbles shampoo. At closing time, all but 18 had been sold. How many bottles were sold during the day?

**47.** Rawhide chips come in packages of 18 or 30. One customer bought one package in each size. How many rawhide chips did the customer buy?

# ESTIMATING DIFFERENCES

Colin takes 72 steps to walk across the school yard. His older brother takes 54 steps to walk across the school yard. About how many more steps does Colin take than his brother?

Estimate the difference by rounding each number to the greatest place value before you subtract.

$$
\begin{array}{r}
72 \rightarrow 70 \\
- 54 \rightarrow - 50 \\
\hline
20
\end{array}
$$

Colin takes about 20 more steps.

 Colin uses a calculator to find the actual difference. He enters 72 [−] 54 [=]. The answer he sees on the calculator is reasonable because the answer and the estimate are close.

## CLASS EXERCISES

What rounded numbers do you use when you estimate the difference?

| **1.** 52 <br> − 22 | **2.** 52 <br> − 25 | **3.** 57 <br> − 25 | **4.** 38 <br> − 18 | **5.** 34 <br> − 18 | **6.** 34 <br> − 13 |
|---|---|---|---|---|---|

Round each number. Then estimate the difference.

| **7.** 73 <br> − 31 | **8.** 73 <br> − 35 | **9.** 77 <br> − 35 | **10.** 46 <br> − 29 | **11.** 46 <br> − 24 | **12.** 42 <br> − 24 |
|---|---|---|---|---|---|

## PRACTICE

Estimate the difference.

| **13.** 79 <br> − 24 | **14.** 93 <br> − 38 | **15.** 41 <br> − 28 | **16.** 88 <br> − 37 | **17.** 64 <br> − 43 | **18.** 92 <br> − 77 |
|---|---|---|---|---|---|
| **19.** 68 <br> − 13 | **20.** 84 <br> − 47 | **21.** 72 <br> − 54 | **22.** 66 <br> − 19 | **23.** 74 <br> − 35 | **24.** 44 <br> − 26 |

**25.**  86   **26.**  45   **27.**  63   **28.**  98   **29.**  74   **30.**  73
   − 35      − 18      − 32      − 29      − 57      − 15

**31.** 79 − 63      **32.** 84 − 59      **33.** 32 − 28      **34.** 91 − 69

Write two subtraction problems for which you could use this estimate.

★ **35.** 40 − 10 = 30  ★ **36.** 80 − 70 = 10  ★ **37.** 50 − 20 = 30  ★ **38.** 60 − 30 = 30

The subtraction was done on a calculator. Is the answer reasonable? Write *yes* or *no*.

**CALCULATOR**

**39.**  71   `24`   **40.**  58   `49`   **41.**  82   `44`
   − 47           − 39           − 38

**42.**  35   `56`   **43.**  43   `406`   **44.**  62   `48`
   − 21           − 27           − 14

## PROBLEM SOLVING APPLICATIONS
### Using Estimation

Estimate the answer.

**45.** From the fourth grade, 56 students signed up for after school activities. From the fifth grade, 43 students signed up. About how many students signed up in all?

**46.** Three classes are on the playground now. One class has 26 students, another class has 31 students, and another class has 24 students. About how many students are on the playground now?

**47.** The music room has 84 chairs. There are 37 chairs in room 403. About how many more chairs are in the music room than in room 403?

**48.** There are 75 boxes of crayons in the supply closet. The first grade class takes 24 boxes. About how many boxes are in the supply closet now?

★ **49.** There are 92 pieces of chalk in the box. If 28 students each take 2 pieces of chalk, about how many pieces of chalk are left in the box?

# THREE-DIGIT SUBTRACTION

To subtract 284 from 475, you have to rename a hundred as 10 tens.

  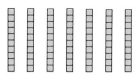

Subtract the ones.

| h | t | o |
|---|---|---|
| 4 | 7 | 5 |
| − 2 | 8 | 4 |
|  |  | 1 |

Rename 4 hundreds 7 tens as 3 hundreds 17 tens.

| h | t | o |
|---|---|---|
| ³4̸ | ¹⁷7 | 5 |
| − 2 | 8 | 4 |
|  |  | 1 |

Subtract the tens and hundreds.

| h | t | o |
|---|---|---|
| ³4̸ | ¹⁷7 | 5 |
| − 2 | 8 | 4 |
| 1 | 9 | 1 |

To subtract 549 from 723, you must rename twice.

Rename the tens.

$$\begin{array}{r} {\scriptstyle 1\ 13} \\ 7\ 2\ 3 \\ -\ 5\ 4\ 9 \\ \hline \end{array}$$

Subtract the ones.

$$\begin{array}{r} {\scriptstyle 1\ 13} \\ 7\ 2\ 3 \\ -\ 5\ 4\ 9 \\ \hline 4 \end{array}$$

Rename the hundreds.

$$\begin{array}{r} {\scriptstyle 11} \\ {\scriptstyle 6\ 1\ 13} \\ 7\ 2\ 3 \\ -\ 5\ 4\ 9 \\ \hline 4 \end{array}$$

Subtract the tens and hundreds.

$$\begin{array}{r} {\scriptstyle 11} \\ {\scriptstyle 6\ 1\ 13} \\ 7\ 2\ 3 \\ -\ 5\ 4\ 9 \\ \hline 1\ 7\ 4 \end{array}$$

 You can find this difference mentally.

$$\begin{array}{r} 364 \\ -\ 132 \\ \hline 232 \end{array}$$

**Think:**   364 − 100 = 264
264 −  30 = 234
234 −   2 = 232

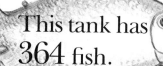

This tank has 364 fish.

## CLASS EXERCISES

Complete.

**1.** 680 = 5 hundreds ▨ tens

**2.** 320 = 2 hundreds ▨ tens

Do you need to rename? Subtract.

**3.**  643
− 211

**4.**  643
− 215

**5.**  643
− 245

**6.**  737
− 524

**7.**  737
− 529

**8.**  737
− 549

# PRACTICE

Subtract.

| 9. | 978<br>− 649 | 10. | 685<br>− 217 | 11. | 754<br>− 343 | 12. | 958<br>− 239 | 13. | 836<br>− 524 | 14. | 795<br>− 736 |
|---|---|---|---|---|---|---|---|---|---|---|---|

| 15. | 754<br>− 362 | 16. | 517<br>− 303 | 17. | 854<br>− 574 | 18. | 677<br>− 495 | 19. | 768<br>− 294 | 20. | 845<br>− 758 |
|---|---|---|---|---|---|---|---|---|---|---|---|

| 21. | 567<br>− 78 | 22. | 443<br>− 356 | 23. | 681<br>− 29 | 24. | 857<br>− 578 | 25. | 534<br>− 73 | 26. | 741<br>− 258 |
|---|---|---|---|---|---|---|---|---|---|---|---|

**27.** 381 − 164    **28.** 743 − 529    **29.** 667 − 574    **30.** 965 − 873

Compare. Write < , > , or = .

★ **31.** 295 − 187 ▥ 334 − 211    ★ **32.** 687 − 165 ▥ 953 − 248

★ **33.** 428 − 269 ▥ 531 − 373    ★ **34.** 856 − 77 ▥ 721 − 56

Use mental math to subtract. Write only the difference.

| 35. | 76<br>− 32 | 36. | 87<br>− 21 | 37. | 417<br>− 205 | 38. | 789<br>− 748 | 39. | 556<br>− 244 |
|---|---|---|---|---|---|---|---|---|---|

**MENTAL MATH**

## PROBLEM SOLVING APPLICATIONS
### Choosing the Operation

Solve.

**40.** The largest fish tank at Allentown Aquarium holds 365 gallons of water. The aquarium plans to get a new tank that holds 542 gallons of water. How many more gallons of water will the new tank hold?

**41.** There is a display of prehistoric sea creatures. It shows that the Tylosaurus was about 22 feet long. The Elasmosaurus was about 50 feet long. The Portheus was about 14 feet long. Which of the three was longest?

★ **42.** There are 476 fish in 1 large tank. The fish will be put into 2 tanks with the same number of fish in each. How many fish will be in each tank?

# ZEROS IN SUBTRACTION

The post office received 305 packages on Monday. By the end of the day, 228 were delivered. To find how many packages were not delivered, subtract 228 from 305. You need to rename a hundred before you can subtract.

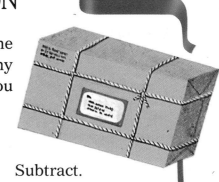

Rename 3 hundreds 0 tens as 2 hundreds 10 tens.

$$\begin{array}{r} {\scriptstyle 2\ 10} \\ \cancel{3}\,\cancel{0}\,5 \\ -\ 2\ 2\ 8 \\ \hline \end{array}$$

Rename 10 tens 5 ones as 9 tens 15 ones.

$$\begin{array}{r} {\scriptstyle\ \ \ 9\ 15} \\ {\scriptstyle 2\ 10} \\ \cancel{3}\,\cancel{0}\,\cancel{5} \\ -\ 2\ 2\ 8 \\ \hline \end{array}$$

Subtract.

$$\begin{array}{r} {\scriptstyle\ \ \ 9\ 15} \\ {\scriptstyle 2\ 10} \\ \cancel{3}\,\cancel{0}\,\cancel{5} \\ -\ 2\ 2\ 8 \\ \hline 7\ 7 \end{array}$$

There were 77 packages not delivered.

When subtracting with zeros, you can combine steps to save time. To subtract 375 from 500, think of 500 as 50 tens.

Rename 50 tens as 49 tens and 10 ones.

$$\begin{array}{r} {\scriptstyle 49\ \ 10} \\ \cancel{5}\,\cancel{0}\,\cancel{0} \\ -\ 3\ 7\ 5 \\ \hline \end{array}$$

Subtract.

$$\begin{array}{r} {\scriptstyle 49\ \ 10} \\ \cancel{5}\,\cancel{0}\,\cancel{0} \\ -\ 3\ 7\ 5 \\ \hline 1\ 2\ 5 \end{array}$$

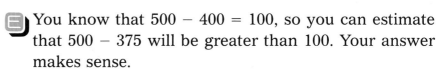

You know that $500 - 400 = 100$, so you can estimate that $500 - 375$ will be greater than 100. Your answer makes sense.

## CLASS EXERCISES

Complete.

**1.** 800 = ▨ tens

**2.** 400 = ▨ tens

**3.** 900 = ▨ tens

**4.** 30 tens = ▨ tens 10 ones

**5.** 70 tens = ▨ tens 10 ones

Subtract.

| **6.** 703<br>− 236 | **7.** 700<br>− 296 | **8.** 305<br>− 124 | **9.** 300<br>− 124 | **10.** 804<br>− 635 | **11.** 804<br>− 735 |
|---|---|---|---|---|---|

# PRACTICE

Subtract.

| | | | | | | |
|---|---|---|---|---|---|---|
| **12.** 750 − 324 | **13.** 670 − 239 | **14.** 430 − 118 | **15.** 280 − 145 | **16.** 630 − 129 | **17.** 450 − 442 | |
| **18.** 309 − 138 | **19.** 707 − 205 | **20.** 508 − 185 | **21.** 602 − 341 | **22.** 405 − 352 | **23.** 307 − 287 | |
| **24.** 605 − 83 | **25.** 902 − 667 | **26.** 803 − 78 | **27.** 310 − 38 | **28.** 802 − 8 | **29.** 901 − 339 | |
| **30.** 400 − 163 | **31.** 500 − 225 | **32.** 900 − 4 | **33.** 700 − 301 | **34.** 300 − 138 | **35.** 500 − 275 | |

**36.** 480 − 299   **37.** 600 − 376   **38.** 704 − 695   **39.** 250 − 144

**40.** 203 − 95   **41.** 302 − 28   **42.** 700 − 5   **43.** 401 − 6

You know 800 − 400 = 400. Estimate. Is the difference *greater than* 400 or *less than* 400?

**ESTIMATE**

| | | | | |
|---|---|---|---|---|
| **44.** 800 − 289 | **45.** 800 − 523 | **46.** 755 − 400 | **47.** 805 − 400 | **48.** 850 − 395 |

## PROBLEM SOLVING APPLICATIONS
### Choosing the Operation

Solve.

**49.** There are 700 letters and 315 post cards to be delivered. How many more letters than post cards must be delivered?

**50.** There are 240 magazines, 34 newspapers, and 109 packages to be delivered. Of these kinds of mail, which has the least number to be delivered?

★ **51.** Donny writes a letter to his cousin Rayleen every 4 weeks. He writes a letter to his Uncle Sal every 6 weeks. After the first week, does Donny ever write to both Rayleen and Uncle Sal in the same week?

# SUBTRACTING GREATER NUMBERS

To subtract 6626 from 8134, you have to rename a thousand as 10 hundreds.

| Rename the tens. | Subtract the ones and the tens. | Rename the thousands. | Subtract the hundreds and the thousands. |
|---|---|---|---|
| 2 14 | 2 14 | 7 11 2 14 | 7 11 2 14 |
| 8 1 3̸ 4̸ | 8 1 3̸ 4̸ | 8̸ 1̸ 3̸ 4̸ | 8̸ 1̸ 3̸ 4̸ |
| − 6 6 2 6 | − 6 6 2 6 | − 6 6 2 6 | − 6 6 2 6 |
|  | 0 8 | 0 8 | 1 5 0 8 |

To subtract 26,917 from 34,641, you have to rename a ten thousand.

$$
\begin{array}{r}
\overset{\phantom{0}\overset{13}{\phantom{0}}}{\overset{2\ \ 3\ 16\ 3\ 11}{3̸\ 4̸,6̸\ 4̸\ 1̸}} \\
-\ 2\ 6,9\ 1\ 7 \\
\hline
7\ 7\ 2\ 4
\end{array}
$$

 To check her answer, Grace uses a calculator to add. 7724 ⊞ 26917 ⊟ On the screen she sees 34641.

**Think:** What are two other ways Grace could check her answer?

## CLASS EXERCISES

Subtract. How many times do you need to rename?

| 1. | 6854 | 2. | 6854 | 3. | 6854 | 4. | 43,295 | 5. | 43,295 |
|---|---|---|---|---|---|---|---|---|---|
|  | − 2432 |  | − 2438 |  | − 5978 |  | − 16,188 |  | − 16,398 |

## PRACTICE

Subtract.

| 6. | 4779 | 7. | 5563 | 8. | 7524 | 9. | 8546 | 10. | 9835 |
|---|---|---|---|---|---|---|---|---|---|
|  | − 1674 |  | − 4038 |  | − 3258 |  | − 7397 |  | − 5469 |

| 11. | 3628 | 12. | 8749 | 13. | 4736 | 14. | 5683 | 15. | 7552 |
|---|---|---|---|---|---|---|---|---|---|
|  | − 1709 |  | − 6638 |  | − 817 |  | − 2946 |  | − 3629 |

| **16.** 87,274<br>$-$ 25,504 | **17.** 46,407<br>$-$ 14,378 | **18.** 98,188<br>$-$ 86,549 | **19.** 67,798<br>$-$ 18,536 | **20.** 85,439<br>$-$ 46,847 |
|---|---|---|---|---|
| **21.** 97,160<br>$-$ 5,046 | **22.** 54,167<br>$-$ 7,453 | **23.** 40,146<br>$-$ 686 | **24.** 86,530<br>$-$ 72,678 | **25.** 70,402<br>$-$ 6,328 |

**26.** 3628 $-$ 1709        **27.** 5048 $-$ 2937        **28.** 6002 $-$ 4774

**29.** 61,123 $-$ 33,467        **30.** 51,726 $-$ 34,530        **31.** 53,259 $-$ 9,494

Complete.

| ★ **32.** 5 3<br>$-$ 2015<br>3208 | ★ **33.** 24▨<br>$-$ 658<br>1837 | ★ **34.** ▨13▨<br>$-$ 1 45<br>7791 | ★ **35.** 56, 54<br>$-$ 7,10▨<br>48,946 |
|---|---|---|---|

Add to check the answer. Use a calculator if you have one.
If the answer is not correct, write the correct answer.

| **36.** 5323<br>$-$ 2015<br>3318 | **37.** 42,302<br>$-$ 38,984<br>3318 | **38.** 80,490<br>$-$ 63,211<br>17,289 | **39.** 23,508<br>$-$ 6,029<br>17,479 |
|---|---|---|---|

**CALCULATOR**

# PROBLEM SOLVING APPLICATIONS
## Using a Table

Use the table to solve.

**40.** How many more people lived in Juneau in 1980 than in 1970?

**41.** Which city had the lowest population in 1980?

★ **42.** Which grew more from 1970 to 1980, the population of Ketchikan or the population of Sitka?

★ **43.** If the population of Juneau increased by the same amount from 1980 to 1990 as it did from 1970 to 1980, what would the population be in 1990?

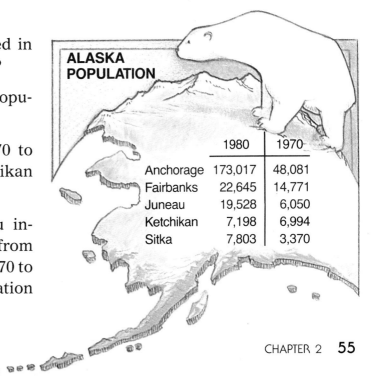

**ALASKA POPULATION**

| | 1980 | 1970 |
|---|---|---|
| Anchorage | 173,017 | 48,081 |
| Fairbanks | 22,645 | 14,771 |
| Juneau | 19,528 | 6,050 |
| Ketchikan | 7,198 | 6,994 |
| Sitka | 7,803 | 3,370 |

# MONEY

To write the value of an amount of money, you can use a cent sign or a dollar sign and a decimal point.

penny
1¢ or $.01

nickel
5¢ or $.05

dime
10¢ or $.10

quarter
25¢ or $.25

half dollar
50¢ or $.50

one dollar
$1.00 or $1

five dollars
$5.00 or $5

ten dollars
$10.00 or $10

twenty dollars
$20.00 or $20

One dollar and 61 cents is 161¢ or $1.61.

## CLASS EXERCISES

What is the value? Use the dollar sign and the decimal point to write the value.

1.

2.

3. 1 dollar 1 quarter

4. 1 dollar 1 quarter 1 dime

5. 5 dollars 1 half dollar

6. 5 dollars 1 half dollar 3 nickels

7. 8 dollars 6 dimes

8. 8 dollars 6 dimes 15 pennies

# PRACTICE

Use a dollar sign and a decimal point to write the value.

**9.** 1 nickel 4 pennies     **10.** 186¢     **11.** 1 half dollar 3 dimes

**12.** 335¢     **13.** 1 dollar 2 nickels     **14.** 403¢

**15.** 207¢     **16.** 2 dimes 1 nickel     **17.** 1 quarter 1 nickel

**18.** 2 dollars     **19.** 5 dollars 1 nickel     **20.** 48¢

**21.** 1 quarter 2 pennies     **22.** 14 dollars 4 pennies     **23.** 801¢

**24.** 4 dollars 2 dimes 1 nickel     **25.** 10 dollars 1 half dollar 3 pennies

**26.** 18 dollars 5 dimes 9 pennies     **27.** 1 dollar 3 quarters 4 nickels

Which amount is greater? Write *a* or *b*. Then use a dollar
sign and a decimal point to write the greater value.

**28. a.** 1 dollar 3 quarters 6 nickels     **b.** 2 half dollars 3 dimes

**29. a.** 9 dimes 7 nickels 10 pennies     **b.** 1 quarter 4 dimes 3 nickels

**30. a.** 1 dollar 2 quarters 2 dimes     **b.** 1 dollar 10 nickels 12 pennies

★ **31. a.** 18 dollars 2 half dollars 4 dimes     **b.** 20 dollars

Write the answer.

**32.**  8    **33.**  13    **34.**  18    **35.**  842
    + 9        − 5        + 9       − 793

**36.**  5653    **37.**  3487    **38.**  27,805    **39.**  56,054
   − 3836      + 6245      − 14,319      + 7,108

**MIXED REVIEW**

## PROBLEM SOLVING APPLICATIONS
### Nonroutine Problems

Suppose you have this amount of money in your bank.
What coins do you have? Some problems may have more
than one answer.

**40.** 7 coins worth 20¢     **41.** 8 coins worth 25¢     **42.** 6 coins worth $.50

**43.** 8 coins worth $1     **44.** 11 coins worth $1     **45.** 12 coins worth $1.50

# ADDING AND SUBTRACTING MONEY

Eileen wants to buy one cassette tape for $5.28 and another for $2.59. To find the total cost, she adds.

$$\begin{array}{r} 1 \\ \$5.28 \\ +\ \ 2.59 \\ \hline \$7.87 \end{array}$$

Eileen needs $7.87 to buy both tapes.

When you add or subtract money, you must keep the decimal points in line.

Zeke buys a record that is on sale for $6.88. The regular price is $8.45. Zeke thinks: $6.88 + $1.00 = $7.88. Zeke estimates that he will save more than $1.00. To find exactly how much he will save, he subtracts.

Zeke will save $1.57.

$$\begin{array}{r} 13 \\ 7\ \ \cancel{3}\,15 \\ \$\cancel{8}\ .\cancel{4}\,\cancel{5} \\ -\ \ 6\ .8\,8 \\ \hline \$1\ .5\,7 \end{array}$$

## CLASS EXERCISES

Add or subtract.

| | | | | | |
|---|---|---|---|---|---|
| **1.** $.25<br>+ .68 | **2.** $4.25<br>+ 3.68 | **3.** $54.25<br>+ 13.68 | **4.** $.84<br>− .79 | **5.** $3.84<br>− 1.79 | **6.** $43.84<br>− 21.79 |

**7.** What is the difference between $7.35 and $2.91?

**8.** What is the sum of $11.18 and $24.47?

## PRACTICE

Add or subtract.

| | | | | |
|---|---|---|---|---|
| **9.** $3.88<br>+ 2.12 | **10.** $5.05<br>+ 1.98 | **11.** $4.19<br>+ 2.87 | **12.** $7.75<br>− 2.32 | **13.** $5.00<br>− 3.67 |

| 14. | $12.97 | 15. | $24.49 | 16. | $53.62 | 17. | $3.75 | 18. | $10.00 |
|---|---|---|---|---|---|---|---|---|---|
| | + 5.59 | | + 18.44 | | − 11.98 | | − .68 | | − 5.99 |

| 19. | $23.62 | 20. | $16.21 | 21. | $27.98 | 22. | $7.93 | 23. | $15.12 |
|---|---|---|---|---|---|---|---|---|---|
| | + 14.28 | | − 7.04 | | + 46.16 | | − 4.75 | | + 8.76 |

| 24. | $1.99 | 25. | $2.08 | 26. | $12.88 | 27. | $19.95 | 28. | $11.08 |
|---|---|---|---|---|---|---|---|---|---|
| | 2.19 | | .98 | | 3.11 | | 12.95 | | 12.98 |
| | + 3.78 | | + 1.88 | | + 1.97 | | + 8.75 | | + 13.87 |

**29.** $.86 + $.49        **30.** $.75 − $.69        **31.** $.57 + $.94

**32.** $5.46 + $.89        **33.** $15.57 − $7.47        **34.** $6.95 − $2.59

**35.** $47.62 − $32.85        **36.** $64.48 + $18.36        **37.** $16.02 − $7.48

**38.** $14.57 + $6.23 + $.78        **39.** $12.65 + $.56 + $1.98

Estimate. Is the amount saved *greater than* or *less than* $1.00?

ESTIMATE

**40.** original price: $1.87
sale price: $1.23

**41.** original price: $4.95
sale price: $3.50

**42.** original price: $18.25
sale price: $17.88

**43.** original price: $21.50
sale price: $18.99

## PROBLEM SOLVING APPLICATIONS
### Choosing the Operation

Solve.

**44.** Antonio spends $27.64 for a jacket and $7.98 for a pair of gloves. How much does Antonio spend altogether?

**45.** Nancy bought a sweater for $21.88. Lenore spent $5.00 more for her sweater. How much did Lenore pay for the sweater?

★ **46.** Len is saving his money to buy a bicycle lock that costs $13.25 and a tire pump that costs $6.99. Len has saved $19.50. Does he have enough money to buy both the lock and the tire pump?

★ **47.** Patricia buys a birthday gift for $18.95, two cards for $.85 each, wrapping paper for $2.25, and ribbon for $.79. She gets $2.36 off the total price. How much does Patricia pay?

# PROBLEM SOLVING
## Making Change

1. Understand
2. Plan
3. Work
4. Answer/Check

Yoshi gives the clerk $10.00 to pay for a bag of food for his dog. The food costs $8.38. What coins and bills can the clerk give Yoshi for his change?

**M)** Here's one way to figure change. Start with the cost and count the change to the amount you are given. Use the fewest coins and bills possible. You can do this mentally.

Count: $8.38    $8.39        $8.40        $8.50        $9.00              $10.00

The clerk can give Yoshi 2 pennies, 1 dime, 1 half dollar, and 1 one-dollar bill. Yoshi gets $1.62 in change.

## CLASS EXERCISES

Count out the change.

| | Price of Item | Amount Given | Change |
|---|---|---|---|
| **1.** | $1.29 | $1.50 | Count: $1.29  $1.30 |
| **2.** | $3.15 | $5.00 | Count: $3.15 |

What coins and bills would you give as change? Count it out.

**3.** price of item: $12.50
amount given: $15.00
Count: $12.50, ▩ , ▩ , ▩

**4.** price of item: $14.62
amount given: $20.00
Count: $14.62, ▩ , ▩ , ▩ , ▩ , ▩ , ▩

# PRACTICE

Solve. When finding the change, use the fewest coins and bills possible.

**5.** Lester buys a record album for $8.98. He gives the clerk a ten-dollar bill. What change does Lester receive?

**6.** Maureen buys school supplies for $11.47. She gives the clerk a twenty-dollar bill. What change does the clerk give Maureen?

**7.** Roberta gave the clerk $30 for a basketball that cost $21.75. She received 5 pennies, 2 nickels, 1 dime, 3 one-dollar bills, 1 five-dollar bill, and 1 ten-dollar bill as change. Was her change correct?

**8.** Martina buys a mystery book. With tax, the total bill comes to $10.44. Martina gives the cashier $20. The cashier has no half dollars. What coins and bills will he give Martina for change?

★ **9.** Soon-Lee gave the clerk $40.00 for a blouse. She received 1 ten-dollar bill, 1 five-dollar bill, 1 one-dollar bill, and 1 nickel for her change. How much did Soon-Lee pay for the blouse?

★ **10.** Eugene spends $2.16 at the hobby shop, but he does not have that exact amount of money. What is the least amount he can give to the clerk to avoid getting any pennies in change?

# CHECKPOINT 2

Estimate the difference. *(pages 48–49)*

**1.**  84
     − 32

**2.**  59
     − 27

**3.**  43
     − 18

Subtract. *(pages 46–47, 50–55)*

**4.**  78
     − 52

**5.**  758
     − 243

**6.**  4572
     − 2649

Add or subtract. *(pages 58–59)*

**7.**  $23.47
     − 18.73

**8.**  $22.49
     +  7.62

Solve using the fewest coins and bills possible. *(pages 60–61)*

**9.** Carl gives the clerk $15 for a paint set that costs $11.48. What is Carl's change?

*Extra practice on page 404*

Estimate the answer. *(pages 38–39)*

| 1. | 2. | 3. | 4. |
|---|---|---|---|
| 14 | 29 | 48 | 73 |
| + 16 | + 31 | + 11 | 24 |
| | | | + 12 |

Write the answer. *(pages 36–37, 40–43)*

| 5. | 6. | 7. | 8. |
|---|---|---|---|
| 59 | 624 | 1321 | 11,963 |
| + 26 | + 337 | + 6984 | + 4,051 |

If the answer is reasonable, write *reasonable*. If it is not, give the correct answer. *(pages 44–45)*

9. Toni made 3 batches of rolls for the party. She made 38 in the first batch, 24 in the second batch, and 26 in the last batch. How many rolls did Toni make?
*Answer:* 78 rolls

Estimate the answer. *(pages 48–49)*

| 10. | 11. | 12. | 13. |
|---|---|---|---|
| 81 | 68 | 79 | 52 |
| − 22 | − 41 | − 36 | − 47 |

Write the answer. *(pages 46–47, 50–55)*

| 14. | 15. | 16. | 17. |
|---|---|---|---|
| 58 | 701 | 9657 | 86,753 |
| − 36 | − 542 | − 8488 | − 59,562 |

Write the answer. *(pages 58–59)*

| 18. | 19. | 20. | 21. |
|---|---|---|---|
| $3.91 | $6.82 | $22.09 | $72.41 |
| + 2.51 | − 3.98 | + 13.75 | − 55.38 |

Use the fewest coins and bills in the answer. *(pages 60–61)*

22. Ben buys a sweater for $17.79. He gives the clerk a twenty-dollar bill. What coins and bills does the clerk give Ben for change?

*Extra practice on page 405*

# MATHEMATICS and ART

People through history used art to record famous events, people, and places. Many artists worked on paper, using pen, pencil, watercolor, crayons, charcoal, or pastels. This table shows the titles, artists, and dates of works of art from American history. Use it to solve the problems.

| TITLE | ARTIST | DATES |
|---|---|---|
| *The Manner of Their Fishing* | John White | 1585-87 |
| *New York from Brooklyn Heights* | Jasper Danckaerts | 1679 |
| *California Indians* | Alexandre-Jean Noel | 1769 |
| *Boston Common from Charles Street Mall* | George Harvey | 1835-40 |
| *In the Rocky Mountains* | Washington F. Friend | 1840 |
| *Madison Street, Chicago* | Alfred R. Waud | 1872 |
| *Gemini IV Launch from Cape Kennedy* | Paul Calle | 1965 |

## HOW DID IT LOOK?

1. How many years were there between the works *California Indians* and *Madison Street, Chicago*?

2. The Declaration of Independence was adopted in 1776. Which work was done closest to this year?

3. In 1958 the United States launched earth satellites. How many years later was the drawing of Gemini IV made?

4. The First Assembly of New York was in 1683. How many years were there between this event and the work of New York by Danckaerts?

5. Some of the Rocky Mountains are in Utah. Utah was admitted into the Union in 1896. *In the Rocky Mountains* was made how much earlier?

# Enrichment

The square below is a magic square. The magic sum in this square is 15.

| | | | 15 |
|---|---|---|---|
| 8 | 3 | 4 | 15 |
| 1 | 5 | 9 | 15 |
| 6 | 7 | 2 | 15 |
| 15 | 15 | 15 | 15 |

You can check to see if a number square is a magic square by adding the numbers in every row, every column, and every diagonal. If all the sums are the same, the square is a magic square.

**1.** Is this a magic square? Tell why or why not.

| 3 | 6 | 2 |
|---|---|---|
| 4 | 5 | 2 |
| 4 | 0 | 7 |

Tell if the square is a magic square. If it is, name the magic sum.

**2.**

| 11 | 6 | 13 |
|---|---|---|
| 12 | 10 | 8 |
| 7 | 14 | 9 |

**3.**

| 28 | 29 | 24 |
|---|---|---|
| 23 | 27 | 31 |
| 30 | 26 | 25 |

**4.**

| 1 | 15 | 14 | 4 |
|---|---|---|---|
| 12 | 6 | 7 | 9 |
| 8 | 10 | 11 | 5 |
| 13 | 3 | 2 | 16 |

**5.**

| 4 | 5 | 8 | 3 |
|---|---|---|---|
| 6 | 7 | 9 | 4 |
| 6 | 4 | 3 | 7 |
| 4 | 4 | 6 | 6 |

**6.**

| 46 | 53 | 48 |
|---|---|---|
| 51 | 49 | 47 |
| 50 | 45 | 52 |

MAGIC
SQUARES

This square is a magic square, but one number is missing.

To find the missing number, find the sum of the numbers in any complete row, column, or diagonal.

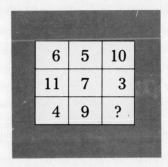

| 6 | 5 | 10 |
|---|---|----|
| 11 | 7 | 3 |
| 4 | 9 | ? |

The sum of the top row is 21.
$$6 + 5 + 10 = 21$$

The sum of the last column must be 21, too.

**Think:** $10 + 3 + ? = 21$. Now find the missing addend.
$$13 + ? = 21$$
$$13 + 8 = 21$$

The missing number is 8.

To check, add the numbers in the last row.

$$4 + 9 + 8 = 21✓$$

Complete each magic square.

**7.**

| 12 | 7 | 14 |
|----|----|----|
| 13 | 11 | 9 |
| 8 | ? | 10 |

**8.**

| ? | 74 | ? |
|----|----|----|
| 80 | 78 | 76 |
| 75 | 82 | ? |

**9.**

| 113 | 120 | 115 |
|-----|-----|-----|
| 118 | ? | 114 |
| 117 | 112 | 119 |

**10.**

| 101 | 115 | 114 | ? |
|-----|-----|-----|-----|
| 112 | 106 | 107 | 109 |
| 108 | 110 | 111 | 105 |
| 113 | 103 | 102 | ? |

# CUMULATIVE REVIEW

Choose the correct answer. Write *a*, *b*, *c*, or *d*.

Find the value of the underlined digit.

**1.** 4947
- **a.** 4
- **b.** 40
- **c.** 400
- **d.** none of these

**2.** 601,734
- **a.** 1000
- **b.** 10,000
- **c.** 100,000
- **d.** none of these

**3.** 513,166,725
- **a.** 3000
- **b.** 3,000,000
- **c.** 30,000,000
- **d.** none of these

Compare the numbers.

**4.** 4131 ▨ 4311
- **a.** >
- **b.** <
- **c.** =
- **d.** none of these

**5.** 60,421 ▨ 6421
- **a.** >
- **b.** <
- **c.** =
- **d.** none of these

**6.** 738,926 ▨ 737,926
- **a.** >
- **b.** <
- **c.** =
- **d.** none of these

Round to the greatest place value.

**7.** 538
- **a.** 540
- **b.** 535
- **c.** 530
- **d.** none of these

**8.** 7007
- **a.** 7000
- **b.** 7010
- **c.** 7100
- **d.** none of these

**9.** 33,584
- **a.** 33,000
- **b.** 30,000
- **c.** 40,000
- **d.** none of these

Find the answer.

**10.** 81 + 928
- **a.** 909
- **b.** 1009
- **c.** 1109
- **d.** none of these

**11.** 373 + 325 + 146
- **a.** 834
- **b.** 744
- **c.** 734
- **d.** none of these

**12.** 21,747 + 6,054
- **a.** 27,891
- **b.** 27,801
- **c.** 27,891
- **d.** none of these

Estimate to find the reasonable answer.

**13.** On Tuesday 124 concert tickets were sold. On Wednesday 103 were sold, and on Thursday 96 were sold. How many tickets were sold altogether?
- **a.** 323 tickets
- **b.** 432 tickets
- **c.** 213 tickets
- **d.** 112 tickets

Estimate to find the reasonable answer.

**14.** Nick collected 52 leaves for his science project. He has already pasted 26 leaves in his notebook. How many more leaves does Nick have to paste?
    **a.** 36 leaves     **b.** 78 leaves     **c.** 26 leaves     **d.** 52 leaves

Find the answer.

| **15.** $\begin{array}{r} 91 \\ -\ 79 \\ \hline \end{array}$ | **16.** $\begin{array}{r} 483 \\ -\ 199 \\ \hline \end{array}$ | **17.** $\begin{array}{r} 6083 \\ -\ 2174 \\ \hline \end{array}$ |
|---|---|---|
| **a.** 2 | **a.** 283 | **a.** 3909 |
| **b.** 12 | **b.** 274 | **b.** 3919 |
| **c.** 28 | **c.** 374 | **c.** 3901 |
| **d.** none of these | **d.** none of these | **d.** none of these |

Find the answer.

| **18.** $\begin{array}{r} \$9.81 \\ -\ 6.44 \\ \hline \end{array}$ | **19.** $\begin{array}{r} \$48.93 \\ +\ 12.99 \\ \hline \end{array}$ | **20.** $\begin{array}{r} \$77.12 \\ -\ 21.08 \\ \hline \end{array}$ |
|---|---|---|
| **a.** $3.38 | **a.** $60.82 | **a.** $56.14 |
| **b.** $3.47 | **b.** $61.02 | **b.** $56.04 |
| **c.** $3.37 | **c.** $61.92 | **c.** $55.04 |
| **d.** none of these | **d.** none of these | **d.** none of these |

# LANGUAGE and VOCABULARY REVIEW

Copy the words on your paper. Write the letter of the matching definition next to each word.

**1.** estimate           **a.** the symbols 0, 1, 2, 3, 4, 5, 6, 7, 8, or 9

**2.** sum                **b.** the answer in subtraction

**3.** digits              **c.** the answer in addition

**4.** difference        **d.** to find the likely answer by rounding the numbers before doing the arithmetic

# INPUT AND OUTPUT PARTS

A computer is a tool that works with data. **Data** are the letters, numbers, and symbols that you give to a computer or get from a computer. Data that you put into a computer are called **input.** Data that you get out of a computer are called **output.**

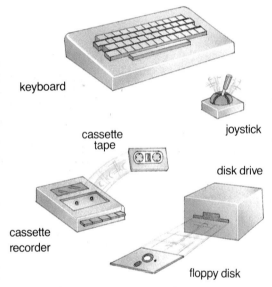

keyboard

joystick

cassette tape

disk drive

cassette recorder

floppy disk

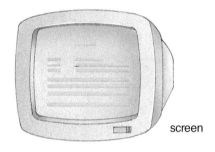

screen

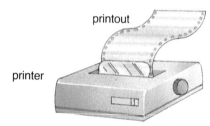

printout

printer

You can use these parts for input.

You can see the output on these parts.

Write *I* if you are working with input. Write *O* if you are working with output.

1. You press the number keys.
2. You move the joystick.
3. You see $50-35=15$ on the printer.
4. You see the word HELLO on the screen.
5. You put a tape in the cassette recorder.
6. You see GOODBYE on the printout.
7. You see your name on the screen.
8. You put a disk into the disk drive.

# 3

The ferry leaves at 8 o'clock each morning and returns 2 hours later. At what time does the ferry return?

CALENDAR, TIME, AND MEASUREMENT

# CALENDAR

There are 7 days in 1 week. The first day of the week is Sunday. There are 365 days in 1 year unless it is a leap year. A leap year has 366 days.

January February March April May June July August September October November December

Each year has 12 months. April, June, September, and November each have 30 days. February has 28 days, except in a leap year when it has 29 days. The other months each have 31 days.

This calendar shows the month of October in a particular year. The first day of October is a Saturday. You read October 1 as *October first*. Numbers like first, second, third, and fourth that show the order of a set of things are called **ordinal numbers.**

**Think:** When else would you use ordinal numbers?

**October**

| S | M | T | W | T | F | S |
|---|---|---|---|---|---|---|
|   |   |   |   |   |   | 1 |
| 2 | 3 | 4 | 5 | 6 | 7 | 8 |
| 9 | 10 | 11 | 12 | 13 | 14 | 15 |
| 16 | 17 | 18 | 19 | 20 | 21 | 22 |
| 23 | 24 | 25 | 26 | 27 | 28 | 29 |
| 30 | 31 |   |   |   |   |   |

## CLASS EXERCISES

Read the date. Use ordinal numbers.

1. January 18
2. December 19
3. August 11

4. March 31
5. July 2
6. April 24

Use the October calendar above.
Write the day of the week.

7. the fifth day of October
8. the fourteenth day of October

9. the twenty-third day of October
10. the last day of October

11. six days after October 9
12. one week before October 18

13. three days after October 31
14. four days before October 1

## PRACTICE

Write the name of the month.

**15.** the twelfth month of the year

**16.** the fifth month of the year

**17.** the seventh month of the year

**18.** the eleventh month of the year

**19.** the second month of the year

**20.** the ninth month of the year

Use the calendar at the right. Write the day of the week and the date.

| APRIL | | | | | | |
|---|---|---|---|---|---|---|
| S | M | T | W | T | F | S |
| | | 1 | 2 | 3 | 4 | 5 |
| 6 | 7 | 8 | 9 | 10 | 11 | 12 |
| 13 | 14 | 15 | 16 | 17 | 18 | 19 |
| 20 | 21 | 22 | 23 | 24 | 25 | 26 |
| 27 | 28 | 29 | 30 | | | |

**21.** the fifth day of the month

**22.** the twenty-ninth day of the month

**23.** the third Tuesday in April

**24.** the second Monday in April

**25.** four days after April 20

**26.** two weeks after April 5

**27.** nine days before April 12

**28.** one week before April 30

★ **29.** two weeks and three days before April 17

★ **30.** one week and six days after April 19

## PROBLEM SOLVING APPLICATIONS
### Days and Dates

Solve.

**31.** Bob's family left on Saturday for a vacation trip to the mountains. They returned 1 week and 5 days later. On what day of the week did they return?

**32.** Bob mailed a postcard to Aunt Liz on Wednesday at noon and it arrived on Saturday at noon. How many days did it take for the postcard to arrive?

★ **33.** School is out on Friday, June 16. We leave on June 30 for a trip. How many days after school is out do we begin our trip? On what day of the week do we leave?

★ **34.** Bill and Reeca are flying to visit their grandfather. Bill leaves on Friday, May 3. Reeca leaves 9 days earlier. On what day and date does Reeca leave?

# TIME

You can read time in different ways.

25 minutes after 11
eleven twenty-five
You write 11:25.

30 minutes after 7
seven thirty
half past seven
You write 7:30.

When the time is later than half past the hour, you can read the time after the hour or before the next hour.

45 minutes after 2
two forty-five

15 minutes before 3
quarter to 3

You write 2:45.

37 minutes after 5
five thirty-seven

23 minutes before 6

You write 5:37.

 To tell time before the hour on a digital clock, subtract the minutes mentally.

**Think:** There are 60 minutes in an hour.

60 − 43 = 17

The time is 17 minutes before 6.

## CLASS EXERCISES

Complete.

**1.**

▨ minutes after ▨

▨ : ▨

**2.**

▨ minutes after ▨

▨ : ▨

**3.**

▨ minutes after ▨
▨ minutes before ▨

▨ : ▨

# ADDING AND SUBTRACTING TIME

There are 60 minutes in 1 hour. There are 60 seconds in 1 minute. You can use these facts when you add and subtract time. Sometimes you have to rename.

Add 2 hours and 35 minutes to 1 hour and 43 minutes to find the total time of a relay race.

Add the minutes. Rename.

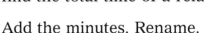

$$\begin{array}{r} \overset{1}{2} \text{ hours } 35 \text{ minutes} \\ + 1 \text{ hour } 43 \text{ minutes} \\ \hline \cancel{78 \text{ minutes}} \\ 18 \text{ minutes} \end{array}$$

**Think:** 60 minutes is 1 hour, so 78 minutes is 1 hour 18 minutes.

Add the hours.

$$\begin{array}{r} \overset{1}{2} \text{ hours } 35 \text{ minutes} \\ + 1 \text{ hour } 43 \text{ minutes} \\ \hline 4 \text{ hours } 18 \text{ minutes} \end{array}$$

Subtract 12 minutes and 26 seconds from 15 minutes and 13 seconds to find the difference between the times of two races.

First rename 1 minute as 60 seconds.

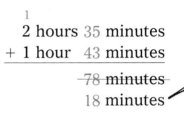

$$\begin{array}{r} \overset{14}{\cancel{15}} \text{ minutes } \overset{73}{\cancel{13}} \text{ seconds} \\ - 12 \text{ minutes } 26 \text{ seconds} \end{array}$$

**Think:** 1 minute is 60 seconds. 60 + 13 = 73

Subtract the minutes and the seconds.

$$\begin{array}{r} \overset{14}{\cancel{15}} \text{ minutes } \overset{73}{\cancel{13}} \text{ seconds} \\ - 12 \text{ minutes } 26 \text{ seconds} \\ \hline 2 \text{ minutes } 47 \text{ seconds} \end{array}$$

## CLASS EXERCISES

Complete.

**1.** 95 seconds = ▦ minute ▦ seconds

**2.** 3 hours = 2 hours ▦ minutes

**3.** 9 minutes 41 seconds = 8 minutes ▦ seconds

Add or subtract. Do you need to rename? Explain why.

**4.**   4 minutes 45 seconds
     + 2 minutes 34 seconds

**5.**   4 minutes 25 seconds
     − 2 minutes 34 seconds

# PRACTICE

Write the time.

**4.**

**5.**

**6.**

**7.**

Match.

| | | | |
|---|---|---|---|
| **8.** 1:30 | **A.** twenty-seven minutes before two |
| **9.** 2:20 | **B.** twenty minutes before two |
| **10.** 1:40 | **C.** one twenty-seven |
| **11.** 1:20 | **D.** twenty minutes after one |
| **12.** 1:33 | **E.** one thirty |
| **13.** 1:27 | **F.** seventeen minutes before two |
| **14.** 1:43 | **G.** twenty minutes after two |

Subtract mentally to complete.

**15.**

▒ minutes
before ▒

**16.**

▒ minutes
before ▒

**17.**

▒ minutes
before ▒

**M**
**MENTAL MATH**

## PROBLEM SOLVING APPLICATIONS
### Comparing Times

Solve.

**18.** Myra arrived at the library at 3:47. Sandy arrived at quarter to four. Who arrived first?

**19.** Don arrived at twenty minutes past two for a game at 2:45. Was he early, on time, or late?

★ **20.** Paul's plane leaves the airport at 6:42. He planned to arrive at the airport by taxi at 6:15. The cab was late and he arrived at quarter to seven. Did he arrive in time for the plane?

★ **21.** Kara's bedtime is 8:30. On weekends her mother allows her to stay up until 9:45. Can Kara watch a television program on Saturday night that begins at 9:00 and lasts for a half-hour?

# PROBLEM SOLVING
## Elapsed Time

1. Understand
2. Plan
3. Work
4. Answer/ Check

There are 24 hours in 1 day, but most clocks show only 12 hours. The hour hand goes around the clock twice in 1 day. A.M. shows a time between 12 midnight and 12 noon. P.M. shows a time between 12 noon and 12 midnight.

Leo leaves for school at 8:45 A.M. He returns for lunch at 11:15 A.M. How long is he gone?

Subtract to solve.

$$
\begin{array}{r}
\overset{10}{\phantom{1}} \qquad \overset{75}{\phantom{1}} \\
11{:}15\ \text{A.M.} \longrightarrow \quad \cancel{11}\ \text{hours}\ \cancel{15}\ \text{minutes} \\
8{:}45\ \text{A.M.} \longrightarrow - \quad 8\ \text{hours}\ 45\ \text{minutes} \\
\hline
2\ \text{hours}\ 30\ \text{minutes}
\end{array}
$$

Leo is gone for 2 hours and 30 minutes.

30 minutes

M) To check your answer, count mentally on the clock.

8:45 A.M. to 9:45 A.M. is 1 hour,
9:45 A.M. to 10:45 A.M. is 1 hour,
10:45 A.M. to 11:15 A.M. is 30 minutes,
so 8:45 A.M. to 11:15 A.M. is 2 hours and 30 minutes.

## CLASS EXERCISES

Is the time A.M. or P.M.?

**1.** Breakfast is at 7:30.   **2.** Sunset is at 6:47.   **3.** Lunch is at 1:00.

How long are you gone? Subtract to answer.

**4.** You leave at 3:30 P.M. You return at 5:00 P.M.

**5.** You leave at 10:20 P.M. You return at 11:30 P.M.

Count on the clock above to solve the problem.

**6.** It is 6:00 A.M. What time will it be in 35 minutes?

**7.** It is 7:30 P.M. What time will it be in 1 hour and 15 minutes?

**8.** It is 1:30 A.M. What time was it 15 minutes ago?

**9.** It is 11:45 P.M. What time was it 3 hours and 30 minutes ago?

# PRACTICE

Add or subtract.

**6.**   3 hours 10 minutes
     + 2 hours  8 minutes

**7.**   17 minutes 45 seconds
     +  2 minutes 36 seconds

**8.**   5 hours 18 minutes
     − 2 hours  5 minutes

**9.**   8 minutes 10 seconds
     − 5 minutes 25 seconds

**10.**   22 hours 23 minutes
     − 10 hours  8 minutes

**11.**   4 minutes 21 seconds
     + 6 minutes 43 seconds

**12.**   9 hours 35 minutes
     − 7 hours 56 minutes

**13.**   7 minutes 38 seconds
     + 8 minutes 12 seconds

Write the answer.

**14.**    69
       + 75

**15.**    984
       − 696

**16.**    598
       + 749

**17.**    62,784
       + 95,487

**18.**    478,321
       −  19,555

**19.**    37,498
       + 74,602

**20.**    $25.61
       +  19.98

**21.**    $13.62
       −  11.81

**MIXED REVIEW**

# PROBLEM SOLVING APPLICATIONS
## Choosing the Operation

Solve.

**22.** The high jump event lasted 68 minutes. The long jump event took 33 minutes. The pole vault event lasted 73 minutes. Which events lasted more than 1 hour?

**23.** Laurel and Denise ran on a relay team. Laurel ran for 6 minutes and 27 seconds. Denise ran for 7 minutes and 3 seconds. What is the difference between the times?

★ **24.** The Olympic record for the men's marathon is 2 hours, 9 minutes, and 55 seconds. In 1896, the marathon was won in a time of 2 hours, 58 minutes, and 50 seconds. What is the difference between the times?

# MATHEMATICS and LANGUAGE ARTS

You know these words in the metric system.

A *kilometer* is 1000 meters.
A *kilogram* is 1000 grams.

Each of these words starts with a group of letters, called a *prefix*, that stands for a number. The prefix *kilo* stands for 1000.

Many words in our language use number prefixes borrowed from ancient Greek and Latin. You can use what you know about prefixes to understand new words.

*uni*: one
*bi*: two
*quadr*: four
*dec* or *decem*: ten

## WHAT'S THE WORD?

*Ped* or *pede* means "foot."

1. How many feet does a quadruped have? List some animals that are quadrupeds.

2. Name some bipeds.

3. What is special about a unicycle?

4. How many birthday candles would you have to blow out if you are a *decade* old on your birthday?

5. In the Roman calendar, December was the tenth month. What do you think the numbers are for *septem*, *octo*, and *novem*?

# Enrichment

By asking no more than three yes-or-no questions, you can discover someone's favorite day of the week. Here is one way to do it.

First think of the days of the week in order. Then pick the day in the middle.

**Sunday   Monday   Tuesday   Wednesday   Thursday   Friday   Saturday**

**First question**

Is the day Wednesday or before Wednesday? Suppose the answer is yes. Make a new list. Pick one of the two days in the middle.

Sunday   Monday   Tuesday   Wednesday

**Second question**

Is the day Monday or before Monday? Suppose the answer is no. The new list then has only two choices. Pick one.

Tuesday   Wednesday

**Third question**

Is the day Tuesday? If yes, the favorite day is Tuesday. If no, the favorite day is Wednesday.

# USING LOGIC FOR SORTING

Use the method above to do these activities.

1. Name the month someone was born. Ask only four questions.

2. Name someone's middle initial by asking only five questions.

3. Have someone choose one word in this sentence. Name the word by asking only three questions.

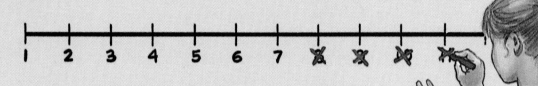

1  2  3  4  5  6  7  ~~8~~  ~~9~~  ~~10~~  ~~11~~                    15

You can use this method to pick numbers on a number line. Draw a number line. Ask your friend to pick a number shown on it. To find your friend's number, pick a number in the middle of the number line. Ask your friend if the number is less than or equal to the number you picked. Cross off the numbers that are ruled out. Repeat until you know your friend's number.

Use the number line to do the activity.

4. Have a friend pick a number. Name the number, asking no more than three questions.

   1  2  3  4  5  6  7  8

5. Have a friend pick a number. Name the number, asking no more than four questions.

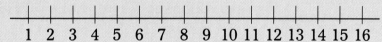

   1  2  3  4  5  6  7  8  9  10  11  12  13  14  15  16

Draw a number line to do the activity.

6. Ask the month of a friend's birthday. Then name the date by asking only five questions.

7. Have a friend think of a number from 1 to 1000. Name the number by asking only ten questions.

Solve.

8. How many questions do you need to guess a number out of 64 numbers? Hint: You need 1 question for two numbers, 2 questions for four numbers, 3 questions for eight numbers, and so on. Draw a chart to help you answer.

Choose the correct answer. Write *a*, *b*, *c*, or *d*.

Round to the place of the underlined digit.

**1.** 3984

  **a.** 3800
  **b.** 3900
  **c.** 4000
  **d.** none of these

**2.** 27,098

  **a.** 27,090
  **b.** 27,100
  **c.** 28,000
  **d.** none of these

**3.** 673,376

  **a.** 673,000
  **b.** 670,000
  **c.** 680,000
  **d.** none of these

Use the graph to answer the questions.

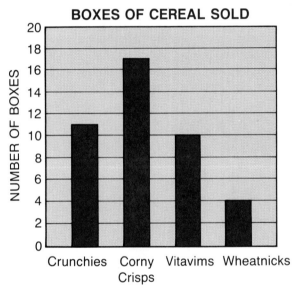

BOXES OF CEREAL SOLD

NUMBER OF BOXES

KINDS OF CEREAL

**4.** How many boxes of Crunchies were sold?

  **a.** 9 boxes    **b.** 10 boxes
  **c.** 11 boxes   **d.** none of these

**5.** Which cereal had the greatest sales?

  **a.** Crunchies   **b.** Corny Crisps
  **c.** Vitavims    **d.** none of these

**6.** How many boxes of cereal were sold in all?

  **a.** 32 boxes   **b.** 41 boxes
  **c.** 42 boxes   **d.** none of these

Which is the best estimate?

**7.**   41
  + 38

  **a.** 100
  **b.** 30
  **c.** 80
  **d.** 0

**8.**   86
  + 19

  **a.** 80
  **b.** 20
  **c.** 70
  **d.** 110

**9.**   18
  + 76

  **a.** 60
  **b.** 100
  **c.** 20
  **d.** 80

**10.**   32
    11
 + 24

  **a.** 30
  **b.** 60
  **c.** 40
  **d.** 20

**11.**   57
    12
 + 21

  **a.** 90
  **b.** 60
  **c.** 10
  **d.** 20

Find the answer.

**12.**  516
509
+ 272

   **a.** 1296
   **b.** 1287
   **c.** 1297
   **d.** none of these

**13.**  6437
945
+ 801

   **a.** 8283
   **b.** 8173
   **c.** 8183
   **d.** none of these

**14.**  71,468
+ 28,702

   **a.** 101,070
   **b.** 100,170
   **c.** 101,170
   **d.** none of these

**15.** 9488 + 688
   **a.** 10,176
   **b.** 10,166
   **c.** 9,176
   **d.** none of these

**16.** 853 + 495
   **a.** 3148
   **b.** 1348
   **c.** 1248
   **d.** none of these

**17.** 93,789 + 7,725
   **a.** 91,514
   **b.** 101,504
   **c.** 101,404
   **d.** none of these

# LANGUAGE and VOCABULARY REVIEW

Find the 15 measurement words hidden in the puzzle. Write them on a piece of paper.

| K | I | L | O | G | R | A | M | N |
|---|---|---|---|---|---|---|---|---|
| I | P | I | N | T | R | C | E | V |
| L | Y | T | F | O | O | T | T | D |
| O | P | E | M | N | U | F | E | E |
| M | G | R | A | M | N | Z | R | G |
| E | M | Q | I | N | C | H | T | R |
| T | I | C | U | P | E | A | C | E |
| E | L | Y | A | R | D | B | W | E |
| R | E | G | A | L | L | O | N | T |

# INPUT
# PROCESS
# OUTPUT

When the computer is given input, it can do two jobs with it. The computer can *store* input. It can also *change* input. Doing a job to change input is called a **process.**

The part of the computer that processes data is called the **Central Processing Unit** or **CPU.** The CPU is inside the computer. You cannot see the CPU unless the computer is opened.

The computer must always be told how to process input. After the process, the computer shows output.

Suppose you want the computer to add 10 and 16. The numbers 10 and 16 are the input. Addition is the process. The answer 26 is the output.

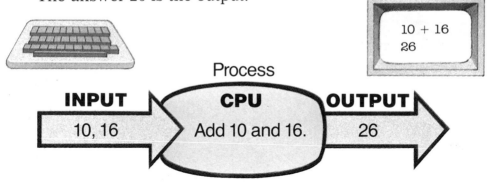

Write the output for each.

|  | INPUT | PROCESS |
|---|---|---|
| 1. | 86, 74 | Add. |
| 2. | 53, 39 | Subtract. |
| 3. | 496, 253 | Add. |
| 4. | 3109, 3901 | Compare to show which is greater. |
| 5. | 743, 487 | Subtract. |

# 4

The large panels reflect sunlight to be used for energy. Each panel is made of 6 mirrors. How many mirrors are in 3 panels?

MULTIPLICATION FACTS

# MEANING OF MULTIPLICATION

There are 3 roses in each bunch of flowers. How many roses are in 4 bunches?

You can add to find out.

$$3 + 3 + 3 + 3 = 12$$

4 threes equal 12

You can also multiply. You can write the multiplication in two ways.

$$4 \times 3 = 12 \qquad \text{or} \qquad \begin{array}{r} 3 \\ \times 4 \\ \hline 12 \end{array}$$

**factors  product**

Four times three equals twelve.

There are 12 roses.

 Skip counting can help you learn the multiplication facts. To find $5 \times 3$, think of 5 groups of 3. Count 3, 6, 9, 12, 15.

$$5 \times 3 = 15$$

## CLASS EXERCISES

Which numbers are factors? Which number is the product?

1. $\begin{array}{r} 2 \\ \times 2 \\ \hline 4 \end{array}$
2. $\begin{array}{r} 4 \\ \times 3 \\ \hline 12 \end{array}$
3. $\begin{array}{r} 2 \\ \times 5 \\ \hline 10 \end{array}$
4. $\begin{array}{r} 4 \\ \times 2 \\ \hline 8 \end{array}$
5. $\begin{array}{r} 3 \\ \times 5 \\ \hline 15 \end{array}$

Find the sum. Find the product. Explain how the addition and multiplication are related.

6. $3 + 3$
   $2 \times 3$

7. $3 + 3 + 3$
   $3 \times 3$

8. $3 + 3 + 3 + 3$
   $4 \times 3$

9. $2 + 2 + 2$
   $3 \times 2$

10. $2 + 2 + 2 + 2$
    $4 \times 2$

11. $2 + 2 + 2 + 2 + 2$
    $5 \times 2$

## PRACTICE

Write the multiplication fact.

**12.** 3 + 3 + 3 + 3 + 3 + 3

**13.** 2 + 2 + 2 + 2 + 2 + 2 + 2 + 2 + 2

**14.** 3 + 3 + 3 + 3 + 3 + 3 + 3

**15.** 4 + 4 + 4 + 4

**16.** 4 + 4 + 4 + 4 + 4 + 4

**17.** 2 + 2 + 2 + 2 + 2 + 2 + 2 ⁓

**18.** 8 twos      **19.** 9 threes      **20.** 8 threes      **21.** 9 twos

**22.** 6 threes      **23.** 7 threes      **24.** 5 twos      **25.** 5 threes

Write the number sentence and the answer.

**26.** Five times three equals ▦.

**27.** Four plus four equals ▦.

★ **28.** Twelve times two equals ▦.

★ **29.** Eleven times three equals ▦.

Use skip counting to answer. Write the product only.

**30.** 5 × 3      **31.** 7 × 2      **32.** 4 × 4      **33.** 5 × 4

**34.** 9 × 2      **35.** 9 × 3      **36.** 6 × 4      **37.** 8 × 3

★ **38.** 11 × 2   ★ **39.** 12 × 4   ★ **40.** 10 × 4   ★ **41.** 12 × 3

**MENTAL MATH**

## PROBLEM SOLVING APPLICATIONS
### Choosing the Operation

Find the cost of 3 tulips at the price given.

**42.** $1 each      **43.** $3 each      **44.** $4 each

Solve.

**45.** Enrico spends $4.50 for flowers and $3.98 for a vase. How much more does he spend for flowers?

**46.** Laura buys 6 carnations. She pays $2 for each. How much does she spend?

**47.** The owner of The Flower Pot earns $4 on every dozen roses sold. She sells 5 dozen roses today. How much does she earn?

★ **48.** Max buys 9 bags of soil for $3 each. He only needs 6 bags of soil so he returns the rest. How much money does he get back?

# MULTIPLYING TWOS, THREES, AND FOURS

Multiplication is repeated addition of the same number. Memorizing the multiplication facts helps you solve problems much faster.

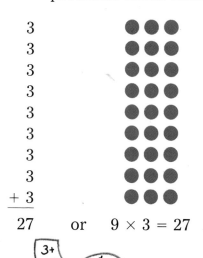

```
  3
  3
  3
  3
  3
  3
  3
  3
+ 3
─────
 27     or     9 × 3 = 27
```

| twos | | threes | | fours | |
|---|---|---|---|---|---|
| × | 2 | × | 3 | × | 4 |
| 0 | 0 | 0 | 0 | 0 | 0 |
| 1 | 2 | 1 | 3 | 1 | 4 |
| 2 | 4 | 2 | 6 | 2 | 8 |
| 3 | 6 | 3 | 9 | 3 | 12 |
| 4 | 8 | 4 | 12 | 4 | 16 |
| 5 | 10 | 5 | 15 | 5 | 20 |
| 6 | 12 | 6 | 18 | 6 | 24 |
| 7 | 14 | 7 | 21 | 7 | 28 |
| 8 | 16 | 8 | 24 | 8 | 32 |
| 9 | 18 | 9 | 27 | 9 | 36 |

## CLASS EXERCISES

Complete the pattern.

**1.** 2, 4, 6, ▢, ▢       **2.** 3, 6, 9, ▢, ▢       **3.** 4, 8, 12, ▢, ▢

**4.** 10, 12, 14, ▢, ▢       **5.** 15, 18, 21, ▢, ▢       **6.** 20, 24, 28, ▢, ▢

Multiply.

**7.** 2 × 3       **8.** 3 × 3       **9.** 4 × 3       **10.** 5 × 3       **11.** 6 × 3

**12.** 2 × 4       **13.** 3 × 4       **14.** 4 × 4       **15.** 5 × 4       **16.** 6 × 4

## PRACTICE

Multiply.

**17.** 4 × 3       **18.** 5 × 2       **19.** 4 × 4       **20.** 3 × 4       **21.** 3 × 2

**22.** $6 \times 2$ **23.** $7 \times 3$ **24.** $5 \times 3$ **25.** $7 \times 2$ **26.** $6 \times 3$

**27.** $\begin{array}{r} 4 \\ \times 7 \\ \hline \end{array}$ **28.** $\begin{array}{r} 2 \\ \times 7 \\ \hline \end{array}$ **29.** $\begin{array}{r} 4 \\ \times 8 \\ \hline \end{array}$ **30.** $\begin{array}{r} 3 \\ \times 9 \\ \hline \end{array}$ **31.** $\begin{array}{r} 3 \\ \times 2 \\ \hline \end{array}$ **32.** $\begin{array}{r} 4 \\ \times 9 \\ \hline \end{array}$

**33.** $\begin{array}{r} 2 \\ \times 8 \\ \hline \end{array}$ **34.** $\begin{array}{r} 3 \\ \times 4 \\ \hline \end{array}$ **35.** $\begin{array}{r} 2 \\ \times 9 \\ \hline \end{array}$ **36.** $\begin{array}{r} 4 \\ \times 5 \\ \hline \end{array}$ **37.** $\begin{array}{r} 3 \\ \times 8 \\ \hline \end{array}$ **38.** $\begin{array}{r} 4 \\ \times 4 \\ \hline \end{array}$

Find the missing factor.

★ **39.** $\boxed{\phantom{x}} \times 3 = 3$ ★ **40.** $9 \times \boxed{\phantom{x}} = 18$ ★ **41.** $7 \times \boxed{\phantom{x}} = 28$ ★ **42.** $\boxed{\phantom{x}} \times 4 = 36$

Draw the keys you would push on a calculator to solve this problem if you could not use the $\boxed{\times}$ key.

CALCULATOR

**43.** $5 \times 3$ **44.** $8 \times 4$ **45.** $9 \times 2$ **46.** $7 \times 3$ **47.** $6 \times 4$

**48. Think:** Which is faster to solve Exercises 43–47, multiplying on a calculator or multiplying mentally?

## PROBLEM SOLVING APPLICATIONS
### Using a Calendar

Solve.

**49.** You borrowed a book on the first Tuesday in November. What date is the book due?

**50.** You borrowed a book on November 10 and returned it on November 28. How much is your fine?

**51.** You borrowed a book on the last Friday in November. What date is the book due?

★ **52.** You borrowed one book on November 3 and another on November 12. You return them both on December 1. What is your fine?

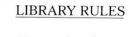

LIBRARY RULES

Borrowing time:
2 weeks

Overdue book fine:
4¢ a day

NOVEMBER

| S | M | T | W | T | F | S |
|---|---|---|---|---|---|---|
|   |   |   |   |   |   | 1 |
| 2 | 3 | 4 | 5 | 6 | 7 | 8 |
| 9 | 10 | 11 | 12 | 13 | 14 | 15 |
| 16 | 17 | 18 | 19 | 20 | 21 | 22 |
| 23 | 24 | 25 | 26 | 27 | 28 | 29 |
| 30 |   |   |   |   |   |   |

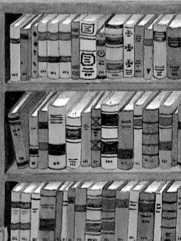

# MULTIPLYING THREES, FOURS, AND FIVES

At the school play there are 8 rows of seats for the chorus. Each row has 4 seats. To find how many seats there are for the chorus, multiply $8 \times 4$.

$$\begin{array}{r} 4 \\ \times 8 \\ \hline 32 \end{array} \quad \text{or} \quad 8 \times 4 = 32$$

There are 32 seats.

**Think:** If you know that $8 \times 5$ is 40, you know that $8 \times 4$ is less than 40. Your answer makes sense.

fours

| × | 4 |
|---|---|
| 0 | 0 |
| 1 | 4 |
| 2 | 8 |
| 3 | 12 |
| 4 | 16 |
| 5 | 20 |
| 6 | 24 |
| 7 | 28 |
| 8 | 32 |
| 9 | 36 |

fives

| × | 5 |
|---|---|
| 0 | 0 |
| 1 | 5 |
| 2 | 10 |
| 3 | 15 |
| 4 | 20 |
| 5 | 25 |
| 6 | 30 |
| 7 | 35 |
| 8 | 40 |
| 9 | 45 |

## CLASS EXERCISES

Complete the multiplication fact.

1. $3 \times 3 = $ ▦

2. $2 \times 5 = $ ▦

3. $3 \times 4 = $ ▦

4. $2 \times 4 = $ ▦

Complete.

5. $1 \times 3 = $ ▦   $2 \times 3 = $ ▦   $3 \times 3 = $ ▦   $4 \times 3 = $ ▦   $5 \times 3 = $ ▦
$6 \times 3 = $ ▦   $7 \times 3 = $ ▦   $8 \times 3 = $ ▦   $9 \times 3 = $ ▦

6. $1 \times 4 = $ ▦   $2 \times 4 = $ ▦   $3 \times 4 = $ ▦   $4 \times 4 = $ ▦   $5 \times 4 = $ ▦
$6 \times 4 = $ ▦   $7 \times 4 = $ ▦   $8 \times 4 = $ ▦   $9 \times 4 = $ ▦

7. $1 \times 5 = $ ▦   $2 \times 5 = $ ▦   $3 \times 5 = $ ▦   $4 \times 5 = $ ▦   $5 \times 5 = $ ▦
$6 \times 5 = $ ▦   $7 \times 5 = $ ▦   $8 \times 5 = $ ▦   $9 \times 5 = $ ▦

# PRACTICE
Multiply.

8. $4 \times 3$   9. $6 \times 4$   10. $4 \times 4$   11. $5 \times 3$   12. $1 \times 5$

13. $8 \times 5$   14. $8 \times 3$   15. $7 \times 5$   16. $1 \times 4$   17. $9 \times 5$

18. $4 \times 5$   19. $6 \times 3$   20. $5 \times 4$   21. $2 \times 5$   22. $9 \times 3$

23. $3 \times 4$   24. $5 \times 5$   25. $7 \times 3$   26. $3 \times 3$   27. $8 \times 4$

28. $\begin{array}{r} 3 \\ \times 2 \\ \hline \end{array}$   29. $\begin{array}{r} 4 \\ \times 9 \\ \hline \end{array}$   30. $\begin{array}{r} 3 \\ \times 4 \\ \hline \end{array}$   31. $\begin{array}{r} 5 \\ \times 1 \\ \hline \end{array}$   32. $\begin{array}{r} 4 \\ \times 2 \\ \hline \end{array}$   33. $\begin{array}{r} 5 \\ \times 6 \\ \hline \end{array}$

34. $\begin{array}{r} 4 \\ \times 7 \\ \hline \end{array}$   35. $\begin{array}{r} 3 \\ \times 1 \\ \hline \end{array}$   36. $\begin{array}{r} 4 \\ \times 5 \\ \hline \end{array}$   37. $\begin{array}{r} 5 \\ \times 3 \\ \hline \end{array}$   38. $\begin{array}{r} 4 \\ \times 8 \\ \hline \end{array}$   39. $\begin{array}{r} 3 \\ \times 7 \\ \hline \end{array}$

40. $\begin{array}{r} 2 \\ \times 6 \\ \hline \end{array}$   41. $\begin{array}{r} 3 \\ \times 8 \\ \hline \end{array}$   42. $\begin{array}{r} 4 \\ \times 1 \\ \hline \end{array}$   43. $\begin{array}{r} 5 \\ \times 7 \\ \hline \end{array}$   44. $\begin{array}{r} 2 \\ \times 9 \\ \hline \end{array}$   45. $\begin{array}{r} 5 \\ \times 9 \\ \hline \end{array}$

Is the product *greater than*, *less than*, or the *same as* the number below?

ESTIMATE

46. $5 \times 3$     47. $4 \times 4$     48. $6 \times 5$     49. $10 \times 5$
   12        20        35        45

## PROBLEM SOLVING APPLICATIONS
### Choosing the Operation

Solve.

50. This year it cost $154 to put on the school play. Ticket sales totaled $192. How much money is left over?

51. Four people make costumes for the play. Three times that number of people make the scenery. How many people make the scenery?

★ 52. For every 4 tickets sold, $2 is given to charity. If 36 tickets are sold, how much goes to charity?

★ 53. The band has 3 rows of stringed instruments, 1 row of flutes and clarinets, and 2 rows of horns. Each row has 5 students. How many are in the band?

# PROPERTIES OF ZERO AND ONE

Here are two ideas that can help you remember some of the multiplication facts.

**Property of One**

The product of one and any number is that number.

$$\begin{array}{r} 1 \\ 1 \\ +\ 1 \\ \hline 3 \end{array} \qquad 3 \times 1 = 3$$

3 groups of 1 are 3.

**Zero Property**

The product of zero and any number is zero.

$$\begin{array}{r} 0 \\ 0 \\ +\ 0 \\ \hline 0 \end{array} \qquad 3 \times 0 = 0$$

3 groups of 0 are 0.

## CLASS EXERCISES

Does the fact show the zero property or the property of one? What is the product?

| | | | | | | |
|---|---|---|---|---|---|---|
| **1.** 1 ×4 | **2.** 0 ×6 | **3.** 0 ×8 | **4.** 1 ×3 | **5.** 1 ×7 | **6.** 0 ×0 | **7.** 1 ×2 |
| **8.** 0 ×7 | **9.** 1 ×9 | **10.** 1 ×1 | **11.** 0 ×5 | **12.** 1 ×6 | **13.** 0 ×4 | **14.** 0 ×1 |

## PRACTICE
Multiply.

| | | | | | | |
|---|---|---|---|---|---|---|
| **15.** 4 ×3 | **16.** 2 ×6 | **17.** 4 ×8 | **18.** 1 ×5 | **19.** 0 ×3 | **20.** 5 ×5 | **21.** 3 ×9 |
| **22.** 1 ×8 | **23.** 0 ×9 | **24.** 3 ×3 | **25.** 4 ×6 | **26.** 5 ×9 | **27.** 2 ×7 | **28.** 0 ×2 |

| 29. 2 ×4 | 30. 5 ×6 | 31. 0 ×8 | 32. 4 ×5 | 33. 5 ×7 | 34. 3 ×0 | 35. 2 ×2 |
|---|---|---|---|---|---|---|
| 36. 4 ×7 | 37. 3 ×7 | 38. 5 ×1 | 39. 2 ×9 | 40. 1 ×4 | 41. 0 ×9 | 42. 4 ×4 |
| 43. 0 ×5 | 44. 2 ×8 | 45. 3 ×6 | 46. 4 ×9 | 47. 3 ×8 | 48. 2 ×5 | 49. 5 ×8 |

Complete.

★ **50.** ▨ × 2 − 8 × 1          ★ **51.** 3 × 4 − ▨ × 2          ★ **52.** 15 > 5 × ▨

Write the answer.

| 53. 8 + 9 | 54. 17 − 3 | 55. 24 + 8 | 56. 36 + 9 | 57. 56 + 7 |
|---|---|---|---|---|
| 58. 11 24 + 36 | 59. 917 − 429 | 60. 268 + 381 | 61. 329 84 + 272 | 62. 3876 2198 + 2477 |

**MIXED REVIEW**

## PROBLEM SOLVING APPLICATIONS
### Writing Number Sentences

Write a number sentence. Solve.

**63.** Four adults each drive a car to the circus. There are 5 children in each car. How many children are driven to the circus?

**64.** The circus is in Edgartown for 8 weeks and in Bonnertown for 9 weeks. How many weeks is the circus in the two towns?

★ **65.** Al sees 3 groups of tigers with 3 tigers in each group. He also sees 7 lions. How many more tigers than lions does he see?

★ **66.** At the circus 5 clowns are performing in each of 2 rings and 4 clowns are in a third ring. How many clowns are in the 3 rings?

# THE ORDER AND GROUPING PROPERTIES

You can think of 24 as 6 fours or as 4 sixes.

**Order Property of Multiplication**

Changing the order of the factors does not change the product.

$6 \times 4 = 24$        $4 \times 6 = 24$

**Grouping Property of Multiplication**

Changing the grouping of the factors does not change the product.

$$(2 \times 2) \times 3 \qquad\qquad 2 \times (2 \times 3)$$
$$\phantom{(}4\phantom{)} \times 3 = 12 \qquad 2 \times \phantom{(}6\phantom{)} = 12$$

Remember, parentheses show you which numbers to work with first.

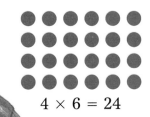 You can multiply $2 \times 2 \times 3$ on a calculator. Enter 2 ⓧ 2 ⓧ and you will see 4. Then enter 3 ⏹ and you will see 12.

## CLASS EXERCISES

Multiply.

**1.** $3 \times 4$
$4 \times 3$

**2.** $0 \times 5$
$5 \times 0$

**3.** $6 \times 3$
$3 \times 6$

**4.** $8 \times 4$
$4 \times 8$

**5.** $9 \times 2$
$2 \times 9$

**6.** $(3 \times 2) \times 3$
$3 \times (2 \times 3)$

**7.** $3 \times (0 \times 9)$
$(3 \times 0) \times 9$

**8.** $4 \times (2 \times 2)$
$(4 \times 2) \times 2$

**9.** $(2 \times 4) \times 1$
$2 \times (4 \times 1)$

## PRACTICE

Multiply.

**10.**  $2$
$\times 7$

**11.**  $4$
$\times 5$

**12.**  $5$
$\times 9$

**13.**  $3$
$\times 5$

**14.**  $5$
$\times 5$

**15.**  $2$
$\times 5$

**16.**  $3$
$\times 8$

**17.** 7
×4

**18.** 9
×2

**19.** 6
×1

**20.** 9
×4

**21.** 6
×3

**22.** 7
×2

**23.** 8
×5

**24.** $(1 \times 2) \times 8$     **25.** $3 \times (2 \times 3)$     **26.** $(4 \times 2) \times 5$     **27.** $7 \times (2 \times 2)$

**28.** $4 \times 2 \times 3$     **29.** $2 \times 9 \times 0$     **30.** $6 \times 1 \times 4$     **31.** $3 \times 3 \times 2$

Complete.

**32.** $2 \times 8 = \blacksquare$     **33.** $5 \times 7 = \blacksquare$     **34.** $(1 \times 9) \times 3 = \blacksquare$     **35.** $3 \times (2 \times 4) = \blacksquare$
$8 \times \blacksquare = 16$     $\blacksquare \times 5 = 35$     $1 \times (\blacksquare \times 3) = 27$     $(3 \times 2) \times \blacksquare = 24$

Write as many multiplication facts as you can for the product.

★ **36.** 24     ★ **37.** 12     ★ **38.** 25     ★ **39.** 1     ★ **40.** 18     ★ **41.** 0

Write the letter of the problem that has the same answer
when entered on the calculator.

**42.** 4 ⊠ 2 ⊠ 5 =     **43.** 4 ⊠ 2 ⊠ 8 =     **44.** 3 ⊠ 2 ⊠ 6 =     CALCULATOR

**A.** 2 ⊠ 6 ⊠ 3 =     **B.** 2 ⊠ 8 ⊠ 4 =     **C.** 2 ⊠ 5 ⊠ 4 =

## PROBLEM SOLVING APPLICATIONS
### Reading Information

Michael and Mia are building a model rocket. Michael
says, "I think it should have 2 sets of landing gear." Mia
says, "It should have 4 windows, 5 control switches, and 3
air locks, too."

Solve.

**45.** It takes 8 boards for each set of
landing gear. How many boards
are needed altogether?

**46.** A control switch is made with 4
screws and 3 nails. How many
screws are needed in all? How
many nails?

The rocket
has 5
stages.

★ **47.** Each window needs 8 strips of
tape. Each air lock needs 6 strips.
How many strips of tape are
needed in all?

★ **48.** Each stage of the rocket needs 6
boxes. If Mia and Michael have 24
boxes, how many more do they
need?

# PROBLEM SOLVING
## Strategy: Using a Diagram

1. Understand
2. Plan
3. Work
4. Answer/Check

You want to have a gift wrapped. You can choose from 2 designs of paper: striped and dotted. Each design comes in 4 different colors: red, blue, yellow, and green. How many different ways can your box be wrapped?

You can draw a **tree diagram** to find the different kinds of gift wrapping. Here's how:

1. Draw two branches to show the two different designs.

2. Draw two sets of four branches to show each of the four different colors.

3. Count the branches at the end of the tree.

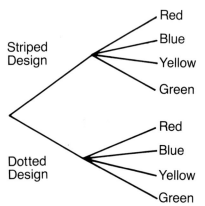

There are 8 different ways your box can be wrapped.

## CLASS EXERCISES

Copy and complete the tree diagram. Solve.

1. Harrison is choosing among 3 stuffed animals: a bear, a cat, and a dog. Each animal comes in 2 sizes, small and large. How many different kinds of stuffed animals are there?

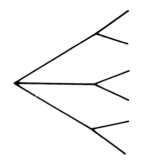

Draw a tree diagram. Solve.

2. The T-Shirt Factory has shirts in 3 different colors and in 2 different print designs. How many different kinds of shirts are there?

3. The Sandwich Shop offers 2 different breads and 4 different fillings. How many different kinds of sandwiches can be made?

# PRACTICE

Draw a tree diagram. Solve.

4. Jeb's sister is buying him a painting. He can choose among 3 different scenes by 3 different artists. How many choices of paintings does Jeb have?

5. The Book Store is having a sale on books of 4 different subjects by 2 different authors. How many different kinds of books are on sale?

6. At one store you can make your own earrings, necklace, or bracelet. You can choose from ruby, pearl, jade, or onyx. How many different kinds of jewelry can you you make?

7. The Card Shop sells a castle puzzle and an airplane puzzle. Each of the puzzles comes in 250 pieces or 500 pieces. How many different puzzles does the Card Shop sell?

★ 8. Marla is ordering a new bicycle. She can choose from 2 different styles, 3 different sizes, and 3 different colors. How many different kinds of bicycles are there?

★ 9. The Card Shop has note cards. There are 3 different pictures in 2 different colors and 4 different sizes. How many different kinds of cards are there?

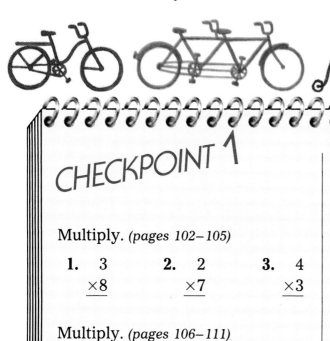

# CHECKPOINT 1

Multiply. *(pages 102–105)*

| 1. | 3 | 2. | 2 | 3. | 4 |
|----|---|----|---|----|---|
|  | ×8 |  | ×7 |  | ×3 |

Multiply. *(pages 106–111)*

4. 8 × 4        5. 2 × 4 × 3

| 6. | 5 | 7. | 5 | 8. | 4 |
|----|---|----|---|----|---|
|  | ×6 |  | ×3 |  | ×0 |

Draw a tree diagram. Solve.
*(pages 112–113)*

9. Frankie found 4 different masks and 4 different hats in his basement. How many different costumes can he make?

*Extra practice on page 408*

# MULTIPLYING SIXES AND SEVENS

If you use the order property and you know that $6 \times 2 = 12$, then you know that $2 \times 6 = 12$. The order property helps you learn the facts in blue below.

There are only four new multiplication facts with 6 as a factor.

There are only four new multiplication facts with 7 as a factor.

$0 \times 6 = 0$
$1 \times 6 = 6$
$2 \times 6 = 12$
$3 \times 6 = 18$
$4 \times 6 = 24$
$5 \times 6 = 30$

You already know these facts.

$0 \times 7 = 0$
$1 \times 7 = 7$
$2 \times 7 = 14$
$3 \times 7 = 21$
$4 \times 7 = 28$
$5 \times 7 = 35$

$6 \times 6 = 36$
$7 \times 6 = 42$
$8 \times 6 = 48$
$9 \times 6 = 54$

These are the new facts.

$6 \times 7 = 42$
$7 \times 7 = 49$
$8 \times 7 = 56$
$9 \times 7 = 63$

The order property of multiplication also helps you memorize two of these new facts together.

$$7 \times 6 = 42 \quad \text{so} \quad 6 \times 7 = 42$$

 **Think:** How many new facts do you have to memorize?

## CLASS EXERCISES

What are the products?

**1.** $2 \times 6$     $4 \times 6$     $6 \times 6$        **2.** $5 \times 7$     $7 \times 7$     $9 \times 7$

**3.** $5 \times 6$     $7 \times 6$     $9 \times 6$        **4.** $4 \times 7$     $6 \times 7$     $8 \times 7$

Write the missing numbers.

**5.**

| 7 | ? | 21 | 28 | ? |
|---|---|----|----|---|

**6.**

| 12 | 18 | ? | 30 | ? |
|----|----|---|----|---|

**7.**

| 30 | 36 | ? | 48 | ? |
|----|----|---|----|---|

**8.**

| 35 | 42 | ? | 56 | ? |
|----|----|---|----|---|

**9.**

| 21 | ? | 35 | ? | 49 |
|----|---|----|---|----|

**10.**

| 24 | ? | 36 | 42 | ? |
|----|---|----|----|---|

# PRACTICE

Multiply.

**11.** $3 \times 7$  **12.** $2 \times 6$  **13.** $1 \times 6$  **14.** $2 \times 7$  **15.** $7 \times 6$  **16.** $3 \times 6$

**17.** $9 \times 6$  **18.** $6 \times 7$  **19.** $4 \times 7$  **20.** $5 \times 6$  **21.** $4 \times 6$  **22.** $1 \times 7$

| | **23.** | **24.** | **25.** | **26.** | **27.** | **28.** | **29.** |
|---|---|---|---|---|---|---|---|
| | 2 | 6 | 6 | 6 | 4 | 7 | 7 |
| | $\times 7$ | $\times 6$ | $\times 9$ | $\times 7$ | $\times 6$ | $\times 0$ | $\times 9$ |

| | **30.** | **31.** | **32.** | **33.** | **34.** | **35.** | **36.** |
|---|---|---|---|---|---|---|---|
| | 6 | 3 | 6 | 7 | 6 | 7 | 7 |
| | $\times 8$ | $\times 7$ | $\times 4$ | $\times 2$ | $\times 3$ | $\times 1$ | $\times 8$ |

| | **37.** | **38.** | **39.** | **40.** | **41.** | **42.** | **43.** |
|---|---|---|---|---|---|---|---|
| | 0 | 6 | 5 | 2 | 7 | 7 | 4 |
| | $\times 6$ | $\times 1$ | $\times 6$ | $\times 6$ | $\times 5$ | $\times 3$ | $\times 7$ |

★ **44.** Write a fact with 6 as one factor and 48 as the product.

★ **45.** Write a fact with 7 as one factor and 49 as the product.

Use mental math to solve. Write only the answer.

**46.** $(4 \times 3) + 3$  **47.** $(5 \times 6) + 2$  **48.** $(8 \times 2) + 6$

**49.** $(9 \times 4) + 4$  **50.** $(4 \times 7) + 1$  **51.** $(9 \times 6) + 7$

**MENTAL MATH**

# PROBLEM SOLVING APPLICATIONS
## Using a Table

Five students walk dogs for the Walk-A-Dog Service. Each student walks the number of dogs shown. It takes 7 minutes to walk each dog.

**52.** How much time does it take Lee to walk the dogs?

**53.** How much time does it take Gary to walk the dogs?

★ **54.** How many more minutes does Lee walk than Erica?

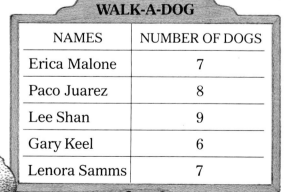

| WALK-A-DOG | |
|---|---|
| NAMES | NUMBER OF DOGS |
| Erica Malone | 7 |
| Paco Juarez | 8 |
| Lee Shan | 9 |
| Gary Keel | 6 |
| Lenora Samms | 7 |

# MULTIPLYING EIGHTS AND NINES

Fay knits 9 squares each day. How many squares does she make in 8 days? To answer, multiply 8 times 9.

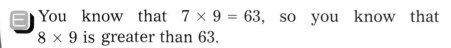 You know that $7 \times 9 = 63$, so you know that $8 \times 9$ is greater than 63.

To find the exact answer, think of 63 plus one more 9.

$$63 + 9 = 72, \text{ so } 8 \times 9 = 72$$

Fay makes 72 squares in 8 days.

Here are four new facts for 8 and 9.

| × | 8 | 9 |
|---|---|---|
| 8 | 64 | 72 |
| 9 | 72 | 81 |

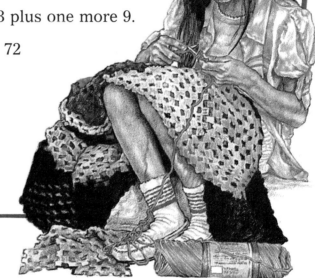

## CLASS EXERCISES

Use the known product. Name the product that is 8 more.

**1.** $2 \times 8 = 16$
$3 \times 8 = $ ▨

**2.** $4 \times 8 = 32$
$5 \times 8 = $ ▨

**3.** $6 \times 8 = 48$
$7 \times 8 = $ ▨

**4.** $8 \times 8 = 64$
$9 \times 8 = $ ▨

Use the known product. Name the product that is 9 more.

**5.** $2 \times 9 = 18$
$3 \times 9 = $ ▨

**6.** $4 \times 9 = 36$
$5 \times 9 = $ ▨

**7.** $6 \times 9 = 54$
$7 \times 9 = $ ▨

**8.** $8 \times 9 = 72$
$9 \times 9 = $ ▨

## PRACTICE

Multiply.

**9.** $8 \times 5$    **10.** $9 \times 3$    **11.** $8 \times 8$    **12.** $8 \times 6$    **13.** $9 \times 7$    **14.** $8 \times 1$

**15.** $9 \times 6$    **16.** $9 \times 4$    **17.** $8 \times 3$    **18.** $9 \times 5$    **19.** $1 \times 9$    **20.** $0 \times 8$

**21.** $9 \times 8$    **22.** $8 \times 2$    **23.** $8 \times 7$    **24.** $8 \times 4$    **25.** $5 \times 9$    **26.** $9 \times 2$

**27.** $9 \times 1$    **28.** $6 \times 8$    **29.** $9 \times 9$    **30.** $5 \times 8$    **31.** $8 \times 9$    **32.** $7 \times 9$

| 33. 8<br>×3 | 34. 8<br>×4 | 35. 8<br>×7 | 36. 9<br>×3 | 37. 8<br>×2 | 38. 8<br>×9 | 39. 0<br>×9 |
|---|---|---|---|---|---|---|
| 40. 8<br>×1 | 41. 9<br>×4 | 42. 9<br>×5 | 43. 3<br>×8 | 44. 9<br>×8 | 45. 9<br>×9 | 46. 9<br>×2 |
| 47. 7<br>×3 | 48. 0<br>×8 | 49. 5<br>×4 | 50. 9<br>×0 | 51. 7<br>×7 | 52. 9<br>×6 | 53. 6<br>×7 |

Write the multiplication facts and their products. Use addition to help if needed.

★ **54.** 1 × 10 through 10 × 10      ★ **55.** 1 × 11 through 11 × 11

★ **56.** 1 × 12 through 12 × 12

You know 7 × 7 = 49. Is the product below greater than or less than 49? Write *greater* or *less*.

**57.** 6 × 5   **58.** 8 × 8   **59.** 5 × 7   **60.** 0 × 8   **61.** 7 × 9

ESTIMATE

## PROBLEM SOLVING APPLICATIONS
### Asking a Question

Write a question for the problem. Then solve.

**62.** Sara is painting with water colors. She paints 2 hours each day for 9 days.

**63.** Katerina filled two photograph albums. She put 36 pictures in one and 45 pictures in the other.

★ **64.** Vincent is writing poetry. His first two poems each have 8 verses. His third poem has 7 verses.

★ **65.** Tony is making vases. He makes 8 blue vases and 4 times as many gold vases. Then he makes 9 red vases.

# MULTIPLICATION TABLE, 0–9

The table shows all the facts through the nines.

The numbers in green are products of a number times itself.

$$9 \times 9 = 81$$

The facts on one side of the green numbers match the facts on the other side.

$$5 \times 4 = 20$$
$$4 \times 5 = 20$$

(M) Patterns like these can help you do multiplication mentally. Look for other patterns in the table.

| × | 0 | 1 | 2 | 3 | 4 | 5 | 6 | 7 | 8 | 9 |
|---|---|---|---|---|---|---|---|---|---|---|
| 0 | 0 | 0 | 0 | 0 | 0 | 0 | 0 | 0 | 0 | 0 |
| 1 | 0 | 1 | 2 | 3 | 4 | 5 | 6 | 7 | 8 | 9 |
| 2 | 0 | 2 | 4 | 6 | 8 | 10 | 12 | 14 | 16 | 18 |
| 3 | 0 | 3 | 6 | 9 | 12 | 15 | 18 | 21 | 24 | 27 |
| 4 | 0 | 4 | 8 | 12 | 16 | 20 | 24 | 28 | 32 | 36 |
| 5 | 0 | 5 | 10 | 15 | 20 | 25 | 30 | 35 | 40 | 45 |
| 6 | 0 | 6 | 12 | 18 | 24 | 30 | 36 | 42 | 48 | 54 |
| 7 | 0 | 7 | 14 | 21 | 28 | 35 | 42 | 49 | 56 | 63 |
| 8 | 0 | 8 | 16 | 24 | 32 | 40 | 48 | 56 | 64 | 72 |
| 9 | 0 | 9 | 18 | 27 | 36 | 45 | 54 | 63 | 72 | 81 |

## CLASS EXERCISES

Multiply.

1. $4 \times 7$
$7 \times 4$

2. $6 \times 3$
$3 \times 6$

3. $9 \times 2$
$2 \times 9$

4. $8 \times 7$
$7 \times 8$

5. $5 \times 6$
$6 \times 5$

6. What is the answer when you multiply zero times any number?

7. Multiply a number by one and what do you get?

## PRACTICE

Multiply.

8. $\begin{array}{r} 7 \\ \times 1 \\ \hline \end{array}$
9. $\begin{array}{r} 4 \\ \times 4 \\ \hline \end{array}$
10. $\begin{array}{r} 9 \\ \times 3 \\ \hline \end{array}$
11. $\begin{array}{r} 4 \\ \times 8 \\ \hline \end{array}$
12. $\begin{array}{r} 7 \\ \times 7 \\ \hline \end{array}$
13. $\begin{array}{r} 8 \\ \times 0 \\ \hline \end{array}$
14. $\begin{array}{r} 4 \\ \times 5 \\ \hline \end{array}$

15. $\begin{array}{r} 5 \\ \times 5 \\ \hline \end{array}$
16. $\begin{array}{r} 4 \\ \times 6 \\ \hline \end{array}$
17. $\begin{array}{r} 8 \\ \times 2 \\ \hline \end{array}$
18. $\begin{array}{r} 9 \\ \times 8 \\ \hline \end{array}$
19. $\begin{array}{r} 7 \\ \times 0 \\ \hline \end{array}$
20. $\begin{array}{r} 6 \\ \times 6 \\ \hline \end{array}$
21. $\begin{array}{r} 1 \\ \times 8 \\ \hline \end{array}$

| 22. | 9 | 23. | 7 | 24. | 6 | 25. | 8 | 26. | 2 | 27. | 7 | 28. | 4 |
|---|---|---|---|---|---|---|---|---|---|---|---|---|---|
| | ×0 | | ×3 | | ×2 | | ×8 | | ×5 | | ×9 | | ×3 |

| 29. | 2 | 30. | 7 | 31. | 3 | 32. | 6 | 33. | 9 | 34. | 9 | 35. | 2 |
|---|---|---|---|---|---|---|---|---|---|---|---|---|---|
| | ×7 | | ×6 | | ×7 | | ×9 | | ×1 | | ×4 | | ×8 |

| 36. | 8 | 37. | 3 | 38. | 9 | 39. | 1 | 40. | 9 | 41. | 8 | 42. | 7 |
|---|---|---|---|---|---|---|---|---|---|---|---|---|---|
| | ×5 | | ×8 | | ×7 | | ×4 | | ×5 | | ×6 | | ×5 |

Patterns can help you check your answers when you multiply by nines. Look at the table at the right.

MENTAL MATH

| × | 9 |
|---|---|
| 1 | 9 |
| 2 | 18 |
| 3 | 27 |
| 4 | 36 |
| 5 | 45 |
| 6 | 54 |
| 7 | 63 |
| 8 | 72 |
| 9 | 81 |

43. **Think:** What is the sum of the digits in each product?

44. **Think:** The number you multiply 9 by is how many more than the number of tens in the product?

★ 45. Complete. 63, 72, 81, ▨, ▨, ▨

## PROBLEM SOLVING APPLICATIONS
### Choosing the Operation

Solve.

46. Centerville had a parade to celebrate its 100th birthday. The parade had 9 bands with 8 members each. How many band members were in the parade?

47. In the parade, 180 women, 153 men, and 229 children marched. How many people marched?

★ 48. The town choir had 6 rows with 8 singers in each row. The children's choir had 5 rows with 9 singers in each row. Which choir had more singers?

★ 49. The Centerville Town Hall received $872 in donations from the history club. The parents' group gave the town hall $168 more than the history club. How much did the town hall receive in all?

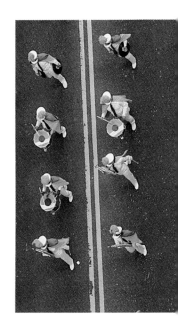

# MULTIPLES AND COMMON MULTIPLES

Because $4 \times 2 = 8$, we say that 8 is a **multiple** of 2.

Some multiples of 2 are 2, 4, 6, 8, 10, 12, 14, 16, 18.

Some multiples of 3 are 3, 6, 9, 12, 15, 18, 21, 24, 27.

The numbers 6, 12, and 18 are multiples of 2 and multiples of 3. We call them **common multiples** of 2 and 3.

Numbers that are multiples of 2 are called **even** numbers. Numbers that are not multiples of 2 are **odd** numbers.

| $\times$ | 2 |
|---|---|
| 1 | 2 |
| 2 | 4 |
| 3 | 6 |
| 4 | 8 |
| 5 | 10 |
| 6 | 12 |
| 7 | 14 |
| 8 | 16 |
| 9 | 18 |

| $\times$ | 3 |
|---|---|
| 1 | 3 |
| 2 | 6 |
| 3 | 9 |
| 4 | 12 |
| 5 | 15 |
| 6 | 18 |
| 7 | 21 |
| 8 | 24 |
| 9 | 27 |

## CLASS EXERCISES

Complete.

**1.** 4, 8, 12, ■, ■, ■, ■, ■, ■

**2.** 5, 10, 15, ■, ■, ■, ■, ■, ■

**3.** 6, 12, 18, ■, ■, ■, ■, ■, ■

**4.** 7, 14, 21, ■, ■, ■, ■, ■, ■

Is the statement true or false? Explain your answer.

**5.** 35 is a multiple of 5.

**6.** 21 is a multiple of 4.

**7.** 24 is a common multiple of 4 and 7.

**8.** 40 is a common multiple of 8 and 5.

## PRACTICE

Is the statement true or false? Write *T* or *F*.

**9.** 49 is a multiple of 7.

**10.** 34 is a multiple of 4.

**11.** 42 is a common multiple of 5 and 6.

**12.** 36 is a common multiple of 6 and 9.

Write the numbers.

**13.** eight multiples of 6

**14.** eight multiples of 8

**15.** two common multiples of 6 and 8

**16.** three common multiples of 2 and 4

**17.** one common multiple of 4 and 5

**18.** three common multiples of 2 and 3

**19.** two common multiples of 3 and 6

**20.** one common multiple of 2 and 5

**21.** the first fifteen even counting numbers

**22.** the first fifteen odd counting numbers

Write *even* or *odd*. Try some examples of your own before you answer.

★ **23.** If two factors are even, the product is .

★ **24.** If two factors are odd, the product is .

★ **25.** If one factor is even and one is odd, the product is .

★ **26.** If two addends are even, their sum is .

★ **27.** If two numbers are odd, their difference is .

★ **28.** If one number is odd and one is even, their difference is .

---

Write $<$ or $>$. Then round each number to its greatest place value.

**29.** 57 ▦ 93

**30.** 45 ▦ 54

**31.** 581 ▦ 245

**32.** 1034 ▦ 2762

**33.** 23,170 ▦ 36,024

**MIXED REVIEW**

## PROBLEM SOLVING APPLICATIONS
### Using Patterns

Delta Springs holds a town election every 2 years. The 1st election was in 1788, the 100th was in 1986. Give the years of the elections listed.

**34.** 101st through 110th    **35.** 2nd through 10th    **36.** 20th

DELTA SPRINGS

100th Election

Elections for President are held in years that are multiples of 4. The elections in 1976, 1980, and 1984 were the 48th, 49th, and 50th elections. Write the year of this election.

★ **37.** 43rd            ★ **38.** 54th            ★ **39.** 2nd

# PROBLEM SOLVING
## Strategy: Two-Step Problems

1. Understand
2. Plan
3. Work
4. Answer/Check

Larry and Caroline like to hike. They hike for 2 hours on 3 days during the week and 4 hours on Saturday. How many hours do they hike in all?

This problem takes not one, but two steps to solve.

Here's what you do first.

MULTIPLY to find the total number of hours hiked during the week.

$$3 \times 2 = 6$$

Here's what you do second.

ADD the hours hiked on Saturday to find the total number of hours hiked.

$$6 + 4 = 10$$

You multiply and then add to find that Larry and Caroline hiked 10 hours in all.

## CLASS EXERCISES

Tell what steps you use to solve the problem. Then give the answer.

1. On Saturday Larry collected 8 leaves from each of 9 different trees. On Sunday he collected 5 different leaves. How many leaves did Larry collect?

2. In three weeks, Caroline saved $14, $16, and $13. She wants to buy hiking boots for $48. How much more does she need to save?

3. During the summer Larry hiked a total of 285 miles. In June he hiked 83 miles and in July he hiked 109 miles. How many miles did he hike in August?

## PRACTICE

Solve. Write the operations you used.

4. On a hike at the beach, Caroline found 12 shells, her mother found 18, and Larry found 15. Eight of the shells were broken. How many were not broken?

**5.** Caroline and Larry buy 2 canteens for $7 each and a compass for $11.58. How much do they spend?

**6.** Larry and Caroline hike for 2 hours and 10 minutes. They stop for lunch and then hike for another 2 hours and 20 minutes. The total trip takes 5 hours and 45 minutes. How long was their lunch break?

The table shows the number of pictures taken by Larry and Caroline. Use the table to solve the problem.

**7.** Larry took 15 pictures of birds and 16 pictures of deer. How many pictures of other animals were taken?

**8.** Caroline took 56 pictures of places. Did Larry take more pictures of places than Caroline did?

★ **9.** Larry took 7 pictures of a stream. He took 5 pictures of each of 3 different plants. How many pictures of other things were taken?

| PICTURES | |
| --- | --- |
| TYPE | NUMBER |
| Animals | 66 |
| Places | 87 |
| Things | 175 |

# CHECKPOINT 2

Multiply. *(pages 114–115)*

| **1.** 7 | **2.** 6 | **3.** 6 |
| --- | --- | --- |
| ×3 | ×7 | ×4 |

Multiply. *(pages 116–119)*

| **4.** 8 | **5.** 9 | **6.** 8 |
| --- | --- | --- |
| ×3 | ×6 | ×8 |

Write the numbers. *(pages 120–121)*

**7.** five multiples of 4

**8.** three common multiples of 3 and 6

Solve. *(pages 122–123)*

**9.** Two kittens each weigh 3 lb. A dog weighs 18 lb. How much do they weigh together?

*Extra practice on page 408*

Write the answer. *(pages 102–105)*

**1.** $\begin{array}{r} 2 \\ \times 6 \\ \hline \end{array}$    **2.** $\begin{array}{r} 3 \\ \times 9 \\ \hline \end{array}$    **3.** $\begin{array}{r} 4 \\ \times 5 \\ \hline \end{array}$    **4.** $\begin{array}{r} 4 \\ \times 7 \\ \hline \end{array}$

Complete. *(pages 106–111)*

**5.** $0 \times 5 = $ ▨     **6.** $4 \times 1 = $ ▨     **7.** $(3 \times 2) \times 4 = $ ▨

$5 \times $ ▨ $ = 0$         ▨ $\times 4 = 4$         ▨ $\times (2 \times 4) = 24$

Draw a tree diagram. Solve. *(pages 112–113)*

**8.** The Salad Palace offers 3 different salads and 4 different dressings. How many different kinds of salads can be made?

Write the answer. *(pages 114–115)*

**9.** $\begin{array}{r} 6 \\ \times 7 \\ \hline \end{array}$    **10.** $\begin{array}{r} 7 \\ \times 8 \\ \hline \end{array}$    **11.** $\begin{array}{r} 6 \\ \times 9 \\ \hline \end{array}$    **12.** $\begin{array}{r} 6 \\ \times 6 \\ \hline \end{array}$

Write the answer. *(pages 116–119)*

**13.** $8 \times 9$     **14.** $6 \times 8$     **15.** $8 \times 8$     **16.** $7 \times 9$

Write the numbers. *(pages 120–121)*

**17.** 8 multiples of 5            **18.** one common multiple of 2 and 7

Solve. *(pages 122–123)*

**19.** For her collection, Lana found 8 scallop shells on each of 5 days. She also found 3 clam shells. How many shells did she find in all?

**20.** Craig bought a puzzle for $1.88 and a game for $4.95. He gave the clerk $10.00. How much change did he receive?

*Extra practice on page 409*

# MATHEMATICS and HEALTH

Does your diet include food from the 4 basic food groups? The groups are listed with some examples from each.

A healthy diet includes 4 or more servings from the bread-cereal group, 4 or more servings from the vegetable-fruit group, and 2 or more servings from the meat group each day. You should also have 3 or more servings from the milk group.

## DOES YOUR DIET COUNT?

**MILK GROUP**

milk
cheese
yogurt

**BREAD-CEREAL GROUP**

bread
crackers
cereal

**MEAT GROUP**

meat
fish
eggs
beans
peanut butter

**VEGETABLE-FRUIT GROUP**

carrots
celery
potatoes
oranges
melon

Suppose you have this food in your refrigerator: whole-wheat bread, tuna salad, milk, apples, celery, peanut butter, pears, and carrots. You plan to drink milk with lunch. You want your lunch to include 1 food from each of the other 3 groups.

1. How many different lunches can you fix? Draw a tree diagram to answer. Use these clues to help you.

   a. Start with the bread.
   b. Then draw branches for the meat group.
   c. Next draw branches for the vegetable-fruit group.

2. List 4 of your menus.

# Enrichment

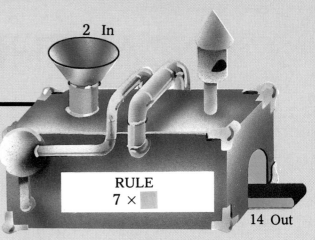

The machine at the right is a function machine. When a number goes in, a different number comes out. The rule for this machine is multiply by 7.

**Think:** If you put 4 in the machine, what number will come out?

Use the function machine rule to complete the table.

**1.**

| IN | 0 | 1 | 2 | 3 | 4 | 5 |
|-----|---|---|---|---|---|---|
| OUT | ? | ? | ? | ? | ? | ? |

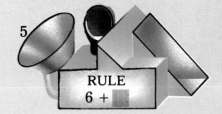

**2.**

| IN | 5 | 9 | 14 | 18 | 23 | 29 |
|-----|---|---|----|----|----|----|
| OUT | ? | ? | ? | ? | ? | ? |

**3.**

| IN | 10 | 18 | 34 | 56 | 82 | 101 |
|-----|----|----|----|----|----|-----|
| OUT | ? | ? | ? | ? | ? | ? |

**4.**

| IN | 9 | 8 | 5 | 4 | 2 | 0 |
|-----|---|---|---|---|---|---|
| OUT | ? | ? | ? | ? | ? | ? |

# FUNCTIONS AND VARIABLES

126

The rule for this machine is written with a letter. A letter that takes the place of a number is called a **variable**. When *n* stands for 6, 24 comes out. What number comes out when *n* stands for 9?

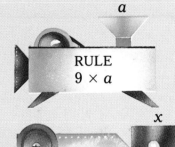

Use the function machine rule to complete the table.

**5.**

| *a* | 2 | 4 | 5 | 6 | 7 | ? |
|-----|---|---|---|---|---|---|
| OUT | ? | ? | ? | ? | ? | 81 |

**6.**

| *x* | 20 | 23 | 31 | 35 | 42 | ? |
|-----|----|----|----|----|----|---|
| OUT | ? | ? | ? | ? | ? | 32 |

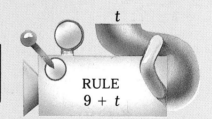

**7.**

| *t* | 5 | 11 | 9 | 23 | ? | ? |
|-----|---|----|---|----|---|---|
| OUT | ? | ? | ? | ? | 25 | 37 |

**8.**

| *s* | 8 | 5 | 7 | 1 | 4 | 6 |
|-----|---|---|---|---|---|---|
| OUT | ? | ? | ? | ? | ? | ? |

Study the table. Write the rule using a variable.

**9.**

| IN | 0 | 1 | 2 | 3 | 4 | 5 |
|----|---|---|---|---|---|---|
| OUT | 11 | 12 | 13 | 14 | 15 | 16 |

**10.**

| IN | 0 | 1 | 2 | 3 | 5 |
|----|---|---|---|---|---|
| OUT | 0 | 6 | 12 | 18 | 30 |

Choose the correct answer. Write *a*, *b*, *c*, or *d*.

Which is the best estimate?

**1.** 71 − 29
  **a.** 10
  **b.** 70
  **c.** 40
  **d.** 100

**2.** 87 − 33
  **a.** 90
  **b.** 120
  **c.** 60
  **d.** 30

**3.** 99 − 67
  **a.** 30
  **b.** 70
  **c.** 100
  **d.** 170

Find the answer.

**4.** 57 − 19
  **a.** 48
  **b.** 38
  **c.** 28
  **d.** none of these

**5.** 893 − 39
  **a.** 834
  **b.** 852
  **c.** 854
  **d.** none of these

**6.** 424 − 106
  **a.** 328
  **b.** 318
  **c.** 320
  **d.** none of these

**7.**
$$\begin{array}{r} 6419 \\ -\ 3828 \\ \hline \end{array}$$
  **a.** 2681
  **b.** 3691
  **c.** 2691
  **d.** none of these

**8.**
$$\begin{array}{r} 50{,}473 \\ -\ 4{,}713 \\ \hline \end{array}$$
  **a.** 46,760
  **b.** 45,160
  **c.** 45,760
  **d.** none of these

**9.**
$$\begin{array}{r} 68{,}292 \\ -\ 46{,}903 \\ \hline \end{array}$$
  **a.** 21,389
  **b.** 21,399
  **c.** 22,389
  **d.** none of these

Find the answer.

**10.**
$$\begin{array}{r} \$23.46 \\ +\ 14.83 \\ \hline \end{array}$$
  **a.** $9.63
  **b.** $38.29
  **c.** $37.29
  **d.** none of these

**11.**
$$\begin{array}{r} \$16.21 \\ -\ 9.99 \\ \hline \end{array}$$
  **a.** $6.22
  **b.** $26.20
  **c.** $6.32
  **d.** none of these

**12.**
$$\begin{array}{r} \$11.08 \\ 3.65 \\ +\ 1.08 \\ \hline \end{array}$$
  **a.** $25.81
  **b.** $15.81
  **c.** $15.71
  **d.** none of these

**13.**
$$\begin{array}{r} \$14.05 \\ -\ 11.49 \\ \hline \end{array}$$
  **a.** $26.05
  **b.** $3.64
  **c.** $2.56
  **d.** none of these

Find the value.

**14.** 1 dollar 2 dimes 3 nickels
    **a.** $1.23
    **b.** $1.33
    **c.** $1.35
    **d.** none of these

**15.** 3 quarters 3 dimes 2 pennies
    **a.** $1.07
    **b.** $.97
    **c.** $1.02
    **d.** none of these

Find the fact needed to solve the problem.

**16.** Bob delivered 74 newspapers in 30 minutes. How many papers does he have left to deliver?
    **a.** the time Bob started delivering
    **b.** the time Bob finished delivering
    **c.** the total number of papers to be delivered
    **d.** none of these

**17.** Friday's high temperature was 5°F higher than Thursday's high. What was Friday's high temperature?
    **a.** Friday's high temperature
    **b.** Friday's low temperature
    **c.** Thursday's high temperature
    **d.** none of these

# LANGUAGE and VOCABULARY REVIEW

Complete the sentences. Write the words on your paper.

**1.** 5, 7, 9, and 11 are examples of _____?_____ numbers.

**2.** In $7 \times 4 = 28$, 28 is the _____?_____.

**3.** In $25 - 18 = 7$, 7 is the _____?_____.

**4.** 3, 6, 9, and 12 are four _____?_____ of 3.

**5.** The _____?_____ of 30 and 50 is 80.

**6.** $0 \times 4 = 0$ is an example of the _____?_____ property.

**7.** $2 \times (3 \times 1) = (2 \times 3) \times 1$ is an example of the _____?_____ property.

# MEMORY

A computer stores data in its **memory.** Computers have two kinds of memory: RAM and ROM.

RAM • Data you put into the computer are stored here.

   • You can change the data anytime.

   • When you turn off the computer, the data are lost.

ROM • You cannot put data into ROM. All the data are put in at the factory.

   • The data are special instructions that cannot be changed.

   • When you turn off the computer, the instructions remain in ROM.

Each letter, number, and symbol that is put in RAM is stored in a special place called an **address.** You do not have to tell the computer to put data at an address. Instructions in ROM tell the computer how to do it.

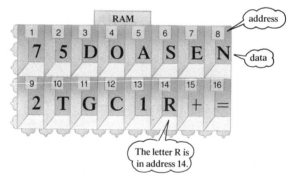

Write the address for the data in RAM.

1. Address: ▦▦
   Data:      2 5

2. Address: ▦▦▦
   Data:     C A T

3. Address: ▦▦▦▦▦
   Data:     7 D O G S

4. Address: ▦▦▦▦▦▦
   Data:     5 + 2 = 7

5. Address: ▦▦▦▦ ▦▦▦▦
   Data:    2 5 7 A N T S

Sixty-four pears have been piled on a tray. They will be packaged 8 to a box. If 8 boxes are filled, will any pears be left on the tray?

5

DIVISION FACTS

Marisa needs 6 party favors. There are 2 favors in each package. How many packages does she need to buy?

You can subtract to find out.

You can subtract 3 twos from 6.

$$\begin{array}{r} 6 \\ -\ 2 \\ \hline 4 \\ -\ 2 \\ \hline 2 \\ -\ 2 \\ \hline 0 \end{array}$$

She needs 3 packages.

You can also divide to find how many twos are in 6. You can write the division in two ways.

$$6 \div 2 = 3 \qquad \text{or} \qquad 2\overline{)6} \xleftarrow{} \text{quotient}$$

dividend   divisor   quotient        divisor   dividend

Six divided by two equals three.

 If you press 6 ⊟ 2 🟰 on a calculator, you will see 4 on the screen. On some calculators, each time you press another = , the calculator will subtract another 2. Count the number of times you press = until you get to 0. This number is the quotient of $6 \div 2$.

6 ⊟ 2 🟰 🟰 🟰 0

3 twos in 6

If you press 6 ➗ 2 🟰 on a calculator, you will see 3.

## CLASS EXERCISES

Use the picture to help name the quotient.

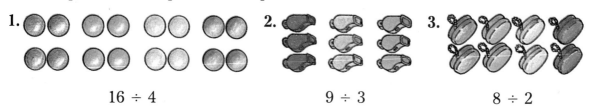

1.        2.        3.

$16 \div 4$        $9 \div 3$        $8 \div 2$

Complete. How are the subtractions and the division related?

4. $12 - 3 = $ ▩   $9 - 3 = $ ▩   $6 - 3 = $ ▩   $3 - 3 = $ ▩   $12 \div 3 = $ ▩

# PRACTICE

Divide.

**5.** $21 \div 3$    **6.** $6 \div 2$    **7.** $3 \div 3$    **8.** $8 \div 4$    **9.** $15 \div 3$

**10.** $16 \div 4$    **11.** $14 \div 2$    **12.** $27 \div 3$    **13.** $2 \div 2$    **14.** $20 \div 4$

**15.** $2\overline{)18}$    **16.** $3\overline{)18}$    **17.** $2\overline{)16}$    **18.** $4\overline{)28}$    **19.** $4\overline{)12}$

**20.** $4\overline{)36}$    **21.** $4\overline{)24}$    **22.** $3\overline{)12}$    **23.** $4\overline{)32}$    **24.** $3\overline{)24}$

How many are there?

**25.** threes in 6    **26.** twos in 10    **27.** fours in 32

**28.** twos in 18    **29.** threes in 21    **30.** threes in 24

**31.** fours in 28    **32.** twos in 16    **33.** fours in 24

**34.** threes in 15    **35.** fours in 12    **36.** threes in 27

**37.** threes in 18    **38.** fours in 20    **39.** twos in 14

Draw the keys you could push on the calculator to solve this problem without using the $\div$ key.

**CALCULATOR**

**40.** $6 \div 3$    **41.** $16 \div 4$    **42.** $28 \div 4$    **43.** $12 \div 3$

**44.** $36 \div 4$    **45.** $10 \div 1$    **46.** $14 \div 2$    **47.** $18 \div 3$

## PROBLEM SOLVING APPLICATIONS
### Choosing the Operation

Solve.

**48.** A small package holds 18 paper cups. If there are 3 of each color, how many colors are there?

**49.** Marisa buys 12 paper hats with feathers and 3 without feathers. How many hats does she buy?

**50.** There are 32 balloons to be blown up. Each person blows up 4 balloons. How many people are needed to blow up the balloons?

**51.** Craig invited 24 people to the party, but only 18 came. How many did not come to the party?

# DIVIDING BY TWO, THREE, AND FOUR

Eddy has 12 magazines that he would like to share with 3 friends. He wants each friend to have the same number of magazines. To find how many each friend gets, you divide.

$$12 \div 3 = 4 \quad \text{or} \quad 3\overline{)12}^{\,4}$$

Each of Eddy's friends gets 4 magazines.

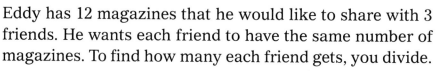

## CLASS EXERCISES

How many will each person get?

**1.** 2 friends share

**2.** 3 friends share

**3.** 4 friends share

**4.** 3 friends share

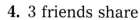

**5.** 2 friends share

**6.** 4 friends share

## PRACTICE

Divide.

**7.** $2 \div 2$      **8.** $15 \div 3$      **9.** $16 \div 2$      **10.** $8 \div 4$      **11.** $3 \div 3$

**12.** $18 \div 3$      **13.** $21 \div 3$      **14.** $6 \div 3$      **15.** $4 \div 4$      **16.** $10 \div 2$

**17.** $28 \div 4$      **18.** $12 \div 2$      **19.** $18 \div 2$      **20.** $36 \div 4$      **21.** $6 \div 2$

**22.** $2\overline{)8}$      **23.** $3\overline{)3}$      **24.** $4\overline{)24}$      **25.** $2\overline{)4}$      **26.** $4\overline{)20}$

**27.** $3\overline{)24}$  **28.** $3\overline{)27}$  **29.** $4\overline{)32}$  **30.** $3\overline{)9}$  **31.** $3\overline{)21}$

**32.** $4\overline{)12}$  **33.** $3\overline{)15}$  **34.** $2\overline{)10}$  **35.** $3\overline{)6}$  **36.** $3\overline{)18}$

**37.** $2\overline{)2}$  **38.** $2\overline{)16}$  **39.** $2\overline{)14}$  **40.** $4\overline{)16}$  **41.** $4\overline{)4}$

**42.** $2\overline{)6}$  **43.** $3\overline{)12}$  **44.** $4\overline{)28}$  **45.** $2\overline{)18}$  **46.** $4\overline{)36}$

Which quotient is different? Write *a*, *b*, or *c*.

**47. a.** $3\overline{)12}$  **b.** $2\overline{)8}$  **c.** $4\overline{)20}$   **48. a.** $4\overline{)24}$  **b.** $3\overline{)15}$  **c.** $2\overline{)12}$

**49. a.** $2\overline{)14}$  **b.** $3\overline{)21}$  **c.** $4\overline{)32}$   **50. a.** $3\overline{)24}$  **b.** $2\overline{)16}$  **c.** $4\overline{)36}$

---

Write the answer.

**51.**  $\begin{array}{r} 8 \\ + 7 \\ \hline \end{array}$  **52.**  $\begin{array}{r} 9 \\ \times 3 \\ \hline \end{array}$  **53.**  $\begin{array}{r} 6 \\ \times 8 \\ \hline \end{array}$  **54.**  $\begin{array}{r} 12 \\ - 5 \\ \hline \end{array}$  **55.**  $\begin{array}{r} 15 \\ + 8 \\ \hline \end{array}$

**56.**  $\begin{array}{r} 5 \\ \times 6 \\ \hline \end{array}$  **57.**  $\begin{array}{r} 7 \\ \times 4 \\ \hline \end{array}$  **58.**  $\begin{array}{r} 6 \\ + 9 \\ \hline \end{array}$  **59.**  $\begin{array}{r} 8 \\ \times 4 \\ \hline \end{array}$  **60.**  $\begin{array}{r} 5 \\ \times 9 \\ \hline \end{array}$

**MIXED REVIEW**

---

# PROBLEM SOLVING APPLICATONS
## Using a Bar Graph

Use the bar graph to solve.

**61.** Eddy shares his *Outdoors* magazines equally with 4 friends. How many does each friend get?

**62.** Eddy stores his *New Crafts* magazines in 2 equal piles. How many magazines are in each pile?

**63.** Eddy gets a *New Crafts* magazine each month. Has he been getting this magazine for more than 1 year? How do you know?

★ **64.** If Eddy gives all his *Science Fun* magazines to 3 friends, will each friend get the same number?

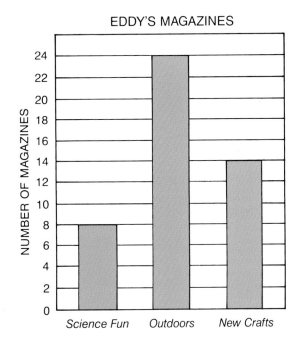

EDDY'S MAGAZINES

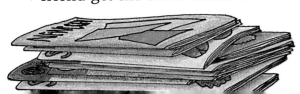

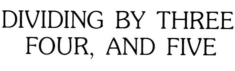

# DIVIDING BY THREE, FOUR, AND FIVE

Stan has a pocket full of nickels. He buys a sandwich for 30¢. How many nickels does he use?

To find out, you use division.

$$30 \div 5 = 6 \qquad \text{or} \qquad 5\overline{)30}^{\,6}$$

Stan uses 6 nickels.

 **Think:** The answer makes sense because $5 + 5 + 5 + 5 + 5 + 5 = 30$.

## CLASS EXERCISES

Write the number of nickels in this amount.

**1.** 15¢     **2.** 20¢     **3.** 40¢     **4.** 10¢     **5.** 45¢     **6.** 35¢

Divide.

**7.** $16 \div 4$     $20 \div 4$     $24 \div 4$     $28 \div 4$     $32 \div 4$     $36 \div 4$

**8.** $9 \div 3$     $12 \div 3$     $15 \div 3$     $18 \div 3$     $21 \div 3$     $24 \div 3$

**9.** $20 \div 5$     $25 \div 5$     $30 \div 5$     $35 \div 5$     $40 \div 5$     $45 \div 5$

## PRACTICE

Divide.

**10.** $40 \div 5$     **11.** $20 \div 4$     **12.** $21 \div 3$     **13.** $36 \div 4$     **14.** $45 \div 5$     **15.** $15 \div 3$

**16.** $28 \div 4$     **17.** $9 \div 3$     **18.** $12 \div 3$     **19.** $6 \div 3$     **20.** $12 \div 4$     **21.** $15 \div 5$

**22.** $3\overline{)15}$ **23.** $5\overline{)10}$ **24.** $4\overline{)12}$ **25.** $4\overline{)20}$ **26.** $5\overline{)35}$

**27.** $3\overline{)21}$ **28.** $5\overline{)40}$ **29.** $3\overline{)9}$ **30.** $3\overline{)6}$ **31.** $3\overline{)27}$

**32.** $4\overline{)16}$ **33.** $5\overline{)30}$ **34.** $5\overline{)45}$ **35.** $5\overline{)25}$ **36.** $5\overline{)15}$

**37.** $2\overline{)18}$ **38.** $4\overline{)32}$ **39.** $5\overline{)20}$ **40.** $2\overline{)14}$ **41.** $4\overline{)8}$

**42.** $3\overline{)24}$ **43.** $2\overline{)12}$ **44.** $4\overline{)28}$ **45.** $5\overline{)5}$ **46.** $2\overline{)6}$

Divide. Write <, >, or = .

★ **47.** $36 \div 4$ ▨ $18 \div 3$   ★ **48.** $12 \div 3$ ▨ $24 \div 4$   ★ **49.** $35 \div 5$ ▨ $28 \div 4$

★ **50.** $24 \div 3$ ▨ $15 \div 3$   ★ **51.** $16 \div 2$ ▨ $20 \div 4$   ★ **52.** $14 \div 2$ ▨ $45 \div 5$

The missing addends in the problem are all the same. Divide to find the missing numbers.

**MENTAL MATH**

**53.** ▨ + ▨ + ▨ = 18   **54.** ▨ + ▨ + ▨ + ▨ = 36

**55.** ▨ + ▨ + ▨ + ▨ = 28   **56.** ▨ + ▨ + ▨ + ▨ + ▨ = 25

## PROBLEM SOLVING APPLICATIONS
### Choosing a Strategy

Solve.

**57.** There will be 28 people selling things at the Pleasure Street Fair. If 4 people share one long table, how many tables are needed?

**58.** The time is 15 minutes after 2 o'clock. Daria leaves work at 5 o'clock. At what time does she start working?

**59.** Taylor can buy 2 kites for a total of $6. If he buys 1 kite and then spends $.50 for string, how much does he spend in all?

★ **60.** Raisin muffins cost 30¢ each. If you buy 4 muffins you get a discount and pay just $1. How much does each cost if you buy 4?

# MULTIPLICATION AND DIVISION

Just as addition and subtraction have fact families, multiplication and division have fact families, too.

You can check a division fact by multiplying.

$5 \times 4 = 20 \qquad 20 \div 4 = 5$

$4 \times 5 = 20 \qquad 20 \div 5 = 4$

Is this correct?　　Check.

$$3 \overline{)15} \quad \begin{array}{r} 5 \\ \end{array}$$

$$\begin{array}{r} 3 \\ \times 5 \\ \hline 15 \checkmark \end{array} \quad \text{It checks.}$$

Suppose you want to divide 0 by 4. Think of multiplication to help you.

$0 \div 4 = \blacksquare$　　What number times 4 equals 0?　$0 \times 4 = 0$　　$\Rightarrow$　　$0 \div 4 = 0$

Now suppose you want to divide 3 by 0.

$3 \div 0 = \blacksquare$　　What number times 0 equals 3? There is no such number!　$\Rightarrow$　No answer is possible.

You cannot divide a number by 0. It is impossible.

When you divide any number except 0 by itself, the quotient is 1. When you divide any number by 1, the quotient is that number.

$8 \div 8 = 1$

$8 \div 1 = 8$

## CLASS EXERCISES

Multiply, then divide. Explain how the facts are related.

**1.** $8 \times 2$      **2.** $5 \times 2$      **3.** $8 \times 4$      **4.** $9 \times 5$      **5.** $7 \times 3$

    $16 \div 2$         $10 \div 2$         $32 \div 4$         $45 \div 5$         $21 \div 3$

## PRACTICE

Divide. Check by multiplying.

**6.** $2 \overline{)2}$      **7.** $3 \overline{)0}$      **8.** $1 \overline{)7}$      **9.** $4 \overline{)16}$      **10.** $1 \overline{)4}$

11. $2\overline{)4}$     12. $3\overline{)9}$     13. $2\overline{)0}$     14. $3\overline{)15}$     15. $4\overline{)12}$

16. $5\overline{)25}$    17. $3\overline{)12}$    18. $5\overline{)20}$    19. $5\overline{)40}$    20. $4\overline{)4}$

21. $1\overline{)1}$     22. $5\overline{)5}$     23. $4\overline{)32}$    24. $5\overline{)10}$    25. $3\overline{)3}$

26. $1\overline{)3}$     27. $3\overline{)21}$    28. $2\overline{)6}$     29. $3\overline{)6}$     30. $1\overline{)8}$

31. $4\overline{)8}$     32. $2\overline{)14}$    33. $5\overline{)30}$    34. $2\overline{)8}$     35. $2\overline{)16}$

36. $3\overline{)27}$    37. $1\overline{)5}$     38. $2\overline{)18}$    39. $4\overline{)0}$     40. $3\overline{)24}$

41. $3\overline{)18}$    42. $4\overline{)36}$    43. $5\overline{)15}$    44. $2\overline{)12}$    45. $4\overline{)28}$

Write the multiplication and division fact family for these numbers.

**46.** 2, 5, 10     **47.** 4, 3, 12     **48.** 5, 4, 20     **49.** 4, 4, 16     ★ **50.** 0, 6, 0

★ **51. Think:** Name a fact family with doubles that uses the same numbers for both addition and multiplication.

---

Compare. Write <, >, or = .

**52.** 24 ▨ 27     **53.** 371 ▨ 317     **54.** 4032 ▨ 4302

**55.** 1 yd ▨ 3 ft     **56.** 7 in. ▨ 7 mi     **57.** 3 qt ▨ 3 pt

**MIXED REVIEW**

## PROBLEM SOLVING APPLICATIONS
### Number Sentences

Write a number sentence. Solve.

**58.** Volunteers at the hospital made 32 puzzles for the children. Another volunteer bought 8 puzzles for the children. How many puzzles did the volunteers have for the children?

**59.** The children's floor has 5 large rooms. The nurse said there are 30 children in the rooms in all. Each room has the same number of children. How many children are in each room?

Write your own word problem for the number sentence.

★ **60.** $18 \div 3 = 6$     ★ **61.** $12 \div 4 = 3$     ★ **62.** $20 \div 5 = 4$

# PROBLEM SOLVING
## Strategy: Choosing the Operation

1. Understand
2. Plan
3. Work
4. Answer/Check

To solve many problems, you must decide whether to add, subtract, multiply, or divide. Remember, you add to find a total. You subtract to find how many more or how many are left. Study these examples for multiplication and division.

8 nails in each box
2 boxes
How many in all?

> MULTIPLY since you have equal groups and you want to find the total.
> $2 \times 8 = 16$

16 nails in all

8 nails to hammer
2 pieces of wood
How many nails for each piece of wood?

> DIVIDE since you want to know how the nails can be shared equally.
> $2\overline{)8}$ $^4$

4 nails for each piece of wood

## CLASS EXERCISES

Would you add, subtract, multiply, or divide to solve the problem? Explain why.

1. Mary has 16 screws. She needs 4 screws for each picture frame. How many frames can she finish?

2. Pedro has a package of 8 nuts and a package of 12 bolts. How many more bolts does he have?

3. Franklin has 2 pliers and 3 hammers. How many tools does Franklin have?

4. Cindy has 5 boxes of chalk. Each box has 6 pieces. How many pieces of chalk does she have?

## PRACTICE

Write *add*, *subtract*, *multiply*, or *divide* for your plan. Then solve.

5. Each section in Elaine's tool chest holds 4 wrenches. Elaine has 16 wrenches. How many sections are in the tool chest?

6. Paula bought 8 paintbrushes. She paid $4 for each of them. How much did Paula spend for the paintbrushes?

7. Gus bought 5 screwdrivers for $15. He paid the same amount for each screwdriver. How much did Gus pay for each screwdriver?

8. Ruth has 4 new tools and Marcus has 5 new tools. How many more new tools does Marcus have than Ruth?

9. Ming has 25 magnets in one box and 5 magnets in another. How many magnets does she have?

10. Julius has 12 cans of stain and 6 cans of paint. How many cans does Julius have?

Solve.

11. Kathleen buys a metal ruler for $2.35, a chisel for $4.58, and a hammer for $9.59. How much does Kathleen spend?

12. Bryan buys 3 screws for 7¢ each, 2 nails for 7¢ each, and 4 bolts for 7¢ each. How much does he spend in all?

★ 13. Ryan bought 4 different tools for $36 at the hardware store. This is $10 more than the tools cost 5 years ago. How much did the tools cost 5 years ago?

★ 14. Eva mailed 3 handmade bookcases to relatives. Each bookcase cost $6 to make. Postage for each bookcase was $4. How much money did Eva spend in all?

# CHECKPOINT 1

Divide. (*pages 132–137*)

1. 2)̅1̅6̅     2. 4)̅2̅4̅

3. 3)̅2̅7̅     4. 5)̅4̅0̅

Divide. Check by multiplying. (*pages 138–139*)

5. 5)̅3̅5̅     6. 3)̅2̅4̅

Write *add, subtract, multiply,* or *divide* for your plan. Then solve. (*pages 140–141*)

7. It takes 5 pieces of wood to make 1 letter holder. How many letter holders can be made with 25 pieces of wood?

*Extra practice on page 410*

# DIVIDING BY SIX AND SEVEN

Centerville School has 30 students on teams for the Math Bowl. There are 6 teams with an equal number of students on each team. How many students are on each team? To answer, you divide.

 When you know a multiplication fact, you know a division fact, too.

**Think:** How many sixes in 30?

$6\overline{)30}$

$\blacksquare \times 6 = 30$

$5 \times 6 = 30$

so $30 \div 6 = 5$

There are 5 students on each team.

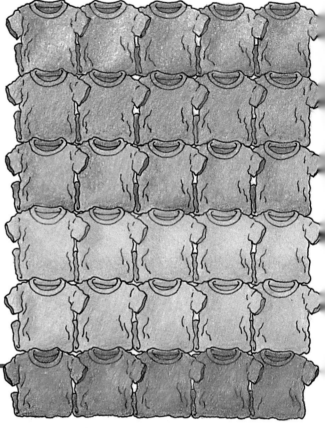

## CLASS EXERCISES

Multiply, then divide.

| | | | | |
|---|---|---|---|---|
| **1.** $5 \times 6$ $30 \div 6$ | **2.** $6 \times 7$ $42 \div 7$ | **3.** $6 \times 6$ $36 \div 6$ | **4.** $5 \times 7$ $35 \div 7$ | **5.** $7 \times 6$ $42 \div 6$ |
| **6.** $8 \times 6$ $48 \div 6$ | **7.** $7 \times 7$ $49 \div 7$ | **8.** $9 \times 6$ $54 \div 6$ | **9.** $8 \times 7$ $56 \div 7$ | **10.** $9 \times 7$ $63 \div 7$ |

## PRACTICE

Divide.

**11.** $12 \div 6$    **12.** $18 \div 6$    **13.** $30 \div 6$    **14.** $24 \div 6$    **15.** $12 \div 2$    **16.** $18 \div 3$

**17.** $14 \div 7$    **18.** $21 \div 7$    **19.** $28 \div 7$    **20.** $35 \div 5$    **21.** $28 \div 4$    **22.** $21 \div 3$

**23.** $0 \div 6$    **24.** $32 \div 4$    **25.** $25 \div 5$    **26.** $42 \div 7$    **27.** $40 \div 5$    **28.** $36 \div 4$

**29.** $6\overline{)6}$    **30.** $7\overline{)56}$    **31.** $6\overline{)54}$    **32.** $6\overline{)18}$    **33.** $6\overline{)42}$    **34.** $7\overline{)7}$

**35.** $5\overline{)25}$    **36.** $1\overline{)6}$    **37.** $3\overline{)15}$    **38.** $4\overline{)36}$    **39.** $3\overline{)12}$    **40.** $4\overline{)32}$

**41.** $5\overline{)20}$    **42.** $7\overline{)35}$    **43.** $7\overline{)0}$    **44.** $3\overline{)18}$    **45.** $4\overline{)28}$    **46.** $7\overline{)42}$

**47.** $6\overline{)48}$    **48.** $3\overline{)21}$    **49.** $6\overline{)36}$    **50.** $5\overline{)35}$    **51.** $4\overline{)20}$    **52.** $6\overline{)24}$

**53.** $6\overline{)12}$    **54.** $3\overline{)27}$    **55.** $7\overline{)14}$    **56.** $4\overline{)24}$    **57.** $5\overline{)30}$    **58.** $7\overline{)49}$

**59.** $2\overline{)14}$    **60.** $5\overline{)15}$    **61.** $3\overline{)24}$    **62.** $6\overline{)0}$    **63.** $1\overline{)7}$    **64.** $5\overline{)40}$

**65.** $7\overline{)63}$    **66.** $4\overline{)16}$    **67.** $7\overline{)28}$    **68.** $5\overline{)45}$    **69.** $7\overline{)21}$    **70.** $6\overline{)30}$

Complete. Write $+$, $-$, $\times$, or $\div$ to make the sentence true.

★ **71.** $45 \div 5 > 18$ ▩ $6$    ★ **72.** $0 \div 8 = 8$ ▩ $8$    ★ **73.** $28$ ▩ $7 = 12$ ▩ $3$

Think of a multiplication or division fact to find the missing number. Write only the missing number.

**74.** ▩ $\div 7 = 4$    **75.** ▩ $\times 6 = 54$    **76.** ▩ $\div 5 = 3$

**77.** ▩ $\times 4 = 32$    **78.** ▩ $\times 3 = 24$    **79.** ▩ $\div 7 = 8$

MENTAL MATH

## PROBLEM SOLVING APPLICATIONS
### Too Little Information

Is there enough information to solve the problem? Write *yes* or *no*. If your answer is *yes*, then solve.

**80.** Brighton School is getting ready for the Math Bowl. The school ordered 36 shirts for the teams. How many shirts does each Math Bowl team get?

**81.** In one day, the team manager can put a number on each of 5 shirts. If the manager works every day for a week, how many shirts will have numbers?

**82.** The Math Bowl teams practiced for 3 hours this week. How long will they practice next week?

**83.** Five students are practicing today. Each gets to answer the same number of questions. If 20 questions are asked, how many questions does each student get to answer?

# DIVIDING BY EIGHT AND NINE

Ann works after school at The Music Loft. She puts 24 records into rows of 8 for a display. How many rows does she make?

You can divide to find the answer.

$$3 \times 8 = 24 \longrightarrow 8)\overline{24} \quad (3)$$

Ann makes 3 rows.

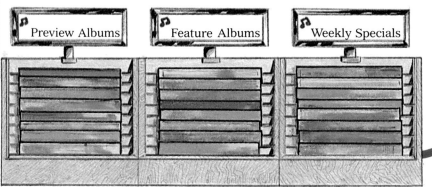

## CLASS EXERCISES

Which multiplication fact helps you find the quotient?

**1.** $32 \div 8$     **2.** $45 \div 9$     **3.** $56 \div 8$     **4.** $27 \div 9$     **5.** $72 \div 8$

**6.** $72 \div 9$     **7.** $54 \div 9$     **8.** $63 \div 9$     **9.** $48 \div 8$     **10.** $64 \div 8$

**11.** $40 \div 8$     **12.** $36 \div 9$     **13.** $8 \div 8$     **14.** $81 \div 9$     **15.** $18 \div 9$

## PRACTICE

Divide.

**16.** $2)\overline{16}$     **17.** $5)\overline{35}$     **18.** $4)\overline{32}$     **19.** $8)\overline{16}$     **20.** $9)\overline{18}$     **21.** $3)\overline{27}$

**22.** $8)\overline{24}$     **23.** $5)\overline{25}$     **24.** $8)\overline{40}$     **25.** $9)\overline{63}$     **26.** $6)\overline{42}$     **27.** $9)\overline{81}$

**28.** $5)\overline{20}$     **29.** $8)\overline{0}$     **30.** $9)\overline{36}$     **31.** $6)\overline{24}$     **32.** $8)\overline{72}$     **33.** $3)\overline{18}$

**34.** $7)\overline{56}$     **35.** $4)\overline{28}$     **36.** $7)\overline{42}$     **37.** $5)\overline{30}$     **38.** $8)\overline{56}$     **39.** $9)\overline{9}$

**40.** $8)\overline{64}$     **41.** $7)\overline{63}$     **42.** $6)\overline{30}$     **43.** $5)\overline{40}$     **44.** $8)\overline{8}$     **45.** $7)\overline{14}$

**46.** 8)32    **47.** 4)24    **48.** 9)54    **49.** 9)72    **50.** 7)21    **51.** 6)36

**52.** 7)35    **53.** 9)45    **54.** 2)18    **55.** 4)36    **56.** 7)49    **57.** 6)48

**58.** 3)24    **59.** 6)54    **60.** 9)0    **61.** 5)45    **62.** 6)18    **63.** 8)48

Write the answer.

**64.**  $5.64    **65.**  $9.45    **66.**  $24.32    **67.**  $15.10
    +  .83        −  1.62        +  5.87        −  8.64

**68.** 1602 − 758          **69.** 3452 + 648 + 82

## PROBLEM SOLVING APPLICATIONS
### Reading a Sign

Use the sign to solve.

**70.** During the first hour of a sale, The Music Loft received $56 for sales of preview albums. How many preview albums were sold?

**71.** Carly received $18 as a birthday gift. Does she have enough money to buy 3 budget albums?

**72.** Dennis has $21 to spend on records. He would like to buy 4 weekly special albums. Does he have enough money?

**73.** Helen bought 3 preview albums on Monday. She returned one of the albums on Tuesday. How much did she spend?

★ **74.** Millicent had a discount coupon. She paid $25 for 3 feature albums. Did she pay more than $8 for each?

★ **75.** William has $23 to spend on records. Which records can he choose?

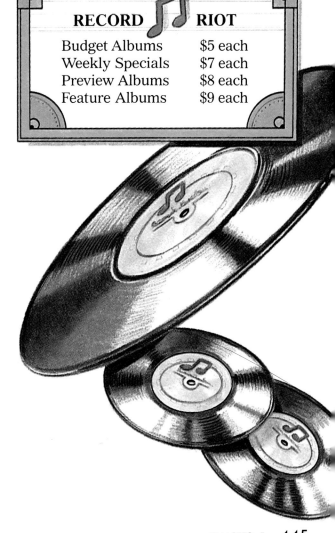

| RECORD 🎵 RIOT | |
|---|---|
| Budget Albums | $5 each |
| Weekly Specials | $7 each |
| Preview Albums | $8 each |
| Feature Albums | $9 each |

# DIVIDING BY 1–9

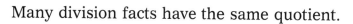

Many division facts have the same quotient.

$$30 \div 5 = 6 \qquad 42 \div 7 = 6 \qquad 6 \div 1 = 6$$

**Think:** What are four more division facts that have 6 as the quotient?

Remember, whether you use mental math or pencil and paper, you can check division by multiplying.

$$12 \div 6 = 2 \qquad 2 \times 6 = 12$$

## CLASS EXERCISES

Divide.

**1.** $2 \div 1$    $3 \div 1$    $4 \div 1$    $5 \div 1$    **2.** $6 \div 1$    $7 \div 1$    $8 \div 1$    $9 \div 1$

**3.** $2 \div 2$    $3 \div 3$    $4 \div 4$    $5 \div 5$    **4.** $6 \div 6$    $7 \div 7$    $8 \div 8$    $9 \div 9$

**5.** $0 \div 2$    $0 \div 3$    $0 \div 4$    $0 \div 5$    **6.** $0 \div 6$    $0 \div 7$    $0 \div 8$    $0 \div 9$

Complete the number sentence. Find three division facts that have the same quotient. Write the letters.

**7.** $12 \div 2 = \ $      **A.** $28 \div 4$      **B.** $35 \div 7$      **C.** $42 \div 6$

**8.** $40 \div 8 = \ $      **D.** $48 \div 8$      **E.** $36 \div 6$      **F.** $15 \div 3$

**9.** $21 \div 3 = \ $      **G.** $18 \div 3$      **H.** $45 \div 9$      **I.** $49 \div 7$

**10.** What is the quotient when you divide 72 by 9?

**11.** What is the quotient when you divide 48 by 6?

# PRACTICE

Divide.

**12.** 54 ÷ 6  **13.** 63 ÷ 9  **14.** 48 ÷ 6  **15.** 32 ÷ 8  **16.** 32 ÷ 4

**17.** 15 ÷ 5  **18.** 42 ÷ 7  **19.** 36 ÷ 6  **20.** 49 ÷ 7  **21.** 64 ÷ 8

**22.** 9)54  **23.** 9)45  **24.** 9)72  **25.** 4)24  **26.** 9)9  **27.** 8)16

**28.** 7)56  **29.** 8)72  **30.** 1)9  **31.** 8)48  **32.** 3)24  **33.** 5)40

**34.** 9)36  **35.** 8)32  **36.** 8)64  **37.** 9)63  **38.** 7)7  **39.** 6)36

**40.** 9)27  **41.** 8)24  **42.** 7)28  **43.** 6)54  **44.** 4)0  **45.** 8)56

Find all the division facts with divisors of 1 through 9 that have this quotient.

**46.** 8  **47.** 9  **48.** 3  **49.** 4  **50.** 2

# PROBLEM SOLVING APPLICATIONS
## Choosing a Strategy

Solve.

**51.** Steve is helping out at the Crosshill Nursery. He has 48 coleus plants to put in boxes. If each box holds 6 plants, how many boxes does he need?

**52.** A hanging begonia needs 4 or more hours of sunshine each day. Is this plant a good one to put in a window that receives sunshine from 9:00 A.M. until noon?

**53.** Phyllis bought 18 tulip bulbs, 25 iris bulbs, and 12 hyacinth bulbs. About how many bulbs did she buy?

★ **54.** Steve has 24 strawberry plants to arrange in rows on a table. If each row has an equal number of plants, how many different ways can Steve arrange the plants? What are they?

# DIVISION WITH REMAINDERS

Joshua and Nell are helping to make flags for the members of their club. Each flag needs 4 stars. Nell has 21 stars. How many flags can Nell make? How many stars are left over?

To divide 21 by 4, you subtract as many fours as possible. The number left over is called the **remainder**.

Subtract 5 fours.
$5 \times 4 = 20$

$$
\begin{array}{r}
5 \\
4\overline{)21} \\
-20 \\
\hline
1 \leftarrow \text{remainder}
\end{array}
$$

5 fours

Write the quotient and the remainder.

$$
\begin{array}{r}
5 \text{ R}1 \\
4\overline{)21} \\
-20 \\
\hline
1
\end{array}
$$

1 left over

The remainder should always be less than the number by which you divide. In this problem the remainder should be less than 4.

Nell can make 5 flags, and 1 star will be left over.

 You use what you know to decide how many groups of 4 are in 21. You know these facts.

$$4 \times 5 = 20 \qquad 4 \times 6 = 24$$

Since 21 is between 20 and 24, the answer must be greater than 5 and less than 6.

## CLASS EXERCISES

Divide. The quotient may or may not have a remainder.

1. $4\overline{)12}$    2. $4\overline{)13}$    3. $4\overline{)14}$    4. $4\overline{)15}$    5. $4\overline{)16}$    6. $4\overline{)17}$

7. $3\overline{)15}$    8. $3\overline{)16}$    9. $3\overline{)17}$    10. $3\overline{)18}$    11. $3\overline{)19}$    12. $3\overline{)20}$

Will the quotient have a remainder? Explain why or why not.

13. $2\overline{)13}$    14. $6\overline{)30}$    15. $3\overline{)27}$    16. $4\overline{)30}$    17. $5\overline{)43}$    18. $7\overline{)28}$

# PRACTICE

Divide.

| | | | | | |
|---|---|---|---|---|---|
| **19.** 2)$\overline{17}$ | **20.** 6)$\overline{15}$ | **21.** 3)$\overline{26}$ | **22.** 5)$\overline{49}$ | **23.** 8)$\overline{41}$ | **24.** 5)$\overline{32}$ |
| **25.** 4)$\overline{19}$ | **26.** 3)$\overline{7}$ | **27.** 6)$\overline{55}$ | **28.** 5)$\overline{43}$ | **29.** 7)$\overline{24}$ | **30.** 2)$\overline{19}$ |
| **31.** 2)$\overline{15}$ | **32.** 5)$\overline{27}$ | **33.** 7)$\overline{45}$ | **34.** 6)$\overline{9}$ | **35.** 9)$\overline{50}$ | **36.** 9)$\overline{75}$ |
| **37.** 3)$\overline{29}$ | **38.** 5)$\overline{8}$ | **39.** 6)$\overline{27}$ | **40.** 4)$\overline{33}$ | **41.** 8)$\overline{54}$ | **42.** 8)$\overline{21}$ |
| **43.** 4)$\overline{22}$ | **44.** 6)$\overline{36}$ | **45.** 9)$\overline{38}$ | **46.** 9)$\overline{63}$ | **47.** 3)$\overline{22}$ | **48.** 2)$\overline{15}$ |
| **49.** 9)$\overline{65}$ | **50.** 7)$\overline{38}$ | **51.** 8)$\overline{64}$ | **52.** 6)$\overline{50}$ | **53.** 7)$\overline{62}$ | **54.** 9)$\overline{55}$ |

Write the two multiplication facts that help you find this quotient.

**55.** 7)$\overline{62}$  **56.** 6)$\overline{28}$  **57.** 8)$\overline{31}$  **58.** 4)$\overline{35}$  **59.** 9)$\overline{49}$

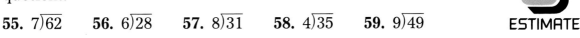

ESTIMATE

## PROBLEM SOLVING APPLICATIONS
### Choosing a Strategy

Solve.

**60.** The club has $18 to spend on fabric for the flags. Each piece of fabric that it buys costs $5. How many pieces does the club buy? How much money is left over?

**61.** While making the flags, the club members take a break to drink some apple juice. How many servings can they get from 58 oz of juice if each serving is 9 oz? How many ounces are left over?

**62.** The background of each flag can be red, blue, or yellow. The stars can be orange or green. How many different kinds of flags can be made?

★ **63.** Rosa has a piece of fabric 3 yd long. She wants to cut it into 9 pieces of equal length. How many cuts must she make? How long will each piece be?

# FACTORS AND COMMON FACTORS

It is possible to divide 16 by many different numbers and have no remainders. Can you name all of them?

$16 \div 1 = 16$     $1 \times 16 = 16$
$16 \div 2 = 8$      $2 \times 8 = 16$
$16 \div 4 = 4$      $4 \times 4 = 16$
$16 \div 8 = 2$      $8 \times 2 = 16$
$16 \div 16 = 1$     $16 \times 1 = 16$

1, 2, 4, 8, and 16 are **factors** of 16.

The numbers 1, 2, 4, 8, and 16 are factors of 16.
The numbers 1, 2, 3, 6, 9, and 18 are factors of 18.
The numbers 1 and 2 are factors of both 16 and 18.
We call them **common factors** of 16 and 18.

## CLASS EXERCISES

Complete to find the factors.

**1.** $2 \div \blacksquare = 2$
    $2 \div \blacksquare = 1$

**2.** $4 \div \blacksquare = 4$
    $4 \div \blacksquare = 2$
    $4 \div \blacksquare = 1$

**3.** $6 \div \blacksquare = 6$     $6 \div \blacksquare = 2$
    $6 \div \blacksquare = 3$     $6 \div \blacksquare = 1$

**4.** $8 \div \blacksquare = 8$
    $8 \div \blacksquare = 4$
    $8 \div \blacksquare = 2$
    $8 \div \blacksquare = 1$

**5.** $10 \div \blacksquare = 10$
    $10 \div \blacksquare = 5$
    $10 \div \blacksquare = 2$
    $10 \div \blacksquare = 1$

**6.** $12 \div \blacksquare = 12$     $12 \div \blacksquare = 3$
    $12 \div \blacksquare = 6$     $12 \div \blacksquare = 2$
    $12 \div \blacksquare = 4$     $12 \div \blacksquare = 1$

Is the statement *true* or *false*? Explain your answer.

**7.** 6 is a factor of 24.

**8.** 8 is a factor of 18.

**9.** 4 is a common factor of 8 and 10.

**10.** 3 is a common factor of 9 and 18.

## PRACTICE

Write the common factors.

**11.** 2 and 4     **12.** 4 and 6     **13.** 2 and 6     **14.** 4 and 8     **15.** 2 and 10

**16.** 8 and 2      **17.** 4 and 10      **18.** 6 and 8      **19.** 8 and 10      **20.** 6 and 10

**21.** 8 and 12      **22.** 15 and 10      **23.** 10 and 12      **24.** 8 and 16      **25.** 15 and 6

**26.** 12 and 6      **27.** 9 and 12      **28.** 12 and 18      **29.** 15 and 18      **30.** 12 and 16

**31.** 27 and 18      **32.** 12 and 14      **33.** 18 and 16      **34.** 15 and 12      **35.** 12 and 21

True or false? Write *T* or *F*.

**36.** Every number has 1 as a factor.

**37.** 3 is a factor of every odd number.

**38.** Every number greater than 1 has at least two different factors.

**39.** Every even number greater than 1 has 2 as a factor.

**40.** Any two numbers have 1 as a common factor.

★**41.** The only common factors of 12, 15, and 18 are 1 and 3.

A *prime* number has only two factors, itself and 1. Is the number prime? Write *yes* or *no*.

★ **42.** 5    ★ **43.** 19    ★ **44.** 24    ★ **45.** 2    ★ **46.** 23    ★ **47.** 33    ★ **48.** 47    ★ **49.** 49

Write the answer.

**50.** 5438 − 2765

**51.** 8910 + 3042

**52.** 27,504 + 11,932

**53.** 16,443 − 8,529

**54.** 4 hours 37 minutes + 6 hours 36 minutes

**MIXED REVIEW**

## PROBLEM SOLVING APPLICATIONS
### Using Patterns

Find the pattern. Copy and complete the table.

**55.**

| NUMBER | FACTORS |
|---|---|
| 2 | 1, 2 |
| 4 | 1, 2, 4 |
| 8 | 1, 2, 4, 8 |
| ? | 1, 2, 4, 8, ? |
| ? | 1, 2, 4, 8, ?, ? |
| ? | 1, 2, 4, 8, ?, ?, ? |

★ **56.**

| NUMBER | FACTORS |
|---|---|
| 3 | 1, 3 |
| 5 | 1, ? |
| ? | 1, 7 |
| 11 | 1, ? |
| ? | 1, ? |
| ? | 1, ? |

# PROBLEM SOLVING
### Strategy: Too Much Information

1. Understand
2. Plan
3. Work
4. Answer/Check

Jake has 25 books at home. He has 10 history books in 2 rows. Each row has the same number of history books. How many history books are in each row?

**Think:** What facts do you need to solve the problem?

10 history books in 2 equal rows

$10 \div 2 = 5$

There are 5 history books in each row.

You did not need to know the total number of books to solve the problem.

## CLASS EXERCISES

Tell which fact you do *not* need. Then solve.

1. Monica has a collection of books. She has 5 large paperbacks and 7 small paperbacks. She has 18 books in all. How many paperbacks does she have in all?

2. Dexter's book is 29 cm high, Roberto's book is 32 cm high, and Dave's book is 18 cm high. How much taller is Dexter's book than Dave's book?

3. An art book costs $25.98. A music book costs $12.95. Marbella has $30.00 to spend. How much change does Marbella get if she buys the art book?

4. Yesterday 8 people went to the library. Each person read 7 books. Today 6 people are at the library. How many books were read yesterday?

## PRACTICE

Solve.

5. The 7 mystery books cost $56 altogether. The sports books cost $36. If each of the mystery books costs the same amount, how much does each cost?

6. Each novel has 6 chapters. Each biography has 9 chapters. How many chapters are in 9 novels?

7. There are 3 pet snakes in Karen's classroom. The library has 11 books about snakes. Karen borrowed 5 of the books. How many books about snakes are left?

8. Carl is putting up bookshelves. Red shelves are 2 ft long, blue shelves are 3 ft long, and yellow shelves are 4 ft long. What is the total length of 4 blue shelves?

9. On Saturday Sid worked in the library 2 hours in the morning and 5 hours in the afternoon. Raymond spent 3 hours working on Saturday morning. How many hours did Sid work on Saturday?

10. Yolanda's book has 16 color photos and 11 black-and-white photos. Randy's book has 18 color photos and 9 black-and-white photos. How many color photos are in both books?

11. Alyce's birthday is 6 days away. She is writing a story. She writes 6 pages each day. She has completed 6 pictures for the story. How many pages will Alyce's story be if she finishes it on her birthday?

12. Book Mart is having a sale. Books are 1 penny for each pound. Debby bought 13 lb of books and Ernie bought 19 lb of books. The price of one book before the sale was $9.95. How much did Debby and Ernie spend in all?

★ 13. Each dictionary weighs 3 times as much as each hard-cover novel and 2 times as much as each encyclopedia. If 4 dictionaries weigh 40 lb, how much does each encyclopedia weigh?

★ 14. Fran wants to buy 4 pens, 2 magazines, and 3 books. A pen costs $1, a magazine costs $2, and a book costs $4. Fran has $15. Does she have enough to buy 4 books and 3 pens?

## CHECKPOINT 2

Divide. *(pages 142–149)*

1. $7\overline{)63}$    2. $9\overline{)54}$    3. $5\overline{)45}$

4. $4\overline{)17}$    5. $8\overline{)49}$    6. $5\overline{)38}$

List the common factors.
*(pages 150–151)*

7. 9 and 12        8. 6 and 21

9. 12 and 18        10. 8 and 16

Solve. *(pages 152–153)*

11. Rae bought 8 book covers and 5 felt-tipped pens. Each book cover cost 9¢. How much did she spend for book covers?

*Extra practice on page 410*

Write the answer. Check by multiplying. *(pages 132–139)*

1. $2\overline{)10}$    2. $3\overline{)18}$    3. $4\overline{)32}$    4. $5\overline{)35}$

5. $3\overline{)27}$    6. $4\overline{)28}$    7. $5\overline{)45}$    8. $2\overline{)16}$

Write *add, subtract, multiply,* or *divide* for your plan. Then solve. *(pages 140–141)*

9. Eva has 4 cats. Each cat uses 3 flea collars during the year. How many collars do Eva's cats use in a year?

10. Sam bought 5 tickets to the school play for $30. He paid the same amount for each ticket. How much did Sam pay for each ticket?

Write the answer. *(pages 142–147)*

11. $6\overline{)42}$    12. $7\overline{)63}$    13. $8\overline{)64}$    14. $9\overline{)54}$

15. $8\overline{)40}$    16. $6\overline{)48}$    17. $9\overline{)27}$    18. $7\overline{)35}$

Write the answer. *(pages 148–149)*

19. $5\overline{)44}$    20. $8\overline{)60}$    21. $7\overline{)53}$    22. $9\overline{)39}$

Write the common factors. *(pages 150–151)*

23. 16 and 24    24. 8 and 14    25. 12 and 15    26. 15 and 9

Solve. *(pages 152–153)*

27. While hiking on Saturday, Marsha saw 6 goldfinches, 8 robins, and 5 sparrows. How many more robins than sparrows did Marsha see?

28. Greg bought 3 rolls of film and 2 packages of flash cubes for his trip. Each roll of film cost $3. How much did Greg spend on film?

*Extra practice on page 411*

# MATHEMATICS and HISTORY

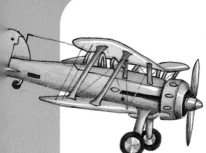

In less than 100 years, there have been some remarkable changes in the way people get from one place to another. The sentences below tell about some of the important events in the history of air travel.

Use the clues below to find the missing dates.

1. Orville Wright successfully flew an aircraft on December A., B., near Kitty Hawk, North Carolina.

2. The first coast-to-coast airplane flight left New York on September A., C., and arrived in Pasadena, California, on November D., C., after many stops.

3. Charles Lindbergh flew alone in a non-stop flight from New York to Paris on May E. and F., G..

4. Amelia Earhart also flew alone in a non-stop flight across the Atlantic on May E. and F., H..

5. On May D., I., Alan Shephard, Jr. was the first American to fly in space.

6. In June J., Sally Ride was one of the astronauts on the six-day flight of the space shuttle *Challenger*.

## DOES TIME FLY?

### CLUES

A. The difference between 189 and 172
B. An odd number between 1901 and 1905
C. The sum of 208 and 1703
D. The quotient of 45 divided by 9
E. The product of 4 and 5
F. The product of 3 and 7
G. An odd number between 1925 and 1929
H. An even number between 1930 and 1934
I. The sum of 1115 and 846
J. The difference of 10,884 and 8901

# Enrichment

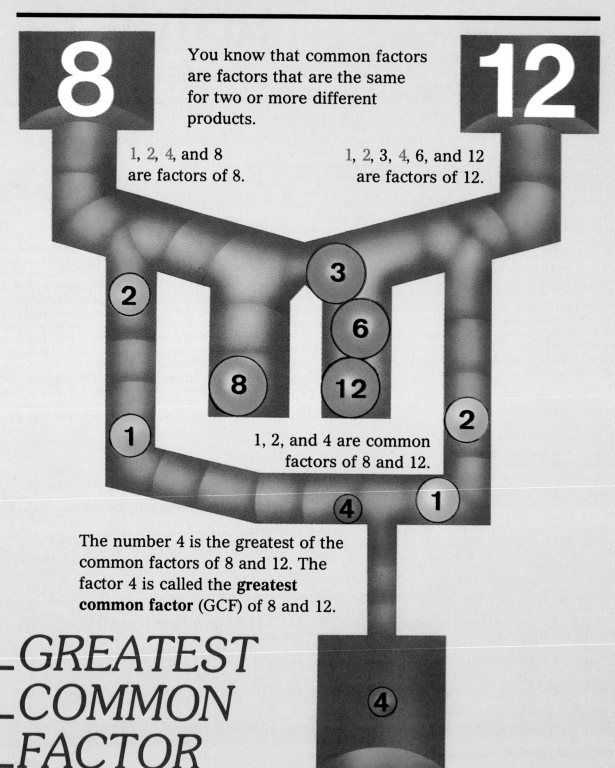

**8**  **12**

You know that common factors are factors that are the same for two or more different products.

1, 2, 4, and 8 are factors of 8.

1, 2, 3, 4, 6, and 12 are factors of 12.

3

2

6

8

12

2

1

1, 2, and 4 are common factors of 8 and 12.

4  1

The number 4 is the greatest of the common factors of 8 and 12. The factor 4 is called the **greatest common factor** (GCF) of 8 and 12.

4

## GREATEST COMMON FACTOR

What is the greatest common factor of 6 and 9?

To answer, first find all the factors for each number.

1, 2, 3, and 6 are factors of 6.

1, 3, and 9 are factors of 9.

Then find the greatest number that is a factor of both.

3 is the greatest common factor of 6 and 9.

Complete.

1. The factors of 10 are ■, ■, ■, and ■.

   The factors of 16 are ■, ■, ■, ■, and ■.

   The common factors of 10 and 16 are ■ and ■.

   The greatest common factor of 10 and 16 is ■.

2. The factors of 14 are ■, ■, ■, and ■.

   The factors of 15 are ■, ■, ■, and ■.

   The common factor of 14 and 15 is ■.

   The greatest common factor of 14 and 15 is ■.

Write the common factors and the greatest common factor.

3. 6 and 10      4. 9 and 12      5. 15 and 25

6. 18 and 27     7. 14 and 21     8. 12 and 18

9. 21 and 16    10. 4 and 20

# CUMULATIVE REVIEW

Choose the correct answer. Write *a, b, c,* or *d.*

Choose the value of the underlined digit.

**1.** 85,320
   **a.** 5000
   **b.** 50,000
   **c.** 8500
   **d.** none of these

**2.** 243,661
   **a.** 4000
   **b.** 400,000
   **c.** 40,000
   **d.** none of these

**3.** 38,871,003
   **a.** 80,000
   **b.** 8000
   **c.** 800,000
   **d.** none of these

Order the numbers from greatest to least.

**4.** 633   608   614
   **a.** 608, 614, 633
   **b.** 633, 614, 608
   **c.** 633, 608, 614
   **d.** none of these

**5.** 8002   8065   8600
   **a.** 8065, 8002, 8600
   **b.** 8002, 8065, 8600
   **c.** 8600, 8065, 8002
   **d.** none of these

**6.** 1742   1723   1732
   **a.** 1742, 1732, 1723
   **b.** 1742, 1723, 1732
   **c.** 1723, 1732, 1742
   **d.** none of these

Round each number to its greatest place value.

**7.** 85
   **a.** 50
   **b.** 80
   **c.** 30
   **d.** none of these

**8.** 329
   **a.** 200
   **b.** 300
   **c.** 400
   **d.** none of these

**9.** 5435
   **a.** 6000
   **b.** 4000
   **c.** 5000
   **d.** none of these

Find the answer.

**10.**   $13.38
       + 11.73
   **a.** $25.11
   **b.** $24.11
   **c.** $25.01
   **d.** none of these

**11.**   $20.00
       − 3.46
   **a.** $16.54
   **b.** $6.54
   **c.** $17.54
   **d.** none of these

**12.**   $7.46
          .59
       + 1.72
   **a.** $8.77
   **b.** $9.77
   **c.** $9.67
   **d.** none of these

Which is the best estimate?

**13.** the width of your thumbnail
   **a.** 7 cm     **b.** 9 cm
   **c.** 5 cm     **d.** 1 cm

**14.** the length of a toothbrush
   **a.** 14 m     **b.** 14 cm
   **c.** 14 km     **d.** 4 cm

**15.** the mass of a crayon
  **a.** 3 g
  **b.** 30 g
  **c.** 300 kg
  **d.** 30 kg

**16.** the paint in a can
  **a.** 40 L
  **b.** 4 mL
  **c.** 4 L
  **d.** 40 mL

Solve.

**17.** There are 34 people on the bus. At each stop, 3 people get on and no one gets off. After 4 stops, how many people are on the bus?
  **a.** 92 people
  **b.** 46 people
  **c.** 38 people
  **d.** none of these

**18.** In 3 days Mr. Yang drove 312 mi. He drove 92 mi the first day and 103 mi the second day. How many miles did Mr. Yang drive on the third day?
  **a.** 117 mi
  **b.** 195 mi
  **c.** 209 mi
  **d.** none of these

# LANGUAGE and VOCABULARY REVIEW

Use the words to label the parts of the problem. Write the words on your paper.

divisor      quotient      remainder      dividend
factors      product       sum            addends

**1.** 5 is the _____?_____.

**2.** 17 is the _____?_____.

**3.** 3 is the _____?_____.

**4.** 2 is the _____?_____.

$$5)\overline{17} \quad \begin{array}{r} 3 \text{ R2} \end{array}$$

**5.** 64 and 18 are the _____?_____.

**6.** 82 is the _____?_____.

$$64 + 18 = 82$$

**7.** 27 is the _____?_____.

**8.** 9 and 3 are the _____?_____.

$$9 \times 3 = 27$$

# FLOWCHART

When you do a job or solve a problem you do one step at a time. A **flowchart** can show the order of the steps. The shapes in a flowchart show different kinds of steps.

Tells when to start or stop

Tells what to do

Asks a question

The flowchart at the right shows 5 steps.

- The first step is start.

- The second step tells you to pick two numbers.

- The third step asks you to decide if the first number is greater than the second.

- If the answer is *Yes*, then the fourth step is find the quotient.

- If the answer is *No*, then the fourth step is find the product.

- The fifth step is stop.

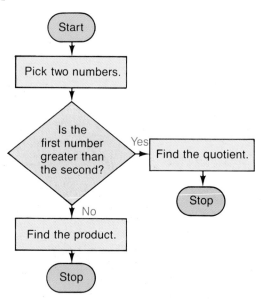

Use the flowchart for the numbers. Write *quotient* or *product* to tell what you find. Then write the answer.

**1.** 14, 7    **2.** 3, 8    **3.** 18, 9    **4.** 5, 7

**5.** 6, 8    **6.** 10, 5    **7.** 7, 9    **8.** 12, 6

# 6

Each of the 9 boxes in this display holds a pair of shoes. How many shoes are in the display? How many shoes are in a display that has twice as many shoes as this display?

# MULTIPLICATION
## BY ONE-DIGIT NUMBERS

# MULTIPLYING TENS, HUNDREDS, AND THOUSANDS

Sometimes patterns can help you multiply large numbers.

| | |
|---|---|
| 4 × 2 ones = 8 ones | 4 × 2 = 8 |
| 4 × 2 tens = 8 tens | 4 × 20 = 80 |
| 4 × 2 hundreds = 8 hundreds | 4 × 200 = 800 |
| 4 × 2 thousands = 8 thousands | 4 × 2000 = 8000 |

You can multiply numbers like these mentally by counting the number of zeros in the factors.

| 3 | 30 | 300 | 3000 | | 4 | 40 | 400 | 4000 |
|---|----|-----|------|---|---|----|-----|------|
| ×5 | ×5 | ×5 | ×5 | | ×5 | ×5 | ×5 | ×5 |
| 15 | 150 | 1500 | 15,000 | | 20 | 200 | 2000 | 20,000 |

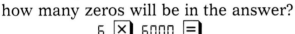 **Think:** If you enter this on a calculator, how many zeros will be in the answer?

6 ✕ 6000 =

*40 glasses on each shelf*

## CLASS EXERCISES

Multiply. Count the zeros in the factors.

| 1. | 1 | 10 | 100 | 1000 | 2. | 2 | 20 | 200 | 2000 |
|----|---|----|-----|------|----|---|----|-----|------|
| | ×8 | ×8 | ×8 | ×8 | | ×3 | ×3 | ×3 | ×3 |

| 3. | 3 | 30 | 300 | 3000 | 4. | 7 | 70 | 700 | 7000 |
|----|---|----|-----|------|----|---|----|-----|------|
| | ×4 | ×4 | ×4 | ×4 | | ×6 | ×6 | ×6 | ×6 |

## PRACTICE

Multiply.

| 5. | 40 | 6. | 200 | 7. | 3000 | 8. | 400 | 9. | 70 | 10. | 100 |
|----|----|----|-----|----|------|----|-----|----|----|-----|-----|
| | ×2 | | ×4 | | ×2 | | ×9 | | ×5 | | ×4 |

| 11. | 6000 | 12. | 30 | 13. | 800 | 14. | 7000 | 15. | 500 | 16. | 20 |
|-----|------|-----|----|-----|-----|-----|------|-----|-----|-----|----|
| | ×6 | | ×3 | | ×3 | | ×8 | | ×8 | | ×4 |

| **17.** 500 | **18.** 50 | **19.** 400 | **20.** 60 | **21.** 9000 | **22.** 6000 |
|---|---|---|---|---|---|
| ×6 | ×3 | ×5 | ×4 | ×7 | ×3 |

| **23.** 8000 | **24.** 4000 | **25.** 7000 | **26.** 900 | **27.** 700 | **28.** 5000 |
|---|---|---|---|---|---|
| ×7 | ×8 | ×3 | ×5 | ×8 | ×9 |

Complete the table.

**29.**

| Meters | 1 | 2 | 3 | 4 | 5 | 6 | 7 | 8 | 9 |
|---|---|---|---|---|---|---|---|---|---|
| Centimeters | 100 | ? | ? | ? | ? | ? | ? | ? | ? |

**30.**

| Kilograms | 1 | 2 | 3 | 4 | 5 | 6 | 7 | 8 | 9 |
|---|---|---|---|---|---|---|---|---|---|
| Grams | 1000 | ? | ? | ? | ? | ? | ? | ? | ? |

Complete.

★ **31.** $5 \times \blacksquare = 450$     ★ **32.** $\blacksquare \times 800 = 4000$     ★ **33.** $\blacksquare \times 300 = 300$

The zero key on Evan's calculator is broken. Draw the keys he could push to help find the product. How many zeros should be in the product?

CALCULATOR

**34.** $9 \times 7000$     **35.** $4 \times 800$     **36.** $6 \times 4000$     **37.** $5 \times 9000$

**38. Think:** Is it faster to use a calculator or mental math to answer Exercises 34–37?

## PROBLEM SOLVING APPLICATIONS
### Choosing the Operation

Solve.

**39.** A glass blower can shape 30 glass pitchers in a week. How many glass pitchers can he shape in 4 weeks?

**40.** There are 230 cups and 40 saucers. How many more saucers must be made to complete the sets?

★ **41.** One person makes 150 glasses in a week. Two others each make 75 in a week. Will the 3 people complete 1150 glasses in 4 weeks?

# ESTIMATING PRODUCTS

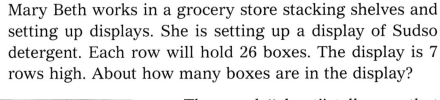

Mary Beth works in a grocery store stacking shelves and setting up displays. She is setting up a display of Sudso detergent. Each row will hold 26 boxes. The display is 7 rows high. About how many boxes are in the display?

The word "about" tells you that you don't need an exact answer. For a quick mental estimate, round the factor greater than 10 to its greatest place value. You don't need to round a one-digit factor.

|  | Round 26. | Multiply. |
|---|---|---|
| 26 | 30 | 30 |
| ×7 | ×7 | ×7 |
|  |  | 210 |

The display holds about 210 boxes.

## CLASS EXERCISES

What is the greatest place value of the number? Round the number to its greatest place value.

**1.** 48     **2.** 728     **3.** 1565     **4.** 807     **5.** 3629     **6.** 92

What factors do you use to estimate the product? What is the estimated product?

**7.** 62
×3

**8.** 47
×4

**9.** 114
×6

**10.** 283
×7

**11.** 5386
×4

## PRACTICE

Round the factor greater than 10 to its greatest place value. Estimate the product.

**12.** 37
×4

**13.** 44
×6

**14.** 26
×9

**15.** 59
×7

**16.** 16
×5

**17.** 19
×6

| 18. 273<br>×9 | 19. 509<br>×6 | 20. 257<br>×5 | 21. 388<br>×7 | 22. 675<br>×4 | 23. 750<br>×8 |
|---|---|---|---|---|---|
| 24. 3624<br>×2 | 25. 6189<br>×8 | 26. 8892<br>×5 | 27. 4583<br>×3 | 28. 7235<br>×5 | 29. 1947<br>×4 |
| 30. 716<br>×6 | 31. 67<br>×4 | 32. 3540<br>×9 | 33. 83<br>×9 | 34. 3322<br>×5 | 35. 586<br>×7 |

**36.** $7 \times 63$      **37.** $6 \times 874$      **38.** $4 \times 1689$      **39.** $7 \times 557$

**40.** $5 \times 148$      **41.** $8 \times 816$      **42.** $9 \times 4460$      **43.** $7 \times 6930$

**44.** $7 \times 42$      **45.** $4 \times 891$      **46.** $7 \times 648$      **47.** $8 \times 75$

★ **48.** $2 \times 38 \times 2$      ★ **49.** $4 \times 95 \times 3$      ★ **50.** $5 \times 52 \times 2$

---

Write the answer.

**MIXED REVIEW**

| 51. 18<br>+ 6 | 52. 9<br>×3 | 53. 27<br>+ 9 | 54. 48<br>+ 3 | 55. 8<br>×6 |
|---|---|---|---|---|

**56.** $56 + 7$      **57.** $7 \times 5$      **58.** $9 \times 9$      **59.** $36 + 5$

---

# PROBLEM SOLVING APPLICATIONS
## Using Estimation

Estimate to solve the problem.

**60.** The new display of cat food has 8 rows of cans with 118 cans in each row. About how many cans of cat food are in the display?

**61.** Manoleto has 9 boxes of paper plates. Each box holds 24 packages. About how many packages does he have?

**62.** There are 2 boxes of paper towels to unpack. One box holds 48 rolls of paper towels. The other box holds 72 rolls. About how many rolls of paper towels need to be unpacked?

★ **63.** The soup display is 14 cans wide, 26 cans deep, and 8 cans high. About how many cans of soup are in the display?

# MULTIPLYING A TWO-DIGIT NUMBER, NO RENAMING

Vista Airlines has 2 flights to Valley City on Monday. There are 32 passengers on each flight. To find how many passengers fly to Valley City on Monday, multiply 2 × 32.

Multiply the 2 ones by 2.

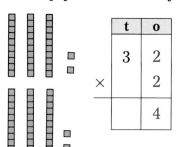

| t | o |
|---|---|
| 3 | 2 |
| × | 2 |
|   | 4 |

Multiply the 3 tens by 2.

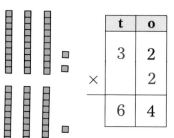

| t | o |
|---|---|
| 3 | 2 |
| × | 2 |
| 6 | 4 |

On Monday 64 passengers fly to Valley City.

Ⓜ If you know your multiplication facts well, you can multiply large numbers quickly.

## CLASS EXERCISES

Multiply.

1.
| t | o |
|---|---|
| 2 | 4 |
| × | 2 |

2.
| t | o |
|---|---|
| 4 | 3 |
| × | 2 |

3.
| t | o |
|---|---|
| 3 | 3 |
| × | 3 |

4.
| t | o |
|---|---|
| 2 | 1 |
| × | 4 |

## PRACTICE

Multiply.

5.  12
    ×2

6.  11
    ×2

7.  30
    ×2

8.  11
    ×4

9.  10
    ×7

10. 13
    ×2

11. 22
    ×2

12. 40
    ×2

13. 11
    ×7

14. 13
    ×3

15. 11
    ×9

16. 14
    ×2

17. 11
    ×6

18. 12
    ×3

19. 22
    ×3

20. 10
    ×4

21. 31
    ×2

22. 11
    ×5

| 23. 10 | 24. 21 | 25. 11 | 26. 22 | 27. 23 | 28. 34 |
|---|---|---|---|---|---|
| ×6 | ×3 | ×8 | ×4 | ×2 | ×2 |

| 29. 31 | 30. 12 | 31. 32 | 32. 23 | 33. 20 | 34. 33 |
|---|---|---|---|---|---|
| ×3 | ×4 | ×2 | ×3 | ×3 | ×2 |

35. $3 \times 11$    36. $3 \times 32$    37. $2 \times 42$    38. $2 \times 20$    39. $3 \times 23$

40. $4 \times 20$    41. $9 \times 11$    42. $3 \times 31$    43. $2 \times 23$    44. $2 \times 44$

45. What is the product of 2 and 24?

46. Is the product of 4 and 12 greater than or less than the product of 3 and 13?

47. Use the symbol < or >. Write a number sentence to tell whether $2 \times 14$ is greater than or less than 30.

Solve mentally. Write only the answer.

48. $(4 \times 8) + 3$    49. $(5 \times 4) + 4$    50. $(2 \times 6) + 1$

51. $(7 \times 4) + 5$    52. $(3 \times 6) + 2$    53. $(8 \times 6) + 6$

**MENTAL MATH**

## PROBLEM SOLVING APPLICATIONS
### Two-Step Problems

Solve.

54. There are 3 rows of seats facing the windows in the airport. In each row there are 11 seats to the left of the aisle and 22 seats to the right. How many seats face the windows in the airport?

55. There are 28 passengers on the plane when it lands in Newtown. Then 7 passengers get off and 9 other passengers get on. How many passengers are on the plane when it leaves Newtown?

56. There were 35 suitcases on each of 2 flights to Raincloud City and 18 suitcases on another flight to Raincloud City. How many suitcases went to Raincloud City altogether?

★ 57. On the morning flight, 8 cartons of grapefruit juice and 23 cartons of orange juice were used. There were twice as many cartons as that on the plane. How many cartons of juice were on the plane?

# MULTIPLYING A TWO-DIGIT NUMBER WITH RENAMING

Sometimes when you multiply, you need to rename 10 ones as 1 ten. Here's how to multiply 47 by 2.

Multiply the 7 ones by 2.
Rename 14 as 1 ten 4 ones.

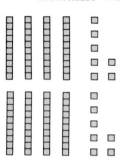

| | t | o |
|---|---|---|
| | 1 | |
| | 4 | 7 |
| × | | 2 |
| | | 4 |

Multiply the 4 tens by 2.
Add the 1 ten.

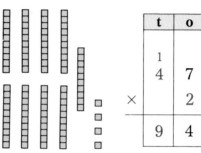

| | t | o |
|---|---|---|
| | 1 | |
| | 4 | 7 |
| × | | 2 |
| | 9 | 4 |

M Sometimes you can multiply mentally without paper and pencil. Multiply $2 \times 47$.

**Think:** $47 = 40 + 7$
Multiply the parts separately.    $2 \times 40 = 80$    $2 \times 7 = 14$
Then add the products.    $80 + 14 = 94$

*47 plants in each row*

## CLASS EXERCISES

Rename the product as tens and ones.

**1.** $3 \times 7 = $ ▦ tens ▦ one

**2.** $5 \times 8 = $ ▦ tens ▦ ones

**3.** $9 \times 6 = $ ▦ tens ▦ ones

**4.** $6 \times 4 = $ ▦ tens ▦ ones

Multiply.

**5.**  13  →  13
    ×3      ×4

**6.**  14  →  14
    ×2      ×3

**7.**  24  →  24
    ×2      ×3

## PRACTICE

Multiply.

**8.**  15
    ×2

**9.**  17
    ×3

**10.**  19
    ×2

**11.**  15
    ×4

**12.**  18
    ×3

**13.**  16
    ×2

**14.** 17
×4

**15.** 19
×3

**16.** 18
×2

**17.** 13
×5

**18.** 17
×2

**19.** 16
×4

**20.** 13
×4

**21.** 16
×5

**22.** 24
×2

**23.** 16
×3

**24.** 19
×4

**25.** 12
×3

**26.** 14
×5

**27.** 27
×2

**28.** 15
×5

**29.** 14
×4

**30.** 40
×2

**31.** 29
×3

**32.** 5 × 18    **33.** 7 × 12    **34.** 3 × 27    **35.** 5 × 17    **36.** 4 × 23

**37.** 6 × 15    **38.** 4 × 24    ★ **39.** 26 × 3    ★ **40.** 19 × 5    ★ **41.** 45 × 2

Use mental math to multiply. Write only the answer.

**42.** 2 × 43    **43.** 4 × 22    **44.** 2 × 34    **45.** 3 × 21

**46.** 7 × 13    **47.** 6 × 16    **48.** 4 × 18    **49.** 3 × 29

MENTAL MATH

## PROBLEM SOLVING APPLICATIONS
### Mental Math or Pencil

Use mental math or paper and pencil to solve the problem.
Write *m* or *p* beside your answer to tell the method you
chose.

**50.** Edgar plants 3 rows of beans with 28 plants in each row. How many bean plants does he use?

**51.** Edgar harvests 40 carrots. He and a friend eat 3 carrots each. How many carrots are left?

**52.** Edgar decides to plant tomatoes in his garden. He buys 16 packs with 6 plants in each pack. How many tomato plants does he buy?

★ **53.** Edgar planted 3 rows of pepper plants with 22 plants in each row and 4 rows of pepper plants with 15 plants in each row. A raccoon ate 16 of the plants during the night. How many pepper plants did Edgar find in the morning?

# MULTIPLYING A TWO-DIGIT NUMBER WITH RENAMING

The Many Shapes Button Factory makes buttons of all sizes and shapes. Each hour, the factory makes 7 boxes of round buttons with 36 buttons in each box. How many round buttons are made in an hour?

To find out, multiply 36 by 7.

Multiply the 6 ones by 7.
Rename 42 as 4 tens 2 ones.

$$\begin{array}{r} {\scriptstyle 4} \\ 36 \\ \times 7 \\ \hline 2 \end{array}$$ 7 × 6 = 42

Multiply the 3 tens by 7.
Add the 4 tens.

$$\begin{array}{r} {\scriptstyle 4} \\ 36 \\ \times 7 \\ \hline 252 \end{array}$$ 7 × 3 tens = 21 tens
21 tens + 4 tens = 25 tens

In an hour, 252 round buttons are made.

You know that 7 × 40 = 280. You can estimate that the actual product of 7 × 36 will be less than 280 because you rounded the greater factor up.

**Think:** If you rounded the greater factor down, would the actual answer be greater than the estimate or less than the estimate?

## CLASS EXERCISES

Complete.

**1.** 48 = ▨ tens ▨ ones

**2.** 72 = ▨ tens ▨ ones

**3.** 35 = ▨ tens ▨ ones

**4.** 63 = ▨ tens ▨ ones

Multiply.

**5.**
$$\begin{array}{r} 50 \\ \times 3 \\ \hline \end{array}$$ →
$$\begin{array}{r} 53 \\ \times 3 \\ \hline \end{array}$$ →
$$\begin{array}{r} 54 \\ \times 3 \\ \hline \end{array}$$

**6.**
$$\begin{array}{r} 60 \\ \times 4 \\ \hline \end{array}$$ →
$$\begin{array}{r} 62 \\ \times 4 \\ \hline \end{array}$$ →
$$\begin{array}{r} 63 \\ \times 4 \\ \hline \end{array}$$

**7.**
$$\begin{array}{r} 40 \\ \times 5 \\ \hline \end{array}$$ →
$$\begin{array}{r} 43 \\ \times 5 \\ \hline \end{array}$$ →
$$\begin{array}{r} 44 \\ \times 5 \\ \hline \end{array}$$

# PRACTICE

Multiply.

| | | | | | |
|---|---|---|---|---|---|
| **8.** 62 ×2 | **9.** 21 ×6 | **10.** 80 ×3 | **11.** 71 ×4 | **12.** 54 ×2 | **13.** 41 ×5 |
| **14.** 57 ×2 | **15.** 66 ×2 | **16.** 53 ×6 | **17.** 70 ×2 | **18.** 53 ×4 | **19.** 67 ×2 |
| **20.** 34 ×3 | **21.** 44 ×5 | **22.** 14 ×7 | **23.** 47 ×3 | **24.** 71 ×7 | **25.** 22 ×4 |

**26.** 5 × 52     **27.** 8 × 60     **28.** 6 × 74     **29.** 4 × 23

**30.** 8 × 36     **31.** 9 × 29     **32.** 4 × 62     **33.** 7 × 49

**34.** 3 × 59     **35.** 4 × 32     **36.** 5 × 37     **37.** 7 × 98

Complete. Write $+$, $-$, or $\times$ to make the sentence true.

★ **38.** $3 \times 28 = 42 \quad 2$     ★ **39.** $60 \quad 5 > 80 - 5$     ★ **40.** $53 \quad 4 < 7 \quad 8$

Estimate the product. Then tell whether the actual product
will be *greater than* or *less than* the estimate.

**41.** 6 × 35    **42.** 9 × 86    **43.** 6 × 62    **44.** 8 × 94

**45.** 5 × 57    **46.** 3 × 61    **47.** 4 × 38    **48.** 7 × 73

**ESTIMATE**

## PROBLEM SOLVING APPLICATIONS
### Too Much or Too Little Information

Some problems have too much or too little information.
Solve the problem if you can.

**49.** Small, square buttons have 2 holes. Each box holds 76 buttons. How many buttons fit in 9 boxes?

**50.** Large, round buttons have 3 holes. How many large, round buttons fit in 6 boxes?

**51.** Round buttons with 4 holes come in packages of 63 buttons. There are 9 buttons in each row. How many rows of buttons are in each package?

★ **52.** Every 10 minutes the Many Shapes Button Factory makes 50 triangle-shaped buttons with 3 holes. How many of these buttons are made in 1 hour?

1. Understand
2. Plan
3. Work
4. Answer/ Check

# PROBLEM SOLVING
## Strategy: Using a Pictograph

A **pictograph** is a graph that uses pictures to show information. Each picture can stand for a number of items.

This pictograph shows the number of instruments played by students at Rachel's school. Each picture stands for 15 instruments. To find how many students play the trumpet, multiply 2 × 15.

$$\begin{array}{r} \overset{1}{15} \\ \times 2 \\ \hline 30 \end{array}$$

Thirty students play the trumpet.

**INSTRUMENTS PLAYED AT RACHEL'S SCHOOL**

| | |
|---|---|
| Clarinet | ⌀ ⌀ ⌀ |
| Drums | ⌀ ⌀ ⌀ ⌀ |
| Trumpet | ⌀ ⌀ |
| Violin | ⌀ ⌀ ⌀ |
| Flute | ⌀ |

Each ⌀ means 15 instruments.

## CLASS EXERCISES

Use the pictograph to solve. Explain your answer.

1. How many students play the drums?

2. How many students play the violin?

3. How many students play the flute?

4. Which instrument do the most students play?

5. Which two instruments do the same number of students play?

## PRACTICE

Use the pictograph to solve.

6. How many trumpets and clarinets are played in all?

7. How many more students play the violin than the flute?

Rachel's class took a survey of the students' favorite music. Use the pictograph to solve.

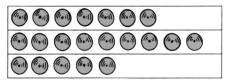

STUDENTS' FAVORITE MUSIC

| Jazz |  |
| Rock | |
| Country | |

Each 🔴 means 25 students.

8. How many students like jazz the best?

9. What kind of music do most of the students like best?

10. What is the total number of students?

11. How many more students like rock music than country music?

★ 12. If 200 students liked country music, how many more records would you draw?

★ 13. The books listed at the right are on the bookshelf in the music room. Make a pictograph to show the information. Let each picture stand for 5 books. Remember to write the title of the graph, the name of each row, and the meaning of each picture.

15 folk music books
25 band music books
35 holiday music books

# CHECKPOINT 1

Estimate the product.
(pages 164–165)

| 1. 37 | 2. 23 | 3. 283 |
|-------|-------|--------|
| ×4    | ×6    | ×3     |

Multiply. (pages 162–163, 166–171)

| 4. 32 | 5. 48 | 6. 73 |
|-------|-------|-------|
| ×3    | ×2    | ×8    |

Use the pictograph to solve.
(pages 172–173)

**RABBITS AT THE PET CENTER**

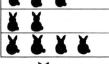

| Spotted | 🐰 🐰 🐰 |
| White | 🐰 🐰 |
| Gray | 🐰 🐰 🐰 🐰 |

Each 🐰 means 5 rabbits.

7. How many rabbits are gray?

8. Are there more gray rabbits or white rabbits?

*Extra practice on page 412*

# MULTIPLYING A THREE-DIGIT NUMBER

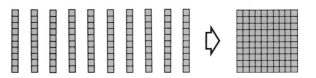

To multiply 3 × 238, you need to rename twice. Remember that 10 tens equal 1 hundred.

Multiply 8 ones by 3. Rename 24 as 2 tens 4 ones.

$$
\begin{array}{r}
\overset{2}{238} \\
\times 3 \\
\hline
4
\end{array}
$$

Multiply 3 tens by 3 and add the 2 tens. Rename 11 tens as 1 hundred 1 ten.

$$
\begin{array}{r}
\overset{12}{238} \\
\times 3 \\
\hline
14
\end{array}
$$

3 × 3 tens = 9 tens

9 tens + 2 tens = 11 tens

Multiply 2 hundreds by 3 and add the 1 hundred.

$$
\begin{array}{r}
\overset{1\,2}{238} \\
\times 3 \\
\hline
714
\end{array}
$$

3 × 2 hundreds = 6 hundreds

6 hundreds + 1 hundred = 7 hundreds

When there are zeros in factors, don't forget to multiply them. Remember, the product of zero and any number is zero.

$$
\begin{array}{r}
\overset{1}{407} \\
\times 2 \\
\hline
814
\end{array}
$$

**WATERVILLE FERRY**
**2 TRIPS DAILY**
407 SEATS

## CLASS EXERCISES

Multiply. Build on what you know.

1. $\begin{array}{r}100 \\ \times 2\end{array}$ → $\begin{array}{r}134 \\ \times 2\end{array}$ → $\begin{array}{r}136 \\ \times 2\end{array}$   2. $\begin{array}{r}300 \\ \times 3\end{array}$ → $\begin{array}{r}302 \\ \times 3\end{array}$ → $\begin{array}{r}308 \\ \times 3\end{array}$   3. $\begin{array}{r}400 \\ \times 2\end{array}$ → $\begin{array}{r}426 \\ \times 2\end{array}$ → $\begin{array}{r}476 \\ \times 2\end{array}$

## PRACTICE

Multiply.

4. $\begin{array}{r}323 \\ \times 3\end{array}$   5. $\begin{array}{r}375 \\ \times 2\end{array}$   6. $\begin{array}{r}117 \\ \times 5\end{array}$   7. $\begin{array}{r}204 \\ \times 2\end{array}$   8. $\begin{array}{r}194 \\ \times 3\end{array}$   9. $\begin{array}{r}287 \\ \times 3\end{array}$

10. $\begin{array}{r}407 \\ \times 2\end{array}$   11. $\begin{array}{r}223 \\ \times 3\end{array}$   12. $\begin{array}{r}308 \\ \times 3\end{array}$   13. $\begin{array}{r}184 \\ \times 4\end{array}$   14. $\begin{array}{r}241 \\ \times 3\end{array}$   15. $\begin{array}{r}152 \\ \times 4\end{array}$

16. $\begin{array}{r}233 \\ \times 3\end{array}$   17. $\begin{array}{r}192 \\ \times 4\end{array}$   18. $\begin{array}{r}141 \\ \times 5\end{array}$   19. $\begin{array}{r}132 \\ \times 2\end{array}$   20. $\begin{array}{r}165 \\ \times 3\end{array}$   21. $\begin{array}{r}124 \\ \times 5\end{array}$

| **22.** 157 | **23.** 135 | **24.** 236 | **25.** 147 | **26.** 273 | **27.** 218 |
|---|---|---|---|---|---|
| ×5 | ×7 | ×4 | ×6 | ×3 | ×4 |

**28.** 2 × 256   **29.** 2 × 208   **30.** 3 × 250   **31.** 4 × 226   **32.** 3 × 194

**33.** 4 × 184   **34.** 3 × 287   **35.** 4 × 212   **36.** 3 × 129   **37.** 5 × 168

Find the missing digits.

★ **38.** ▢2   ★ **39.** 3▢6   ★ **40.** ▢3▢   ★ **41.** ▢▢▢
      ×3             ×2              ×7              ×8
      72▢            ▢9▢             9▢5             984

---

Write the standard form. Then round the number to its greatest place value.

**MIXED REVIEW**

**42.** 5 hundreds 6 tens 4 ones      **43.** 8 hundreds 9 ones

**44.** 7 thousands 3 hundreds 4 tens 7 ones

**45.** 4 thousands 7 hundreds 2 tens 3 ones

**46.** 6 thousands 3 tens 9 ones

---

# PROBLEM SOLVING APPLICATIONS
## Choosing a Strategy

Solve.

**47.** The ferry to Crestview can carry no more than 312 people on one trip. How many people can it carry altogether in 2 trips?

**48.** The ferry carried 248 people on the first trip and 78 people on the second trip. Were there more than 3 times as many people on the first trip as on the second?

★ **49.** As the ferry arrives, Danielle hears a clock chiming. If the clock chimes the number of the hour, how many times does it chime each day? If the clock also chimes once each half-hour, how many times does the clock chime each day?

# MULTIPLYING A THREE-DIGIT NUMBER

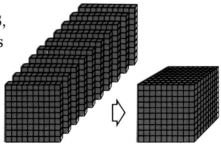

4
hours of tennis

298
Calories burned
each hour

When you multiply 4 × 298, remember that 10 hundreds equal 1 thousand.

| Multiply the 8 ones by 4. Rename 32 as 3 tens 2 ones. | Multiply the 9 tens by 4 and add the 3 tens. Rename 39 tens as 3 hundreds 9 tens. | Multiply the 2 hundreds by 4 and add the 3 hundreds. |
|---|---|---|
| $\begin{array}{r} 3 \\ 29\!8 \\ \times 4 \\ \hline 2 \end{array}$ | $\begin{array}{r} 33 \\ 298 \\ \times 4 \\ \hline 92 \end{array}$ | $\begin{array}{r} 33 \\ 298 \\ \times 4 \\ \hline 1192 \end{array}$ |

**Think:** 4 × 300 = 1200, so you can estimate that 4 × 298 is about 1200. The answer makes sense.

## CLASS EXERCISES

Multiply.

**1.**  27 ⟶ 271
      ×4        ×4

**2.**  86 ⟶ 863
      ×5        ×5

**3.**  42 ⟶ 429
      ×8        ×8

**4.** Explain the steps of the multiplication.

**a.** $\begin{array}{r} 1 \\ 345 \\ \times 3 \\ \hline 5 \end{array}$  **b.** $\begin{array}{r} 11 \\ 345 \\ \times 3 \\ \hline 35 \end{array}$  **c.** $\begin{array}{r} 11 \\ 345 \\ \times 3 \\ \hline 1035 \end{array}$

## PRACTICE

Multiply.

**5.**  536
      ×3

**6.**  624
      ×4

**7.**  727
      ×9

**8.**  612
      ×8

**9.**  409
      ×5

| 10. 604 | 11. 591 | 12. 673 | 13. 361 | 14. 842 |
|---|---|---|---|---|
| ×3 | ×7 | ×6 | ×4 | ×8 |

| 15. 360 | 16. 452 | 17. 946 | 18. 533 | 19. 238 |
|---|---|---|---|---|
| ×4 | ×9 | ×3 | ×9 | ×2 |

| 20. 999 | 21. 145 | 22. 847 | 23. 510 | 24. 648 |
|---|---|---|---|---|
| ×7 | ×5 | ×6 | ×5 | ×8 |

**25.** 5 × 345    **26.** 4 × 303    **27.** 6 × 607    **28.** 8 × 326

**29.** 6 × 670    **30.** 4 × 830    **31.** 7 × 346    **32.** 9 × 487

★ **33.** 3 × (5 × 37)    ★ **34.** 6 × (8 × 54)    ★ **35.** 9 × (5 × 76)

You know that 4 × 250 = 1000. Estimate. Will the product be *less than* or *greater than* 1000?

| 36. 226 | 37. 287 | 38. 257 | 39. 218 | 40. 254 |
|---|---|---|---|---|
| ×4 | ×4 | ×5 | ×3 | ×2 |

ESTIMATE

## PROBLEM SOLVING APPLICATIONS
### Using a Table

Use the table to solve.

**41.** How many Calories would Simon burn in 4 hours of skiing?

**42.** Will Ben burn more than 500 Calories if he skates for 2 hours?

**43.** Julie went horseback riding for 1 hour, then rested for 1 hour. How many Calories did she burn altogether?

★ **44.** In which activity will Jeannette burn more Calories, playing 2 hours of table tennis or 3 hours of volleyball?

**CALORIES BURNED IN 1 HOUR**

| Activity | Number of Calories |
|---|---|
| Skating | 240 |
| Horseback riding | 198 |
| Skiing | 396 |
| Volleyball | 121 |
| Table tennis | 240 |
| Resting | 43 |

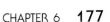

# MULTIPLYING A FOUR-DIGIT NUMBER

You need to rename when you multiply 4586 by 3.

Multiply the 6 ones by 3. Write the 8. Remember the 1 ten.

4586
×3
─────
8

$3 \times 6 = 18$

Multiply the 8 tens by 3 and add the 1 ten. Write the 5. Remember the 2 hundreds.

4586
×3
─────
58

$3 \times 8$ tens = 24 tens
24 tens + 1 ten = 25 tens

Multiply the 5 hundreds by 3 and add the 2 hundreds. Write the 7. Remember the 1 thousand.

4586
×3
─────
758

$3 \times 5$ hundreds
= 15 hundreds
15 hundreds + 2 hundreds
= 17 hundreds

Multiply the 4 thousands by 3 and add the 1 thousand.

4586
×3
─────
13,758

$3 \times 4$ thousands
= 12 thousands
12 thousands + 1 thousand
= 13 thousands

When you multiply 4586 by 3 on a calculator, your answer will not show a comma. When you write a number greater than 9999, be sure to write the comma.

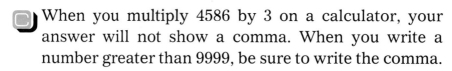

3 ✕ 4586 ꞊ 13758

## CLASS EXERCISES

Multiply. In which places do you need to rename?

| **1.** 1323 | **2.** 1363 | **3.** 1367 | **4.** 5367 | **5.** 5867 |
|---|---|---|---|---|
| ×3 | ×3 | ×3 | ×3 | ×3 |

## PRACTICE

Multiply.

| **6.** 3714 | **7.** 2963 | **8.** 5317 | **9.** 9306 | **10.** 3062 |
|---|---|---|---|---|
| ×2 | ×3 | ×4 | ×2 | ×4 |

| 11. 4825 | 12. 9760 | 13. 2158 | 14. 8156 | 15. 2032 |
|---|---|---|---|---|
| ×2 | ×7 | ×4 | ×5 | ×3 |

| 16. 4059 | 17. 1742 | 18. 3862 | 19. 3884 | 20. 4935 |
|---|---|---|---|---|
| ×8 | ×5 | ×6 | ×7 | ×9 |

| 21. 1239 | 22. 2785 | 23. 2647 | 24. 1434 | 25. 5948 |
|---|---|---|---|---|
| ×8 | ×8 | ×7 | ×2 | ×7 |

**26.** 3 × 9050  **27.** 4 × 7086  **28.** 6 × 6805  **29.** 6 × 5914

★ **30.** Complete the multiplication problem at the right using each of the digits 1, 2, 5, 6, and 7 to make the greatest product and the least product possible.

Use a calculator or paper and pencil to find two numbers from the box at the right with this product. You can use a number more than once.

**31.** 35,058  **32.** 22,430  **33.** 36,095

**34.** 50,533  **35.** 37,152  **36.** 43,344

| 5 | 5843 |
|---|---|
| 6192 | 8 |
| 7219 | 6 |
| 4486 | 7 |

CALCULATOR

## PROBLEM SOLVING APPLICATIONS
### Choosing the Operation

Solve.

**37.** The Sears Tower in Chicago is 1454 ft tall without its mast. Its mast is 105 ft tall. How tall is the Sears Tower with its mast?

**38.** The World Trade Center in New York is 1353 ft tall. If a building were 5 times as tall, how tall would it be?

★ **39.** Peachtree Center Plaza in Atlanta is 723 ft tall. The Empire State Building in New York is 1472 ft tall with its mast. Is the Empire State Building more than twice the height of Peachtree Center Plaza?

# MULTIPLYING MONEY

$29.25

When you multiply dollars and cents, the answer must be in dollars and cents. Multiply as you would with other numbers. Then write the decimal point and a dollar sign in the product. Here are some examples.

| $7.48 | $29.25 | $.77 |
|---|---|---|
| ×6 | ×4 | ×8 |
| $44.88 | $117.00 | $6.16 |

**Think:** How many digits are always to the right of the decimal point?

$7.48

Most calculators do not have a dollar sign. To multiply 6 × $4.25 enter 6 ☒ 4.25 ▣. You will probably see 25.5, for the answer. You can write $25.50.

## CLASS EXERCISES

Write the product with a dollar sign and decimal point.

| **1.** $.25 | **2.** $.59 | **3.** $3.49 | **4.** $1.25 | **5.** $2.50 |
|---|---|---|---|---|
| ×3 | ×2 | ×2 | ×5 | ×3 |
| 75 | 118 | 698 | 625 | 750 |

| **6.** $6.20 | **7.** $8.54 | **8.** $3.16 | **9.** $48.20 | **10.** $21.37 |
|---|---|---|---|---|
| ×5 | ×3 | ×6 | ×5 | ×4 |
| 3100 | 2562 | 1896 | 24100 | 8548 |

## PRACTICE

Multiply.

| **11.** $.50 | **12.** $.44 | **13.** $1.33 | **14.** $2.50 | **15.** $3.20 |
|---|---|---|---|---|
| ×3 | ×4 | ×2 | ×3 | ×4 |

| **16.** $.75 | **17.** $.95 | **18.** $1.78 | **19.** $2.72 | **20.** $13.43 |
|---|---|---|---|---|
| ×3 | ×5 | ×3 | ×4 | ×5 |

**21.** $.69
   ×3

**22.** $4.35
   ×4

**23.** $21.88
   ×2

**24.** $4.95
   ×7

**25.** $3.02
   ×6

**26.** $20.45
   ×4

**27.** $.89
   ×3

**28.** $4.96
   ×8

**29.** $10.98
   ×6

**30.** $99.99
   ×9

**31.** 7 × $6.49     **32.** 8 × $8.74     **33.** 7 × $21.09     **34.** 6 × $.48

The multiplication was done on a calculator. Is the answer correct? Write *yes* or *no*. If the answer is wrong, write the correct answer.

CALCULATOR

**35.** $8.52
   ×4
   [340.8]

**36.** $6.75
   ×4
   [27.]

**37.** $.07
   ×8
   [5.6]

**38.** $4.80
   ×3
   [14.4]

# PROBLEM SOLVING APPLICATIONS
## Using a Catalog

Use the information below to solve the problem.

**Bob's Bike Shop**

ORDERED BY

| CATALOG NUMBER | ITEM | PRICE | QUANTITY | TOTAL |
|---|---|---|---|---|
| 20 A | WATER BOTTLE | $2.95 | | |
| 30 A | SADDLEBAG | $19.96 | | |
| 41 B | HELMET | $29.08 | | |
| 52 C | MIRROR | $6.45 | | |
| 61 B | HEADLIGHT | $6.98 | | |

**39.** How much will 4 mirrors cost altogether?

**40.** How much will 1 headlight and 1 water bottle cost?

**41.** Will 3 saddlebags cost more than $58.00?

**42.** Does a headlight cost more than 2 water bottles?

★ **43.** The delivery charge depends on the total amount of the order. Calvin and his sister order 2 water bottles, 2 helmets, and 1 headlight. How much is the delivery charge? How much do they pay in all?

| TOTAL AMOUNT OF ORDER | DELIVERY CHARGE |
|---|---|
| Up to $15.00 | $2.25 |
| $15.01–$50.00 | $3.25 |
| More than $50.00 | $4.25 |

# PROBLEM SOLVING

## Strategy: Estimating with Money

1. Understand
2. Plan
3. Work
4. Answer/Check

For a quick mental estimate when you work with money, you can round the amount to its greatest place value.

Ellen buys 8 postcards for $.42 each. About how much does she spend?

Round to the nearest ten cents. Then multiply.

$.42 ⟶ $.40
×8        ×8
            $3.20

Ellen spends about $3.20.

Harold buys 3 travel books for $6.75 each. About how much does he spend?

Round to the nearest dollar. Then multiply.

$6.75 ⟶ $7.00
×3            ×3
                $21.00

Harold spends about $21.00.

## CLASS EXERCISES

Round the amount to its greatest place value.

**1.** $.84     **2.** $.37     **3.** $3.88     **4.** $5.26     **5.** $31.72     **6.** $57.35

Round to the greatest place value to estimate the answer. Write *A*, *B*, or *C*. Explain your answer.

**7.** A ticket for the bus ride from Craigville to Parker Beach costs $2.25 . About how much do 2 tickets from Craigville to Parker Beach cost?

**8.** Joe buys a pair of running shoes for $18.88 and a sweatshirt for $11.99. About how much more do the shoes cost than the sweatshirt?

**9.** Sandra pays $5.37 to mail a package to her cousin and $2.55 to mail a package to her aunt. About how much does Sandra pay to mail both packages?

**A.** about $10.00

**B.** about $4.00

**C.** about $8.00

# PRACTICE

Round to the greatest place value to estimate the answer.

**10.** Each of the maps that Sofia buys costs $.76. Sofia buys 4 maps for her trip. About how much does she spend?

**11.** A book on sailing costs $9.65. A book about hiking costs $6.85. About how much more does the book on sailing cost?

**12.** Morgan's lunch costs $4.22 and his dinner costs $6.53. About how much does Morgan spend for both of his meals?

**13.** Luanne buys 4 packages of film for her camera. Each costs $2.78. About how much does Luanne spend for film?

**14.** Michiko wants to buy a softball bat that costs $18.99 and a glove that costs $27.99. About how much do they cost altogether?

**15.** Vera can buy a plain T-shirt for $4.35 or a printed T-shirt for $6.88. About how much less does the plain T-shirt cost?

★ **16.** Richard buys a pair of sunglasses for $4.57, 2 paperback books for $3.28 each, and a magazine for $2.25. About how much does Richard spend?

★ **17.** Ellen traveled to 8 national parks. She bought 3 posters at Grand Canyon National Park. She bought 1 poster at each of the other parks. Each poster cost $2.65. About how much did Ellen spend?

# CHECKPOINT 2

Multiply. *(pages 174–181)*

| | | |
|---|---|---|
| **1.** 109<br>$\times 4$ | **2.** 284<br>$\times 3$ | **3.** 347<br>$\times 6$ |
| **4.** 8142<br>$\times 5$ | **5.** $.89<br>$\times 4$ | **6.** $5.35<br>$\times 7$ |

Estimate the answer.
*(pages 182–183)*

**7.** Kelly buys 6 packages of pencils for $.59 each. About how much does she spend?

**8.** Paolo buys a paint set for $4.85 and a package of brushes for $1.27. About how much does he spend?

*Extra practice on page 412*

Estimate the product. *(pages 164–165)*

**1.** 38
　×5

**2.** 73
　×8

**3.** 467
　×6

**4.** 7950
　×7

Write the answer. *(pages 162–163, 166–171)*

**5.** 800
　×9

**6.** 34
　×2

**7.** 15
　×6

**8.** 83
　×7

Use the pictograph to solve each problem. *(pages 172–173)*

**9.** How many students like movies the best?

**10.** Do more than 4 students like sports the best?

**11.** How many more students like movies than sports?

**STUDENTS' FAVORITE ACTIVITIES**

Each ▯ means 15 students.

Write the answer. *(pages 174–179)*

**12.** 836
　×7

**13.** 597
　×4

**14.** 3751
　×6

**15.** 4608
　×9

Write the answer. *(pages 180–181)*

**16.** $.74
　×5

**17.** $.87
　×4

**18.** $5.95
　×6

**19.** $72.49
　×8

Estimate the answer. *(pages 182–183)*

**20.** A baseball cap costs $5.25. A visor costs $2.95. About how much more does the cap cost than the visor?

**21.** Don buys 4 pairs of socks. Each pair costs $1.09. About how much does Don spend for his new socks?

*Extra practice on page 413*

# MATHEMATICS and SCIENCE

Temperature can be measured in many different ways. Around the world there are over 3500 weather observation stations that record the temperature every hour. Many stations release balloons that use radio transmitters to send information back to Earth.

## HOW DOES THE TEMPERATURE SOUND?

One way to estimate the temperature is by listening to the crickets chirp. Count the number of chirps in 15 seconds. Then add 40. This will give you an estimate of the temperature in degrees Fahrenheit.

**1.** Suppose a cricket chirps 35 times in 15 seconds. About what is the temperature?

**2.** Suppose a cricket chirps about 3 times in one second. About what is the temperature?

**3.** How many times does a cricket chirp in 15 seconds if the temperature is 88°F?

**4.** If the temperature is 60°F, will a cricket chirp more than 25 times in 15 seconds?

# Enrichment

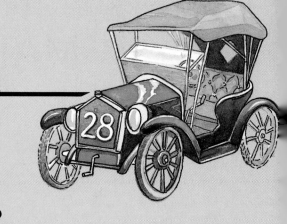

The numbers 1, 2, and 3 are *consecutive* numbers. The numbers 28, 29, and 30 are also consecutive numbers. Name 3 consecutive numbers whose sum is 159.

**Think:** You want numbers in order that add up to 159. You can guess the first number.

Trial 1:  Guess 50.
The 3 consecutive numbers are 50, 51, 52.
$50 + 51 + 52 = 153$
153 is less than 159.
Your guess is too low. Try a greater number.

Trial 2:  Guess 54.
The 3 consecutive numbers are 54, 55, 56.
$54 + 55 + 56 = 165$
165 is greater than 159.
Your guess is too high. Try a number between 50 and 54.

Trial 3:  Guess 52.
$52 + 53 + 54 = 159$
Your guess is correct. The three numbers are 52, 53, and 54.

## TRIAL AND ERROR

1. Why was 50 used as a first guess in Trial 1?

2. Find three consecutive numbers whose sum is 249.

3. Find three consecutive numbers whose sum is 222.

4. Find three consecutive even numbers whose sum is 96.

5. Find three consecutive even numbers whose sum is 60.

6. **Think:** Can you always solve a problem in 3 trials? Why or why not?

Peter collects model cars and motorcycles. He has a total of 9 models and 24 wheels. How many cars and how many motorcycles does Peter have?

To solve this problem, make a table to keep track of your guesses. You know there are 9 models, so try 5 motorcycles and 4 cars. Each car has 4 wheels and each motorcycle has 2 wheels.

Too high. Try fewer cars and more motorcycles.

| TRIAL | CARS | CAR WHEELS | MOTORCYCLES | MOTORCYCLE WHEELS | TOTAL WHEELS |
|-------|------|-----------|-------------|-------------------|--------------|
| 1 | 4 | 16 | 5 | 10 | 26 |
| 2 | 3 | 12 | 6 | 12 | 24 |

There are 3 cars and 6 motorcycles.

This time it took only 2 trials. Sometimes, if your first guess is not close, it may take 4, 5, or more trials.

Solve. Make a table to keep track of your guesses.

**7.** 9 models and 30 wheels    **8.** 9 models and 22 wheels

**9.** 10 models and 32 wheels    **10.** 8 models and 32 wheels

**11.** 6 models and 14 wheels

Sometimes a problem may not have a solution. It is not possible to have 9 models and 21 wheels.

2 cars and 7 motorcycles have $8 + 14 = 22$ wheels
1 car and 8 motorcycles have $4 + 16 = 20$ wheels

**12.** It is also impossible to have 23, 25, 27, or 29 wheels. Why?

**13.** If Peter sees 28 wheels but he can't see how many models there are, how many cars and motorcycles are there? Find all answers. There is more than one answer.

187

# CUMULATIVE REVIEW

Choose the correct answer. Write *a*, *b*, *c*, or *d*.

Find the answer.

**1.** the eighth month
of the year
   **a.** March
   **b.** August
   **c.** October
   **d.** none of these

**2.** a week before
June 12
   **a.** June 2
   **b.** June 5
   **c.** June 3
   **d.** none of these

**3.** 3:35
   **a.** 35 minutes before 4
   **b.** 25 minutes before 3
   **c.** 25 minutes before 4
   **d.** none of these

Choose the most likely measurement.

**4.** width of a piece
of paper
   **a.** 8 ft
   **b.** 8 in.
   **c.** 8 yd
   **d.** 8 mi

**5.** weight of a
birthday card
   **a.** 1 lb
   **b.** 1·T
   **c.** 1 oz
   **d.** 1 pt

**6.** small milk carton
   **a.** 1 gal
   **b.** 1 qt
   **c.** 1 c
   **d.** 1 oz

Find the answer.

**7.** 59 + 35
   **a.** 94
   **b.** 84
   **c.** 24
   **d.** none of these

**8.** 429 + 46 + 408
   **a.** 873
   **b.** 1297
   **c.** 883
   **d.** none of these

**9.** 16,798 + 45,843
   **a.** 62,541
   **b.** 62,531
   **c.** 62,641
   **d.** none of these

Find the answer.

**10.**    81
       − 38
   **a.** 53
   **b.** 43
   **c.** 42
   **d.** none of these

**11.**    601
       − 374
   **a.** 237
   **b.** 327
   **c.** 337
   **d.** none of these

**12.**    7032
       − 2958
   **a.** 4184
   **b.** 4174
   **c.** 4084
   **d.** none of these

Find the matching value.

**13.** 509¢
    **a.** $509
    **b.** $5.90
    **c.** $5.09
    **d.** none of these

**14.** 8 dollars 1 quarter
    **a.** $81.25
    **b.** $825
    **c.** $8.01
    **d.** none of these

**15.** 3 dimes 4 nickels
    **a.** $.34
    **b.** $.45
    **c.** $.50
    **d.** none of these

Find the answer.

**16.** $.94 − $.69
    **a.** $.25
    **b.** $.35
    **c.** $1.63
    **d.** none of these

**17.** $8.25 − $3.57
    **a.** $11.82
    **b.** $4.68
    **c.** $4.72
    **d.** none of these

**18.** $46.99 + $17.18
    **a.** $64.17
    **b.** $64.07
    **d.** $63.17
    **d.** none of these

# LANGUAGE and VOCABULARY REVIEW

Copy the word or words on your paper. Write the letter of the matching definition.

**1.** Property of One

**A.** Graph that uses pictures to show information

**2.** Grouping Property

**B.** The answer in division

**3.** Tree diagram

**C.** One of the numbers multiplied to make a product

**4.** Pictograph

**D.** Product of one and any number is the number

**5.** Factor

**E.** Drawing that shows the number of possible combinations

**6.** Quotient

**F.** One of the numbers used to find a sum

**7.** Addend

**G.** Changing the grouping of factors does not change the product

# LOGIC

Instructions with "If" and "then" mean that a decision should be made. For example:

> *If* the first number is greater than the second, *then* write >.

The part that begins with "If" is called the *condition*. It tells what decision should be made.

> If the first number is greater than the second,

The part that begins with "then" is called the *action*. It tells you what to do.

> then write >.

When you can say *yes* to the condition, you do the action.

|  First number | Second number |
|:---:|:---:|
| 30 | 20 |

Is the first number greater than the second? Yes. So, you can write >.

When you say *no* to the condition, you cannot do the action.

|  First number | Second number |
|:---:|:---:|
| 25 | 45 |

Is the first number greater than the second? No. So you do not write anything.

---

Would you say *yes* or *no* to the condition? Write *yes* or *no*. Do the action if you say *yes*.

> If the first number is less than the second, then write <.

|  | 1. | 2. | 3. | 4. | 5. | 6. |
|---|---|---|---|---|---|---|
| First Number | 79 | 404 | 570 | 8904 | 9 × 42 | 5 × 70 |
| Second Number | 97 | 440 | 507 | 894 | 400 | 3500 |

Suppose you have 21 L of liquid to pour into jars that hold 2 L each. Will 10 jars be enough to hold all the liquid? Can you fill 11 jars?

7

DIVISION
ONE-DIGIT DIVISORS

191

# TWO-DIGIT QUOTIENTS, NO REMAINDERS

It takes just one step to divide 16 by 2.
It takes two steps to divide 86 by 2.

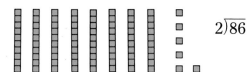

$$2\overline{)86}$$

Divide the 8 tens by 2.

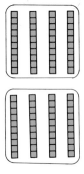

$$\begin{array}{r} 4 \\ 2\overline{)86} \\ -8 \\ \hline 0 \end{array}$$

Subtract 4 × 2.

Divide the 6 ones by 2.

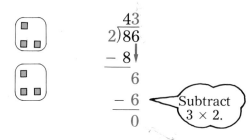

$$\begin{array}{r} 43 \\ 2\overline{)86} \\ -8\downarrow \\ \hline 6 \\ -6 \\ \hline 0 \end{array}$$

Subtract 3 × 2.

To check your answer, multiply the quotient by the divisor.

$$\begin{array}{r} 43 \\ \times\ 2 \\ \hline 86\checkmark \end{array}$$

To divide 86 by 2 on a calculator, press 86 ÷ 2 =.
You will see 43. To check the answer, press × 2 =.

## CLASS EXERCISES

The first step of the division is done. Is the digit in the quotient tens or ones? Explain how you know.

1. $2\overline{)24}^{\,1}$   2. $2\overline{)12}^{\,6}$   3. $4\overline{)80}^{\,2}$   4. $3\overline{)27}^{\,9}$   5. $2\overline{)64}^{\,3}$

Divide.

6. $2\overline{)20}$   $2\overline{)40}$   $2\overline{)60}$      7. $3\overline{)63}$   $3\overline{)66}$   $3\overline{)69}$

## PRACTICE

Divide and check.

8. $2\overline{)22}$      9. $3\overline{)30}$      10. $4\overline{)44}$      11. $4\overline{)80}$      12. $3\overline{)60}$

**13.** 8)80    **14.** 4)48    **15.** 4)88    **16.** 7)77    **17.** 3)96

**18.** 2)42    **19.** 5)55    **20.** 2)44    **21.** 3)99    **22.** 2)80

**23.** 2)46    **24.** 8)88    **25.** 2)82    **26.** 2)64    **27.** 4)40

**28.** 4)84    **29.** 9)99    **30.** 2)66    **31.** 2)48    **32.** 3)93

**33.** 2)68    **34.** 2)84    **35.** 3)90    **36.** 6)66    **37.** 2)62

Look at the division problem at the right. Then write *dividend, divisor,* or *quotient* to complete the sentence.

**38.** The 4 is called the ___?___.

**39.** The 22 is called the ___?___.

$$\frac{22}{4)88}$$

**40.** The 88 is called the ___?___.

Draw the keys you would push to divide and check the answer on a calculator.

**41.** 2)82    **42.** 4)88    **43.** 9)90    **44.** 2)46

**CALCULATOR**

## PROBLEM SOLVING APPLICATIONS
### Choosing a Strategy

Solve.

**45.** The local radio station is giving away 68 tickets to the Tornado's concert. If 2 tickets are given away for each phone call, how many callers will receive tickets?

**46.** The radio station asked if the listeners liked a song. About 5 people called each minute to say "yes" and 3 called each minute to say "no." About how many people called in 15 minutes?

**47.** The station played 18 songs without breaks. If each song was 4 minutes long, about how many minutes of music were played?

★ **48.** The radio station has 9 records to give away. One record is given to every 5th caller, beginning with the 5th call. How many records are left after the 36th call?

# TWO-DIGIT QUOTIENTS, WITH REMAINDERS

When you divide
64 by 3, you have
a remainder.

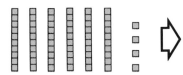   

Divide the 6 tens by 3.    Divide the 4 ones by 3.    Write the remainder next to the quotient.

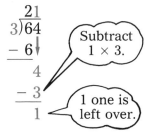

$$\begin{array}{r} 2 \\ 3\overline{)64} \\ -6 \\ \hline 0 \end{array}$$
Subtract 2 × 3.

$$\begin{array}{r} 21 \\ 3\overline{)64} \\ -6\downarrow \\ \hline 4 \\ -3 \\ \hline 1 \end{array}$$
Subtract 1 × 3.
1 one is left over.

$$\begin{array}{r} 21 \text{ R1} \\ 3\overline{)64} \\ -6 \\ \hline 4 \\ -3 \\ \hline 1 \end{array}$$

The remainder always must be less than the divisor.

Use multiplication and addition to check the answer.

| Multiply the quotient by the divisor. | Then add the remainder. |
|---|---|
| 21 | 63 |
| ×3 | + 1 |
| 63 | 64✓ |

 You can use mental math to divide 64 by 3.
**Think:**   64 = 60 + 4
Divide the parts separately.     60 ÷ 3 ◊ 20     4 ÷ 3 ◊ 1 R1
Then add the answers.     20 + 1 R1 ◊ 21 R1

## CLASS EXERCISES

Divide.

**1.** $2\overline{)46}$ ⟶ $2\overline{)47}$        **2.** $6\overline{)60}$ ⟶ $6\overline{)63}$        **3.** $4\overline{)84}$ ⟶ $4\overline{)86}$

Check the problem. If the answer is not correct, tell what
went wrong. Then write the correct answer.

**4.** $\begin{array}{r}22\text{ R2}\\3\overline{)68}\end{array}$    **5.** $\begin{array}{r}4\text{ R5}\\2\overline{)85}\end{array}$    **6.** $\begin{array}{r}12\text{ R1}\\3\overline{)67}\end{array}$    **7.** $\begin{array}{r}31\text{ R1}\\2\overline{)63}\end{array}$    **8.** $\begin{array}{r}23\text{ R1}\\2\overline{)27}\end{array}$

# PRACTICE

Divide and check.

| | | | | |
|---|---|---|---|---|
| **9.** $2\overline{)23}$ | **10.** $5\overline{)58}$ | **11.** $2\overline{)25}$ | **12.** $4\overline{)49}$ | **13.** $3\overline{)34}$ |
| **14.** $2\overline{)47}$ | **15.** $2\overline{)83}$ | **16.** $4\overline{)47}$ | **17.** $2\overline{)49}$ | **18.** $3\overline{)94}$ |
| **19.** $2\overline{)63}$ | **20.** $4\overline{)87}$ | **21.** $2\overline{)67}$ | **22.** $3\overline{)95}$ | **23.** $7\overline{)78}$ |
| **24.** $3\overline{)98}$ | **25.** $5\overline{)55}$ | **26.** $2\overline{)89}$ | **27.** $4\overline{)85}$ | **28.** $3\overline{)69}$ |
| **29.** $3\overline{)65}$ | **30.** $4\overline{)86}$ | **31.** $2\overline{)64}$ | **32.** $4\overline{)89}$ | **33.** $2\overline{)65}$ |

★ **34.** Write two divisions with 12 R1 as the answer.

★ **35.** Write two divisions with 11 R3 as the answer.

Use mental math to divide. Write only the answer.

| | | | |
|---|---|---|---|
| **36.** $4\overline{)45}$ | **37.** $6\overline{)67}$ | **38.** $5\overline{)56}$ | **39.** $8\overline{)89}$ |
| **40.** $3\overline{)64}$ | **41.** $2\overline{)43}$ | **42.** $4\overline{)46}$ | **43.** $3\overline{)35}$ |

**MENTAL MATH**

## PROBLEM SOLVING APPLICATIONS
### Choosing the Operation

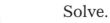

Solve.

**44.** There are 65 new desks to be divided equally among 3 floors at the High-rise Tower Building. How many new desks will be on each floor? How many will be left over?

**45.** The second floor has 7 large meeting rooms that have 18 chairs each. How many chairs are in the meeting rooms altogether?

★ **46.** Christy Adams has 1 hour and 20 minutes to deliver packages on 4 different floors. She spends the same amount of time on each floor. How many minutes does she spend on each floor?

# TWO-DIGIT QUOTIENTS
# WITH REMAINDERS

This is how you divide 54 by 4.

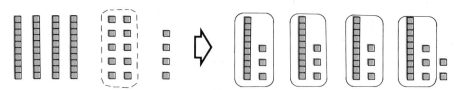

Divide the 5 tens by 4.

Divide the 14 ones by 4. Write the remainder with the quotient.

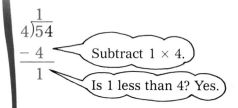

Subtract 1 × 4.

Is 1 less than 4? Yes.

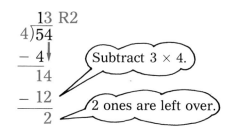

Subtract 3 × 4.

2 ones are left over.

To estimate 54 ÷ 4, think this way. You know that 40 ÷ 4 is 10. Since 54 is greater than 40, you can estimate that the quotient will be greater than 10.

## CLASS EXERCISES

Divide.

**1.** 2)30 $\longrightarrow$ 2)32

**2.** 3)72 $\longrightarrow$ 3)75

**3.** 5)75 $\longrightarrow$ 5)79

Look at the division at the right.

$$\begin{array}{r} 19 \text{ R2} \\ 4\overline{)78} \\ -4 \phantom{0} \\ \hline 38 \\ -36 \\ \hline 2 \end{array}$$

**4.** Explain the steps in the division.

**5.** How many tens are in the quotient?

**6.** How many ones are in the quotient?

**7. Think:** What is the greatest number you could have as a remainder when 4 is the divisor?

# PRACTICE

Divide.

| | | | | |
|---|---|---|---|---|
| **8.** $3\overline{)57}$ | **9.** $4\overline{)72}$ | **10.** $2\overline{)38}$ | **11.** $5\overline{)65}$ | **12.** $3\overline{)51}$ |
| **13.** $2\overline{)53}$ | **14.** $2\overline{)95}$ | **15.** $3\overline{)71}$ | **16.** $3\overline{)41}$ | **17.** $4\overline{)73}$ |
| **18.** $4\overline{)65}$ | **19.** $6\overline{)96}$ | **20.** $4\overline{)57}$ | **21.** $3\overline{)56}$ | **22.** $5\overline{)60}$ |
| **23.** $5\overline{)85}$ | **24.** $5\overline{)61}$ | **25.** $6\overline{)90}$ | **26.** $6\overline{)78}$ | **27.** $7\overline{)97}$ |
| **28.** $5\overline{)90}$ | **29.** $3\overline{)85}$ | **30.** $5\overline{)62}$ | **31.** $7\overline{)91}$ | **32.** $5\overline{)73}$ |
| **33.** $2\overline{)52}$ | **34.** $8\overline{)96}$ | **35.** $6\overline{)75}$ | **36.** $7\overline{)82}$ | **37.** $4\overline{)57}$ |
| **38.** $4\overline{)84}$ | **39.** $6\overline{)86}$ | **40.** $5\overline{)66}$ | **41.** $3\overline{)75}$ | **42.** $6\overline{)84}$ |
| **43.** $2\overline{)54}$ | **44.** $4\overline{)95}$ | **45.** $2\overline{)57}$ | **46.** $4\overline{)61}$ | **47.** $3\overline{)74}$ |

★ **48. Think:** If you divide an even number by 2, will the answer ever have a remainder? Why?

Estimate. Will the quotient be greater than 10? Write *yes* or *no*.

**ESTIMATE**

| | | | |
|---|---|---|---|
| **49.** $5\overline{)47}$ | **50.** $3\overline{)65}$ | **51.** $2\overline{)24}$ | **52.** $7\overline{)79}$ |
| **53.** $4\overline{)78}$ | **54.** $5\overline{)59}$ | **55.** $8\overline{)74}$ | **56.** $6\overline{)38}$ |

## PROBLEM SOLVING APPLICATIONS
### Choosing the Operation

Solve.

**57.** Each Whirlybird car seats 3 children. If 79 children are on the ride, how many cars will be filled? Will there be a car with fewer than 3 children?

**58.** There are 36 cars on the space ride. Each car will hold 4 people. How many people can go on the space ride at the same time?

★ **59.** The train to the park carries 97 people, including the driver. Each car holds 8 people, not including the driver. The train has 1 driver. How many cars are there?

# DIVIDING THREE-DIGIT NUMBERS

Big Pine Construction Company has 367 sheets of plywood. Can all the wood be put into just 5 equal stacks?

To find out, divide 367 by 5. There are not enough hundreds to divide by 5. Think of 3 hundreds 6 tens as 36 tens.

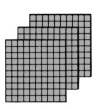  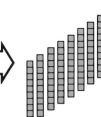 

Divide the 36 tens by 5.

$$
\begin{array}{r}
7 \\
5\overline{)367} \\
-35 \\
\hline
1
\end{array}
$$

Divide the 17 ones by 5. Write the remainder with the quotient.

$$
\begin{array}{r}
73 \text{ R}2 \\
5\overline{)367} \\
-35\downarrow \\
\hline
17 \\
-15 \\
\hline
2
\end{array}
$$

No. There will be 5 stacks of 73 and 2 pieces left over.

## CLASS EXERCISES

Divide.

**1.** 3)‾16̅    3)‾165̅    3)‾167̅    **2.** 5)‾22̅    5)‾225̅    5)‾228̅

**3.** 6)‾48̅    6)‾486̅    6)‾489̅    **4.** 7)‾58̅    7)‾588̅    7)‾589̅

## PRACTICE

Divide.

**5.** 6)‾210̅    **6.** 3)‾147̅    **7.** 5)‾440̅    **8.** 4)‾249̅    **9.** 2)‾138̅

10. 3)292　　11. 7)457　　12. 7)328　　13. 2)155　　14. 5)456

15. 6)204　　16. 7)359　　17. 6)555　　18. 4)194　　19. 9)567

20. 3)281　　21. 3)174　　22. 6)319　　23. 3)189　　24. 4)352

25. 6)518　　26. 2)127　　27. 8)736　　28. 6)499　　29. 5)458

30. 8)576　　31. 5)423　　32. 8)489　　33. 4)176　　34. 7)481

Using each of the numbers 1 through 12 as a divisor, write 12 divisions that have this quotient with no remainder.

★ **35.** 10　　　　★ **36.** 11　　　　★ **37.** 12

Write the answer.

**38.** 3 × 59　　　**39.** 521 + 521　　　**40.** 4 × 386

**41.** 3 × 4462　　**42.** 3 × $6.95　　**43.** 864 − 281

**MIXED REVIEW**

## PROBLEM SOLVING APPLICATIONS
### Using a Table

Use the information from the table to solve the problem.

**44.** The pine is to be put into 8 equal stacks. Is this possible? Why?

**45.** What is the total number of boards delivered?

**46.** The redwood was delivered by 2 trucks in equal batches. How much did each truck carry?

**47.** By the end of the week, Big Pine Construction expects to receive a total of 6 deliveries of hemlock. Each will equal today's delivery. Can the hemlock delivered be stored equally in 3 sheds?

| LUMBER DELIVERED TODAY | |
|---|---|
| TYPE | NUMBER OF BOARDS |
| Douglas Fir | 657 |
| Pine | 738 |
| Redwood | 956 |
| Hemlock | 837 |

# PROBLEM SOLVING
## Strategy: Interpreting Answers

Lucia and her friends are making costumes for a play. Each costume needs 4 yd of material. There are 18 yd of material. How many costumes can be made?

$$\begin{array}{r} 4 \text{ R2} \\ 4\overline{)18} \\ -16 \\ \hline 2 \end{array}$$

Remainders can have different meanings. For this problem, you can leave out the remainder. Even though Lucia and her friends have material left over, they can make only 4 orange costumes.

For other problems, the remainder is a clue to increase the quotient by 1.

One spool has enough thread to make 3 costumes. How many spools of thread are needed to make 10 costumes?

$$\begin{array}{r} 3 \text{ R1} \\ 3\overline{)10} \\ -9 \\ \hline 1 \end{array}$$

If there were 3 spools, there would not be enough thread to sew the last costume. To answer, increase the quotient by 1. You need 4 spools to make 10 costumes.

## CLASS EXERCISES

Should you leave out the remainder or increase the quotient by 1? Explain why. Solve.

1. Ed has 24 tape measures. He puts the same number of tape measures on each of 5 tables. How many does he put on each table?

2. Each sewing table has room for 4 people to work. If 19 people are working on the costumes, how many sewing tables are needed?

## PRACTICE

Solve.

3. Mona has made 15 striped pockets. Each costume needs 2 matching pockets. How many costumes will have striped pockets?

4. One package of yarn is enough to make 4 wigs for the costumes. How many packages are needed to make 14 wigs?

5. Casper has 13 yd of material to use to make shirts. Each shirt needs 2 yd of material. How many shirts can Casper make?

6. Buttons come in packages of 4. If Lucia wants to buy 54 buttons for the costumes, how many packages should she buy?

7. Dale has 138 sequins. He wants to put the same number of sequins on each of 5 coats. How many sequins are put on each coat?

8. Coats for the costumes need 6 yd of material. If Ruby Mae has 23 yd of material for coats, how many coats can she make?

9. Karson is making hats for the costumes. Each hat needs 3 feathers. Karson has 29 feathers. How many hats can he finish?

10. Karson measures his material and finds that he has 41 ft. Each hat needs 2 ft of material. Can Karson make 21 hats?

★ 11. Each costume that Maxine makes has a pair of pants and a vest of the same color. She has 5 yd of green material, 4 yd of red, and 3 yd of blue. Each pair of pants needs 2 yd, and each vest needs 1 yd. How many costumes can Maxine make with matching pants and vest?

# CHECKPOINT 1

Divide. *(pages 192–199)*

1. $3\overline{)63}$    2. $6\overline{)60}$

3. $7\overline{)79}$    4. $4\overline{)87}$

5. $5\overline{)70}$    6. $3\overline{)82}$

7. $2\overline{)175}$    8. $8\overline{)497}$

Solve. *(pages 200–201)*

9. One box of oatmeal cereal is enough for 7 servings. How many boxes should a scout leader buy to feed 23 scouts?

*Extra practice on page 414*

# THREE-DIGIT QUOTIENTS, NO FINAL REMAINDERS

Darcy, Miguel, and Frankie have 387 bottle caps to share equally. How many bottle caps does each receive? To answer, divide 387 by 3.

Divide the hundreds by 3.          Divide the tens by 3.          Divide the ones by 3.

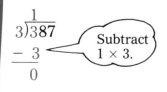

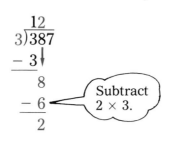

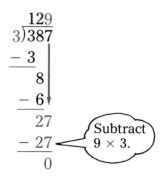

Each gets 129 bottle caps.

When you use a calculator, check the number of digits in your answer. **Think:** How many digits will be in the quotient of 387 ÷ 3? You can divide 3 hundreds by 3, so the quotient will have a digit in the hundreds' place. The quotient will have 3 digits.

387 ÷ 3 = 129

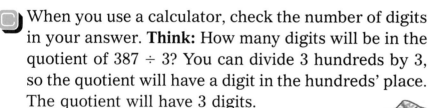

## CLASS EXERCISES

The first step of the division is done. Is the number in the quotient hundreds, tens, or ones? Explain how you know.

| | | | | |
|---|---|---|---|---|
| $\overset{1}{}$ | $\overset{1}{}$ | $\overset{9}{}$ | $\overset{8}{}$ | $\overset{2}{}$ |
| **1.** 4)564 | **2.** 6)726 | **3.** 5)455 | **4.** 7)623 | **5.** 3)849 |

Divide.

**6.** 2)24          2)246          **7.** 3)37          3)375          **8.** 5)84          5)845

# PRACTICE

Divide.

9. $3\overline{)300}$      10. $4\overline{)844}$      11. $2\overline{)264}$      12. $3\overline{)966}$      13. $4\overline{)488}$

14. $2\overline{)468}$      15. $3\overline{)639}$      16. $2\overline{)824}$      17. $2\overline{)682}$      18. $7\overline{)777}$

19. $4\overline{)848}$      20. $5\overline{)550}$      21. $3\overline{)936}$      22. $2\overline{)484}$      23. $2\overline{)842}$

24. $3\overline{)723}$      25. $6\overline{)672}$      26. $2\overline{)364}$      27. $8\overline{)968}$      28. $4\overline{)928}$

29. $7\overline{)917}$      30. $6\overline{)846}$      31. $2\overline{)566}$      32. $4\overline{)892}$      33. $7\overline{)987}$

34. $4\overline{)768}$      35. $7\overline{)266}$      36. $6\overline{)786}$      37. $2\overline{)198}$      38. $6\overline{)744}$

39. $3\overline{)246}$      40. $4\overline{)756}$      41. $7\overline{)875}$      42. $5\overline{)420}$      43. $4\overline{)976}$

Write the number of digits that will be in the quotient.
Then divide. Use a calculator if you have one.

**CALCULATOR**

44. $3\overline{)336}$      45. $4\overline{)884}$      46. $4\overline{)176}$      47. $8\overline{)488}$

48. $7\overline{)847}$    ★ 49. $2\overline{)4862}$    ★ 50. $3\overline{)3453}$    ★ 51. $6\overline{)5586}$

## PROBLEM SOLVING APPLICATIONS
### Choosing the Operation

Solve.

52. Darcy and Frankie collected a total of 268 cans. If they both collected the same number, how many cans did each collect?

53. Darcy collects 329 aluminum cans, Miguel collects 568, and Frankie collects 297. How many cans do they collect in all?

54. Together, Darcy, Miguel, and Frankie think they have walked a total of 693 km during the last year while collecting aluminum cans. If each walked the same distance, how far did each walk?

★ 55. Darcy, Frankie, Miguel, and 5 friends are collecting cans. Each collects 112 cans. If the cans are divided equally into 4 bags, how many cans are in each bag?

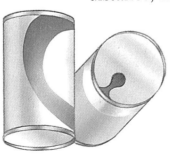

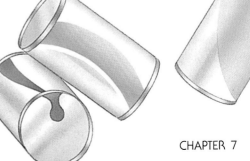

# ZEROS IN THE QUOTIENT

Clarissa did this division problem and then used multiplication and addition to check her answer. She saw she had made a mistake.

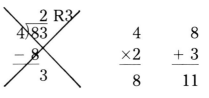

$$\begin{array}{r} 2\ R3 \\ 4\overline{)83} \\ -8 \\ \hline 3 \end{array}$$

$$\begin{array}{r} 4 \\ \times 2 \\ \hline 8 \end{array} \qquad \begin{array}{r} 8 \\ +3 \\ \hline 11 \end{array}$$

Clarissa left out a zero. She should have divided this way.

The correct answer is 20 R3.

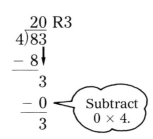

$$\begin{array}{r} 20\ R3 \\ 4\overline{)83} \\ -8\downarrow \\ \hline 3 \\ -0 \\ \hline 3 \end{array}$$

Subtract $0 \times 4$.

Now divide 812 by 4.

Divide the hundreds by 4.

$$\begin{array}{r} 2 \\ 4\overline{)812} \\ -8 \\ \hline 0 \end{array}$$

Subtract $2 \times 4$.

Divide the tens by 4.

$$\begin{array}{r} 20 \\ 4\overline{)812} \\ -8\downarrow \\ \hline 1 \\ -0 \\ \hline 1 \end{array}$$

Subtract $0 \times 4$.

Divide the ones by 4.

$$\begin{array}{r} 203 \\ 4\overline{)812} \\ -8 \\ \hline 1 \\ -0\downarrow \\ \hline 12 \\ -12 \\ \hline 0 \end{array}$$

Subtract $3 \times 4$.

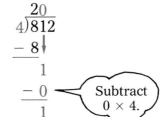

M Sometimes you can use mental math to divide.

$$3\overline{)618}$$

**Think:** 6 hundreds ÷ 3 = 2 hundreds,
1 ten ÷ 3 = 0 tens,
18 ones ÷ 3 = 6 ones,
so 618 ÷ 3 = 206.

## CLASS EXERCISES

Divide.

**1.** $2\overline{)20}$  $2\overline{)21}$  $2\overline{)212}$  **2.** $4\overline{)40}$  $4\overline{)43}$  $4\overline{)438}$

**3.** $7\overline{)70}$  $7\overline{)75}$  $7\overline{)756}$  **4.** $3\overline{)60}$  $3\overline{)62}$  $3\overline{)627}$

## PRACTICE

**Divide.**

5. $4\overline{)83}$     6. $6\overline{)62}$     7. $5\overline{)53}$     8. $2\overline{)61}$     9. $7\overline{)74}$

10. $5\overline{)520}$     11. $2\overline{)214}$     12. $6\overline{)642}$     13. $3\overline{)927}$     14. $2\overline{)816}$

15. $8\overline{)872}$     16. $5\overline{)52}$     17. $3\overline{)621}$     18. $4\overline{)832}$     19. $9\overline{)98}$

20. $7\overline{)735}$     21. $6\overline{)654}$     22. $4\overline{)82}$     23. $3\overline{)924}$     24. $8\overline{)864}$

25. $4\overline{)816}$     26. $3\overline{)91}$     27. $4\overline{)820}$     28. $7\overline{)72}$     29. $3\overline{)912}$

30. $6\overline{)612}$     31. $4\overline{)824}$     32. $8\overline{)856}$     33. $3\overline{)618}$     34. $3\overline{)62}$

35. $4\overline{)836}$     36. $9\overline{)97}$     37. $3\overline{)921}$     38. $7\overline{)742}$     39. $4\overline{)812}$

★ 40. **Think:** Suppose you can divide a number by 5 with no remainder. There are only two digits that can be in the ones' place. What are the two digits?

**Use mental math to divide. Write only the quotient.**

41. $2\overline{)200}$     42. $7\overline{)770}$     43. $8\overline{)888}$     44. $5\overline{)525}$

45. $2\overline{)414}$     46. $4\overline{)844}$     47. $3\overline{)399}$     48. $4\overline{)408}$

MENTAL MATH

## PROBLEM SOLVING APPLICATIONS
### Choosing a Strategy

**Solve.**

49. Howard has 236 pieces of track that he keeps in 4 boxes. If each box holds the same number of pieces, how many pieces of track are in each box?

50. At 6:15, Howard begins to work on his electric train. He spends 45 minutes putting it together and 9 minutes testing it. Does he work on his train for more than 1 hour?

★ 51. Howard uses 50 cars to put together 5 trains. Each train that he makes has one more car than the train before it. How many cars does Howard use for the first train?

# DIVIDING MONEY

Tony pays $9 for 4 bird feeders for his windows. How much does each bird feeder cost?

To find out, divide $9 by 4. Remember that $9 also can be written as $9.00. When dividing money, first put the dollar sign and decimal point in the quotient.

$$\begin{array}{r} \$\ . \\ 4\overline{)\$9.00} \end{array}$$

**Divide 9 by 4.**

$$\begin{array}{r} \$2. \\ 4\overline{)\$9.00} \\ -\ 8 \\ \hline 1 \end{array}$$

Subtract 2 × 4.

**Divide 10 by 4.**

$$\begin{array}{r} \$2.2 \\ 4\overline{)\$9.00} \\ -\ 8 \\ \hline 1\ 0 \\ -\ 8 \\ \hline 2 \end{array}$$

Subtract 2 × 4.

**Divide 20 by 4.**

$$\begin{array}{r} \$2.25 \\ 4\overline{)\$9.00} \\ -\ 8 \\ \hline 1\ 0 \\ -\ 8 \\ \hline 20 \\ -\ 20 \\ \hline 0 \end{array}$$

Subtract 5 × 4.

Each bird feeder costs $2.25.

To estimate the cost of each bird feeder, look at the first step of the division.

$$\begin{array}{r} \$2. \\ 4\overline{)\$9.00} \end{array}$$

You know that the quotient is $2 and some cents, but it is not as much as $3.

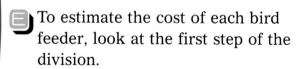

## CLASS EXERCISES

Are the dollar sign and decimal point in the correct place?
If not, write the answer correctly.

1. $\begin{array}{r}\$2.14\\3\overline{)\$6.42}\end{array}$
2. $\begin{array}{r}\$.250\\3\overline{)\$7.50}\end{array}$
3. $\begin{array}{r}\$2.22\\3\overline{)\$6.66}\end{array}$
4. $\begin{array}{r}\$10.0\\5\overline{)\$5.00}\end{array}$

# PRACTICE

Divide. Remember the dollar sign and decimal point.

**5.** 3)$\overline{\$9.33}$   **6.** 4)$\overline{\$8.48}$   **7.** 2)$\overline{\$6.44}$   **8.** 5)$\overline{\$5.50}$   **9.** 4)$\overline{\$9.52}$

**10.** 3)$\overline{\$8.49}$   **11.** 5)$\overline{\$8.40}$   **12.** 7)$\overline{\$8.19}$   **13.** 9)$\overline{\$9.18}$   **14.** 6)$\overline{\$7.08}$

**15.** 8)$\overline{\$9.92}$   **16.** 4)$\overline{\$8.76}$   **17.** 2)$\overline{\$7.08}$   **18.** 5)$\overline{\$9.35}$   **19.** 3)$\overline{\$5.25}$

Divide. Write the quotient in dollars and cents.

**20.** 2)$\overline{\$7}$   **21.** 4)$\overline{\$5}$   **22.** 5)$\overline{\$7}$   **23.** 4)$\overline{\$6}$   **24.** 5)$\overline{\$9}$

Without completing the division, estimate whether the answer will be *more than* or *less than* $2.00.

**ESTIMATE**

**25.** 4)$\overline{\$7.00}$   **26.** 5)$\overline{\$6.00}$   **27.** 2)$\overline{\$5.00}$   **28.** 4)$\overline{\$6.00}$

**29.** 2)$\overline{\$7.18}$   **30.** 2)$\overline{\$8.74}$   **31.** 4)$\overline{\$9.50}$   **32.** 3)$\overline{\$7.28}$

## PROBLEM SOLVING APPLICATIONS
### Estimation, Mental Math, or Pencil

Use estimation, mental math, or paper and pencil to solve the problem. Write *e, m,* or *p* to tell the method you chose.

**33.** Tony buys 3 bags of sunflower seeds for $4.59 to use in the new bird feeders. How much does Tony pay for each bag?

**34.** One bag of mixed birdseed costs $.99. The bag holds 2 lb of seed. Does the birdseed cost more than $.40 for each pound?

**35.** Tony spends $18.54 for supplies. He gives the clerk $20.00. Using the fewest coins and bills possible, what is Tony's change?

★ **36.** A package of Bright seeds costs $3.48 for 3 lb. A package of Wilder's seeds costs $2.36 for 2 lb. Which costs less for each pound?

# THREE-DIGIT QUOTIENTS, WITH REMAINDERS

This summer 639 scouts are at the jamboree. Each tent can hold 4 scouts. How many tents are needed for the scouts?

To find out, divide 639 by 4.

Divide the hundreds by 4.

$$\begin{array}{r} 1 \\ 4\overline{)639} \\ -4 \\ \hline 2 \end{array}$$

Is 2 less than 4? Yes.

Divide the tens by 4.

$$\begin{array}{r} 15 \\ 4\overline{)639} \\ -4\downarrow \\ \hline 23 \\ -20 \\ \hline 3 \end{array}$$

Is 3 less than 4? Yes.

Divide the ones by 4.

$$\begin{array}{r} 159 \text{ R3} \\ 4\overline{)639} \\ -4\ \ \ \\ \hline 23\ \ \\ -20\downarrow \\ \hline 39 \\ -36 \\ \hline 3 \end{array}$$

Is 3 less than 4? Yes.

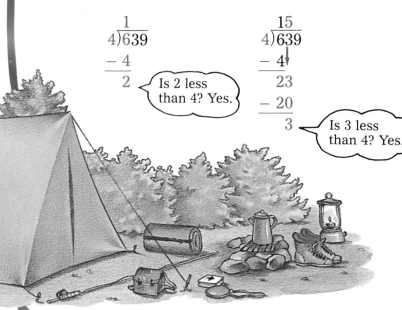

The answer 159 R3 means that 159 tents will have 4 people and 1 tent will have 3 people. For 639 scouts, 160 tents are needed.

## CLASS EXERCISES

Is the division correct? If not, what went wrong?

1. $\begin{array}{r} 115 \text{ R5} \\ 4\overline{)465} \end{array}$
2. $\begin{array}{r} 113 \text{ R2} \\ 5\overline{)567} \end{array}$
3. $\begin{array}{r} 133 \text{ R4} \\ 3\overline{)403} \end{array}$
4. $\begin{array}{r} 141 \text{ R7} \\ 6\overline{)853} \end{array}$
5. $\begin{array}{r} 211 \text{ R1} \\ 2\overline{)423} \end{array}$

6. $\begin{array}{r} 174 \text{ R6} \\ 5\overline{)876} \end{array}$
7. $\begin{array}{r} 215 \text{ R2} \\ 4\overline{)862} \end{array}$
8. $\begin{array}{r} 332 \text{ R2} \\ 3\overline{)998} \end{array}$
9. $\begin{array}{r} 153 \text{ R1} \\ 6\overline{)919} \end{array}$
10. $\begin{array}{r} 122 \text{ R11} \\ 8\overline{)987} \end{array}$

## PRACTICE

Divide.

11. $2\overline{)875}$
12. $8\overline{)893}$
13. $7\overline{)783}$
14. $3\overline{)494}$
15. $2\overline{)323}$

16. $3\overline{)334}$
17. $7\overline{)919}$
18. $6\overline{)827}$
19. $5\overline{)587}$
20. $7\overline{)874}$

21. $3\overline{)524}$    22. $7\overline{)921}$    23. $4\overline{)729}$    24. $5\overline{)958}$    25. $6\overline{)967}$

26. $2\overline{)834}$    27. $4\overline{)648}$    28. $3\overline{)214}$    29. $8\overline{)832}$    30. $5\overline{)856}$

31. $7\overline{)917}$    32. $3\overline{)829}$    33. $4\overline{)872}$    34. $6\overline{)773}$    35. $5\overline{)274}$

★ 36. $4\overline{)5366}$   ★ 37. $4\overline{)5452}$   ★ 38. $5\overline{)6750}$   ★ 39. $3\overline{)6279}$   ★ 40. $6\overline{)7573}$

---

Write the answer.

**MIXED REVIEW**

41.
```
   324
 −  38
```

42.
```
   516
 − 339
```

43.
```
  $8.25
 + 3.99
```

44.
```
  $36.54
 − 21.28
```

45.
```
   33
   27
 + 19
```

46.
```
   644
    82
 + 117
```

47.
```
  $7.11
   9.24
 + 3.82
```

48.
```
  $21.40
   2.16
 + 9.87
```

---

## PROBLEM SOLVING APPLICATIONS
### Choosing a Strategy

Solve.

49. Each scout without a sleeping bag gets 2 blankets. The supply clerk has 595 blankets. How many scouts can get blankets from the supply clerk?

50. Yesterday, 217 scouts went swimming, 523 scouts went canoeing, and 426 scouts went hiking. How many more scouts went canoeing than swimming?

51. There are 529 scouts who want to be on badminton teams. Each team must have 4 people. How many badminton teams will there be?

★ 52. Of the 639 scouts at the jamboree, 379 will be in short races. The other scouts will run in a relay race in pairs. How many pairs will run in the relay race?

# AVERAGES

The table at the left shows the temperatures in Des Moines, Iowa, for 7 days in May. Some temperatures are higher than others. You can find the **average** temperature for these days. Finding the average temperature takes two steps.

DAILY TEMPERATURES

| Date | Temperature |
|------|-------------|
| May 5 | 58°F |
| May 6 | 64°F |
| May 7 | 68°F |
| May 8 | 63°F |
| May 9 | 59°F |
| May 10 | 55°F |
| May 11 | 60°F |

Add the temperatures.

```
   58
   64
   68
   63
   59
   55
 + 60
  427
```

Divide the sum by the number of days.

```
        61 ← Average
   7)427
    - 42
        7
      - 7
        0
```

The average temperature was 61°F.

Sometimes you can estimate the average mentally. Estimate the average of these numbers.

53     48     52     47

**Think:** All of the numbers are about 50, so the average will be about 50.

## CLASS EXERCISES

Use the chart to solve.

1. What is the sum of the temperatures?

2. How many dates are recorded?

3. To find the average, divide the ___?___ by the number of ___?___.

4. What is the average temperature?

**DAILY TEMPERATURES**

| Date | Temperature |
|------|-------------|
| March 15 | 38°F |
| March 16 | 42°F |
| March 17 | 45°F |
| March 18 | 39°F |
| March 19 | 46°F |

# PRACTICE

Write the average.

5. 10, 8, 9, 13

6. 8, 9, 15, 12

7. 11, 20, 14, 22, 13

8. 15, 11, 28, 15, 21

9. 23, 18, 24, 19

10. 13, 11, 9, 10, 12

11. 27, 36, 47, 34

12. 64, 52, 43, 33

13. 20, 19, 18, 16, 16, 14, 9

14. 35, 24, 16, 24, 29, 46

15. 255, 310, 424, 383

16. 153, 95, 207, 197

The *median* of a group of numbers is the number in the middle. When the numbers are in order, there are as many numbers in the group above the median as below it. Find the median.

★ 17. 12, 15, 18, 17, 20

★ 18. 18, 24, 35, 19, 27

Estimate the average.

19. 18, 21, 19, 22

20. 29, 32, 31, 28

21. 87, 94, 92, 89, 88

22. 146, 154, 147, 153

ESTIMATE

## PROBLEM SOLVING APPLICATIONS
### Choosing the Operation

Solve.

23. The normal temperatures in Anchorage, Alaska, are 13°F in January, 24°F in March, 46°F in May, 58°F in July, 48°F in September, and 21°F in November. What is the average temperature?

24. In Phoenix, Arizona, one year, the highest temperature recorded was 113°F and the lowest temperature recorded was 34°F. What is the difference between the two temperatures?

★ 25. I am thinking of 3 numbers. The first two numbers are 49 and 51. The average of the 3 numbers is 52. What is the third number?

# PROBLEM SOLVING
## Strategy: Using a Line Graph

1. Understand
2. Plan
3. Work
4. Answer/Check

**Line graphs** help you see changes. This graph shows how a television ad for Gourmet Dog Food affects dog food sales at Big Buy markets. The bottom of the graph shows the days the ad is shown on television. The left side shows the number of boxes of dog food sold.

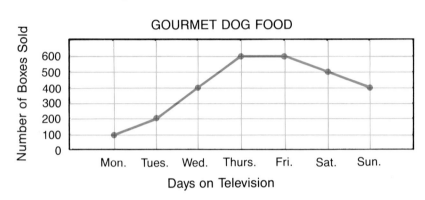

GOURMET DOG FOOD

Number of Boxes Sold

Days on Television

The line graph shows when sales are increasing or decreasing. On Wednesday 400 boxes were sold. On Thursday the sales increased to 600 boxes.

## CLASS EXERCISES

Use the graph above to answer the question. How many boxes are sold on this day?

**1.** Monday      **2.** Tuesday      **3.** Friday      **4.** Saturday      **5.** Sunday

On which day does this happen?

**6.** Exactly 500 boxes are sold.      **7.** Sales begin to decrease.

## PRACTICE

Use the graph above to answer the question.

**8.** What are the total sales for all 7 days?

**9.** What are the average sales for a day this week?

This line graph shows the estimated number of people who watched the local television show, *Smitty, the Hero Dog.*

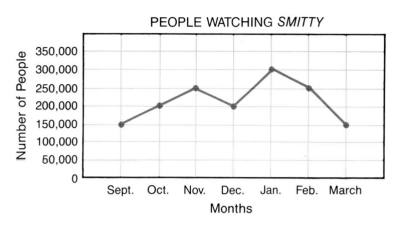

PEOPLE WATCHING *SMITTY*

Use the graph to answer the question.

**10.** How many more people watched in November than in September?

**11.** Did more people watch in February or in October?

**12.** Between which two months did the number who watched the show increase the most?

**13.** Between which two months did the number who watched the show decrease the most?

★ **14.** Each year Harbor City holds a local dog show. Copy and complete the line graph to show the number of ribbons awarded each year. Don't forget to add labels.

1984, 15 ribbons      1985, 10 ribbons
1986, 25 ribbons      1987, 20 ribbons

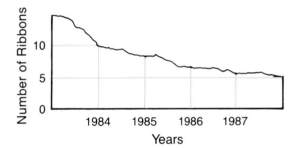

# CHECKPOINT 2

Divide. *(pages 202–209)*

**1.** 4)844          **2.** 7)714

**3.** 6)$8.10       **4.** 4)957

Find the average. *(pages 210–211)*

**5.** 10, 8, 15, 6, 16

**6.** 13, 8, 7, 12, 11, 3

Use the graph at the top of the page. *(pages 212–213)*

**7.** In which month did the most people watch?

**8.** How many people watched in March?

*Extra practice on page 414*

Write the answer. *(pages 192–199)*

1. $3\overline{)63}$

2. $5\overline{)59}$

3. $4\overline{)85}$

4. $4\overline{)64}$

5. $5\overline{)58}$

6. $7\overline{)89}$

7. $6\overline{)216}$

8. $5\overline{)359}$

Solve. *(pages 200–201)*

9. One can of fruit punch is enough for 8 servings. How many cans are needed to serve 28 people?

10. Each paper cup holds 5 oz. There are 48 oz of fruit punch left. How many cups can be filled?

Write the answer. *(pages 202–209)*

11. $3\overline{)726}$

12. $6\overline{)648}$

13. $7\overline{)756}$

14. $4\overline{)\$8.68}$

15. $6\overline{)\$7.14}$

16. $7\overline{)924}$

17. $8\overline{)915}$

18. $5\overline{)937}$

Write the average. *(pages 210–211)*

19. 24, 19, 25, 20, 27

20. 36, 33, 22, 45

21. 144, 260, 145, 187

22. 12, 11, 10, 8, 8, 15, 13

Use the graph to solve the problems. *(pages 212–213)*

PEOPLE BUYING BIKES

23. How many people bought bikes in November?

24. How many more people bought bikes in June than in August?

*Extra practice on page 415*

# MATHEMATICS and HISTORY

The U.S. Constitution says that a candidate for President must be at least 35 years old. This table gives information about the first five Presidents of the United States.

| PRESIDENT | YEAR OF BIRTH | YEARS IN OFFICE | AGE AT INAUGURATION |
|---|---|---|---|
| George Washington | 1732 | 1789–1797 | 57 |
| John Adams | 1735 | 1797–1801 | 61 |
| Thomas Jefferson | 1743 | 1801–1809 | 57 |
| James Madison | 1751 | 1809–1817 | 57 |
| James Monroe | 1758 | 1817–1825 | 58 |

# WHAT WAS THE AVERAGE?

Use the table to answer the question.

1. Of these Presidents, who was the oldest at his inauguration?

2. What was the average age of these Presidents at their inaugurations?

3. Which of these Presidents was in office for the shortest time?

4. How old was George Washington when James Madison was born?

★5. Abraham Lincoln took office 72 years after George Washington did. He was 52 years old at his inauguration. When was Abraham Lincoln born?

# Enrichment

Using the word *and* instead of *or* in a sentence can make a real difference.

Can you find the box that each person wrapped?

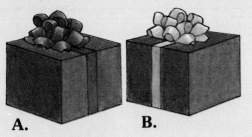

**A.**   **B.**   **C.**   **D.**   **E.**

Jenny wrapped the box with red paper *and* a yellow ribbon. Box B is the only box that has both red paper and a yellow ribbon, so you know that Jenny wrapped box B.

Marty wrapped the box with blue paper *or* a blue ribbon. Box D and box E have blue paper. Box C and box E have blue ribbons. You cannot tell which box Marty wrapped.

Match the balloon with the description.

**1.** It is yellow and it has red dots.

**2.** It is blue or it has white dots.

**3.** It is purple or it has yellow dots.

**4.** It is yellow and it has blue dots.

# LOGICAL THINKING

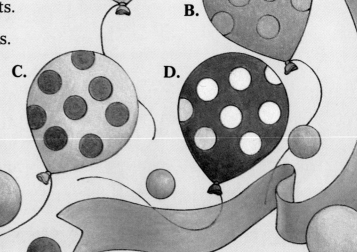

**A.**   **B.**   **C.**   **D.**

Look at the shirts above. Write the name or names on the shirts described.

5. Blue shirt and red letters
6. Blue shirt or red letters
7. Red shirt and blue letters
8. Red shirt or blue letters
9. Yellow shirt or blue letters
10. Green shirt or red letters
11. Who has the colors blue and red?
12. Who has the colors yellow or blue?

13. Herbie, Muff, Rufus, and Taffy won ribbons at the dog show. Use the picture above and the clues below to name the dog that won each ribbon.

A. Rufus is a red dog and did not win first place.
B. Taffy has spots and is next to Herbie.
C. Herbie won first or second place.
D. Muff is next to Herbie and next to Rufus.

Choose the correct answer. Write *a*, *b*, *c*, or *d*.

Find the answer.

**1.** $6 \times 3$
  **a.** 9
  **b.** 24
  **c.** 18
  **d.** none of these

**2.** $9 \times 4$
  **a.** 36
  **b.** 32
  **c.** 33
  **d.** none of these

**3.** $8 \times 5$
  **a.** 20
  **b.** 40
  **c.** 60
  **d.** none of these

**4.** $5 \times (2 \times 3)$
  **a.** 21
  **b.** 13
  **c.** 10
  **d.** none of these

**5.** $3 \times 8 \times 0$
  **a.** 24
  **b.** 11
  **c.** 0
  **d.** none of these

**6.** $(1 \times 4) \times 7$
  **a.** 35
  **b.** 28
  **c.** 1
  **d.** none of these

Find the answer.

**7.** $7 \times 6$
  **a.** 42
  **b.** 48
  **c.** 46
  **d.** none of these

**8.** $9 \times 7$
  **a.** 56
  **b.** 63
  **c.** 58
  **d.** none of these

**9.** $8 \times 7$
  **a.** 54
  **b.** 56
  **c.** 64
  **d.** none of these

Find the answer.

**10.** $8 \times 9$
  **a.** 17
  **b.** 89
  **c.** 72
  **d.** none of these

**11.** $8 \times 8$
  **a.** 16
  **b.** 61
  **c.** 65
  **d.** none of these

**12.** $9 \times 9$
  **a.** 99
  **b.** 81
  **c.** 18
  **d.** none of these

Find the answer.

**13.** 6 multiples of 7
  **a.** 0, 1, 2, 3, 4, 5
  **b.** 7, 13, 20, 26, 32, 38
  **c.** 7, 14, 21, 28, 35, 42
  **d.** none of these

**14.** one common multiple of 5 and 9
  **a.** 45
  **b.** 59
  **c.** 54
  **d.** none of these

**15.** two common multiples of 4 and 8
  **a.** 8, 12
  **b.** 4, 16
  **c.** 8, 16
  **d.** none of these

**16.** three common multiples of 3 and 6
  **a.** 9, 15, 18
  **b.** 3, 6, 12
  **c.** 6, 12, 18
  **d.** none of these

Solve.

**17.** Movie tickets cost $3. Tickets to the concert are $7. If Staci buys 4 movie tickets, how much does she spend?
  **a.** $28
  **b.** $12
  **c.** $10
  **d.** none of these

**18.** A book of 7 movie tickets costs $28. John saw 2 westerns and 1 space movie last month. How much does each movie ticket cost?
  **a.** $4
  **b.** $3
  **c.** $7
  **d.** none of these

# LANGUAGE and VOCABULARY REVIEW

Choose the correct word to complete the sentence. Write the word on your paper.

1. The answer in a division problem is called the (quotient, dividend).

2. In any division problem, the remainder must be less than the (divisor, difference).

3. To check your answer in a division problem, multiply the quotient by the divisor, then add the (sum, remainder).

4. If you add the ages of the students in your class and divide the sum by the number of students, the answer will be the (average, estimated) age.

5. The answer in a multiplication problem is called the (factor, product).

6. To find the difference of two numbers, you (subtract, divide).

# PLANNING A PROGRAM

A **program** is a list of instructions. It tells the computer to do a process in step-by-step order.

Jorge wants to write a program. He wants the computer to tell if he is taller than the average 4th grader. Jorge asks himself questions. He uses the questions and answers to plan a program.

| QUESTIONS | PLAN |
|---|---|
| **1.** Do I need to know my height? Yes | **a.** Write Jorge's height. |
| **2.** Do I need to know the height of the average 4th grader? Yes | **b.** Write the height of the average 4th grader. |
| **3.** Do I need to know my teacher's height? No | |
| **4.** Do I need to know what to do with the heights? Yes | **c.** Compare the heights. If Jorge's height is greater than the average then write "Taller." If not, write "Not taller." |

Jorge wants the computer to find the average height of his classmates.

**1.** Which questions should Jorge ask? Write the letters.

**a.** Do I need the number of classmates?

**b.** Do I need the height of each classmate?

**c.** Do I need the weight of each classmate?

**d.** Do I need to know what to do with the numbers?

**2.** Which steps are in his plan? Write the letters.

**a.** Write the number of classmates.

**b.** Write the height of each classmate.

**c.** Write the weight of each classmate.

**d.** Add the heights and divide by the number of classmates.

8

The Golden Gate Bridge hangs from two steel cables that are 93 cm thick. Think of dividing 1 m into centimeters. Is a cable more than 1 m thick?

DECIMALS

# TENHS

The square has been divided into 10 equal parts. Each part is one tenth of the square. You can write a **decimal** to show one tenth.

0.1

You read the decimal as *one tenth*.

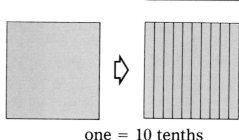

one = 10 tenths

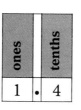

**Lookout Point**

**1.4 km**

One whole square and 4 tenths of a square are shaded. You can write the decimal 1.4 to show what is shaded. You read the decimal as *one and four tenths*.

## CLASS EXERCISES

Write the decimal for the shaded part.

**1.**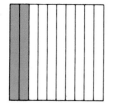

**2.**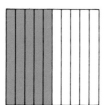

**3.**

Write the decimal. Then read the decimal.

**4.**

| ones | tenths |
|------|--------|
| 3 . | 7 |

**5.**

| ones | tenths |
|------|--------|
| 5 . | 2 |

**6.**

| ones | tenths |
|------|--------|
| 0 . | 8 |

**7.**

| tens | ones | tenths |
|------|------|--------|
| 1 | 9 . | 5 |

## PRACTICE

Write the decimal.

**8.** 5 tenths

**9.** 9 tenths

**10.** 4 tenths

**11.** 7 tenths
**12.** 1 tenth
**13.** 3 tenths

**14.** 2 tenths
**15.** 8 tenths
**16.** 6 tenths

**17.** 2 and 6 tenths
**18.** 5 and 3 tenths
**19.** 4 and 7 tenths

**20.** 16 and 4 tenths
**21.** 28 and 8 tenths
**22.** 17 and 5 tenths

**23.** three tenths
**24.** six tenths
**25.** five tenths

**26.** fifty-seven and four tenths
**27.** thirty and nine tenths

★ **28.** 60 + 4 + 0.8
★ **29.** 300 + 20 + 9 + 0.5

Write the number in words.

**30.** 8.3
**31.** 3.7
**32.** 4.5
**33.** 49.2
**34.** 100.1

Choose the better estimate. Write *a* or *b*.

**35.** width of a calculator      **a.** 7 cm     **b.** 7 m

**36.** distance of a bicycle ride    **a.** 2 m      **b.** 2 km

**37.** weight of a postcard       **a.** 2 g       **b.** 2 kg

**38.** gasoline needed for a trip    **a.** 50 mL    **b.** 50 L

**MIXED REVIEW**

## PROBLEM SOLVING APPLICATIONS
### Tenths in Measurement

This picture shows part of a centimeter ruler. Each centimeter is divided into tenths.

Use a centimeter ruler with tenths of a centimeter. Measure to the nearest tenth of a centimeter.

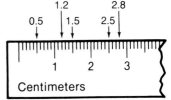

**39.**

**40.**

**41.**

**42.**

**43.**

**44.**

# HUNDREDTHS

You can use a decimal when a whole is divided into 100 equal parts. Each part is 1 hundredth. You write 1 hundredth as 0.01.

one = 100 hundredths

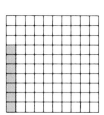

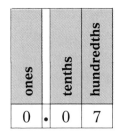

| ones | tenths | hundredths |
|------|--------|------------|
| 0 .  | 0      | 7          |

7 hundredths are shaded. You write the decimal as 0.07. You read it as *seven hundredths.*

 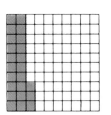

| ones | tenths | hundredths |
|------|--------|------------|
| 1 .  | 2      | 3          |

The greatest rainfall recorded in 1 minute was 1.23 in.

1 and 23 hundredths are shaded. You write the decimal as 1.23. You read it as *one and twenty-three hundredths.*

## CLASS EXERCISES

Write the decimal for the shaded part. Then read the decimal.

**1.**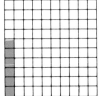

**2.**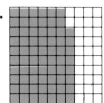

**3.**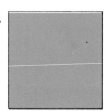

Complete.

**4.** 2.65 = ▢ and ▢ hundredths

**5.** 11.02 = ▢ and ▢ hundredths

# PRACTICE

Write the decimal.

**6.** 58 hundredths      **7.** 12 hundredths      **8.** 8 hundredths

**9.** 3 hundredths      **10.** 99 hundredths      **11.** 10 hundredths

**12.** 5 hundredths      **13.** 46 hundredths      **14.** 50 hundredths

**15.** 3 and 26 hundredths    **16.** 8 and 53 hundredths    **17.** 7 and 17 hundredths

**18.** 9 and 21 hundredths    **19.** 6 and 5 hundredths    **20.** 5 and 8 hundredths

**21.** 5 and 7 tenths      **22.** 17 and 36 hundredths    **23.** 25 and 6 hundredths

**24.** 36 and 93 hundredths      **25.** 8 and 2 tenths

**26.** 3 tenths and 9 hundredths      **27.** 14 and 3 hundredths

**28.** 48 and 59 hundredths      **29.** 62 and 8 hundredths

**30.** 4 ones 5 tenths 1 hundredth      **31.** 2 tens 3 tenths 8 hundredths

**32.** 9 tens 1 tenth 6 hundredths      **33.** 4 tens 4 tenths

★ **34.** one hundred and one hundredth    ★ **35.** one thousand and one tenth

★ **36.** thirty-five hundreds and five tenths    ★ **37.** three hundred five and one hundredth

## PROBLEM SOLVING APPLICATIONS
### Writing Mathematical Information

Write the underlined words as a decimal.

**38.** The largest hailstone ever recorded weighed <u>one and sixty-seven hundredths</u> pounds.

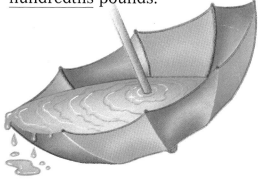

**39.** The greatest rainfall in one day was <u>seventy-three and sixty-two hundredths</u> inches.

**40.** The greatest rainfall in one month was <u>three hundred sixty-six and fourteen hundredths</u> inches.

★ **41.** For one year, the record rainfall was <u>one thousand forty-one and seventy-eight hundredths</u> inches.

# COMPARING AND ORDERING DECIMALS

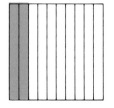 

$$0.2 < 0.9$$

 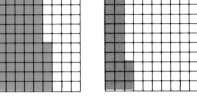

$$0.65 > 0.23$$

You compare decimals in the same way as whole numbers. Start at the left with the greatest place value and compare the digits.

Compare 3.56 and 3.52. The ones are the same. The tenths are the same. Compare the hundredths.

| ones | | tenths | hundredths |
|---|---|---|---|
| 3 | . | 5 | 6 |
| 3 | . | 5 | 2 |

6 hundredths > 2 hundredths
so 3.56 > 3.52

 To order decimals, compare them mentally. These decimals are in order from least to greatest.

2.25    2.48    2.73

**Think:** 2.25 < 2.48 and 2.48 < 2.73.

## CLASS EXERCISES

Write < or > to compare the decimals.

**1.**

| ones | | tenths |
|---|---|---|
| 0 | . | 6 |
| 0 | . | 8 |

0.6 ▓ 0.8

**2.**

| ones | | tenths |
|---|---|---|
| 5 | . | 3 |
| 4 | . | 9 |

5.3 ▓ 4.9

**3.**

| ones | | tenths | hundredths |
|---|---|---|---|
| 0 | . | 0 | 8 |
| 0 | . | 8 | 0 |

0.08 ▓ 0.80

**4.** Are these numbers in order from greatest to least? Answer *yes* or *no*. Explain why or why not.

4.88    4.86    4.54    4.73

## PRACTICE

Write < or > to compare the decimals.

**5.** 0.4 ▦ 0.9      **6.** 0.5 ▦ 0.3      **7.** 0.2 ▦ 2.0

**8.** 0.32 ▦ 0.37      **9.** 0.90 ▦ 0.70      **10.** 0.05 ▦ 0.50

**11.** 5.6 ▦ 5.3      **12.** 0.08 ▦ 0.09      **13.** 4.23 ▦ 4.32

**14.** 2.60 ▦ 2.06      **15.** 8.3 ▦ 8.8      **16.** 0.9 ▦ 1.0

**17.** 3.35 ▦ 3.36      **18.** 2.47 ▦ 2.40      **19.** 4.37 ▦ 3.40

**20.** 9.8 ▦ 8.9      **21.** 34.5 ▦ 35.4      **22.** 3.80 ▦ 3.81

Complete.

**23.**
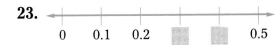
0    0.1    0.2    ▦    ▦    0.5

**24.**
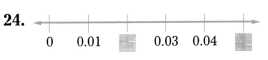
0    0.01    ▦    0.03    0.04    ▦

**25.**
0.41    0.42    0.43    ▦    ▦

**26.**
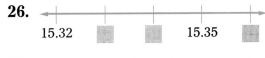
15.32    ▦    ▦    15.35    ▦

**27.**
2.10    2.11    ▦    ▦    2.14

★ **28.**

22.5    ▦    22.7    ▦    ▦    ▦

Compare the numbers mentally. Write them in order from greatest to least.

**29.** 0.5, 0.8, 1.1, 0.3

**30.** 8.7, 6.9, 5.4, 7.2

**31.** 0.54, 0.45, 0.52, 0.42

**32.** 13.32, 12.23, 12.32, 13.33

**MENTAL MATH**

## PROBLEM SOLVING APPLICATIONS
### Nonroutine Problems

You have this amount of money in your pocket. List the coins you could have. There is more than one answer.

**33.** You have $.30, but you can't make change for a quarter.

**34.** You have $.55, but you can't make change for a half dollar.

★ **35.** You have $1.19, but you can't make change for $1.

# TENTHS AND HUNDREDTHS

When you write a zero after the last digit of a decimal, the value of the decimal stays the same.

  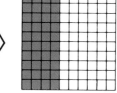

4 tenths          40 hundredths

0.4 = 0.40

1 and 7 tenths is the same as 1 and 70 hundredths.

1.7 = 1.70

2 is the same as 2 and 0 tenths or 2 and 0 hundredths.

2 = 2.0 = 2.00

Which is greater, 1.5 or 1.52? To compare, write a zero after 1.5.

 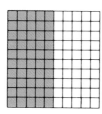           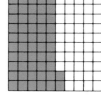

1.5 = 1.50                           1.52

1.50 < 1.52

so 1.5 < 1.52

 If you enter 1.50 ▣ on a calculator, 1.5 will appear.

## CLASS EXERCISES

Complete the decimal.

**1.**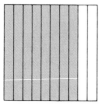

0.8 = 0.8⬚

**2.**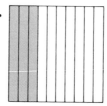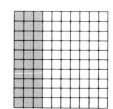

0.3 = 0.3⬚

Which is greater? Explain how you know.

**3.** 0.13 or 1.3          **4.** 2.3 or 2.34          **5.** 6.2 or 6.45

# PRACTICE

Write as a decimal that shows hundredths.

**6.** 0.2     **7.** 0.6     **8.** 0.9     **9.** 0.1     **10.** 0.3     **11.** 0.5

**12.** 5.4     **13.** 8.9     **14.** 7.6     **15.** 8.7     **16.** 4.8     **17.** 1.0

**18.** 21.5     **19.** 32.7     **20.** 18.8     **21.** 24     **22.** 35     **23.** 46

Compare. Write $<$ , $>$ , or $=$.

**24.** 0.8 ▓ 0.86       **25.** 0.34 ▓ 0.4       **26.** 5.2 ▓ 5.23

**27.** 1.5 ▓ 1.25       **28.** 6.5 ▓ 6.50       **29.** 4.3 ▓ 3.48

Write in order from greatest to least. Write zeros after the last digits of the decimals when needed.

★ **30.** 2.3, 0.23, 23      ★ **31.** 0.7, 7.7, 0.77      ★ **32.** 0.12, 0.2, 0.1

★ **33.** 0.32, 0.33, 0.3      ★ **34.** 0.04, 1.04, 1.24      ★ **35.** 3.5, 3.35, 3.53

If you enter the number shown and press ⊟ on a calculator, what number will appear on the screen?

CALCULATOR

**36.** 2.0     **37.** 40.3     **38.** 17.00     **39.** 5.90

**40.** 0.04     **41.** 7.02     **42.** 30.09     **43.** 60.00

# PROBLEM SOLVING APPLICATIONS
## Using a Table

Use the information in the table. Solve.

**44.** Which comet takes the least time to go around the sun once?

**45.** Does Comas Sola take more than 8.5 years to go around the sun once?

★ **46.** Write the comets in order from the one that takes the most time to the one that takes the least time to go around the sun once.

**COMETS TRAVELING
AROUND THE SUN**

| Comet | Number of Years to Go Around the Sun Once |
|---|---|
| Comas Sola | 8.78 |
| Forbes | 6.26 |
| Halley | 76.0 |
| Harrington | 6.84 |
| Wild 1 | 13.3 |

# ROUNDING DECIMALS

In the 1984 Olympics, the winning time for the women's 100 m freestyle race was 55.92 seconds. You can round the decimal if you don't need to know the exact time.

You round decimals as you round whole numbers. Look at the digit to the right of the place to be rounded. This digit tells you whether to round up or down.

| NUMBER | ROUND TO THE NEAREST | DIGIT TO THE RIGHT | IS IT 5 OR MORE? | ROUND THE NUMBER |
|---|---|---|---|---|
| 55.92 | whole number | 9 | yes | up to 56 |
| 55.92 | tenth | 2 | no | down to 55.9 |

To round 55.92 to its greatest place value, look at the digit to the right of the tens' place. Round 55.92 up to 60.

## CLASS EXERCISES

Round to the nearest whole number.

**1.** 9.1    **2.** 6.5    **3.** 8.95    **4.** 54.31    **5.** 28.96

Round to the nearest tenth.

**6.** 6.44    **7.** 4.79    **8.** 8.01    **9.** 53.11    **10.** 17.87

## PRACTICE

Round to the place of the underlined digit.

**11.** 17.8    **12.** 42.3    **13.** 2.83    **14.** 4.36    **15.** 20.39

**16.** 64.34    **17.** 91.87    **18.** 28.91    **19.** 14.32    **20.** 19.76

**21.** 42.23    **22.** 61.89    **23.** 84.96    **24.** 24.76    **25.** 113.39

**26.** 185.62    **27.** 100.14    **28.** 210.9    **29.** 0.85    **30.** 330.45

Round to the greatest place value.

**31.** 8.7    **32.** 11.6    **33.** 4.32    **34.** 9.16    **35.** 38.5

**36.** 21.8          **37.** 59.42          **38.** 137.4          **39.** 482.6          **40.** 300.55

★ **41. Think:** Rounded to its greatest place value, the number at the right is 5. What is the greatest the number could be? What is the least the number could be?

## PROBLEM SOLVING APPLICATIONS
### Decimals and Time

Use the information at the right to answer the question.

**42.** To the nearest tenth of a second, what was the winning time in 1972?

**43.** Was the winning time faster in 1976 or in 1984?

**44.** To the nearest whole number, in which years were the winning times about 50 seconds?

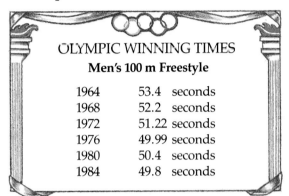

OLYMPIC WINNING TIMES
**Men's 100 m Freestyle**

| 1964 | 53.4 seconds |
| 1968 | 52.2 seconds |
| 1972 | 51.22 seconds |
| 1976 | 49.99 seconds |
| 1980 | 50.4 seconds |
| 1984 | 49.8 seconds |

**45.** Round the times in the table to their greatest place values. In which years were the winning times about 50 seconds?

★ **46.** In 1912 the winning time was 1 minute and 3.4 seconds. Is the difference between this time and the winning time in 1964 more than 1 minute?

# CHECKPOINT 1

Write the decimal. *(pages 222–225)*

**1.** 7 tenths

**2.** 14 and 6 tenths

**3.** 45 hundredths

**4.** 3 and 18 hundredths

Complete. Write $<$ , $>$ , or $=$ .
*(pages 226–229)*

**5.** 0.4 ▓ 0.6     **6.** 4.13 ▓ 4.03

**7.** 6.1 ▓ 6.10     **8.** 0.37 ▓ 0.7

Round to the place of the underlined digit. *(pages 230–231)*

**9.** 2̲7.8     **10.** 16.4̲1     **11.** 9̲2.4

*Extra practice on page 416*

# PROBLEM SOLVING
## Strategy: Estimating with Decimals

1. Understand
2. Plan
3. Work
4. Answer/Check

Virginia is helping her parents with their errands. Her mother asks her to buy about 5 lb of fruit. She weighs the fruit as she picks it out. She gets 1.38 lb of bananas and 3.67 lb of apples. Does she have enough fruit?

Sometimes you don't need an exact answer. An estimate is all you need to solve the problem. To estimate the sum, round to the greatest place value.

$$1.38 \longrightarrow \phantom{+} 1$$
$$3.67 \longrightarrow + 4$$
$$\overline{\phantom{+}5}$$

Virginia has about 5 lb of fruit. She has enough.

## CLASS EXERCISES

Choose the best estimate. Write *a*, *b*, or *c*. Explain how you found your answers.

1. Virginia buys 6.75 lb of potatoes, 3.23 lb of onions, and 2.64 lb of broccoli. About how many pounds of vegetables does she buy?

   **a.** 6 lb      **b.** 13 lb      **c.** 7 lb

2. Virginia buys 8.37 lb of chicken and 3.24 lb of beef. About how many more pounds of chicken than beef does she buy?

   **a.** 11 lb      **b.** 3 lb      **c.** 5 lb

## PRACTICE

Estimate to solve.

3. Virginia's family drives 2.8 mi from home to the grocery store. Then they drive 9.4 mi from the grocery store to the post office. About how far do they drive from home to the post office?

**4.** At the post office Virginia mails 3 packages. The packages cost $6.27, $3.64, and $4.32. About how much does it cost to mail all the packages?

**5.** A 2.75 lb package costs $3.01 to send by priority mail. It costs $1.73 to send by parcel post. About how much more will it cost to send the package by priority mail?

**6.** Virginia and her brother try out digital scales at the department store. Virginia weighs 61.8 lb and her brother weighs 72.3 lb. About how much more does Virginia's brother weigh?

**7.** At the Feed and Seed Store, the Michaels buy 3.27 lb of thistle seed, 4.65 lb of sunflower seed, and 6.87 lb of mixed seed. About how many pounds of seed do they buy?

**8.** At their last stop, the Michaels ordered crushed rock for the driveway. It was delivered in 2 loads. One load weighed 3.86 t and the other weighed 5.24 t. About how many tons of crushed rock were delivered?

★ **9.** The Feed and Seed Store charges $1.89 a pound for thistle seed and $1.09 a pound for mixed seed. Estimate which will cost more, 2.7 lb of thistle seed or 3.8 lb of mixed seed.

★ **10.** Crushed rock sells for $6.85 a ton. There is a delivery charge of $30. The Michaels receive 9.1 t of crushed rock. Estimate the total cost of the crushed rock.

---

Write the answer.

| | | |
|---|---|---|
| **11.** 525 − 108 | **12.** 56 ÷ 7 | **13.** 4876 + 3721 |
| **14.** 34 ÷ 4 | **15.** 46 ÷ 3 | **16.** 6 × $4.88 |
| **17.** $2.51 + $3.09 | **18.** $21 ÷ 3 | **19.** $17.50 − $3.21 |

**MIXED REVIEW**

# ADDING DECIMALS, SAME PLACE VALUES

One of Kevin's bookcases is 3.14 m long. The other bookcase is 2.77 m long. How much space does Kevin need to put the bookcases side by side?

To find out, add 3.14 and 2.77. Because you must add hundredths to hundredths, tenths to tenths, and ones to ones, it is important to keep the decimal points in line.

Line up the decimal points.

$$\begin{array}{r} 3.14 \\ +\ 2.77 \\ \hline \end{array}$$

Add.

$$\begin{array}{r} 1\phantom{.00} \\ 3.14 \\ +\ 2.77 \\ \hline 5.91 \end{array}$$

Remember to write the decimal point in the answer.

The space must be at least 5.91 m.

To estimate the sum of 3.14 and 2.77, think of a whole number that is close to both addends. That number is 3. **Think:** $2 \times 3 = 6$. The total space is about 6 m so your answer makes sense.

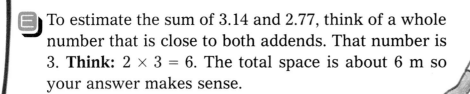

# CLASS EXERCISES

Are the decimal points lined up correctly? If not, tell what you would do to correct the problem.

1.
$$\begin{array}{r} 2.7 \\ +\ 3.8 \\ \hline \end{array}$$

2.
$$\begin{array}{r} 2.07 \\ +\ 5.70 \\ \hline \end{array}$$

3.
$$\begin{array}{r} 36.10 \\ +\ 8.70 \\ \hline \end{array}$$

4.
$$\begin{array}{r} 9.7 \\ +\ 0.3 \\ \hline \end{array}$$

5.
$$\begin{array}{r} 20.18 \\ +\ 3.57 \\ \hline \end{array}$$

Write the sum with a decimal point. Then read the sum.

6. $4.6 + 2.7 = 73$

7. $0.5 + 8.2 = 87$

8. $62.97 + 54.63 = 11760$

# PRACTICE

Add.

| | | | | |
|---|---|---|---|---|
| **9.** 2.3 <br> + 1.4 | **10.** 5.6 <br> + 0.5 | **11.** 7.61 <br> + 8.43 | **12.** 8.05 <br> + 7.61 | **13.** 15.43 <br> + 2.07 |
| **14.** 5.6 <br> + 7.3 | **15.** 7.9 <br> + 4.5 | **16.** 8.50 <br> + 3.45 | **17.** 5.64 <br> + 6.70 | **18.** 73.52 <br> + 8.05 |
| **19.** 8.7 <br> + 3.2 | **20.** 9.2 <br> + 0.9 | **21.** 3.69 <br> + 5.80 | **22.** 7.93 <br> + 8.70 | **23.** 7.60 <br> + 50.73 |

**24.** 8.5 + 6.6    **25.** 7.65 + 50.73    **26.** 56.79 + 2.80    **27.** 86.07 + 8.90

**28.** 53.2 + 76.4    **29.** 5.90 + 17.67    **30.** 7.06 + 8.49    **31.** 79.80 + 8.64

**32.** 16.37 + 4.90    **33.** 87.40 + 15.63    **34.** 23.60 + 9.67    **35.** 7.60 + 83.92

★ **36.** 14.86 + 8.07 + 32.65    ★ **37.** 67.59 + 95.04 + 7.16

Think of a whole number that is close to both addends.
Then multiply that number by 2 to estimate the sum.

**ESTIMATE**

**38.** 9.4 + 8.9    **39.** 6.5 + 7.4    **40.** 4.65 + 5.47

**41.** 10.24 + 9.87    **42.** 15.38 + 14.92    **43.** 99.6 + 100.4

## PROBLEM SOLVING APPLICATIONS
### Decimals and Length

Solve.

**44.** A couch is 1.85 m long and a table is 0.55 m long. How much space is needed to fit the couch and the table side by side?

**45.** A plant stand is 0.6 m wide. It sits under a window that is 0.58 m wide. Which is wider, the plant stand or the window?

**46.** Amy has 4 new books. The widths of the books are 6.2 cm, 2.4 cm, 5.8 cm, and 3.6 cm. How much space does she need to fit the books side by side?

★ **47.** Tamara wants to put a chair that is 46 cm wide next to a bookcase that is 104 cm wide. Will 2 m be enough space to fit both?

# SUBTRACTING DECIMALS, SAME PLACE VALUES

The average body temperature of humans is 37.0°C. Goldfish have an average body temperature of 23.5°C. How much lower is the average temperature of goldfish?

To find out, subtract 23.5 from 37.0.

Line up the decimal points.

$$\begin{array}{r} 37.0 \\ -\ 23.5 \\ \hline \end{array}$$

Subtract.

$$\begin{array}{r} {\scriptstyle 6\ 10} \\ 37.\cancel{0} \\ -\ 23.5 \\ \hline 13.5 \end{array}$$

Remember to write the decimal point in the answer.

The average temperature of goldfish is 13.5°C lower.

 You can add on mentally to check your answers. First add on the tenths, then add on the whole number.

**Think:** $23.5 \xrightarrow{+\ 0.5} 24.0 \xrightarrow{+\ 13.0} 37.0\checkmark = 13.5$

## CLASS EXERCISES

Which digits are in the tenths' place? How would you copy the problem correctly?

| 1. | 2. | 3. | 4. | 5. |
|---|---|---|---|---|
| 2.00 | 12.59 | 28.9 | 0.76 | 98.60 |
| − 0.24 | − 1.43 | − 8.1 | − 0.24 | − 7.23 |
| 1.76 | 11.16 | 20.8 | 0.52 | 91.37 |

Write the difference with a decimal point. Then read the difference.

**6.** 2.67 − 1.34 = 133      **7.** 25.49 − 22.29 = 320      **8.** 0.78 − 0.59 = 019

**9.** 6.1 − 3.8 = 23      **10.** 19.7 − 8.9 = 108      **11.** 7.62 − 0.06 = 756

## PRACTICE

Subtract.

| **12.** 0.9<br>− 0.6 | **13.** 7.7<br>− 4.3 | **14.** 6.8<br>− 3.5 | **15.** 23.8<br>− 1.8 | **16.** 56.9<br>− 34.5 |
|---|---|---|---|---|
| **17.** 8.1<br>− 2.5 | **18.** 3.6<br>− 2.8 | **19.** 56.1<br>− 49.7 | **20.** 10.3<br>− 7.6 | **21.** 24.2<br>− 5.2 |

**22.** 0.67 − 0.54   **23.** 6.98 − 3.76   **24.** 3.50 − 1.75   **25.** 8.02 − 2.64

**26.** 11.68 − 10.55   **27.** 24.45 − 3.45   **28.** 36.64 − 12.39   **29.** 25.25 − 2.46

**30.** 20.59 − 12.58   **31.** 25.95 − 0.88   **32.** 24.75 − 5.79   **33.** 36.11 − 9.72

Write + or − to make the number sentence true.

★ **34.** 89.07 − 7.01 > 94.25 ▨ 12.20     ★ **35.** 25.95 − 0.88 < 20.59 ▨ 12.58

★ **36.** 53.72 ▨ 8.61 < 69.36 − 18.37     ★ **37.** 41.07 ▨ 9.11 = 49.80 ▨ 17.84

Is the answer correct? Add on mentally to check. Write *yes* or *no*.

MENTAL MATH

| **38.** 7.0<br>− 2.3<br>5.7 | **39.** 23.0<br>− 9.8<br>13.2 | **40.** 10.00<br>− 9.86<br>0.14 | **41.** 50.00<br>− 39.91<br>20.09 |
|---|---|---|---|

## PROBLEM SOLVING APPLICATIONS
### Working with Temperature

Solve.

**42.** A goat's temperature is 39.9°C. A polar bear has a temperature of 37.3°C. What is the difference between these two temperatures?

**43.** A crocodile's temperature is 25.6°C. An owl's temperature is 14.6°C higher. What is the owl's temperature?

★ **44.** A spiny anteater has a temperature of 23.3°C. Double the temperature and then subtract 8.6°C. This was Jay's temperature when he had the flu. What was Jay's temperature?

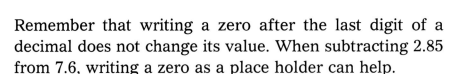

# ADDING AND SUBTRACTING, DIFFERENT PLACE VALUES

Remember that writing a zero after the last digit of a decimal does not change its value. When subtracting 2.85 from 7.6, writing a zero as a place holder can help.

Line up the
decimal points.

$$
\begin{array}{r}
7.6 \\
- 2.85 \\
\end{array}
$$

Write a zero in the
hundredths' place.

$$
\begin{array}{r}
7.60 \\
- 2.85 \\
\end{array}
$$

Subtract.

$$
\begin{array}{r}
{\scriptstyle 6\ 15\ 10} \\
7.\cancel{6}\,\cancel{0} \\
- 2.8\,5 \\
\hline
4.7\,5 \\
\end{array}
$$

When you add or subtract, write a decimal point and the zeros you need.

$$
\begin{array}{r}
63 \\
+ 10.7 \\
\end{array}
\quad\Rightarrow\quad
\begin{array}{r}
63.0 \\
+ 10.7 \\
\hline
73.7 \\
\end{array}
$$

$$
\begin{array}{r}
37 \\
- 8.59 \\
\end{array}
\quad\Rightarrow\quad
\begin{array}{r}
{\scriptstyle 16\ 9} \\
{\scriptstyle 2\ \cancel{6}\ \cancel{10}\ 10} \\
\cancel{3}\,7.\cancel{0}\,\cancel{0} \\
- \quad 8.5\,9 \\
\hline
2\,8.4\,1 \\
\end{array}
$$

When you use a calculator, you don't need to enter zeros after the last digit of the decimal.

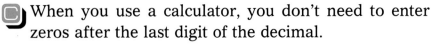

37.00 − 8.59 = 28.41     or     37 − 8.59 = 28.41

**Think:** What is another way to enter this problem on the calculator?

## CLASS EXERCISES

Copy the problem. Line up the decimal points. Then add or subtract.

| | | | | |
|---|---|---|---|---|
| **1.** 7 <br> + 8.9 | **2.** 6.9 <br> + 9.26 | **3.** 8.45 <br> + 9.7 | **4.** 24 <br> + 8.3 | **5.** 6.78 <br> + 18 |
| **6.** 8 <br> − 4.6 | **7.** 8.6 <br> − 3.18 | **8.** 5.19 <br> − 2.3 | **9.** 43 <br> − 6.7 | **10.** 13 <br> − 5.61 |

# PRACTICE

Add or subtract.

| | | | | |
|---|---|---|---|---|
| **11.** 5.6 <br> + 4 | **12.** 8.7 <br> − 6 | **13.** 9.64 <br> + 7.9 | **14.** 7.96 <br> − 5.5 | **15.** 18.97 <br> + 7.6 |
| **16.** 9 <br> − 4.5 | **17.** 4.8 <br> + 7 | **18.** 4.51 <br> + 8.6 | **19.** 9.8 <br> − 5.92 | **20.** 24.8 <br> − 16.24 |

**21.** 0.9 + 7   **22.** 7 − 1.2   **23.** 14.1 − 9   **24.** 0.9 − 0.86

**25.** 15 − 9.8   **26.** 3.9 + 8   **27.** 56.4 + 18   **28.** 6.1 − 4.36

**29.** 4 + 9.6   **30.** 56.3 + 18.76   **31.** 63.1 − 9.83   **32.** 82 − 9.56

Complete.

★ **33.** $4.3 + \rule{1cm}{0.15mm} = 2.16 + 4.3$   ★ **34.** $37.25 = \rule{1cm}{0.15mm} + 37.25$

★ **35.** $19.8 - \rule{1cm}{0.15mm} = 35.2 - 27.51$   ★ **36.** $14.58 - \rule{1cm}{0.15mm} = 4 + 9.6$

Is the answer correct? Write *yes* or *no*. Write *e*, *m*, or *c* to tell whether you use estimation, mental math, or a calculator to check.

**CALCULATOR**

**37.** 9 − 0.8 $\boxed{8.2}$   **38.** 7.36 + 4 $\boxed{11.6}$

**39.** 8 − 7.45 $\boxed{0.55}$   **40.** 92.81 − 37.98 $\boxed{64.83}$

## PROBLEM SOLVING APPLICATIONS
### Choosing a Strategy

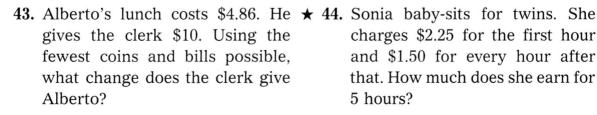

Solve.

**41.** Craig earns $10.50 baby-sitting, $8.45 walking the neighbor's dog, and $14 mowing lawns. How much more does he earn mowing lawns than walking the dog?

**42.** Lila has $5. She wants to buy oil paint for $2.79 and a paintbrush for $1.69. Does she have enough money to buy the paint and the brush?

**43.** Alberto's lunch costs $4.86. He gives the clerk $10. Using the fewest coins and bills possible, what change does the clerk give Alberto?

★ **44.** Sonia baby-sits for twins. She charges $2.25 for the first hour and $1.50 for every hour after that. How much does she earn for 5 hours?

# PROBLEM SOLVING
### Strategy: Organizing Information in a Table

1. Understand
2. Plan
3. Work
4. Answer/Check

Emily Robinson's car needs an oil change and a safety inspection. Emily reads these ads to decide where to take her car. She decides to make a table to organize the information.

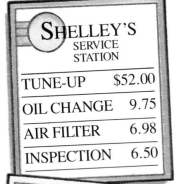

**SHELLEY'S SERVICE STATION**

| | |
|---|---|
| TUNE-UP | $52.00 |
| OIL CHANGE | 9.75 |
| AIR FILTER | 6.98 |
| INSPECTION | 6.50 |

**Todd's Tune-Ups**

| | |
|---|---|
| TUNE-UP | $39.95 |
| INSPECTION | 5.98 |
| AIR FILTER | 7.95 |
| OIL CHANGE | 12.00 |

**COSTS FOR SERVICE**

| Place | Safety Inspection | Oil Change | Total |
|---|---|---|---|
| Shelley's | $6.50 | $9.75 | $16.25 |
| Todd's | $5.98 | $12.00 | $17.98 |

Her table has rows that go across and columns that go down. She writes titles of the columns across the top of the table. Emily can see from the *Total* column in her table that it will cost less to take her car to Shelley's.

## CLASS EXERCISES

Jan, Fred, and Gil work at the 3rd Street Garage. They are paid $3 for each oil change, $5 for a safety inspection, $4 for tire rotations, and $20 for tune-ups.

> +++ means 5

Schedule for Monday

| | Jan | Fred | Gil |
|---|---|---|---|
| Oil Changes | /// | | // |
| Safety Inspections | | +++ | /// |
| Tire Rotations | // | / | / |
| Tune-ups | / | / | |

Use the work schedule for Monday to complete the table.

**MONEY EARNED**

| | Mechanic | Oil Changes | Safety Inspections | Tire Rotations | Tune-Ups | Total |
|---|---|---|---|---|---|---|
| 1. | Jan | $9 | ? | ? | ? | ? |
| 2. | Fred | ? | ? | ? | $20 | ? |
| 3. | Gil | ? | ? | $4 | ? | ? |

4. How much did Jan, Fred, and Gil earn in all for tune-ups?

# PRACTICE

The owner of the garage keeps a record of how much gasoline is sold each day. Copy and complete the table. Use the owner's records.

**WEEKLY RECORD OF GASOLINE SOLD**

| | Days | Liters of Regular | Liters of Unleaded | Number of Liters Per Day |
|---|---|---|---|---|
| | Monday | 3496.5 | 6542.3 | 10,038.8 |
| 5. | Tuesday | ? | ? | ? |
| 6. | Wednesday | ? | ? | ? |
| 7. | Thursday | ? | ? | ? |
| 8. | Friday | ? | ? | ? |

> Monday
> Regular
> 3496.5 L
> Unleaded
> 6542.3 L

> Tuesday
> Regular
> 3512.06 L
> Unleaded
> 7583.73 l.

> Wednesday
> Regular
> 5406.7 L
> Unleaded
> 7917.31 L

> Thursday
> Regular
> 5367.9 L
> Unleaded
> 7432.25 L

> Friday
> Regular
> 6542.27 L
> Unleaded
> 8718.5 L

Use the table to answer the question.

9. On which day was the most gasoline sold?

10. Was more regular or unleaded gas sold this week?

11. How many liters of gas were sold altogether this week?

★ 12. The owner has hired part-time help. Which days would be best for them to work? Why?

# CHECKPOINT 2

**Estimate to solve.** *(pages 232–233)*

1. Manuel bicycled 18.2 km on Saturday and 11.6 km on Sunday. About how far did he bicycle?

**Add or subtract.** *(pages 234–239)*

2.  16.4
  + 39.8

3.  5.4
  − 3.2

4.  16
  − 2.5

**Make a table to solve.** *(pages 240–241)*

5. On Monday Jan worked 5 hours and Fred worked 6 hours. On Tuesday Jan worked 7 hours and Fred worked 5 hours. What was the total number of hours for each person for the two days?

**HOURS WORKED**

| Name | Monday | Tuesday | Total |
|---|---|---|---|
| | | | |

*Extra practice on page 416*

# CHAPTER 8 TEST

Write the decimal. *(pages 222–225)*

**1.** 9 tenths

**2.** 6 and 4 tenths

**3.** twenty-eight and five tenths

**4.** 72 hundredths

**5.** 5 and 13 hundredths

**6.** two hundred and two hundredths

Compare. Write <, >, or =.
*(pages 226–229)*

**7.** 0.6 ▢ 6.6

**8.** 0.81 ▢ 0.18

**9.** 2.23 ▢ 2.3

Round to the place of the underlined digit. *(pages 230–231)*

**10.** 1<u>5</u>.7

**11.** <u>4</u>3.4

**12.** 26.<u>7</u>8

**13.** 35.<u>5</u>1

Use estimation to solve the problem. *(pages 232–233)*

**14.** Brian's fish tank holds 9.25 L of water. Beverly's tank holds 4.75 L of water. About how much less water does Beverly's tank hold than Brian's?

**15.** Joe Fillmore added 3.6 L of water to the guppy tank, 4.2 L to the goldfish tank, and 2.9 L to the minnow tank. About how much water did he add to the three tanks?

Write the answer. *(pages 234–239)*

**16.**
$$9.2 + 33.7$$

**17.**
$$11.05 - 4.38$$

**18.**
$$8.7 + 6.41$$

**19.**
$$32.4 - 15.52$$

Make a table to solve the problem. *(pages 240–241)*

**20.** On Monday Dan biked 17.5 km and Joy biked 23.7 km. On Tuesday Dan biked 19.2 km and Joy biked 10.5 km. What was the total distance each one biked in two days?

*Extra practice on page 417*

# MATHEMATICS and PHYSICAL EDUCATION

The members of the Clifton Cubs baseball team keep track of their batting and scores. This table shows information for 6 of the players on the team. Each number is the player's total for 8 games played so far this season.

| PLAYER | TIMES AT BAT | RUNS | HITS | HOME RUNS |
|--------|--------------|------|------|-----------|
| Kevin | 27 | 2 | 4 | 1 |
| Mary Ann | 32 | 3 | 6 | 1 |
| Alicia | 25 | 1 | 5 | 0 |
| Man-Sun | 24 | 2 | 4 | 0 |
| James | 36 | 4 | 8 | 2 |
| Cathy | 18 | 1 | 3 | 0 |

## WHAT'S THE SCORE?

Use the table to answer the question.

1. Who was at bat the fewest times?

2. Did Mary Ann have more than twice as many hits as Cathy?

3. Which two people had the same number of hits?

4. Who had fewer home runs than Kevin?

5. Which players were at bat 6 times as often as they had hits?

6. What was the total number of hits for the 6 players?

# Enrichment

Of the first 100 students to arrive at the class picnic, 84 were wearing sneakers. You can write the decimal 0.84 to show 84 hundredths, or you can write a **percent.** Percent means per hundred.

$$0.84 = 84\%$$

This symbol means percent.

You read 84% as *eighty-four percent.*

In this square, 0.70 is shaded. You can say that 70 hundredths or 70% of the square is shaded.

30% of the square is not shaded.

**Think:** What percent shows the sum of the part that is shaded and the part that is not shaded?

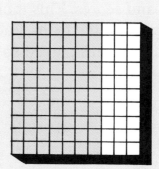

Complete.

1.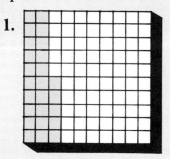

0.25 = ▨ hundredths = ▨ %

2.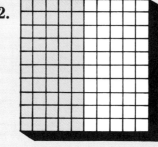

0.50 = ▨ hundredths = ▨ %

**3.** 0.40 = ▨ hundredths = ▨ %     **4.** 0.85 = ▨ hundredths = ▨ %

**5.** 0.95 = ▨ hundredths = ▨ %     **6.** 0.07 = ▨ hundredths = ▨ %

Write as a percent.

**7.** 0.30     **8.** 0.20     **9.** 0.70     **10.** 0.80

**11.** 0.64     **12.** 0.82     **13.** 0.66     **14.** 0.52

**15.** 0.23     **16.** 0.05

**17.** 0.08     **18.** 0.02

# PERCENT

Write as a decimal.

**19.** 90%     **20.** 30%     **21.** 20%     **22.** 60%     **23.** 75%     **24.** 32%

**25.** 84%     **26.** 93%     **27.** 7%     **28.** 4%     **29.** 1%     **30.** 100%

Match the decimal first to the percent, then to the words.

| | | |
|---|---|---|
| **31.** 0.44 | **A.** 4% | **G.** eight percent |
| **32.** 0.89 | **B.** 89% | **H.** four percent |
| **33.** 0.08 | **C.** 40% | **I.** forty-four percent |
| **34.** 0.40 | **D.** 80% | **J.** forty percent |
| **35.** 0.80 | **E.** 44% | **K.** eighty-nine percent |
| **36.** 0.04 | **F.** 8% | **L.** eighty percent |

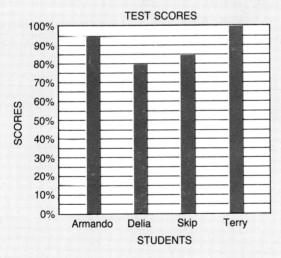

The graph shows the scores of four students on a test.

**37.** Who received the highest score? What was the score?

**38.** Who received the lowest score? What was the score?

**39.** Who received the third highest score? What was the score?

**40.** Who received a perfect score on the test?

**41.** Can you tell how many items were on the test? Tell why or why not.

# CUMULATIVE REVIEW

Choose the correct answer. Write *a*, *b*, *c*, or *d*.

Find the answer.

**1.** $16 \div 2$
 **a.** 6
 **b.** 8
 **c.** 9
 **d.** none of these

**2.** $21 \div 3$
 **a.** 3
 **b.** 5
 **c.** 7
 **d.** none of these

**3.** $20 \div 4$
 **a.** 4
 **b.** 5
 **c.** 6
 **d.** none of these

**4.** $\boxed{\phantom{x}} \times 3 = 3$
 **a.** 1
 **b.** 3
 **c.** 9
 **d.** none of these

**5.** $\boxed{\phantom{x}} \times 5 = 45$
 **a.** 4
 **b.** 5
 **c.** 9
 **d.** none of these

**6.** $\boxed{\phantom{x}} \times 4 = 24$
 **a.** 4
 **b.** 5
 **c.** 8
 **d.** none of these

Solve.

**7.** Martin buys 5 photo albums. Each album costs $6. How much does Martin spend?
 **a.** $1
 **b.** $11
 **c.** $30
 **d.** none of these

**8.** Jenny bought 4 scrapbooks for $28. She paid the same amount for each scrapbook. How much did each scrapbook cost?
 **a.** $7
 **b.** $24
 **c.** $32
 **d.** none of these

Find the answer.

**9.** $42 \div 6$
 **a.** 8
 **b.** 7
 **c.** 6
 **d.** none of these

**10.** $49 \div 7$
 **a.** 7
 **b.** 8
 **c.** 9
 **d.** none of these

**11.** $72 \div 8$
 **a.** 6
 **b.** 8
 **c.** 9
 **d.** none of these

**12.** $7\overline{)56}$
 **a.** 6
 **b.** 7
 **c.** 8
 **d.** none of these

**13.** $8\overline{)48}$
 **a.** 4
 **b.** 6
 **c.** 8
 **d.** none of these

**14.** $9\overline{)81}$
 **a.** 6
 **b.** 8
 **c.** 9
 **d.** none of these

Find the answer.

**15.** $7\overline{)54}$
 a. 7 R5
 b. 8 R1
 c. 7 R4
 d. none of these

**16.** $6\overline{)56}$
 a. 7
 b. 8 R7
 c. 8 R6
 d. none of these

**17.** $8\overline{)66}$
 a. 9 R2
 b. 8 R2
 c. 8 R4
 d. none of these

**18.** $5\overline{)47}$
 a. 9
 b. 9 R1
 c. 9 R2
 d. none of these

**19.** $3\overline{)22}$
 a. 7 R1
 b. 7 R7
 c. 8 R1
 d. none of these

**20.** $9\overline{)62}$
 a. 6 R7
 b. 7
 c. 6 R8
 d. none of these

Find the common factors.

**21.** 6 and 12
 a. 6, 12
 b. 3, 6, 12
 c. 1, 2, 3, 6
 d. none of these

**22.** 8 and 24
 a. 1, 2, 4, 8
 b. 1, 2, 4, 6, 8
 c. 1, 2, 4, 6, 12
 d. none of these

**23.** 21 and 27
 a. 1, 3, 7, 9
 b. 1, 3
 c. 3, 7, 9
 d. none of these

# LANGUAGE and VOCABULARY REVIEW

Use the words to complete the sentence. Write the word on your paper.

tenths    hundredths    factors    common factors    round

decimal    number sentence    ordinal numbers

**1.** One tenth can be written as a ___?___ .

**2.** Five ___?___ (or 0.5) is greater than five ___?___ (or 0.05).

**3.** You can ___?___ 5.81 up to 6 when you estimate.

**4.** 1, 2, 4, 5, 10, and 20 are ___?___ of 20.

**5.** Numbers like first, second, third, and fourth are called ___?___ .

**6.** $18 + 3 = 21$ is called a ___?___ .

# DATABASE

A computer can store very large amounts of data. A **database** is a group of data that the computer has put in a certain order according to a plan you give it. When data are put in order, you can quickly get the information you need.

Part of a database from a library is shown below. It shows books that have been borrowed. The words at the top of the table are called **keywords.**

This database shows titles of the books first. This is one way to put the books in order.

| BOOK | BORROWED | RETURNED | STUDENT |
|---|---|---|---|
| Magic Tricks | May 20 | May 27 | Tommy Lee |
| Making Puppets | May 7 | No | Jennie Barker |
| Maps to Draw | May 1 | May 14 | Mary Sue Miller |
| Math Puzzles | May 11 | May 22 | Pat Parrish |

Solve.

1. What do you call the order in which the titles are listed?

2. How many keywords are shown? What are they?

3. Choose two keywords about the books that you might add to the database.
   a. author   b. age   c. subject   d. number of books

4. Here are data for another database. They are not in any order. Write 3 keywords for the data. Then order the data by students' names.

| | | |
|---|---|---|
| Class 3A | Bob Smith | 105 Second Avenue |
| Diane Lapari | Class 4B | 392 Park Avenue |
| James Maloney | 15 Artista Drive | Class 3B |
| 24 Cherry Lane | Lin Chow | Class 4A |

9

The right and left sides of this window are alike. Lead holds the pieces of glass together. There are 4 pieces of glass from the top to the center. How many pieces are there across the bottom of the window?

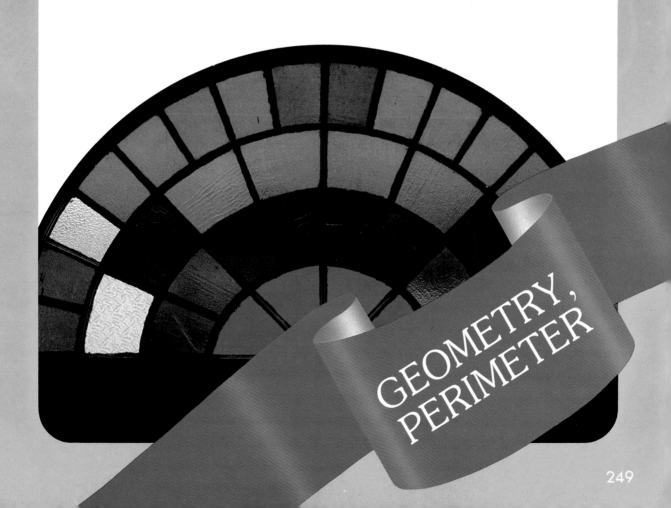

GEOMETRY, PERIMETER

# POINTS AND LINES

A and B are **points.**

A •        B •

The straight path between points A and B is a line **segment.** A and B are its endpoints. You write *segment AB* or *segment BA.*

A •————————• B

segment AB or BA

A segment is part of a **line.** The arrows show that the line goes on and on in both directions. A and B are points on the line. You write *line AB* or *line BA.*

←•————————•→ A        B

line AB or BA

A **ray** is part of a line. It has only one endpoint. It goes on and on in one direction. You write *ray AB.*

A •————————•——→ B

ray AB

 You can draw 6 line segments through 4 points. Each line segment connects 2 of the points. **Think:** How many line segments can you draw through 3 points?

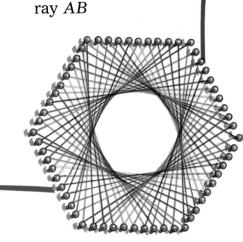

## CLASS EXERCISES

Complete the name.

**1.**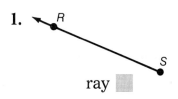

ray ▨

**2.**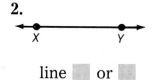

line ▨ or ▨

**3.**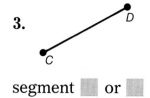

segment ▨ or ▨

Complete.

**4.** A figure with one endpoint that goes on and on in one direction is called a __?__.

**5.** The part of a straight line between two endpoints is called a __?__.

**6.** A straight path with no endpoints is called a __?__.

# PRACTICE

Name the figure.

**7.**

**8.**

**9.**

**10.**

**11.**

**12.**

**13.**

**14.**

**15.**

Draw and label the segment, line, or ray.

**16.** line segment *RP*

**17.** ray *KL*

**18.** line *OR*

**19.** line *MZ*

**20.** line segment *LM*

**21.** ray *XP*

Use mental math to complete the chart. Look
for patterns. Write only the answer.

**MENTAL MATH**

|                              | **22.** | **23.** |   | **24.** | ★ **25.** |
| ---------------------------- | --- | --- | --- | --- | --- |
| Number of points             | 2   | 3   | 4   | 5   | 6   |
| Total number of line segments | ?   | ?   | 6   | ?   | ?   |

## PROBLEM SOLVING APPLICATIONS
### Mental Math or Pencil

Use mental math or paper and pencil to solve. Write *m* or *p*
to tell which method you chose.

**26.** Each dash in a dashed white line
on a road is a segment. If each
segment is 8 ft long, how long
will 9 segments be?

**27.** There is a total of 56 ft of space
between segments on the road.
Each space is 7 ft long. How
many spaces are there?

★ **28.** Each segment is 8 ft long. Each
space between the segments is
7 ft long. Find the total distance
from the beginning of the first
segment to the end of the sixth
segment.

# CLASSIFYING ANGLES

When you put two rays together such as those at the right, you form an **angle.**

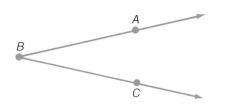

An angle is named by the three points shown on it. The letter of the point where the rays meet always goes in the middle. This point is called the **vertex.**

angle *ABC* or angle *CBA*

The corner of a ticket forms a **right** angle. Angle *LMN* is a right angle.

An angle less than a right angle is **acute.** Angle *QRS* is an acute angle.

An angle greater than a right angle is **obtuse.** Angle *XYZ* is an obtuse angle.

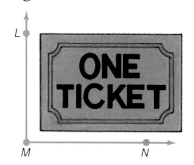

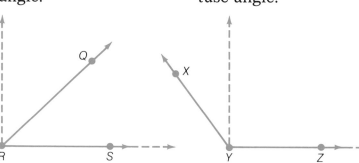

 You can estimate whether an angle is obtuse or acute. Use a right angle or the corner of a piece of paper as a guide.
**Think:** Is the angle *less than* or *greater than* a right angle?

## CLASS EXERCISES

Is it a right angle? Write *yes* or *no*. Test with the corner of a sheet of paper.

1.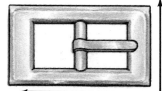

2.

3.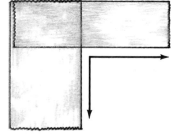

Complete.

4. An angle that is greater than a right angle is __?__.

5. An angle that is less than a right angle is __?__.

# PRACTICE

Name the angle and the vertex. Then write *R* for right, *A* for acute, or *O* for obtuse.

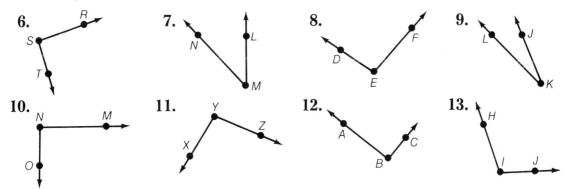

6.   7.   8.   9.

10.   11.   12.   13.

Draw the figure.

**14.** obtuse angle *MPN*    **15.** acute angle *DEF*    **16.** segment *XY*

Estimate to decide whether the angle is right, acute, or obtuse. Use the corner of a piece of paper to check your answer.

ESTIMATE

 **17.**     **18.**    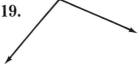 **19.**

## PROBLEM SOLVING APPLICATIONS
### Using Angles

Use the picture to answer the questions.

**20.** Name 4 right angles.

**21.** Name 4 acute angles.

**22.** Name 3 obtuse angles.

★ **23.** If angle *HGF* and angle *FGA* are put together, what kind of angle do they make?

★ **24.** Name an angle that looks the same size as angle *EFC*.

★ **25.** Name an angle that looks the same size as angle *DCF*.

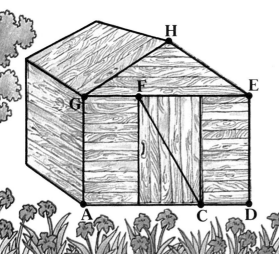

# PARALLEL AND PERPENDICULAR LINES

Lines that never meet are called **parallel.**

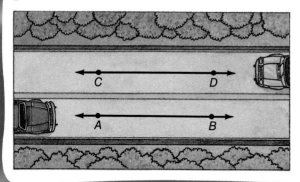

Lines that meet at right angles are called **perpendicular.**

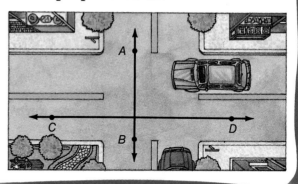

## CLASS EXERCISES

Match the lines and the description.

1.   2.   3.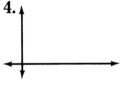

**A.** perpendicular

**B.** parallel

**C.** neither parallel nor perpendicular

## PRACTICE

Write *parallel* if two lines seem to be parallel. Write *perpendicular* if two lines seem to be perpendicular.

4. 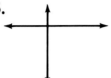  5. 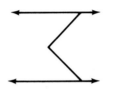  6. 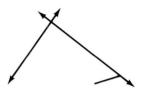  7.

8.   9. 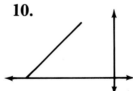  10. 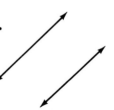  11.

**12.** 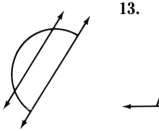  **13.** 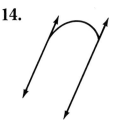  **14.** 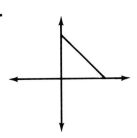  **15.**

Solve.

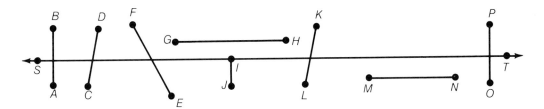

## A E F H I L N T V

**16.** Which of the letters above have parallel line segments?

**17.** Which of the letters above have perpendicular line segments?

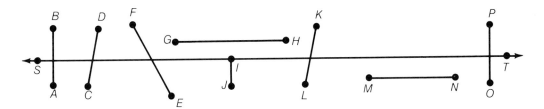

**18.** Name the line segments that are perpendicular to line *ST*.

**19.** Name the line segments that are parallel to line *ST*.

## PROBLEM SOLVING APPLICATIONS
### Using Pictures

Look carefully at the picture to answer the question.

**20.** *PR* seems parallel to which other segment?

**21.** *EF* seems perpendicular to which other segment?

**22.** *CB* seems parallel to which segments?

**23.** *DC* seems perpendicular to which four segments?

**24.** *DC* seems parallel to which two segments? (*WA, WB, WZ, AB, AZ,* and *BZ* all name the same segment.)

★ **25.** Name six right angles.

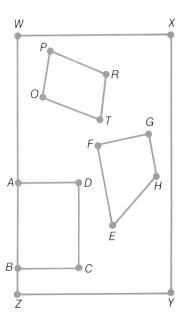

# LOCATING POINTS

A **grid** is formed with parallel and perpendicular lines. A grid can help you find points on a map. To locate points on a grid, you start at 0. Count across first and then count up.

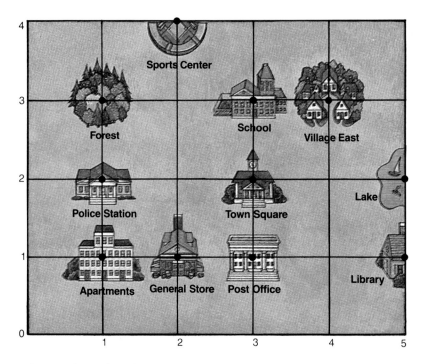

The **ordered pair** (3, 1) shows you where the post office is. To find the post office, go 3 spaces across and 1 space up.

The forest is at point (1, 3). To find the forest, go 1 space across and 3 spaces up.

## CLASS EXERCISES

Use the grid above. Name the place at this point.

**1.** 1 space across, 2 spaces up

**2.** 2 spaces across, 1 space up

**3.** 5 spaces across, 1 space up

**4.** 4 spaces across, 3 spaces up

## PRACTICE

Use the grid above. Name the place at the point.

**5.** (1, 1)  **6.** (4, 3)  **7.** (2, 4)  **8.** (3, 2)  **9.** (5, 2)  **10.** (3, 3)

Complete.

11. Bank is at (▒, ▒).

12. Diner is at (▒, ▒).

13. Park is at (▒, ▒).

14. Library is at (▒, ▒).

15. Hospital is at (▒, ▒).

16. School is at (▒, ▒).

17. Hotel is at (▒, ▒).

18. Movies are at (▒, ▒).

19. Store is at (▒, ▒).

20. Airport is at (▒, ▒).

★ 21. Pool is at (▒, ▒).

★ 22. Home is at (▒, ▒).

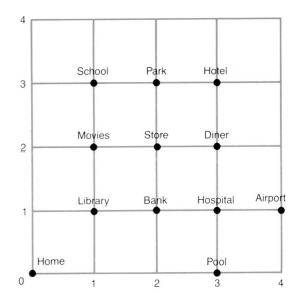

Complete. Write <, >, or =.

| | | |
|---|---|---|
| 23. 291 ▒ 306 | 24. 4285 ▒ 428 | 25. 1193 ▒ 1095 |
| 26. 11.3 ▒ 11.7 | 27. 0.38 ▒ 0.24 | 28. 6.19 ▒ 6.08 |

MIXED REVIEW

## PROBLEM SOLVING APPLICATIONS
### Using a Map

Use the map to solve the problem.

29. Which city is located near (6, A)?

30. At what point is South Portland located?

31. Is Westbrook closer to point (1, D) or (1, C)?

32. Which is closer to (4, F), South Portland or Portland International Jetport?

★ 33. What type of angle is formed if you draw segments from (2, B) to Westbrook to (3, E)?

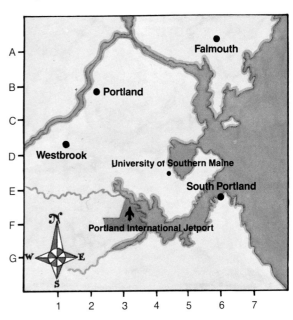

# PROBLEM SOLVING
## Strategy: Sorting and Classifying

1. Understand
2. Plan
3. Work
4. Answer/ Check

You can use the words *all*, *some*, and *no* to sort and classify things. Diagrams like the ones below can help.

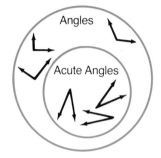

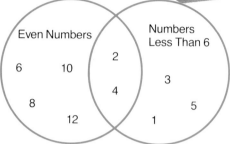

*All* acute angles are angles.

*Some* even numbers are less than 6.

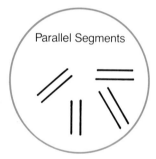

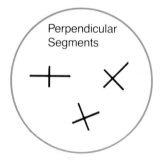

*No* parallel segments are perpendicular.

## CLASS EXERCISES

Write *all*, *some*, or *no* to complete the sentence. Then write the letter of the diagram that is correct for the sentence.

**A.**

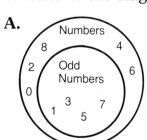

**B.**

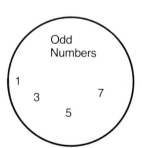

1. __?__ numbers are odd numbers.

2. __?__ odd numbers are numbers.

# PRACTICE

Write *all, some,* or *no* to complete the sentence.

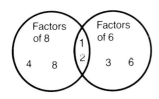

**3.** ___?___ factors of 6 are factors of 8.

**4.** ___?___ factors of 8 are factors of 6.

**5.** ___?___ odd numbers are even numbers.

**6.** ___?___ even numbers are odd numbers.

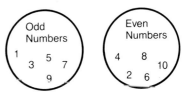

True or false? Write *T* or *F*.

**7.** Some angles are obtuse angles.

**8.** No lines have endpoints.

**9.** All perpendicular lines form right angles.

**10.** All obtuse angles are right angles.

**11.** No acute angles are greater than right angles.

**12.** Some perpendicular lines are parallel.

**13.** All numbers less than 15 are greater than 9.

**14.** All multiples of 8 are multiples of 4.

## CHECKPOINT 1

Name the figure. *(pages 250–251)*

**1.** **2.**

Name the angles. Then write *R* for right, *A* for acute, or *O* for obtuse. *(pages 252–253)*

**3.** **4.**

Write *parallel* or *perpendicular* to describe the lines.
*(pages 254–255)*

 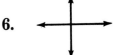

**5.** **6.**

Write *all, some,* or *no.*
*(pages 258–259)*

**7.** ___?___ perpendicular lines are parallel.

**8.** ___?___ obtuse angles are angles.

*Extra practice on page 418*

# POLYGONS

A **polygon** is a shape formed by three or more line segments called its **sides.** The sides of a polygon meet to form angles. The points where the sides meet are called **vertexes.**

These are polygons.          These are not polygons.

A polygon with three sides is a **triangle.**

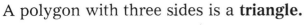

A polygon with four sides is a **quadrilateral.**

A polygon with five sides is a **pentagon.**

## CLASS EXERCISES

Is it a polygon? Answer *yes* or *no*. Explain why or why not.

1.     2.     3.

4.     5.     6.

# PRACTICE

Match. Write *A, B, C, D, E,* or *F.*

**7.** A quadrilateral with just two parallel sides

**8.** A triangle with a right angle

**9.** A pentagon with two right angles

**10.** A quadrilateral with four right angles

**11.** A triangle with three acute angles

**12.** A triangle with an obtuse angle

A 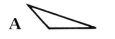   B

C    D

E    F

Classify the shape. Write *T* for triangle, *Q* for quadrilateral, or *P* for pentagon.

**13.** 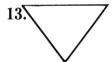   **14.** 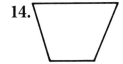   **15.** 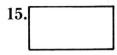   **16.**

**17.** 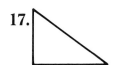   **18.** 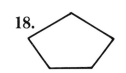   ★ **19.** 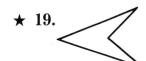   ★ **20.**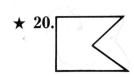

## PROBLEM SOLVING APPLICATIONS
### Sides and Angles

Copy and complete the chart.

|  | **21.** | **22.** | **23.** | ★ **24.** | ★ **25.** |
|---|---|---|---|---|---|
| NAME OF POLYGON | triangle | ? | ? | hexagon | octagon |
| Number of Sides | 3 | 4 | ? | 6 | ? |
| Number of Angles | ? | ? | 5 | ? | ? |
| Number of Vertexes | ? | ? | ? | ? | 8 |

★ **26.** Copy each shape and try to join *A* to *B* with a curve that goes through each side only once like the one shown on the triangle. When does it work?

# PARALLELOGRAMS

A **parallelogram** is a special kind of quadrilateral.

*ABCD* is a parallelogram. The opposite sides are parallel and the same length.

Sides *AB* and *DC* are parallel.
Sides *BC* and *AD* are parallel.

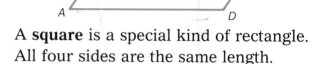

A **rectangle** is a parallelogram with four right angles.

A **square** is a special kind of rectangle. All four sides are the same length.

**Think:** How many parallelograms do you see in the stained glass?

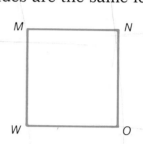

## CLASS EXERCISES

Write the letter or letters of the polygon that best match the description.

1. quadrilateral
2. parallelogram
3. rectangle
4. square
5. rectangle, but not a square
6. parallelogram, but not a rectangle or a square

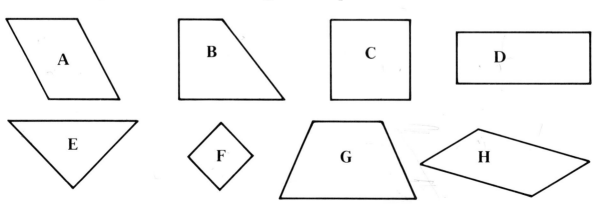

## PRACTICE

Complete.

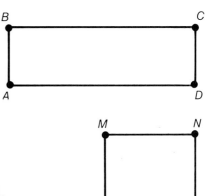

7. Rectangle *ABCD* has ▦ right angles.

8. Side *AB* is parallel to side ▦.

9. Side *AD* is parallel to side ▦.

10. Square *LMNO* has ▦ right angles.

11. Side *LM* is parallel to side ▦.

12. Side *NO* is perpendicular to sides ▦ and ▦.

13. Side *LO* is the same length as sides ▦, ▦, and ▦.

True or false? Write *T* or *F*.

14. All rectangles are parallelograms.

15. All parallelograms are rectangles.

16. All squares are rectangles.

17. All rectangles are squares.

18. All parallelograms are quadrilaterals.

19. All quadrilaterals are parallelograms.

★ 20. Some quadrilaterals have parallel sides.

★ 21. No pentagons have parallel sides.

## PROBLEM SOLVING APPLICATIONS
### Nonroutine Problems

There are three triangles hidden in the figure at the right.

Use the figure at the right below to answer.

22. How many triangles are hidden in the figure?

23. How many parallelograms are hidden?

★ 24. How many pentagons are hidden?

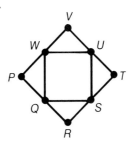

# PERIMETER

The picture at the right shows a new pool being built at the zoo. How many meters of fencing would you need to go around it?

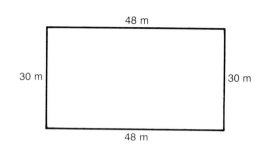

48 m

30 m       30 m

48 m

The **perimeter** of a shape is the distance around it. You find the perimeter of the pool by adding the lengths of the sides.

$$30 + 48 + 30 + 48 = 156$$

You need 156 m of fencing.

You can use a calculator to find the perimeter of the square shown at the right. Enter the length of one side. Press $\boxed{+}$. On some calculators you can press $\boxed{=}$ once for each of the sides.

8 cm

8 cm    8 cm

8 cm

$8\ \boxed{+}\ \boxed{=}\ \boxed{=}\ \boxed{=}\ \boxed{=}\ 32$

**Think:** What is another way to find the perimeter of the square above?

## CLASS EXERCISES

What is the perimeter? Explain how you find your answer.

**1.**

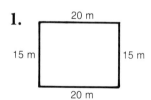

20 m

15 m    15 m

20 m

**2.**

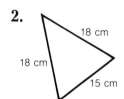

18 cm

18 cm

15 cm

**3.**

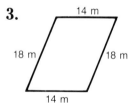

14 m

18 m    18 m

14 m

## PRACTICE

Find the perimeter.

**4.**

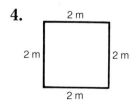

2 m

2 m    2 m

2 m

**5.**

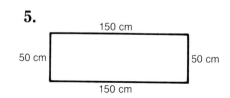

150 cm

50 cm    50 cm

150 cm

**6.**

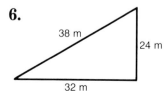

38 m

24 m

32 m

**7.**
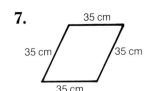
35 cm
35 cm
35 cm
35 cm

**8.**
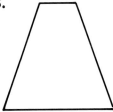
13 cm
14 cm
13 cm

**9.**
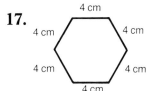
15 cm
11 cm
15 cm
23 cm

**10.**
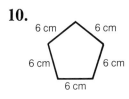
6 cm
6 cm
6 cm
6 cm
6 cm

★ **11.** A square, 24 cm each side

★ **12.** A pentagon, each side 12 m

Measure the sides to the nearest centimeter. Find the perimeter.

**13.**
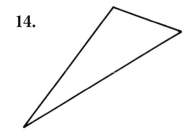

**14.**
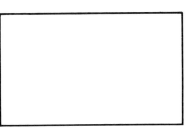

**15.**

The  on your calculator is broken. What keys can you press to find the perimeter? What is the perimeter?

**16.**

3 cm
3 cm
3 cm

**17.**
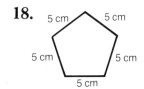
4 cm
4 cm
4 cm
4 cm
4 cm
4 cm

**18.**

5 cm
5 cm
5 cm
5 cm
5 cm

CALCULATOR

## PROBLEM SOLVING APPLICATIONS
### Working with Geometric Figures

Solve.

**19.** The area for the bears has five sides. Each side is a different length. What is the shape of the area for the bears?

**20.** The seal pool looks as if two triangles are placed on opposite sides of a square. What is the shape of the seal pool?

★ **21.** Sal needs a frame for the poster he bought at the zoo. The poster is a rectangle. One side is 24 cm. The other is 33 cm. What is the perimeter of the poster?

# CIRCLES

A **circle** is a figure made up of points that are all the same distance from the **center** point. Point $O$ is at the center of the circle.

The distance from the center of a circle to a point on the circle is called the **radius.** Segment $OA$ is a radius.

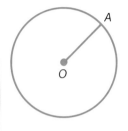

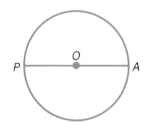

The distance across a circle through its center is called the **diameter.** Segment $PA$ is a diameter.

## CLASS EXERCISES

Use the figure at the right to complete the sentence.

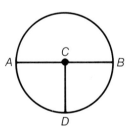

**1.** Segment $AB$ is a ___?___ of the circle.

**2.** Segment $CD$ is a ___?___ of the circle.

**3.** Point ___?___ is at the center of the circle.

## PRACTICE

Name the center, a radius, and a diameter.

**4.**
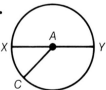

**5.**
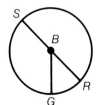

**6.**
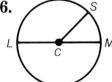

**7.**

**8.**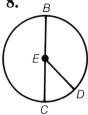

**9.**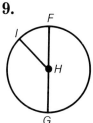

True or false? Write *T* or *F*.

**10.** Segment *LN* is longer than segment *MS*.

**11.** Segment *SM* is a diameter of the circle.

**12.** Angle *NMS* is a right angle.

**13.** Angle *LMS* is an obtuse angle.

★ **14.** The distance around the circle is longer than the length of segment *LN*.

Write the answer.

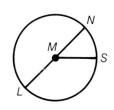
**15.** $3 \times 48$

**16.** $54 \div 3$

**17.** $318 \div 6$

**18.** $317 \times 5$

**19.** $3 \times \$5.20$

**20.** $7 \times \$.59$

**21.** $4.15 + 3.95$

**22.** $11.9 - 4.17$

**23.** $2.3 + 8.42$

# PROBLEM SOLVING APPLICATIONS
## Drawing Circles

You can use a compass or a pencil, a tack, and a strip of cardboard with a hole in it to draw a circle.

Draw the circle or circles. Label the points.

**24.** A circle with center *X*, radius *XY*, and diameter *WZ*

**25.** A circle with center *L*, radius *LM*, radius *LN*, and diameter *ST*

★ **26.** Two circles with the same center.

★ **27.** Suppose you draw a circle with a radius of 2 cm. How long is the diameter?

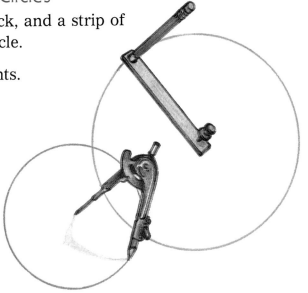

# PROBLEM SOLVING
## Strategy: Drawing a Picture

1. Understand
2. Plan
3. Work
4. Answer/Check

Kern County is building a pioneer village to show what living was like in the area 100 years ago. A fence will go around the property. The property is a rectangle 275 m long and 150 m wide. How many meters of fence are needed?

You can draw a picture to help solve the problem. From the picture you see that you need to add to find the perimeter.

$$275 + 150 + 275 + 150 = 850$$

The amount of fence needed is 850 m.

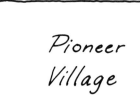

275 m

150 m    Pioneer Village    150 m

275 m

## CLASS EXERCISES

Copy and complete the picture. Then solve.

1. A low fence is needed around the main house. It will measure 35 m long and 25 m wide. How many meters of fence are needed?

2. String is used to mark off the foundation of a shed for winter supplies. The shed will be a square 8.5 m on a side. How many meters of string are used?

## PRACTICE

Draw a picture. Solve.

3. The barn will be a rectangle. It will be 20 m long and 15 m wide. What will the perimeter of the barn be?

4. The parking lot will be a rectangle 30 m long and 26.5 m wide. What will the distance around the parking lot be?

5. The map of the village is a rectangle 185 cm long and 115 cm wide. The village director wants to put a rope border around the map. How much rope does she need?

6. The picnic area will be shaped like a parallelogram. One side will be 34 m and another will be 26 m. What will the perimeter of the picnic area be?

7. The information building will be a special shape. The building will be a pentagon that is 8 m on each side. What will the perimeter of the building be?

8. One garden is a square 6 m on a side. The other is a rectangle measuring 8 m by 5 m. How many meters of fence are needed for both gardens?

★ 9. Five planks are used for a path along the front of the house. Each plank measures 5 m long by 50 cm wide. How many meters is it around each plank?

★ 10. The museum building will be a rectangle that is 25 m wide. It is 10 m longer than it is wide. How many meters will it be around the building?

# CHECKPOINT 2

Match the name with a picture. *(pages 260–261)*

1. pentagon    A.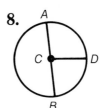

2. triangle    B.

3. quadrilateral    C.

Choose the name. *(pages 262–263)*

4.    a. triangle
      b. parallelogram

5.    a. rectangle
      b. square

What is the perimeter? *(pages 264–265)*

6.  3 cm  3 cm  4 cm

7. 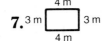 4 m  3 m  3 m  4 m

Name the center, a radius, and a diameter. *(pages 266–267)*

8.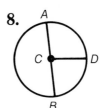

9.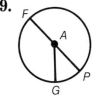

Draw a picture. Solve. *(pages 268–269)*

10. A bulletin board is 145 cm long and 95 cm wide. How many centimeters of crepe paper does it take to make a border around the bulletin board?

Name the figure. Then write *R* for right, *A* for acute, or *O* for obtuse if the figure is an angle. *(pages 250–253)*

1.

2.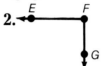

3.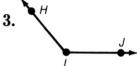

Solve. *(pages 254–255)*

4. Name the line segments that are perpendicular to line KL.

5. Name the line segments that are parallel to line KL.

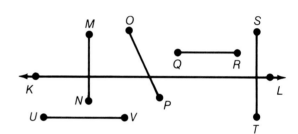

Write *all*, *some*, or *no*. *(pages 258–259)*

6. ___?___ lines are parallel or perpendicular.

7. ___?___ lines are both parallel and perpendicular.

Choose the name that best describes each polygon. *(pages 260–263)*
   triangle   square   parallelogram   pentagon

8.

9.

10.

11.

Find the perimeter of the figure.
*(pages 264–265)*

12. 27 cm / 23 cm / 31 cm

13. 56 m / 42 m / 42 m / 56 m

Name the center, a radius, and a diameter of the circle. *(pages 266–267)*

14.

15.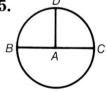

Draw a picture to solve. *(pages 268–269)*

16. Marcia's patio is a rectangle 23 m long and 18 m wide. What is the perimeter of her patio?

*Extra practice on page 419*

# MATHEMATICS and ART

One way of creating rhythm in a piece of art is through geometry. One drawing may create rhythm through the use of parallel line segments, while another one shows the repetition of the same or similar shapes. The drawing below does both. Study the drawing as you answer these questions.

## CAN YOU REPEAT THAT?

1. A line segment drawn in this position is vertical. Two vertical line segments in a drawing are parallel. How many vertical line segments can you find?

2. A line segment drawn in this position is horizontal. Two horizontal line segments are parallel. How many horizontal line segments can you find?

3. The circle is repeated on the drawing. How many complete circles can you find?

4. How many half circles are there?

5. How many times is this figure repeated?

6. Draw another shape that appears more than once.

# Enrichment

Some figures that we draw are *closed* figures. Some are not. Closed figures have an inside and an outside. There is no inside or outside for figures that are not closed.

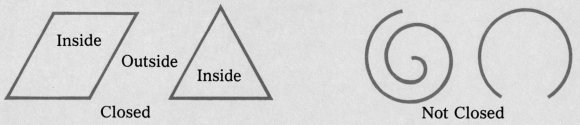

Closed                           Not Closed

Is the figure closed? Write *Yes* or *No.*

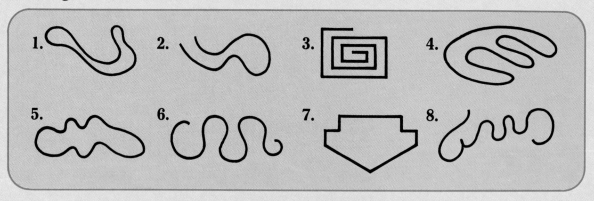

**9.** Draw a closed figure.          **10.** Draw an open figure.

Are both endpoints of the segments inside the figure?
Write *Yes* or *No.*

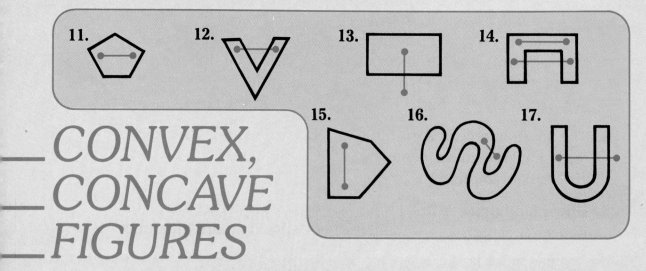

CONVEX,
CONCAVE
FIGURES

272

A closed figure may be *convex* or *concave*. Read the descriptions to tell which is which.

**Convex**
Choose two points inside the figure. Draw a line segment from one to the other. The line segment will be inside the figure, too. To be a convex figure, *all* line segments you could draw must be inside the figure.

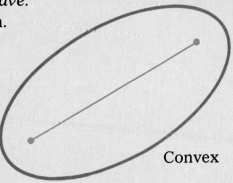

Convex

Concave          Concave

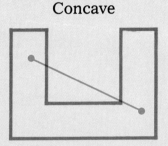 

**Concave**
Choose two points inside the figure. Draw a line segment from one to the other. Part of the line segment may be outside the figure.

Copy and test each figure by connecting pairs of points.
Is the figure convex or concave?

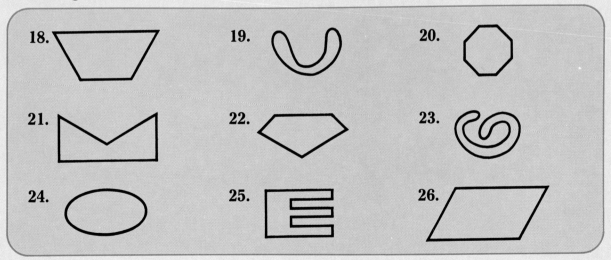

18.

19.

20.

21.

22.

23.

24.

25.

26.

27. **Think:** Is a point convex? a line?

28. Give an example of a convex figure that is a closed curve with every point on the curve the same distance from a center point.

# CUMULATIVE REVIEW

Choose the correct answer. Write *a*, *b*, *c*, or *d*.

Estimate the product.

**1.**  17
     ×4
  **a.** 40
  **b.** 20
  **c.** 80
  **d.** 100

**2.** 266
     ×8
  **a.** 2400
  **b.** 1000
  **c.** 1600
  **d.** 3000

**3.** 9330
     ×5
  **a.** 90,000
  **b.** 15,000
  **c.** 45,000
  **d.** 40,000

Find the answer.

**4.**  25
     ×3
  **a.** 28
  **b.** 65
  **c.** 75
  **d.** none of these

**5.**  43
     ×8
  **a.** 324
  **b.** 344
  **c.** 364
  **d.** none of these

**6.**  37
     ×7
  **a.** 219
  **b.** 259
  **c.** 224
  **d.** none of these

Use the pictograph to solve.

**CARNIVAL BOOTHS**

Food
Games
Music

Each ■ means 5 booths

**7.** How many booths offer food?

  **a.** 4 booths    **b.** 16 booths
  **c.** 20 booths   **d.** none of these

**8.** How many more booths offer games than offer music?

  **a.** 3 booths    **b.** 15 booths
  **c.** 30 booths   **d.** none of these

Find the answer.

**9.** 347
    ×2
  **a.** 664
  **b.** 349
  **c.** 694
  **d.** none of these

**10.** 754
     ×6
  **a.** 4204
  **b.** 4224
  **c.** 4524
  **d.** none of these

**11.** 618
     ×9
  **a.** 5462
  **b.** 5562
  **c.** 5492
  **d.** none of these

**12.** 4032
$\times 3$

a. 1296
b. 12,096
c. 12,196
d. none of these

**13.** 3957
$\times 5$

a. 15,555
b. 19,755
c. 15,785
d. none of these

**14.** 8684
$\times 7$

a. 60,768
b. 60,588
c. 60,788
d. none of these

Find the answer.

**15.** $.41
$\times 4$

a. $1.64
b. $16.40
c. $.45
d. none of these

**16.** $9.49
$\times 8$

a. $75.97
b. $75.92
c. $75.32
d. none of these

**17.** $3.98
$\times 6$

a. $21.74
b. $18.48
c. $23.88
d. none of these

**18.** $22.85
$\times 5$

a. $114.25
b. $114.05
c. $110.25
d. none of these

**19.** $5.95
$\times 8$

a. $40.20
b. $40.60
c. $47.60
d. none of these

**20.** $42.93
$\times 9$

a. $366.37
b. $386.37
c. $396.37
d. none of these

# LANGUAGE and VOCABULARY REVIEW

Copy the words on your paper. Write the letter of the matching definition next to each word.

**1.** line segment

**A.** A metric unit used to measure length

**2.** line

**B.** Part of a line with only one endpoint

**3.** ray

**C.** Part of a line with two endpoints

**4.** gram

**D.** A straight path that goes on and on in both directions

**5.** meter

**E.** A metric unit of mass

**6.** liter

**F.** An answer that is not exact

**7.** estimate

**G.** A metric unit for measuring liquids

# PRINT

COMPUTER
LITERACY

A computer needs instructions to process data. A **program** is a list of instructions. It tells the computer to do a process in step-by-step order. *Line numbers* show the order of steps.

You use a computer language to write a program. One language some computers understand is BASIC.

**PRINT** is a special word in BASIC. You can use PRINT two ways.

| | |
|---|---|
| If you tell the computer PRINT 7 * 6, it will do the arithmetic. Then it will show the output. <br><br>        Output <br><br> `PRINT 7 * 6`     `42` | If you tell the computer PRINT "7 * 6", it will show exactly what is between the quotation marks. <br><br>        Output <br><br> `PRINT "7 * 6"`     `7 * 6` |

(Multiply)

Here is a program that uses PRINT both ways.

Press the RETURN or ENTER key after you type each line.

Output

```
10 PRINT "WHEN YOU"
20 PRINT "DIVIDE 40 BY 8"
30 PRINT "THE QUOTIENT IS"
40 PRINT 40/8        (Divide)
50 END        (End of program)
```

```
WHEN YOU
DIVIDE 40 BY 8
THE QUOTIENT IS
5
```

Write the output for each program.

1.
```
10 PRINT "IF YOU DIVIDE"
20 PRINT "63 BY 9"
30 PRINT 63/9
40 PRINT "IS THE QUOTIENT"
50 END
```

2.
```
10 PRINT "WHEN YOU MULTIPLY"
20 PRINT " 32 BY 9"
30 PRINT "THE PRODUCT IS"
40 PRINT 32 * 9
50 END
```

10

In a factory, 1 person can test 35 engines. How many engines can 5 people test? How many engines can 10 people test?

MULTIPLICATION
BY TWO-DIGIT NUMBERS

# MULTIPLYING BY TEN

Each elevator in Daily's Department Store holds 10 passengers. One elevator makes 8 trips in one hour. What is the greatest number of passengers that can ride in the elevator during one hour?

To find out, multiply 8 × 10 or 10 × 8.

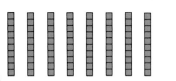

$$\begin{array}{r} 10 \\ \times 8 \\ \hline 80 \end{array} \qquad \begin{array}{r} 8 \\ \times 10 \\ \hline 80 \end{array}$$

In one hour, 80 passengers can ride.

**Think:** You know that 8 × 10 has the same product as 10 × 8. What property tells you that 8 × 10 = 10 × 8?

 A pattern will help you multiply other numbers by ten.

$$\begin{array}{r} 6 \\ \times 10 \\ \hline 60 \end{array}$$ 10 sixes are 60.

$$\begin{array}{r} 16 \\ \times 10 \\ \hline 160 \end{array}$$ 10 sixteens are 160.

$$\begin{array}{r} 166 \\ \times 10 \\ \hline 1660 \end{array}$$ 10 one hundred sixty-sixes are 1660.

## CLASS EXERCISES

Multiply.

1. $\begin{array}{r} 10 \\ \times 7 \end{array}$  $\begin{array}{r} 7 \\ \times 10 \end{array}$

2. $\begin{array}{r} 10 \\ \times 3 \end{array}$  $\begin{array}{r} 3 \\ \times 10 \end{array}$

3. $\begin{array}{r} 10 \\ \times 22 \end{array}$  $\begin{array}{r} 22 \\ \times 10 \end{array}$

4. $\begin{array}{r} 3 \\ \times 10 \end{array}$  $\begin{array}{r} 13 \\ \times 10 \end{array}$  $\begin{array}{r} 133 \\ \times 10 \end{array}$

5. $\begin{array}{r} 2 \\ \times 10 \end{array}$  $\begin{array}{r} 82 \\ \times 10 \end{array}$  $\begin{array}{r} 782 \\ \times 10 \end{array}$

6. $\begin{array}{r} 6 \\ \times 10 \end{array}$  $\begin{array}{r} 60 \\ \times 10 \end{array}$  $\begin{array}{r} 600 \\ \times 10 \end{array}$

## PRACTICE

Multiply.

7. $\begin{array}{r} 12 \\ \times 10 \end{array}$

8. $\begin{array}{r} 16 \\ \times 10 \end{array}$

9. $\begin{array}{r} 11 \\ \times 10 \end{array}$

10. $\begin{array}{r} 15 \\ \times 10 \end{array}$

11. $\begin{array}{r} 13 \\ \times 10 \end{array}$

| 12. 26 $\times 10$ | 13. 38 $\times 10$ | 14. 43 $\times 10$ | 15. 77 $\times 10$ | 16. 89 $\times 10$ |
|---|---|---|---|---|
| 17. 126 $\times 10$ | 18. 137 $\times 10$ | 19. 176 $\times 10$ | 20. 189 $\times 10$ | 21. 180 $\times 10$ |
| 22. 238 $\times 10$ | 23. 339 $\times 10$ | 24. 400 $\times 10$ | 25. 683 $\times 10$ | 26. 952 $\times 10$ |
| 27. 450 $\times 10$ | 28. 800 $\times 10$ | 29. 968 $\times 10$ | 30. 500 $\times 10$ | 31. 849 $\times 10$ |

32. $10 \times 29$    33. $10 \times 87$    34. $10 \times 266$    35. $10 \times 720$

★ 36. $10 \times 5000$    ★ 37. $100 \times 92$    ★ 38. $1000 \times 78$    ★ 39. $10,000 \times 45$

Use mental math to solve. Write just $<$, $>$, or $=$.

40. $10 \times 50$ ▓ $50 \times 10$    41. $10 \times 62$ ▓ $61 \times 10$

42. $521 \times 10$ ▓ $10 \times 512$    43. $789 \times 10$ ▓ $10 \times 798$

MENTAL MATH

# PROBLEM SOLVING APPLICATIONS
## Choosing the Operation

Solve.

44. On Monday an elevator made 87 trips with 10 people on each trip. How many people rode on the elevator Monday?

45. On Tuesday 392 people rode on the elevator. If 7 people rode on each trip, how many trips were made Tuesday?

★ 46. On Wednesday 88 trips were made with 10 people on each trip. On Thursday 104 trips were made with 10 people on each trip. How many people rode on the elevator altogether on both days?

★ 47. On Friday 138 trips were made with 10 people on each trip. On Saturday 274 trips were made with 7 people on each trip. How many more people rode on the elevator Saturday than Friday?

# MULTIPLYING BY TENS

A man climbed 40 ft up a coconut tree in record time. How many inches did he climb?

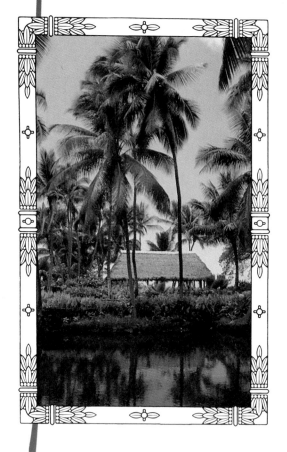

You know that 1 ft is the same as 12 in. To find the number of inches in 40 ft, you multiply 40 × 12.

| Multiply 12 by 0. Write a 0 in the ones' place. | Multiply 12 by 4 tens. |
|---|---|
| 12<br>×40<br>―――<br>0 | 12<br>×40<br>―――<br>480 |

The man climbed 480 in.

Here is another example. Multiply 20 × 157.

| Multiply 157 by 0. Write a 0 in the ones' place. | Multiply 157 by 2 tens. |
|---|---|
| 157<br>×20<br>―――<br>0 | 157<br>×20<br>―――<br>3140 |

 You know that 4 × 12 = 48.
**Think:** What is the product of 40 × 12?

## CLASS EXERCISES

Will the product be ten thousands, thousands, hundreds, or tens? Find the product.

1. 13    13
    ×6    ×60

2. 54    54
    ×5    ×50

3. 83    83
    ×8    ×80

4. 213    213
    ×6    ×60

5. 326    326
    ×8    ×80

6. 648    648
    ×9    ×90

# PRACTICE

Multiply.

| 7. 72<br>×20 | 8. 34<br>×40 | 9. 65<br>×30 | 10. 92<br>×20 | 11. 10<br>×50 | 12. 87<br>×20 |
|---|---|---|---|---|---|
| 13. 33<br>×30 | 14. 61<br>×30 | 15. 52<br>×40 | 16. 21<br>×90 | 17. 41<br>×70 | 18. 71<br>×60 |
| 19. 938<br>×20 | 20. 193<br>×90 | 21. 465<br>×40 | 22. 766<br>×50 | 23. 653<br>×60 | 24. 536<br>×40 |
| 25. 653<br>×70 | 26. 296<br>×80 | 27. 389<br>×50 | 28. 544<br>×30 | 29. 914<br>×80 | 30. 649<br>×70 |

**31.** 30 × 45      **32.** 50 × 67      **33.** 80 × 762      **34.** 60 × 395

**35.** 70 × 79      **36.** 60 × 84      **37.** 40 × 847      **38.** 70 × 596

**39.** 50 × 85   ★ **40.** 900 × 76   ★ **41.** 8000 × 485   ★ **42.** 60,000 × 673

Without multiplying, match the factors and the product.
Write the letter.

**MENTAL MATH**

**43.** 30 × 26  **44.** 300 × 26  **45.** 3000 × 26  **46.** 30,000 × 26

**A.** 78,000      **B.** 780      **C.** 780,000      **D.** 7800

## PROBLEM SOLVING APPLICATIONS
### Time and Measurement

Solve.

**47.** Marcus Hooper was the youngest person to swim the English Channel. He swam from England to France in about 15 hours. How many minutes did it take?

**48.** The weight of the average fourth-grader is 66 lb. About how much do 10 fourth-graders weigh?

★ **49.** A camel is 7 ft tall. A giraffe is 20 ft tall. How many inches taller is the giraffe than the camel?

★ **50.** Old Billy is said to be the horse that lived the longest. Old Billy lived for about 60 years. How many days did it live? how many hours? (Do not include leap years.)

# ESTIMATING PRODUCTS

Donna counts 36 words that are defined on one page of her dictionary. There are 712 pages in the dictionary. About how many words are defined in the dictionary?

To find the exact number of words, you would have to count the words on every page. Instead of looking for the exact answer, you can estimate.

**Think:** Which word in the problem tells you that you can estimate?

712 ⟶ Round to the greatest place value. ⟶ 700
×36 ⟶ Round to the greatest place value. ⟶ ×40

You have to be careful when there are many zeros to multiply. Here is one way.

Write 0 in the ones' place.      Multiply 700 by 4 tens.

$$
\begin{array}{r}
700 \\
\times 40 \\
\hline
0
\end{array}
\qquad
\begin{array}{r}
700 \\
\times 40 \\
\hline
28{,}000
\end{array}
$$

About 28,000 words are defined in the dictionary.

## CLASS EXERCISES

What is the greatest place value of the number? Round the number to its greatest place value.

**1.** 27　　　**2.** 349　　　**3.** 88　　　**4.** 629　　　**5.** 606　　　**6.** 935

What factors do you multiply to estimate the product? What is the estimated product?

**7.**　46　　**8.**　54　　**9.**　72　　**10.**　191　　**11.**　514　　**12.**　308
　　×28　　　　×17　　　　×35　　　　×46　　　　　×62　　　　　×12

# PRACTICE

Round to the greatest place value and estimate the product.

| 13. | 14 | 14. | 43 | 15. | 67 | 16. | 78 | 17. | 85 |
|---|---|---|---|---|---|---|---|---|---|
| | ×26 | | ×72 | | ×92 | | ×56 | | ×32 |

| 18. | 636 | 19. | 782 | 20. | 568 | 21. | 824 | 22. | 656 |
|---|---|---|---|---|---|---|---|---|---|
| | ×56 | | ×42 | | ×43 | | ×79 | | ×52 |

| 23. | 498 | 24. | 92 | 25. | 785 | 26. | 53 | 27. | 746 |
|---|---|---|---|---|---|---|---|---|---|
| | ×55 | | ×84 | | ×63 | | ×45 | | ×45 |

**28.** $37 \times 41$    **29.** $52 \times 382$    **30.** $71 \times 62$    **31.** $25 \times 465$

**32.** $68 \times 276$    **33.** $84 \times 58$    **34.** $43 \times 361$    **35.** $92 \times 88$

★ **36.** $37 \times 53 \times 52$    ★ **37.** $18 \times 41 \times 79$    ★ **38.** $95 \times 18 \times 21$

---

Write the answer.

**39.** $5 \times 7$    **40.** $9 \times 6$    **41.** $8 \times 4$    **42.** $7 \times 3$

**43.** $35 + 7$    **44.** $48 + 4$    **45.** $32 + 7$    **46.** $45 + 9$

**47.** $4 \times 18$    **48.** $9 \times 42$    **49.** $7 \times 64$    **50.** $6 \times 37$

**MIXED REVIEW**

---

## PROBLEM SOLVING APPLICATIONS
### Using Estimation

Estimate to solve.

**51.** Charles's dictionary defines about 55 words on a page. There are 16 pages of words starting with K. About how many words starting with K are defined?

**52.** The first page of Stephanie's story has 295 words. There are 88 pages in the story. About how many words are in Stephanie's story?

**53.** Mary Jane took 30 seconds to count the words defined on one page of a 696-page dictionary. About how many seconds would it take her to count the words defined in the whole dictionary?

★ **54.** In a dictionary words beginning with W take 32 pages and words beginning with Z take 18 pages. Each page defines about 55 words. About how many words are defined on the pages for W and Z?

# MULTIPLYING BY A NUMBER BETWEEN 10 AND 20

There are 52 rooms on each floor of the Deluxe Hotel. The hotel has 14 floors. How many rooms are in the hotel?

Multiply 52 by 14.

| Multiply 52 by 4 ones. | Multiply 52 by 1 ten. | Add. |
|---|---|---|
| 52<br>×14<br>___<br>208 | 52<br>×14<br>___<br>208<br>520<br>___ | 52<br>×14<br>___<br>208<br>520<br>___<br>728 |

728 ← 208 + 520

There are 728 rooms in the Deluxe Hotel.

 You know 10 × 50 = 500. You can estimate that the product of 14 × 52 will be greater than 500 because you rounded both factors down. **Think:** If you rounded both factors up, would the exact product be greater than or less than the estimate?

## CLASS EXERCISES

Complete.

**1.** 18 = ▓ ten ▓ ones

**2.** 16 = ▓ ten ▓ ones

**3.** 12 = ▓ ten ▓ ones

**4.** 19 = ▓ ten ▓ ones

Multiply. How are the products related?

**5.**
| 34<br>×2 | 34<br>×10 | 34<br>×12 |
|---|---|---|

**6.**
| 93<br>×9 | 93<br>×10 | 93<br>×19 |
|---|---|---|

## PRACTICE

Multiply.

**7.** 42<br>×12

**8.** 62<br>×11

**9.** 54<br>×16

**10.** 13<br>×13

**11.** 65<br>×14

**12.** 24<br>×12

| **13.** 42<br>×14 | **14.** 23<br>×13 | **15.** 93<br>×12 | **16.** 63<br>×12 | **17.** 53<br>×15 | **18.** 37<br>×11 |
|---|---|---|---|---|---|
| **19.** 21<br>×17 | **20.** 49<br>×11 | **21.** 51<br>×19 | **22.** 38<br>×11 | **23.** 31<br>×12 | **24.** 44<br>×12 |
| **25.** 18<br>×10 | **26.** 17<br>×12 | **27.** 33<br>×18 | **28.** 81<br>×17 | **29.** 86<br>×11 | **30.** 92<br>×13 |
| **31.** 93<br>×11 | **32.** 82<br>×12 | **33.** 12<br>×14 | **34.** 41<br>×15 | **35.** 43<br>×13 | **36.** 73<br>×12 |

**37.** 15 × 37     **38.** 13 × 63     **39.** 11 × 79     **40.** 15 × 18

**41.** 10 × 66     **42.** 17 × 85     **43.** 14 × 28     **44.** 19 × 57

Complete.

★ **45.** ▓ × 37 = 0     ★ **46.** 18 × 56 = 56 × ▓

★ **47.** 74 × ▓ = 74     ★ **48.** (2 × 9) × 37 = 2 × (▓ × 37)

Estimate the product. Write *T* for true or *F* for false.

**49.** 10 × 49 > 500     **50.** 19 × 79 < 1600     **51.** 14 × 52 > 500

**52.** 12 × 84 > 800     **53.** 15 × 44 < 400     **54.** 13 × 63 > 600

ESTIMATE

## PROBLEM SOLVING APPLICATIONS
### Choosing a Strategy

Solve.

**55.** One hotel has 224 rooms. It has 7 floors. Each floor has the same number of rooms. How many rooms are on each floor?

**56.** A new hotel has 32 rooms on each floor. How many floors are in the new hotel?

**57.** A large hotel has 28 floors. There are 15 people working on each floor. How many people work on all the floors of the hotel?

★ **58.** The Elegant Hotel has 18 floors. There are 12 large rooms and 16 small rooms on each floor. There are 45 balconies. How many rooms are in the Elegant Hotel?

# MULTIPLYING BY TWO-DIGIT NUMBERS

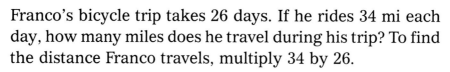

Franco's bicycle trip takes 26 days. If he rides 34 mi each day, how many miles does he travel during his trip? To find the distance Franco travels, multiply 34 by 26.

Multiply 34 by 6 ones.

```
  34
×26
 204
```

Multiply 34 by 2 tens.

```
  34
×26
 204
 680
```

Add.

```
  34
×26
 204
 680
 884
```

Franco travels 884 mi.

Some calculators have a memory key, **M+**. If you enter a number and press **M+**, the calculator remembers the number. To see the number again, press **MR**. To multiply 26 × 34 and 26 × 42, put 26 in the memory to use with 34 and 42.

[2] [6] [M+] [×] [3] [4] [=] 884

[MR] 26 [×] [4] [2] [=] 1092

## CLASS EXERCISES

Multiply.

**1.**
```
 25    25    25
 ×3   ×20   ×23
```

**2.**
```
 27    27    27
 ×3   ×40   ×43
```

**3.**
```
 29    29    29
 ×4   ×50   ×54
```

## PRACTICE

Multiply.

**4.**
```
  24
×23
```

**5.**
```
  39
×54
```

**6.**
```
  16
×22
```

**7.**
```
  43
×15
```

**8.**
```
  49
×41
```

**9.**
```
  95
×31
```

| | | | | | |
|---|---|---|---|---|---|
| **10.** 72 ×25 | **11.** 12 ×80 | **12.** 81 ×29 | **13.** 63 ×53 | **14.** 52 ×72 | **15.** 27 ×52 |
| **16.** 26 ×38 | **17.** 39 ×23 | **18.** 39 ×61 | **19.** 38 ×17 | **20.** 26 ×36 | **21.** 73 ×59 |
| **22.** 55 ×55 | **23.** 36 ×63 | **24.** 68 ×74 | **25.** 56 ×47 | **26.** 79 ×45 | **27.** 48 ×73 |
| **28.** 57 ×68 | **29.** 69 ×46 | **30.** 33 ×77 | **31.** 47 ×28 | **32.** 91 ×18 | **33.** 86 ×36 |

Complete.

| | | | | |
|---|---|---|---|---|
| ★ **34.** 2▓ ×16 ───── 448 | ★ **35.** 34 ×2▓ ───── 850 | ★ **36.** ▓9 ×32 ───── 1888 | ★ **37.** 62 ×▓6 ───── 2852 | ★ **38.** 97 ×▓2 ───── 213▓ |

Multiply. Use a calculator with a memory key if you have one. Notice that all problems have a factor of 36.

**39.** 36 × 18    **40.** 36 × 35    **41.** 36 × 27    **42.** 36 × 59

CALCULATOR

# PROBLEM SOLVING APPLICATIONS
## Choosing the Operation

Solve.

**43.** Sondra bicycles 32 mi each day for 21 days. How far does she travel?

**44.** Franco spends $28 each day during his 7-day trip. How much money does he spend?

**45.** Alex's family bicycles 132 mi in 4 days from Yosemite Valley to Mono Lake. If the family rides the same number of miles each day, how far does it travel each day?

★ **46.** The first 16 days of the trip, Allison rides 38 mi each day. For 2 days, she rests. Then she rides 27 mi each day for the next 14 days. How far does she travel?

# PROBLEM SOLVING
## Strategy: Using Patterns

1. *Understand*
2. *Plan*
3. *Work*
4. *Answer/ Check*

Eva puts coins in her bank every day. The first day she puts 3¢ in her bank, the second day she puts in 6¢, the third day she puts in 9¢, and the fourth day she puts in 12¢. If she continues this pattern, how much does she put in the bank on the fourteenth day?

You can use a table to continue the pattern.

## MY MONEY CHART

| DAY | 1 | 2 | 3 | 4 | 5 | 6 | 7 | 8 | 9 | 10 | 11 | 12 | 13 | 14 |
|---|---|---|---|---|---|---|---|---|---|---|---|---|---|---|
| CENTS | 3 | 6 | 9 | 12 | 15 | 18 | 21 | 24 | 27 | 30 | 33 | 36 | 39 | 42 |

Eva will put 42¢ in her bank on the fourteenth day.

The table shows that the pattern Eva used is to increase the amount she put in the bank by 3¢ each day. So, another way to solve the problem is to multiply the last day by 3¢.

$$14 \times 3¢ = 42¢$$

## CLASS EXERCISES

Copy and complete the table to solve each problem.

| Day | 1 | 2 | 3 | 4 | 5 | 6 | 7 | 8 | 9 | 10 | 11 | 12 |
|---|---|---|---|---|---|---|---|---|---|---|---|---|
| Cents | ? | ? | ? | ? | ? | ? | ? | ? | ? | ? | ? | ? |

**1.** Ed plans to put 1¢ in his bank today, 2¢ tomorrow, 4¢ the next day, 8¢ on the fourth day, and 16¢ the fifth day. If he continues this pattern, how much will he put in his bank on the tenth day?

**2.** Emily plans to put 1¢ in her bank today, 4¢ tomorrow, 9¢ the third day, 16¢ the fourth day, and 25¢ the fifth day. If she continues this pattern, how much will she put in her bank on the twelfth day?

# PRACTICE

Solve. Look for a pattern. Use a table if needed.

3. Ricardo saved $2 the first week, $4 the second week, $6 the third week, and $8 the fourth week. How much did Ricardo save the fifth week? the ninth week?

4. Joy practiced piano 8 hours in January, 16 hours in February, 24 hours in March, and 32 hours in April. How long did she practice in May? in June? in July?

5. A store clerk wants to stack cereal in a display 12 rows high. One box will be on the top row, 3 boxes on the next row, 5 boxes will be on the third row, and so on. How many boxes will she use to make the twelfth row?

6. Tim ran 5 minutes the first day and rested the second day. He ran 6 minutes the third day, rested the fourth, and ran 7 minutes the fifth day. If the pattern continues, how many minutes does he run on the eleventh day? on the sixteenth?

★ 7. On the first day Mary swam 20 laps. On all other odd days she swam 25 laps. On the second day and all other even days, Mary swam 15 laps. How many laps did Mary swim in 14 days?

★ 8. Emily is saving for a bike bag that costs $5.30. She saves 10¢ the first week. She plans to double the amount she saves each week until she has saved enough. When will she have enough money?

## CHECKPOINT 1

Multiply. *(pages 278–281, 284–287)*

| 1. | 170 | 2. | 81 | 3. | 65 |
|---|---|---|---|---|---|
| | ×10 | | ×60 | | ×19 |

Round to the greatest place value and estimate.
*(pages 282–283)*

| 4. | 14 | 5. | 87 | 6. | 846 |
|---|---|---|---|---|---|
| | ×36 | | ×22 | | ×55 |

Solve. Look for a pattern.
*(pages 288–289)*

7. Bryan reads 10 minutes the 1st day, 20 minutes the 2nd day, 10 minutes the 3rd day, 30 minutes the 4th day, 10 minutes the 5th day, 40 minutes the 6th day, and 10 minutes the 7th day. If this pattern continutes, how long will he read on the 14th day?

*Extra practice on page 420*

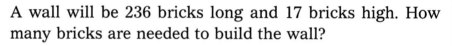

# MULTIPLYING A THREE-DIGIT NUMBER

A wall will be 236 bricks long and 17 bricks high. How many bricks are needed to build the wall?

To find the number of bricks, multiply 236 by 17.

| Multiply 236 by 7 ones. | Multiply 236 by 1 ten. | Add. |
|---|---|---|
| 236<br>×17<br>——<br>1652 | 236<br>×17<br>——<br>1652<br>2360 | 236<br>×17<br>——<br>1652<br>2360<br>——<br>4012 |

To build the wall, 4012 bricks are needed.

## CLASS EXERCISES

Multiply.

1. 816    816    816
   ×6    ×10    ×16

2. 723    723    723
   ×4    ×10    ×14

3. 563    563    563
   ×5    ×10    ×15

4. 654    654    654
   ×6    ×10    ×16

## PRACTICE

Multiply.

5. 715
   ×16

6. 243
   ×15

7. 174
   ×12

8. 261
   ×13

9. 631
   ×17

10. 323
    ×16

11. 236
    ×14

12. 529
    ×16

13. 919
    ×12

14. 816
    ×14

15. 472
    ×13

16. 524
    ×15

| 17. 352<br>×14 | 18. 423<br>×15 | 19. 179<br>×10 | 20. 346<br>×16 | 21. 664<br>×13 | 22. 243<br>×14 |
|---|---|---|---|---|---|
| 23. 652<br>×15 | 24. 558<br>×13 | 25. 743<br>×16 | 26. 727<br>×17 | 27. 256<br>×15 | 28. 327<br>×19 |
| 29. 567<br>×15 | 30. 347<br>×16 | 31. 465<br>×14 | 32. 195<br>×18 | 33. 288<br>×17 | 34. 493<br>×18 |
| 35. 724<br>×16 | 36. 467<br>×18 | 37. 678<br>×16 | 38. 529<br>×17 | 39. 842<br>×19 | 40. 748<br>×15 |

**41.** 18 × 674　　　**42.** 15 × 763　　　**43.** 17 × 893　　　**44.** 16 × 592

★ **45.** (19 × 27) × 376　　　　　★ **46.** 18 × (475 × 18)

★ **47.** (17 × 678) × 16　　　　　★ **48.** (19 × 92) × 146

---

Write the numbers in order from greatest to least. Then round each number to its greatest place value.

**MIXED REVIEW**

**49.** 23, 87, 69

**50.** 106, 215, 84

**51.** 6875, 4482, 3109

**52.** 13.8, 7.6, 25.2

**53.** 4.09, 12.34, 6.85

**54.** 0.98, 2.16, 2.49

---

## PROBLEM SOLVING APPLICATIONS
### Choosing a Strategy

Solve.

**55.** There are 5 people building a brick wall. Each row of the wall takes 975 bricks. The wall is 18 bricks high. How many bricks are needed?

**56.** Gene has 632 bricks. He plans to build a wall 8 rows high. He wants the same number of bricks in each row. How many bricks will be in each row?

**57.** Myra spends $26.94 for flower seedlings to plant in front of a wall. She spends $37.86 for vegetable seedlings. About how much does she spend in all?

★ **58.** Part of a wall is 279 bricks long and 12 bricks high. Another part is 16 bricks high and twice as long as the first part. How many bricks are used for both parts?

# MULTIPLYING A THREE-DIGIT NUMBER

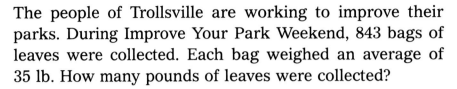

The people of Trollsville are working to improve their parks. During Improve Your Park Weekend, 843 bags of leaves were collected. Each bag weighed an average of 35 lb. How many pounds of leaves were collected?

To find out, you multiply 843 by 35.

Multiply 843 by 5 ones.    Multiply 843 by 3 tens.    Add.

```
      843              843              843
     ×35              × 35             ×35
     ----             -----            -----
     4215             4215             4215
                     25290            25290
                                      ------
                                      29,505
```

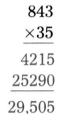

There were 29,505 lb of leaves collected.

You can multiply 843 by 35 on a calculator this way.

$$35 \boxed{\times} \; 843 \; \boxed{=} \; 29505$$

**Think:** What is another way to find the product on a calculator?

## CLASS EXERCISES

Complete.

**1.** 25 = ▓ tens ▓ ones     **2.** 43 = ▓ tens ▓ ones     **3.** 36 = ▓ tens ▓ ones

Multiply.

**4.**
```
357      357      357
 ×6      ×30      ×36
```
**5.**
```
476      476      476
 ×5      ×80      ×85
```

## PRACTICE

Multiply.

**6.**
```
423
×24
```
**7.**
```
224
×32
```
**8.**
```
153
×25
```
**9.**
```
236
×32
```
**10.**
```
342
×26
```
**11.**
```
252
×42
```

| **12.** 190 | **13.** 706 | **14.** 605 | **15.** 358 | **16.** 534 | **17.** 364 |
|---|---|---|---|---|---|
| ×34 | ×52 | ×92 | ×27 | ×48 | ×54 |

| **18.** 349 | **19.** 719 | **20.** 663 | **21.** 493 | **22.** 149 | **23.** 452 |
|---|---|---|---|---|---|
| ×56 | ×34 | ×52 | ×62 | ×83 | ×36 |

| **24.** 536 | **25.** 105 | **26.** 573 | **27.** 307 | **28.** 508 | **29.** 836 |
|---|---|---|---|---|---|
| ×64 | ×92 | ×45 | ×72 | ×64 | ×24 |

**30.** 59 × 468   **31.** 63 × 894   **32.** 72 × 585   **33.** 87 × 467

**34.** 49 × 856   **35.** 56 × 763   **36.** 67 × 764   **37.** 85 × 399

Complete. Write +, −, or ×.

★ **38.** 23 ▓ 426 > 4672 + 5014      ★ **39.** 93 ▓ 368 = 58,954 ▓ 24,730

★ **40.** 18 × 528 = 528 ▓ 18      ★ **41.** 27,924 ▓ 6180 < 58 × 588

Write <, >, or =. Remember 1 hour equals 60 minutes, 1 minute equals 60 seconds, and 1 day equals 24 hours.

**CALCULATOR**

**42.** 1 hour ▓ 3000 seconds      **43.** 1 hour ▓ 4000 seconds

**44.** 1 day ▓ 2000 minutes      **45.** 125 days ▓ 3000 hours

**46.** 275 days ▓ 7000 hours      ★ **47.** 1 year ▓ 8000 hours

## PROBLEM SOLVING APPLICATIONS
### Mental Math, Pencil, or Calculator

Use mental math, paper and pencil, or a calculator to solve the problem. Write *m*, *p*, or *c* to tell the method you chose.

**48.** If each of 600 people planted 17 flowers, how many flowers were planted?

**49.** The 600 people were divided into teams of 3 each. How many teams were formed?

**50.** A fund drive to improve the parks lasted 4 weeks. The amounts collected were $8472, $4698, $3687, and $5804. About how much was collected?

★ **51.** The park director wrote down the amount of wood chips she ordered for the gardens. She forgot the multiplication signs. The total amount ordered was 684 lb. Where do the signs belong?

5   7   2   6

# MULTIPLYING MONEY

Professional tennis players use many tennis balls during practice. If one can of tennis balls costs $2.98, how much do 28 cans cost?

To find out, multiply $2.98 by 28.

$2.98   ← This amount is in dollars
×28        and cents.
23 84
59 60
$83.44  ← The answer is in dollars and cents. Don't forget the dollar sign and the decimal point.

The cost of 28 cans is $83.44.

To estimate the cost, round each factor to its greatest place value.

$2.98 ⟶ $3
×28 ⟶ ×30
$90

3 tens × 3 is 9 tens, or $90.

The estimate and the answer are close.
The answer makes sense.

## CLASS EXERCISES

Write the answer with a dollar sign and a decimal point.

| 1. $1.32 | 2. $2.29 | 3. $6.65 | 4. $.68 | 5. $.85 |
|---|---|---|---|---|
| ×12 | ×18 | ×25 | ×52 | ×67 |
| 264 | 1832 | 3325 | 136 | 595 |
| 1320 | 2290 | 13300 | 3400 | 5100 |
| 1584 | 4122 | 16625 | 3536 | 5695 |

# PRACTICE

Multiply.

| | | | | |
|---|---|---|---|---|
| **6.** $4.23 ×11 | **7.** $.27 ×31 | **8.** $4.32 ×22 | **9.** $.78 ×12 | **10.** $3.59 ×35 |
| **11.** $8.78 ×12 | **12.** $.37 ×29 | **13.** $6.95 ×32 | **14.** $.45 ×52 | **15.** $3.38 ×45 |
| **16.** $7.13 ×25 | **17.** $.69 ×42 | **18.** $4.82 ×51 | **19.** $.56 ×46 | **20.** $9.32 ×35 |
| **21.** $6.45 ×43 | **22.** $.87 ×37 | **23.** $8.76 ×59 | **24.** $.98 ×47 | **25.** $6.85 ×64 |

Estimate the product.

**26.** 76 × $4.95    **27.** 94 × $.76    **28.** 48 × $7.86

**29.** 74 × $.93    **30.** 89 × $7.87    **31.** 96 × $1.05

ESTIMATE

# PROBLEM SOLVING APPLICATIONS
## Using a Table

Use the information in the table to solve the problem.

**32.** Which kind of ball costs more than a soccer ball?

**33.** How much will 15 basketballs cost?

**34.** About how much more would you pay for a basketball than a baseball?

**35.** One baseball team used 48 baseballs in a game. What was the cost of baseballs for the game?

| PRICE LIST | |
|---|---|
| 3 tennis balls | $2.98 |
| 1 baseball | $2.79 |
| 2 racquetballs | $3.99 |
| 1 basketball | $9.98 |
| 1 soccer ball | $7.49 |

★ **36.** Each tennis match requires 6 tennis balls. What is the total cost for 34 women's matches and 28 men's matches?

★ **37.** A sponsor for a racquetball tournament donated 100 racquetballs. What is the value of the sponsor's donation?

# PROBLEM SOLVING
## Strategy: Open-Ended Problems

Denise paid $4.90 for yarn. She gave the clerk $5 and received $.10 in change. What coins could she have received?

There is more than one correct answer to this problem. Since Denise does not receive more than $.10, each coin she receives must be $.10 or less.

Some answers are:    1 dime

                       1 nickel, 5 pennies

There are 4 ways to solve this problem.

**Think:** What are the other 2 ways?

## CLASS EXERCISES

Solve. There is more than one answer.

**1.** How would you make change for $.10? Why?

**2.** List all the ways you can make change for $.15.

## PRACTICE

Use the picture to solve the problem. Give two possible answers.

**3.** Liz has $7. She does not spend it all. What could she buy?

**4.** Todd plans to spend between $8 and $10. What could he buy?

**5.** Lee bought a truck, 2 boxes of crayons, and a shirt. He gave the clerk $19. He received 8 coins for change. What coins did he receive for change?

Overalls $13.50

Shirt $10.99

record $5.98

$3.92

$1.60

Solve. There is more than one answer.

**6.** Robert has exactly 6 coins that total $.30. What coins might Robert have?

**7.** Maggie received no pennies in her change for $.20. What coins might she have received?

**8.** The temperature dropped 3 degrees in 2 hours. How many degrees could the temperature have dropped during each hour?

**9.** Ella needs 20 sewing needles for her scout troop. Needles are sold in packages of 4, 5, or 10. How many packages does she buy?

**10.** Evan needs 15 buttons. Buttons are sold in packages of 3 or 5. How many packages of buttons does Evan buy?

**11.** Pete, John, and Ralph are standing in line. In what order might they be standing if Ralph is ahead of John?

**12.** Dottie had to go to the library, the market, and to Audrey's house. In what order might she run her errands if she ends up at Audrey's house?

★ **13.** Joanie built a rectangular jewelry box. Its perimeter is 24 in. If the measurements are odd numbers, what might the lengths of its sides be?

★ **14.** Matthew is thinking of a 3-digit number. The tens' digit is twice the ones' digit. The hundreds' digit is twice the tens' digit. What numbers might Matthew be thinking of?

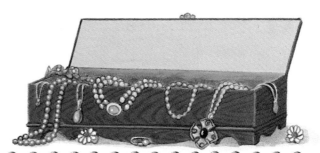

# CHECKPOINT 2

Multiply. *(pages 290–295)*

| | | |
|---|---|---|
| **1.** 163 | **2.** 246 | **3.** 354 |
| ×16 | ×13 | ×27 |
| **4.** 236 | **5.** 617 | **6.** 534 |
| ×24 | ×36 | ×35 |

| | | |
|---|---|---|
| **7.** $2.46 | **8.** $1.86 | **9.** $4.08 |
| ×35 | ×45 | ×29 |

Solve. There is more than one answer. *(pages 296-297)*

**10.** Sharon has $10. She has no coins. What bills could she have?

*Extra practice on page 420*

Write the answer. *(pages 278–281, 284–287)*

| **1.** 75 | **2.** 38 | **3.** 26 | **4.** 19 |
|---|---|---|---|
| ×10 | ×70 | ×40 | ×90 |

| **5.** 45 | **6.** 63 | **7.** 84 | **8.** 39 |
|---|---|---|---|
| ×18 | ×66 | ×57 | ×72 |

| **9.** 88 | **10.** 71 | **11.** 96 | **12.** 38 |
|---|---|---|---|
| ×14 | ×16 | ×47 | ×89 |

Estimate the product. *(pages 282–283)*

| **13.** 58 | **14.** 77 | **15.** 619 | **16.** 948 |
|---|---|---|---|
| ×12 | ×83 | ×48 | ×36 |

Solve. Look for a pattern. Use a table if needed. *(pages 288–289)*

**17.** Jennifer biked 2 mi the first day, 3 mi the second day, 2 mi the third day, 4 mi the fourth day, 2 mi the fifth day, and 5 mi the sixth day. How many miles did she bike on the twelfth day?

**18.** Leroy saved $9 in March, $27 in April, and $45 in May. If this pattern continues, how much will Leroy save in June? How much will he save in July? How much will he save in August?

Write the answer. *(pages 290–295)*

| **19.** 925 | **20.** 607 | **21.** 743 | **22.** 638 |
|---|---|---|---|
| ×38 | ×53 | ×58 | ×76 |

| **23.** $4.69 | **24.** $8.84 | **25.** $1.34 | **26.** $8.92 |
|---|---|---|---|
| ×24 | ×72 | ×49 | ×53 |

Solve. There is more than one answer. *(pages 296-297)*

**27.** Sheila is thinking of a three-digit number with the digits 5, 3, and 2. What number might the number be?

*Extra practice on page 421*

# MATHEMATICS and SCIENCE

Lightning may be described as an electrical flash of light. The sound that follows a flash of lightning is called thunder. It takes one second for the sound to travel 1090 ft. This means it takes about 5 seconds for thunder to travel a mile.

To determine how far away lightning is, you can count the number of seconds between lightning and thunder. Then multiply 1090 by the number of seconds.

## DID YOU HEAR THAT?

**1.** Copy and complete the chart.

| TIME BETWEEN LIGHTNING AND THUNDER | DISTANCE |
|---|---|
| 1 second | 1090 ft |
| 2 seconds | ? ft |
| 3 seconds | ? ft |
| 4 seconds | ? ft |
| 5 seconds | 5450 ft, about 1 mi |

**2.** Jim saw a lightning flash. He counted 8 seconds before he heard the thunder. How far away was the storm?

**3.** Janet estimated that a storm was about 2 mi away. How many seconds did she count between the lightning and thunder?

# Enrichment

Taking a **survey** means asking people questions and recording their answers. Surveys are used for many purposes. Companies use surveys to find out what people will buy. Scientists use them to learn more about people.

Suppose three students are planning a car wash. They are not sure what price to charge. They decide to take a survey of all the families in the neighborhood. They ask what price each family would pay for a car wash.

Smith $ 2.00
Connor    4.00
Sanchez   3.00
White     5.00
Miller    4.00
Lee       3.00
Leister   2.00
Chin      4.00
Gray      3.00
Muecci    2.00
Wong      3.00
Blum      4.00
Walker    2.00
Forbes    3.00
Adler     3.00

Use the answers above. Copy and complete the table.

1.

| PRICE | TALLY MARKS | NUMBER |
|-------|-------------|--------|
| $2.00 | //// | 4 |
| $3.00 | ? | ? |
| $4.00 | ? | ? |
| $5.00 | ? | ? |

Use the answers from the survey. Solve.

2. How many families did the students survey?

3. Which price did most of the families choose?

4. Suppose the students charged $2.00 for the car wash, and each family in the survey brought a car. How much money would the students earn?

5. Suppose the students charged $3.00 and only the families who said they would pay $3.00 or more brought cars. How much would the students earn?

# USING SURVEYS

Some surveys need a very large group of people. It would take too long to survey every person. Instead, a **sample,** or part of the group, is questioned. The sample helps estimate what the entire group would say.

Suppose 100 scouts are having a picnic. They will vote to decide if the picnic will be at Oak Park or Eagle Park. Carol can't wait to find out. She picks 20 names from the scout list and surveys them. Here are the results.

| CHOICE OF PARK | OUT OF 20 | OUT OF 100 |
|---|---|---|
| Oak Park | 14 | $5 \times 14 = 70$ |
| Eagle Park | 6 | $5 \times 6 = 30$ |

The large group is 5 times the size of the sample. Multiply the results of the sample by 5. Now you have an estimate of what all the scouts will say.

$5 \times 20 = 100$

About 70 scouts will choose Oak Park. About 30 will choose Eagle Park.

Copy and complete the table.

### COLOR OF EYES

| | COLOR | OUT OF 30 | OUT OF 900 |
|---|---|---|---|
| | Blue | 4 | 120 |
| 6. | Green | 5 | ? |
| 7. | Brown | 21 | ? |

### FAVORITE PETS

| | PET | OUT OF 40 | OUT OF 80 |
|---|---|---|---|
| 11. | Dog | 17 | ? |
| 12. | Cat | 14 | ? |
| 13. | Fish | 5 | ? |
| 14. | Bird | 4 | ? |

### NUMBER OF CAVITIES

| | NUMBER | OUT OF 25 | OUT OF 750 |
|---|---|---|---|
| 8. | None | 5 | ? |
| 9. | One | 9 | ? |
| 10. | More than one | 11 | ? |

### BROTHERS AND SISTERS

| | NUMBER | OUT OF 25 | OUT OF 500 |
|---|---|---|---|
| 15. | None | 4 | ? |
| 16. | One | 11 | ? |
| 17. | Two | 7 | ? |
| 18. | More than two | 3 | ? |

Choose the correct answer. Write *a, b, c,* or *d.*

Find the answer.

**1.** 6)94

   **a.** 10 R4
   **b.** 15
   **c.** 15 R4
   **d.** none of these

**2.** 8)296

   **a.** 37
   **b.** 36 R7
   **c.** 47
   **d.** none of these

**3.** 7)642

   **a.** 90 R2
   **b.** 91 R5
   **c.** 96
   **d.** none of these

Solve.

**4.** Loretta has 75 yd of material to use to make tablecloths for a craft show. Each tablecloth takes 8 yd of material. How many table-cloths can Loretta make?

   **a.** 8 tablecloths
   **b.** 9 tablecloths
   **c.** 10 tablecloths
   **d.** none of these

**5.** One box of rice is enough for 6 servings. How many boxes should Stan buy for 28 guests at his dinner party?

   **a.** 28 boxes
   **b.** 4 boxes
   **c.** 5 boxes
   **d.** none of these

Find the answer.

**6.** 9)963

   **a.** 107
   **b.** 177
   **c.** 17
   **d.** none of these

**7.** 5)$8.05

   **a.** $1.70
   **b.** $1.60
   **c.** $1.61
   **d.** none of these

**8.** 4)951

   **a.** 237
   **b.** 237 R1
   **c.** 237 R2
   **d.** none of these

Find the average.

**9.** 12, 20, 16, 24, 13

   **a.** 17
   **b.** 16
   **c.** 15
   **d.** none of these

**10.** 37, 41, 54, 33, 42, 39

   **a.** 54
   **b.** 42
   **c.** 41
   **d.** none of these

**11.** 264, 88, 309, 195

   **a.** 195
   **b.** 214
   **c.** 264
   **d.** none of these

Use the graph to solve the problem.

BICYCLES SOLD

**12.** In which month were the most bikes sold?
  **a.** March  **b.** April
  **c.** May  **d.** none of these

**13.** How many more bikes were sold in June than in April?
  **a.** 50 bikes  **b.** 100 bikes
  **c.** 150 bikes  **d.** none of these

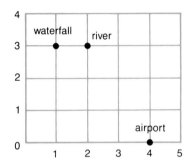

Complete.

**14.** Airport is at
  **a.** (4, 0)
  **b.** (0, 4)
  **c.** (0, 0)
  **d.** none of these

**15.** River is at
  **a.** (2, 3)
  **b.** (3, 2)
  **c.** (2, 2)
  **d.** none of these

Find the perimeter.

**16.**
140 cm
25 cm    25 cm
140 cm
  **a.** 165 cm
  **b.** 190 cm
  **c.** 330 cm
  **d.** none of these

**17.**
18 cm    18 cm
17 cm
  **a.** 53 cm
  **b.** 54 cm
  **c.** 62 cm
  **d.** none of these

# LANGUAGE and VOCABULARY REVIEW

Choose the correct word to complete the sentence. Write the word on your paper.

**1.** The distance across a circle through the center is called a (radius, diameter).

**2.** An angle that is less than a right angle is an (acute, obtuse) angle.

**3.** A (gram, meter) is a unit for measuring length.

**4.** A (grid, ray) is formed with parallel and perpendicular lines.

**5.** A (square, triangle) is a special kind of rectangle.

# LET

**LET** tells the computer to make a letter stand for a number. You can use PRINT and LET to show an output.

```
10 LET A = 5
20 PRINT A
30 END
RUN
```

Output

5

The computer does not show the letter. It shows only the number.

Here are some other ways to use LET and PRINT together.

```
10 LET B = 12 - 9
20 PRINT B
30 END
RUN
```

Output

3

The computer does the arithmetic and shows only the answer.

```
10 LET C = 6
20 LET D = 14
30 PRINT D - C
40 END
RUN
```

Output

8

The computer finds the numbers for *D* and *C*. It does the arithmetic in line 30 and shows only the answer.

You must always type RUN to make the computer follow the instructions. RUN is not part of the program so it does not need a line number.

Write the output you would see after typing RUN.

1. 
```
10 LET L = 42
20 LET R = 6
30 PRINT "IF YOU DIVIDE"
40 PRINT "42 BY 6"
50 PRINT "THE QUOTIENT IS"
60 PRINT L/R
70 END
```

2. 
```
10 LET S = 15 + 9
20 LET T = 5 - 2
30 PRINT "WHEN YOU ADD"
40 PRINT "15 PLUS 9"
50 PRINT "AND 5 MINUS 2"
60 PRINT "THE SUM IS"
70 PRINT S + T
80 END
```

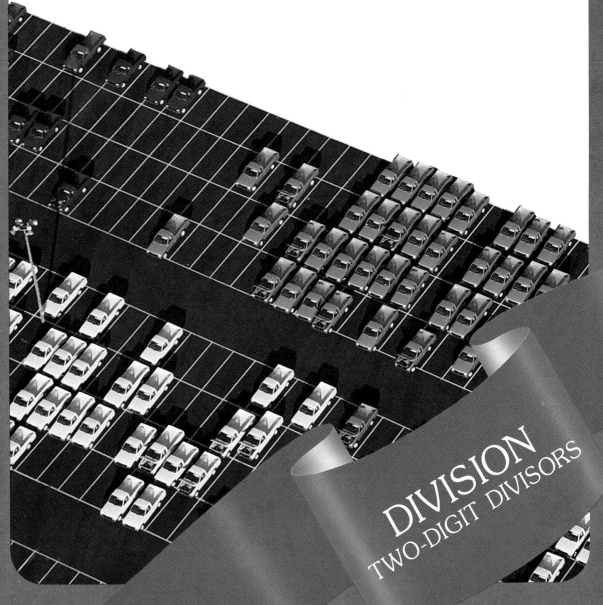

An over-the-road trailer can carry 7 pickup trucks. A railroad trailer can carry twice as many pickup trucks. How many railroad trailers are needed to carry 210 pickup trucks?

## 11

## DIVISION
## TWO-DIGIT DIVISORS

305

# DIVIDING BY TENS

Can 65 soccer uniforms be put into equal groups of 20 uniforms?

To find out, divide 65 by 20.

Think of $2\overline{)6}$.

$$\begin{array}{r} 3 \\ 20\overline{)65} \\ -\ 60 \\ \hline 5 \end{array}$$

Subtract $3 \times 20$.

Write the remainder with the quotient.

$$\begin{array}{r} 3 \text{ R5} \\ 20\overline{)65} \\ -\ 60 \\ \hline 5 \end{array}$$

No, there are 3 groups of 20 uniforms with 5 left over.

Here is how you divide 150 by 20.

Think of $2\overline{)15}$.

$$\begin{array}{r} 7 \\ 20\overline{)150} \\ -\ 140 \\ \hline 10 \end{array}$$

Subtract $7 \times 20$.

Write the remainder with the quotient.

$$\begin{array}{r} 7 \text{ R10} \\ 20\overline{)150} \\ -\ 140 \\ \hline 10 \end{array}$$

**M** Use mental math to check the answer.
**Think:** $7 \times 20 = 140$, and $140 + 10 = 150.$ ✓

## CLASS EXERCISES

Divide.

1. $3\overline{)3}$      $30\overline{)30}$      $30\overline{)36}$      2. $4\overline{)8}$      $40\overline{)80}$      $40\overline{)84}$

3. $2\overline{)6}$      $20\overline{)60}$      $20\overline{)67}$      4. $1\overline{)7}$      $10\overline{)70}$      $10\overline{)77}$

5. $3\overline{)12}$      $30\overline{)120}$      $30\overline{)127}$      6. $5\overline{)18}$      $50\overline{)180}$      $50\overline{)184}$

# PRACTICE

Divide.

**7.** $20\overline{)83}$ **8.** $20\overline{)67}$ **9.** $40\overline{)83}$ **10.** $30\overline{)92}$ **11.** $20\overline{)48}$

**12.** $80\overline{)89}$ **13.** $20\overline{)45}$ **14.** $30\overline{)62}$ **15.** $30\overline{)96}$ **16.** $20\overline{)88}$

**17.** $90\overline{)90}$ **18.** $40\overline{)81}$ **19.** $50\overline{)58}$ **20.** $20\overline{)80}$ **21.** $30\overline{)63}$

**22.** $20\overline{)132}$ **23.** $30\overline{)251}$ **24.** $50\overline{)267}$ **25.** $20\overline{)187}$ **26.** $30\overline{)173}$

**27.** $40\overline{)320}$ **28.** $60\overline{)493}$ **29.** $30\overline{)142}$ **30.** $50\overline{)250}$ **31.** $40\overline{)248}$

**32.** $20\overline{)78}$ **33.** $30\overline{)219}$ **34.** $20\overline{)123}$ **35.** $10\overline{)78}$ **36.** $70\overline{)95}$

Complete.

**37.** $4 \times 20 = 80$
$80 \div \blacksquare = 4$

**38.** $5 \times 30 = 150$
$\blacksquare \div 30 = 5$

★ **39.** $9 \times \blacksquare = 360$
$\blacksquare \div 40 = 9$

Is the answer correct? Write *yes* or *no*. Use mental math to check.

**MENTAL MATH**

**40.** $20\overline{)32}^{\,1\ R2}$ **41.** $30\overline{)51}^{\,2\ R9}$ **42.** $40\overline{)160}^{\,40}$ **43.** $20\overline{)190}^{\,9\ R10}$

## PROBLEM SOLVING APPLICATIONS
### Choosing a Strategy

Solve.

**44.** There are 72 shirts. If each of the 20 members gets an equal number of shirts, how many shirts does each person get?

**46.** Kay buys 2 pairs of shoes. Each pair costs $18.98. About how much change does she get from $50?

**47.** Look at the picture at the right. What is the least number of clothespins needed to hang 72 shirts on the same line?

**45.** Patches for the team jackets come in packages of 10. The coach needs 26 patches. How many packages should he buy?

# ONE-DIGIT QUOTIENTS

Video World has cassette racks that hold 21 cassettes each.
If 87 cassettes are displayed, how many racks are filled?

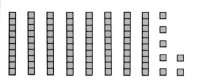     

To divide 87 by 21, first round the divisor.

Round 21 down to 20.

Think of $2\overline{)8}$.

Write the remainder with the quotient.

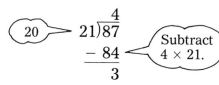

Only 4 racks are filled. There are 3 cassettes left over.

A calculator is handy to check your work. Multiply and then add.

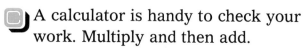

## CLASS EXERCISES

Divide.

**1.** $20\overline{)45}$     $22\overline{)45}$     **2.** $40\overline{)84}$     $38\overline{)84}$     **3.** $30\overline{)93}$     $31\overline{)93}$

**4.** $40\overline{)162}$     $35\overline{)162}$     **5.** $50\overline{)255}$     $48\overline{)255}$     **6.** $60\overline{)379}$     $59\overline{)379}$

## PRACTICE

Divide.

**7.** $66\overline{)98}$     **8.** $77\overline{)89}$     **9.** $17\overline{)65}$     **10.** $23\overline{)46}$     **11.** $36\overline{)45}$

**12.** $25\overline{)68}$     **13.** $34\overline{)68}$     **14.** $58\overline{)99}$     **15.** $67\overline{)89}$     **16.** $89\overline{)97}$

**17.** $22\overline{)67}$　**18.** $32\overline{)96}$　**19.** $18\overline{)67}$　**20.** $12\overline{)39}$　**21.** $11\overline{)68}$

**22.** $22\overline{)134}$　**23.** $36\overline{)281}$　**24.** $43\overline{)396}$　**25.** $21\overline{)147}$　**26.** $18\overline{)160}$

**27.** $87\overline{)298}$　**28.** $93\overline{)605}$　**29.** $19\overline{)183}$　**30.** $85\overline{)457}$　**31.** $75\overline{)586}$

**32.** $30\overline{)156}$　**33.** $32\overline{)262}$　**34.** $21\overline{)193}$　**35.** $19\overline{)126}$　**36.** $64\overline{)272}$

**37.** $13\overline{)27}$　**38.** $44\overline{)352}$　**39.** $43\overline{)86}$　**40.** $37\overline{)132}$　**41.** $58\overline{)93}$

What number makes both number sentences true?

★ **42.** $3 \times \blacksquare = 81$
　　$81 \div \blacksquare = 3$

★ **43.** $4 \times \blacksquare = 140$
　　$140 \div \blacksquare = 4$

★ **44.** $7 \times \blacksquare = 112$
　　$112 \div \blacksquare = 7$

Is the answer correct? Write *yes* or *no*. If you have a calculator use it to check the answer.

CALCULATOR

**45.** $18\overline{)62}$ $\overset{3\ R8}{}$　**46.** $27\overline{)92}$ $\overset{3\ R11}{}$　**47.** $10\overline{)99}$ $\overset{9}{}$　**48.** $39\overline{)96}$ $\overset{1\ R16}{}$

**49.** $41\overline{)56}$ $\overset{1\ R1}{}$　**50.** $56\overline{)75}$ $\overset{1\ R19}{}$　**51.** $12\overline{)49}$ $\overset{4}{}$　**52.** $26\overline{)72}$ $\overset{2}{}$

**53. Think:** Which of Exercises 45–52 would be easier to check using mental math?

## PROBLEM SOLVING APPLICATIONS
### Too Much Information

Solve.

**54.** Big Hit Video received a shipment of 88 tapes. Each display case holds 19 tapes. The price of each tape is $9.98. How many cases are needed to display the new tapes?

**55.** On Friday 61 people rented tapes. There were 189 tapes rented in all. Forty-seven of the tapes were children's tapes. How many of the tapes that were rented were not children's tapes?

**56.** On Tuesday 84 children's tapes, 63 jazz tapes, and 127 other tapes were rented. There were 72 customers on Tuesday. How many tapes were rented in all?

★ **57.** For one week only, the store gave a free tape to every 75th customer. During that week 2520 tapes were rented to 672 people. How many free tapes were given out?

# PROBLEM SOLVING
## Strategy: Reasonable Answers

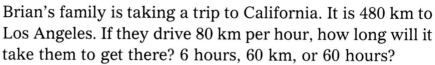

Brian's family is taking a trip to California. It is 480 km to Los Angeles. If they drive 80 km per hour, how long will it take them to get there? 6 hours, 60 km, or 60 hours?

To solve the problem, you divide.

$$80\overline{)480}$$

**Think:** How many digits will be in the answer?

Since you cannot divide 48 tens by 80, the answer will not have a digit in the tens' place.

The question asks for time, so the most likely answer is 6 hours.

## CLASS EXERCISES

Choose the answer. Explain your choice.

1. Brian and his parents decided to have lunch in San Diego. Each of them ordered the same item. The total cost of lunch was $9.87. How much did each lunch cost?

   **a.** $29.61   **b.** $3.29   **c.** $9.87

2. The Wilsons went to visit the giant trees in Sequoia National Park. The Park is 365 km from Los Angeles. If Brian's mother drove at a speed of 73 km per hour, how long did the trip take?

   **a.** 5 hours **b.** 292 hours **c.** 5 km

3. The Giant Sequoia tree is 12 times as tall as the tree in Brian's back yard. If Brian's tree is 7 m tall, how tall is the giant tree?

   **a.** 19 m   **b.** 56 cm   **c.** 84 m

4. Brian's mother bought 28 L of gasoline. The gas cost $.37 per liter. What was the total cost of the gas?

   **a.** $1036   **b.** $10.36   **c.** $.65

# PRACTICE

If the answer makes sense, write *correct*. If it does not make sense, give the correct answer.

**5.** Brian and his grandparents took a tour. There were 3 buses for 111 people. An equal number of people rode on each bus. How many people were on each bus?
*Answer:* 37 buses

**6.** Brian's mother drove slowly through the Sierra Nevada mountains. If she drove at a speed of 52 km per hour, how long did it take to drive 156 km?
*Answer:* 8112 hours

**7.** Mount Whitney, California's highest mountain, is 4418 m high. There is only one mountain in the USA that is higher. Mount McKinley, in Alaska, is 6190 m. How much taller is Mount McKinley than Mount Whitney?
*Answer:* 1772 m

**8.** Brian wants to visit Lassen Peak, an old volcano. It is 616 km from Los Angeles to Sacramento, 258 km from Sacramento to Redding, and 77 km from Redding to Lassen Peak. How far will he travel if he follows this route?
*Answer:* 951 km

**9.** Brian's father bought food for a picnic in the park. The food cost $7.28. How much change did he get from $20.00?
*Answer:* $27.28

★ **10.** When he visited Hollywood, Brian bought 12 postcards for $.15 each. How much change did he get from $10.00?
*Answer:* $1.80

★ **11.** The Wilsons are 420 km from home. If they drive 88 km before lunch and twice that far after lunch, how much farther must they drive before they are home?
*Answer:* 156 km

Write the answer.

| **12.** | **13.** | **14.** | **15.** | **16.** |
|---|---|---|---|---|
| 257 | 358 | 842 | 987 | 382 |
| + 463 | ×27 | ×78 | − 178 | + 657 |

| **17.** | **18.** | **19.** | **20.** | **21.** |
|---|---|---|---|---|
| 620 | 518 | 700 | 608 | 863 |
| − 487 | ×65 | − 429 | − 599 | + 140 |

**MIXED REVIEW**

# TWO-DIGIT QUOTIENTS

At Pine Woods there are 384 trees to be planted in rows of 20 trees each. How many rows will be planted? Will any trees be left over?

To answer, divide 384 by 20. Think of 3 hundreds 8 tens as 38 tens.

Divide 38 by 20.
Think of $2\overline{)3}$.

$$\begin{array}{r} 1\phantom{00} \\ 20\overline{)384} \\ -20\phantom{0} \\ \hline 18\phantom{0} \end{array}$$

Subtract 1 × 20.

Divide 184 by 20.
Think of $2\overline{)18}$.

$$\begin{array}{r} 19\phantom{0} \\ 20\overline{)384} \\ -20\phantom{0} \\ \hline 184 \\ -180 \\ \hline 4 \end{array}$$

Subtract 9 × 20.

Write the remainder.

$$\begin{array}{r} 19\,\text{R4} \\ 20\overline{)384} \\ -20\phantom{0} \\ \hline 184 \\ -180 \\ \hline 4 \end{array}$$

There are 19 rows of 20 trees with 4 trees left over.

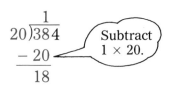

You can estimate the answer. **Think:** $200 \div 20 = 10$ and $400 \div 20 = 20$. Because 384 is between 200 and 400, $384 \div 20$ must be between 10 and 20.

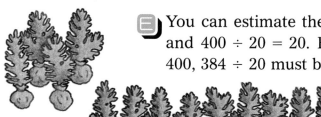

## CLASS EXERCISES

Divide.

**1.** $30\overline{)64}$   $30\overline{)640}$   **2.** $20\overline{)52}$   $20\overline{)523}$   **3.** $60\overline{)75}$   $60\overline{)755}$

Look at the division problem at the right.

**4.** Explain the steps in the division problem.

**5.** How many tens are in the quotient?

**6.** How many ones are in the quotient?

**7. Think:** What is the greatest number you could ever have as a remainder when 40 is the divisor?

$$\begin{array}{r} 16\,\text{R25} \\ 40\overline{)665} \\ -40\phantom{0} \\ \hline 265 \\ -240 \\ \hline 25 \end{array}$$

# PRACTICE

Divide. Remember to put zeros in the quotient when they are needed.

**8.** $20\overline{)400}$     **9.** $60\overline{)600}$     **10.** $40\overline{)840}$     **11.** $50\overline{)500}$     **12.** $30\overline{)630}$

**13.** $30\overline{)304}$     **14.** $40\overline{)806}$     **15.** $20\overline{)402}$     **16.** $30\overline{)907}$     **17.** $10\overline{)808}$

**18.** $20\overline{)226}$     **19.** $30\overline{)642}$     **20.** $40\overline{)451}$     **21.** $50\overline{)574}$     **22.** $30\overline{)952}$

**23.** $30\overline{)406}$     **24.** $20\overline{)317}$     **25.** $50\overline{)615}$     **26.** $40\overline{)523}$     **27.** $60\overline{)752}$

**28.** $30\overline{)338}$     **29.** $50\overline{)562}$     **30.** $90\overline{)810}$     **31.** $80\overline{)279}$     **32.** $60\overline{)735}$

**33.** $50\overline{)255}$     **34.** $80\overline{)408}$     **35.** $80\overline{)999}$     **36.** $80\overline{)560}$     **37.** $90\overline{)986}$

★ **38.** $20\overline{)5030}$    ★ **39.** $40\overline{)9380}$    ★ **40.** $30\overline{)4600}$    ★ **41.** $60\overline{)6270}$    ★ **42.** $70\overline{)9330}$

Match the division problem and the estimated answer.

**43.** $20\overline{)741}$     **A.** between 10 and 20

**44.** $30\overline{)786}$     **B.** between 20 and 30

**45.** $40\overline{)698}$     **C.** between 30 and 40

**ESTIMATE**

## PROBLEM SOLVING APPLICATIONS
### Mental Math or Pencil

Use mental math or paper and pencil to solve the problem. Write *m* or *p* to tell the method you chose.

**46.** One out of every 30 trees will be cut down for lumber. There are 845 trees. How many trees will be cut down?

**47.** At the sawmill a large tree can be cut to make 20 boards. How many boards can be made from 58 large trees?

**48.** A tree trunk is 80 ft long. It is cut to make 20 logs of equal length. How long is each log?

**49.** A small truck can carry 40 logs. A larger one can carry 135. How many more logs can the larger truck carry?

★ **50.** A log is 88 ft long. It can be cut in either 4 ft or 8 ft lengths, or in a combination of both. What are two ways in which the log can be cut?

# TWO-DIGIT QUOTIENTS

The Albert Einstein Planetarium at the Smithsonian Institution in Washington, D.C., can hold 230 people. How many groups of 18 people can it hold?

To divide 230 by 18, think of the divisor rounded to a multiple of 10.

Round 18 to 20.
Think of $2\overline{)2}$.

Think of $2\overline{)5}$.

Write the remainder with the quotient.

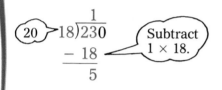

$$\begin{array}{r} 1 \\ 18\overline{)230} \\ -18 \\ \hline 5 \end{array}$$

Subtract $1 \times 18$.

$$\begin{array}{r} 12 \\ 18\overline{)230} \\ -18\downarrow \\ \hline 50 \\ -36 \\ \hline 14 \end{array}$$

Subtract $2 \times 18$.

$$\begin{array}{r} 12\ \text{R}14 \\ 18\overline{)230} \\ -18 \\ \hline 50 \\ -36 \\ \hline 14 \end{array}$$

The planetarium can hold 12 groups of 18 people. There are 14 seats left over.

## CLASS EXERCISES

Divide.

1. $20\overline{)403}$   $18\overline{)403}$   2. $60\overline{)632}$   $56\overline{)632}$

3. $30\overline{)812}$   $32\overline{)812}$   4. $20\overline{)530}$   $23\overline{)530}$

5. $50\overline{)799}$   $48\overline{)799}$   6. $30\overline{)680}$   $28\overline{)680}$

## PRACTICE

Divide.

7. $28\overline{)603}$   8. $76\overline{)853}$   9. $32\overline{)400}$   10. $27\overline{)615}$   11. $72\overline{)811}$

12. $50\overline{)649}$   13. $53\overline{)616}$   14. $44\overline{)517}$   15. $81\overline{)905}$   16. $68\overline{)791}$

17. $19\overline{)522}$   18. $83\overline{)913}$   19. $30\overline{)490}$   20. $59\overline{)743}$   21. $45\overline{)802}$

**22.** 38)712  **23.** 66)826  **24.** 79)914  **25.** 36)646  **26.** 47)889

**27.** 29)572  **28.** 60)815  **29.** 48)815  **30.** 39)523  **31.** 83)977

**32.** 46)772  **33.** 37)542  **34.** 53)901  **35.** 28)491  **36.** 18)210

## PROBLEM SOLVING APPLICATIONS
### Choosing a Strategy

Solve.

**37.** The parking garage holds 390 cars. There are 30 parking spaces in each section. How many sections are in the garage?

**38.** The National Air and Space Museum is built of Tennessee pink marble. It is 635 ft long and 225 ft wide. The floor of the building is the shape of a rectangle. What is the perimeter of the building?

**40.** A student ticket for the Langley Theater costs $.75. About how many tickets can you buy for $8.00?

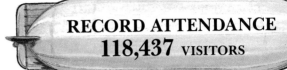

**RECORD ATTENDANCE**
**118,437** VISITORS

**39.** April 14, 1984, was a record attendance day. On that day, 118,437 people visited the museum. That amount was 51,437 more than the average daily attendance. What is the average daily attendance?

★ **41.** The theater has 12 shows daily from 9:30 A.M. to 5:30 P.M. If there are no breaks between the shows, how long is each show?

## CHECKPOINT 1

Divide. *(pages 306–309, 312–315)*

**1.** 30)92  **2.** 18)63

**3.** 71)320  **4.** 83)442

**5.** 30)489  **6.** 40)567

**7.** 27)942  **8.** 56)810

If the answer makes sense, write *correct*. If not, give the correct answer. *(pages 310–311)*

**9.** Isabel walked 160 km during a 20-day trip. She walked the same distance each day. How far did she walk in one day?
*Answer:* 8 km

*Extra practice on page 422*

# ADJUSTING THE QUOTIENT

Sometimes when you divide you have to adjust the quotient.

Divide 843 by 27.

Round 27 to 30.
Think of 3)8.

$$
\begin{array}{r}
2 \\
27\overline{)843} \\
-54 \\
\hline
30
\end{array}
$$

Is 30 less than 27? No.

Change the quotient.
Try 3.

$$
\begin{array}{r}
3 \\
27\overline{)843} \\
-81 \\
\hline
3
\end{array}
$$

Is 3 less than 27? Yes.

Divide 33 by 27.
Think of 3)3.

$$
\begin{array}{r}
31 \text{ R6} \\
27\overline{)843} \\
-81\downarrow \\
\hline
33 \\
-27 \\
\hline
6
\end{array}
$$

Is 6 less than 27? Yes.

Now divide 618 by 32.

Round 32 to 30.
Think of 3)6.

$$
\begin{array}{r}
2 \\
32\overline{)618} \\
-64
\end{array}
$$

64 is too large.

Change the quotient.
Try 1.

$$
\begin{array}{r}
1 \\
32\overline{)618} \\
-32 \\
\hline
29
\end{array}
$$

Is 29 less than 32? Yes.

Divide 298 by 32.
Think of 3)29.

$$
\begin{array}{r}
19 \text{ R10} \\
32\overline{)618} \\
-32\downarrow \\
\hline
298 \\
-288 \\
\hline
10
\end{array}
$$

Is 10 less than 32? Yes.

## CLASS EXERCISES

Does the quotient need adjusting? Explain why or why not.
Finish the problem.

1. $\begin{array}{r} 2 \\ 26\overline{)882} \\ -52 \\ \hline 36 \end{array}$
2. $\begin{array}{r} 2 \\ 42\overline{)814} \\ -84 \end{array}$
3. $\begin{array}{r} 1 \\ 35\overline{)743} \\ -35 \\ \hline 39 \end{array}$
4. $\begin{array}{r} 1 \\ 47\overline{)991} \\ -47 \\ \hline 52 \end{array}$
5. $\begin{array}{r} 3 \\ 16\overline{)682} \\ -48 \\ \hline 20 \end{array}$

## PRACTICE

Divide. Adjust the quotient if needed.

6. $28\overline{)592}$
7. $37\overline{)786}$
8. $19\overline{)779}$
9. $47\overline{)989}$
10. $15\overline{)478}$

**11.** $46\overline{)968}$  **12.** $16\overline{)388}$  **13.** $23\overline{)427}$  **14.** $31\overline{)609}$  **15.** $32\overline{)615}$

**16.** $36\overline{)765}$  **17.** $25\overline{)575}$  **18.** $18\overline{)752}$  **19.** $27\overline{)845}$  **20.** $13\overline{)413}$

**21.** $45\overline{)973}$  **22.** $37\overline{)784}$  **23.** $26\overline{)571}$  **24.** $32\overline{)929}$  **25.** $35\overline{)748}$

**26.** $17\overline{)594}$  **27.** $14\overline{)599}$  **28.** $22\overline{)639}$  **29.** $29\overline{)892}$  **30.** $21\overline{)823}$

Estimate the answer.

**31.** $48 + 76$    **32.** $19 \times 27$    **33.** $97 - 23$

**34.** $6.8 + 3.4$    **35.** $247 \times 9$    **36.** $\$.28 + \$.52$

**MIXED
REVIEW**

# PROBLEM SOLVING APPLICATIONS
## Choosing the Operation

Solve.

**37.** Parícutin, a volcano in Mexico, erupted for about 9 years. How many months is that?

**38.** Parícutin built up a cone 457 m high in 26 weeks. How many meters is that per week?

**39.** When Parícutin erupted in 1943, it was the first volcano to form in the Western Hemisphere since 1770. For how many years were there no new volcanoes?

★ **40.** Parícutin threw out 40,909 kg of ash every second it erupted for the first few months. How many kilograms is that in one day?

★ **41.** The volcano erupted in a cornfield. Follow the steps below to find the distance in kilometers from the cornfield to Mexico City.
  **a.** Add 1 to the year Parícutin erupted.
  **b.** Divide the sum by the number of years it erupted.
  **c.** Add 72 to the quotient.

# PROBLEM SOLVING
## Strategy: Simplifying a Problem

1. Understand
2. Plan
3. Work
4. Answer/Check

Sometimes numbers in a problem make it look more difficult than it is. You may not know whether to add, subtract, multiply, or divide to solve it. Using easier numbers may help you choose the correct operation.

**Original Problem**

Beth and her parents took a ride through Windy Knoll. The total cost of their tickets was $8.55. How much did each ticket cost?

**Easier Problem**

Three people took a ride. The total cost was $6. How much was each ticket?

You can see from the easier problem that you divide $6 by 3 to find the cost of each ticket.

Now go back to the original problem and divide.

The cost of each ticket was $2.85.

$$\begin{array}{r} \$2.85 \\ 3)\overline{\$8.55} \\ -\underline{6} \phantom{.55} \\ 2\,5 \\ -\underline{2\,4} \\ 15 \\ -\underline{15} \\ 0 \end{array}$$

Visit Windy Knoll

## CLASS EXERCISES

Rewrite the problem using easier numbers. Next write *add, subtract, multiply,* or *divide* to tell what operation to use to solve it. Then give the answer.

1. The trip from Rainy Forest to Pokey Point is 26.2 km along flat land and then 12.7 km through the mountains. What is the total distance between these places?

2. The train through Pokey Point can carry 816 people. Each car on the train can hold 48 people. How many cars are there on the train?

# PRACTICE

Use easier numbers to decide which operation to use. Then solve.

**3.** Carl's trip to Rainy Forest cost $32.50. Matt paid $20.75 less for his trip to Dry Gulch. How much did Matt's trip cost?

**4.** Tickets for Warm Springs are $9.50. The Smiths buy 5 tickets. How much do they spend for the tickets?

**5.** During the week, you can ride the train for half price. If a regular ticket is $18.90, what is the reduced rate?

**6.** An outdoor theater at Dry Gulch holds 1150 people. There are 25 rows of seats. How many seats are in each row?

**7.** At the theater, 789 people attended the first show and 153 fewer people attended the second show. What was the total attendance for the two shows?

**8.** The conductor makes 9 round trips a week from Pokey Point to Windy Knoll. He travels 4464 km in all. What is the distance of each round trip?

**9.** Last month, the three conductors with the longest total trips were:

Jan 19,261.3 km
Marty 21,800.2 km
Helen 9920.8 km

Who traveled farther than anyone else?

**10.** Emily bought a ticket to Windy Knoll for $12.85 and a ticket to Harbor City for $7.60. She received $4.55 in change. How much money did she give the ticket seller?

★ **11.** From 8:00 to 8:05 the ticket seller sold these tickets:

5 tickets for $32 each
4 tickets for $12 each
6 tickets for $29 each
1 ticket for $31

At 8:00 she had $175 in the cash drawer. How much did she have at 8:05?

# ESTIMATING QUOTIENTS

The students sold 314 tickets for the school art festival. The festival will last for 4 days. If the same number of people come to the festival each day, about how many will attend each day?

You can estimate to answer the question. Rounding to the greatest place value will not help to make the division easier.

$$314 \div 4 \longrightarrow 300 \div 4$$

In cases like this, it is easier to estimate by using numbers that divide easily.

$$4\overline{)314} \qquad \text{Try: } 4\overline{)320}^{\,80}$$

About 80 people will attend each day.

**Think:** Will the actual answer be greater than or less than 80?

When you work with a 2-digit divisor, first round the divisor to the nearest ten. Then think of numbers that divide easily.

$$32\overline{)263} \longrightarrow 30\overline{)270}^{\,9}$$

## CLASS EXERCISES

Choose the easier way to estimate the answer. Write *a* or *b*.
Then write the estimate.

1. $8\overline{)326}$    a. $8\overline{)300}$    b. $8\overline{)320}$    2. $7\overline{)624}$    a. $7\overline{)620}$    b. $7\overline{)630}$

3. $21\overline{)585}$    a. $20\overline{)600}$    b. $20\overline{)590}$    4. $28\overline{)194}$    a. $30\overline{)200}$    b. $30\overline{)180}$

What numbers would you use to estimate the answer?

5. $3\overline{)187}$        6. $9\overline{)277}$        7. $6\overline{)431}$        8. $39\overline{)352}$        9. $43\overline{)158}$

# PRACTICE

Estimate the answer.

**10.** 6)368     **11.** 6)127     **12.** 9)255     **13.** 6)523     **14.** 3)862

**15.** 8)714     **16.** 7)297     **17.** 8)412     **18.** 4)351     **19.** 9)437

**20.** 58)340     **21.** 33)188     **22.** 79)542     **23.** 44)219     **24.** 66)549

**25.** 11)932     **26.** 21)748     **27.** 17)345     **28.** 85)953     **29.** 45)998

## PROBLEM SOLVING APPLICATIONS
### Using Estimation

Estimate the answer.

**30.** Eight students hand out 730 name tags. About how many will each student hand out?

**31.** One display area has 7 rows of seats. Each row has 14 seats. Are there enough seats for 65 people?

**32.** There are 17 display areas for 143 drawings. About how many drawings will be in each area?

★ **33.** Orange juice will be served each day. A 2 L pitcher serves 12 people. About how many liters of juice will be needed to serve 200 people?

# CHECKPOINT 2

Divide. *(pages 316–317)*

**1.** 36)786     **2.** 23)429

**3.** 13)415     **4.** 32)931

Estimate the answer.
*(pages 320–321)*

**5.** 3)239     **6.** 4)784

**7.** 68)736     **8.** 32)219

Use easier numbers to decide which operation to use. Then solve. *(pages 318–319)*

**9.** Mario must display 540 postcards in cases that hold 38 cards each. How many cases will he fill?

*Extra practice on page 424*

Write the answer. *(pages 306–309)*

**1.** $60\overline{)394}$     **2.** $38\overline{)87}$     **3.** $92\overline{)705}$     **4.** $53\overline{)218}$

If the answer makes sense, write *correct*. If it does not make sense, give the correct answer. *(pages 310–311)*

**5.** Julie bought one record for $8.45 and another record for $7.98. What was the total cost of the two records?
*Answer:* $.74

**6.** The theater has 432 seats. There are 12 rows with an equal number of seats in each. How many seats are in each row?
*Answer:* 36 seats

Write the answer. *(pages 312–317)*

**7.** $80\overline{)968}$     **8.** $29\overline{)714}$     **9.** $47\overline{)821}$     **10.** $36\overline{)563}$

**11.** $30\overline{)746}$     **12.** $52\overline{)658}$     **13.** $28\overline{)625}$     **14.** $44\overline{)963}$

**15.** $75\overline{)902}$     **16.** $43\overline{)824}$     **17.** $12\overline{)400}$     **18.** $26\overline{)651}$

Use easier numbers to decide which operation to use. Then solve. *(pages 318–319)*

**19.** Joe's lunch cost $5.84 and his dinner cost $3.75 more than lunch. What was the total cost of both meals?

**20.** The distance from Fairview Park to Lookout Point is 24.8 km. The distance from Lookout Point to Forest Hills is 35.3 km. How much farther is it from Lookout Point to Forest Hills than from Fairview Park to Lookout Point?

Estimate the answer. *(pages 320–321)*

**21.** $7\overline{)361}$     **22.** $18\overline{)793}$     **23.** $63\overline{)491}$     **24.** $48\overline{)367}$

*Extra practice on page 423*

# MATHEMATICS and GEOGRAPHY

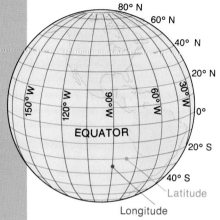

EQUATOR

Latitude

Longitude

You can think of the earth divided into parts. The parts are formed by *lines of longitude* and *lines of latitude*. Lines of longitude run north and south. Lines of latitude run east and west. Together the lines form a grid.

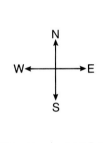

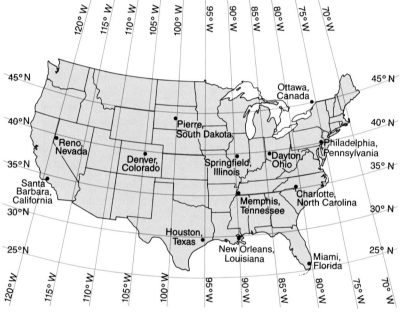

# WHAT'S THE POINT?

You can see that Philadelphia, Pennsylvania, is near 40°N and 75°W.

Use the map above.
Name the city that is located near this point.

**1.** 30°N, 95°W

**2.** 40°N, 90°W

**3.** 35°N, 120°W

**4.** 40°N, 120°W

**5.** 25°N, 80°W

**6.** 45°N, 100°W

**7.** 35°N, 80°W

**8.** 30°N, 90°W

**9.** 40°N, 85°W

**10.** 40°N, 105°W

**11.** 45°N, 75°W

**12.** 35°N, 90°W

# Enrichment

Scientists often use photographs to estimate the number of animals in an area. Let's see how they do it.

Suppose you want to know how many animals are in this wildlife park. A guess may not be close enough. And it would take a long time to count all the animals. What you can do is take a **sample.**

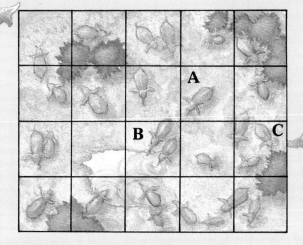

A grid can help you estimate the number of animals. This grid divides the lot into 20 equal sections. First take a sample by counting the number of animals in one section. Then multiply that number by 20 to get an estimate of the total number of animals.

Count the number of animals in the section indicated. Then complete the table to answer the question.

1.

| SECTION | NUMBER | ESTIMATE OF TOTAL |
|---------|--------|-------------------|
| A | ? | ? |
| B | ? | ? |
| C | ? | ? |

Compare your estimates. How close are they? Why are they different?

# SAMPLING AND ESTIMATING

When you count objects in only one section of a grid, your estimate may not be very close to the actual number. To get a closer estimate, you can count the number of objects in several sections. Then you can make several estimates and average them.

A photograph is helpful when you have to count moving objects. Notice that the grid lines go through some of the objects. When that happens, count an object only if the greatest part of its body lies within a section.

Count the number of fish in the section indicated. Then complete the table and average the estimates.

**2.**

| SECTION | NUMBER | ESTIMATE OF TOTAL |
|---------|--------|-------------------|
| A | ? | ? |
| B | ? | ? |
| C | ? | ? |
| D | ? | ? |

Average of Estimates = ___?___

Solve.

**3.** Choose 4 different sections of the photo and make another estimate. Compare your estimate with your classmates' estimates. How close are they?

**4.** Which would give you a closer estimate, 4 sections or 8 sections? Why?

325

# CUMULATIVE REVIEW

Choose the correct answer. Write *a*, *b*, *c*, or *d*.

Find the numbers.

**1.** six multiples of 7
  **a.** 1, 7, 14, 21, 28, 35
  **b.** 7, 14, 21, 28, 35, 42
  **c.** 14, 21, 28, 35, 42, 49
  **d.** none of these

**2.** three common multiples of 4 and 6
  **a.** 4, 6, 12      **b.** 12, 16, 24
  **c.** 12, 24, 36    **d.** none of these

Find the common factors.

**3.** 12 and 16
  **a.** 1, 2, 4
  **b.** 1, 2, 3, 4
  **c.** 2, 6, 8
  **d.** none of these

**4.** 9 and 15
  **a.** 1, 3, 5
  **b.** 1, 3
  **c.** 1, 9, 15
  **d.** none of these

**5.** 28 and 20
  **a.** 1, 2, 4
  **b.** 4, 5, 7
  **c.** 1, 4, 5, 7
  **d.** none of these

Find the decimal.

**6.** 18 and 8 tenths
  **a.** 0.188
  **b.** 18.08
  **c.** 18.8
  **d.** none of these

**7.** 66 hundredths
  **a.** 0.66
  **b.** 0.066
  **c.** 0.0066
  **d.** none of these

**8.** 54 and 7 hundredths
  **a.** 0.547
  **b.** 54.7
  **c.** 54.07
  **d.** none of these

Compare the numbers.

**9.** 0.5 ▓ 0.53

  **a.** >      **b.** <
  **c.** +      **d.** =

**10.** 3.5 ▓ 3.50

  **a.** <      **b.** >
  **c.** =      **d.** +

**11.** 7.61 ▓ 6.71

  **a.** +      **b.** >
  **c.** <      **d.** =

Find the answer.

**12.**   3.29
      + 5.06
      _____

  **a.** 8.35
  **b.** 8.89
  **c.** 8.25
  **d.** none of these

**13.**   9.4
      + 4.86
      _____

  **a.** 13.26
  **b.** 14.26
  **c.** 13.6
  **d.** none of these

**14.**   21.5
      +  6.8
      _____

  **a.** 14.7
  **b.** 28.3
  **c.** 27.3
  **d.** none of these

Find the answer.

| 15. | 16. | 17. |
|---|---|---|
| 18.5 | 23.7 | 5.1 |
| − 11.7 | − 6.7 | − 3.82 |
| **a.** 7.8 | **a.** 27.1 | **a.** 9.92 |
| **b.** 17.8 | **b.** 17.0 | **b.** 8.92 |
| **c.** 6.8 | **c.** 30.4 | **c.** 1.38 |
| **d.** none of these | **d.** none of these | **d.** none of these |

Estimate to solve.

**18.** Brenda bicycled 3.7 km on Monday, 2.8 km on Tuesday, and 1.6 km on Wednesday. About how far did she bicycle?

**a.** about 9 km    **b.** about 4 km    **c.** about 3 km    **d.** about 5 km

Use the table. Solve.

**19.** How much more do an inner tube and a new chain cost at Sally's than at Bill's?
**a.** $18.40          **b.** $9.98
**c.** $1.47           **d.** none of these

**20.** What is the total cost of the three repairs at Sally's?
**a.** $29.35          **b.** $39.95
**c.** $39.45          **d.** none of these

**BIKE REPAIRS**

| PLACE | BILL'S | SALLY'S |
|---|---|---|
| Chain | $6.95 | $7.98 |
| Inner Tube | $9.98 | $10.42 |
| Brake Adjustment | $11.50 | $10.95 |

# LANGUAGE and VOCABULARY REVIEW

Read the sentence. On your paper write *True* or *False*.

**1.** A right angle is always less than 90°.

**2.** A quadrilateral is a polygon with four sides.

**3.** The symbol for "is greater than" is <.

**4.** A medium-sized pitcher holds about 1 mL of water.

**5.** Numbers that answer the question "Which one?" are called ordinal numbers.

# GOTO AND LET

A **loop** makes the computer do lines over and over.
You can use **GOTO** to make the computer loop.
Each time through the program is one loop.

This program makes the computer count.

Output

```
        10 LET A = 0
      → 20 LET A = A + 1
Loop    30 PRINT A
      ─ 40 GOTO 20
        50 END
```

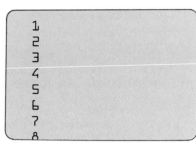

Line 10   *LET A = 0* makes *A* stand for zero.
Line 20   For *A* + 1, the computer adds 1 to zero.   $0 + 1 = 1$
          Now *A* stands for 1.
Line 30   The computer shows the number 1.
Line 40   The computer goes back to line 20. The computer
          adds 1 to 1 and shows the number 2.

The computer will continue adding 1 to *A*
until you make the program stop.

> On some computers, press the CONTROL and BREAK keys to stop the program.

Write the output for five loops.

**1.**
```
10 LET B = 0
20 LET B = B + 2
30 PRINT B
40 GOTO 20
50 END
```

**2.**
```
10 LET C = 21
20 LET C = C - 3
30 PRINT C
40 GOTO 20
50 END
```

**3.**
```
10 PRINT "COUNT BY 5"
20 LET D = 0
30 LET D = D + 5
40 PRINT D
50 GOTO 30
60 END
```

# 12

This parachute is divided into 9 parts. How many of the 9 parts are white? How many of the 9 parts are not white?

FRACTIONS

329

# FRACTIONS AND PARTS

Pedro and Joyce want a spinner with one half shaded red.

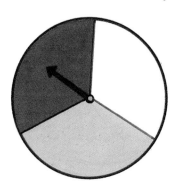 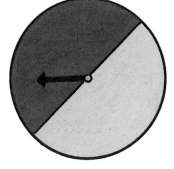 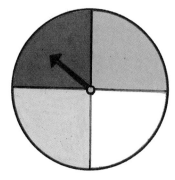

Spinner A       Spinner B       Spinner C

They pick spinner B. Spinner B has two equal parts or two halves. One part, or one half, is shaded red.

You write one half as the **fraction** $\frac{1}{2}$.

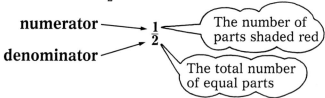

**numerator** $\longrightarrow$ $\frac{1}{2}$ $\longleftarrow$ The number of parts shaded red

**denominator** $\longrightarrow$ The total number of equal parts

**Think:** What fraction of spinner A is shaded red?

## CLASS EXERCISES

Read the fraction. Which number is the numerator? Which number is the denominator?

**1.** $\frac{1}{3}$      **2.** $\frac{1}{4}$      **3.** $\frac{2}{5}$      **4.** $\frac{3}{8}$      **5.** $\frac{1}{10}$

Complete the fraction for the shaded part.

**6.** 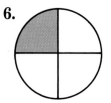   $\frac{\phantom{0}}{4}$

**7.** 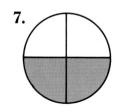   $\frac{2}{\phantom{0}}$

**8.** 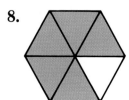   $\frac{\phantom{0}}{\phantom{0}}$

# PRACTICE

Write the fraction for the shaded part.

**9.**

**10.**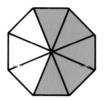

**11.**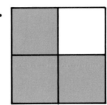

**12.**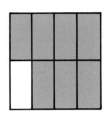

**13.**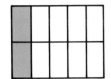

**14.**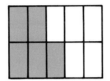

**15.**

**16.**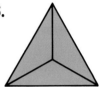

**17.**

**18.**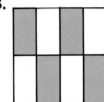

★ **19.**

★ **20.**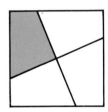

## PROBLEM SOLVING APPLICATIONS
### Choosing a Strategy

Solve.

**21.** Two friends come to play a game with Pedro and Joyce. They make a spinner with 1 part for each player. How many parts does it have?

**22.** Pedro and Joyce invite Marcia, Juan, Cecilia, Homer, and Helene to play a game. The spinner has 1 part for each player. How many parts does the spinner have?

**23.** Steve has first choice of markers for a board game. The markers come in 3 different shapes and 2 different colors. From how many markers can Steve choose?

**24.** Gerry is making a spinner. She marks off 1 part for every 2 players. How many parts does Gerry mark off if there are 8 players?

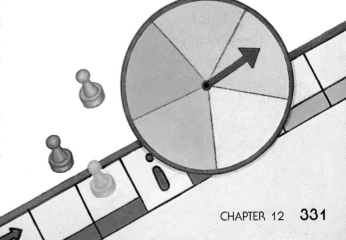

# FRACTIONS AND GROUPS

**TYPES OF DOGS**

| Boxer | ✓ |
|---|---|
| Chow Chow | ✓ |
| Cocker Spaniel | ✓ |
| Poodle | |
| Beagle | ✓ |
| Collie | |
| Labrador | ✓ |
| Shepherd | |

Sometimes you can write a fraction to show a part of a group.

The table at the left shows 8 types of dogs. In Bernie's class, students have the 5 types of dogs that are checked. Five eighths of the types are checked.

You can write the fraction $\frac{5}{8}$.

Three eighths of the types are not checked. You can write $\frac{3}{8}$.

## CLASS EXERCISES

Complete.

1. ▨ of the 6 squares are shaded.
   $\frac{□}{6}$ of the squares are shaded.

2. 3 of the ▨ circles are shaded.
   $\frac{3}{□}$ of the circles are shaded.

3. ▨ of the ▨ triangles are shaded.
   $\frac{□}{□}$ of the triangles are shaded.

## PRACTICE

What fraction of the shapes is shaded?

4.

5.

6.

**7.**

**8.**

**9.**

**10.**

**11.**

**12.**

Complete.

★ **13.**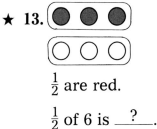

$\frac{1}{2}$ are red.

$\frac{1}{2}$ of 6 is ___?___.

★ **14.**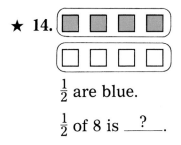

$\frac{1}{2}$ are blue.

$\frac{1}{2}$ of 8 is ___?___.

★ **15.**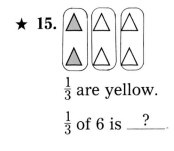

$\frac{1}{3}$ are yellow.

$\frac{1}{3}$ of 6 is ___?___.

★ **16.**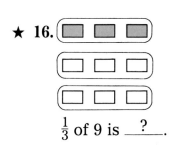

$\frac{1}{3}$ of 9 is ___?___.

★ **17.**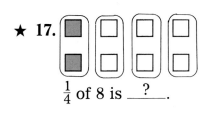

$\frac{1}{4}$ of 8 is ___?___.

★ **18.**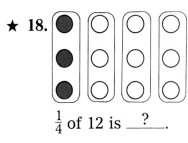

$\frac{1}{4}$ of 12 is ___?___.

## PROBLEM SOLVING APPLICATIONS
### Using a Table

Carol surveyed the 20 students in her class. The table shows the results. Solve.

**19.** How many students have dogs?

**20.** How many students do not have a dog?

**21.** What fraction of students have dogs?

**22.** What fraction of students do not have a dog?

**23.** What fraction of students have beagles?

**24.** Which dog is the most popular?

★ **25.** What fraction of students who have dogs have a beagle, a collie, or a poodle?

| TYPE OF DOG | NUMBER |
|---|---|
| Boxer | 1 |
| Cocker Spaniel | 3 |
| Beagle | 2 |
| Labrador | 6 |
| Collie | 2 |
| Poodle | 1 |
| No Dog | 5 |

# EQUIVALENT FRACTIONS

This piece of paper is folded into three equal parts. One of the three parts is blue. The fraction $\frac{1}{3}$ tells how much of the paper is blue.

The same piece of paper is folded into six equal parts. Two of the six parts are blue. The fraction $\frac{2}{6}$ tells how much of the paper is blue.

 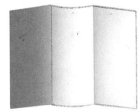

1 part is blue.

3 parts in all

$\frac{1}{3}$

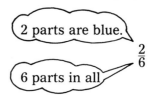 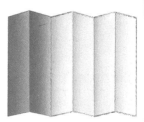

2 parts are blue.

6 parts in all

$\frac{2}{6}$

The fractions $\frac{1}{3}$ and $\frac{2}{6}$ name the same amount of blue parts.

They are **equivalent** fractions.

$$\frac{1}{3} = \frac{2}{6}$$

## CLASS EXERCISES

Complete the number sentence to show equivalent fractions.

**1.**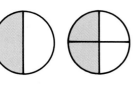

$\frac{1}{2} = \frac{\phantom{0}}{4}$

**2.**

$\frac{1}{3} = \frac{3}{\phantom{0}}$

**3.**

$\frac{\phantom{0}}{5} = \frac{\phantom{0}}{10}$

## PRACTICE

Write a number sentence to show equivalent fractions.

**4.**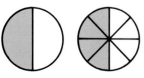

**5.**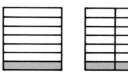

**6.**

**7.**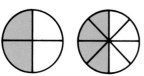

**8.**

**9.**

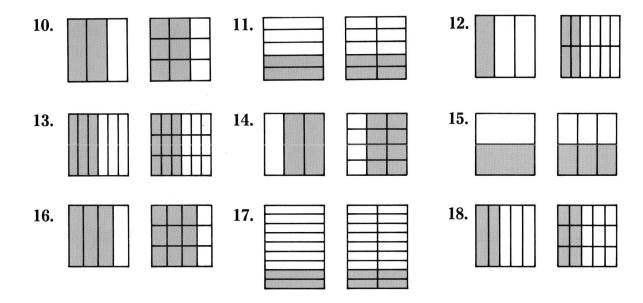

**10.** **11.** **12.**

**13.** **14.** **15.**

**16.** **17.** **18.**

Write the numbers.

**19.** Five multiples of 3

**20.** All the factors of 12

**21.** Three common multiples of 4 and 6

**22.** All the common factors of 4 and 8

**MIXED
REVIEW**

## PROBLEM SOLVING APPLICATIONS
### Using a Picture

Write the letter of the picture that
shows the equivalent fraction.

**23.** Tim painted two thirds of a
fence.

**24.** Cleo painted three fourths
of a fence.

★ **25.** Patty painted two sixths of
a fence.

★ **26.** Mandy painted four eighths
of a fence.

A.

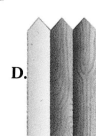

B.

C.

D.

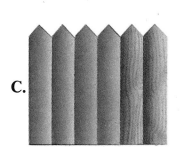

# FRACTIONS IN LOWEST TERMS

You can find a fraction equivalent to another fraction by dividing the numerator and the denominator by a common factor greater than one.

You can divide the numerator and the denominator of $\frac{4}{8}$ by 2.

$$\frac{4}{8} = \frac{4 \div 2}{8 \div 2} = \frac{2}{4}$$

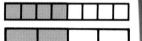

Sometimes you can divide more than once. Divide the numerator and the denominator by 2 again.

$$\frac{2}{4} = \frac{2 \div 2}{4 \div 2} = \frac{1}{2}$$

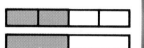

To save a step, you could have divided the numerator and the denominator by 4.

$$\frac{4}{8} = \frac{4 \div 4}{8 \div 4} = \frac{1}{2}$$

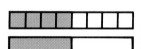

The numerator and the denominator of the fraction $\frac{1}{2}$ cannot be divided by a factor greater than 1. The fraction $\frac{1}{2}$ is in **lowest terms.**

If the numerator and the denominator are the same, the fraction is equal to 1.

$$\frac{4}{4} = \frac{4 \div 4}{4 \div 4} = \frac{1}{1} = 1$$

 If you know your division facts, you can divide mentally to find the lowest terms.

## CLASS EXERCISES

Complete.

**1.** $\frac{2}{4} = \frac{2 \div 2}{4 \div 2} = \frac{\blacksquare}{2}$

**2.** $\frac{6}{6} = \frac{6 \div 6}{6 \div 6} = \frac{\blacksquare}{1} = \blacksquare$

**3.** $\frac{2}{10} = \frac{2 \div 2}{10 \div 2} = \frac{\blacksquare}{\blacksquare}$

**4.** $\frac{3}{9} = \frac{3 \div 3}{9 \div 3} = \frac{\blacksquare}{\blacksquare}$

**5.** $\frac{6}{8} = \frac{6 \div 2}{8 \div 2} = \frac{\blacksquare}{\blacksquare}$

**6.** $\frac{5}{15} = \frac{5 \div \blacksquare}{15 \div \blacksquare} = \frac{\blacksquare}{\blacksquare}$

Complete.

**7.** $\frac{4}{20} = \frac{\blacksquare}{5}$

**8.** $\frac{8}{20} = \frac{\blacksquare}{5}$

**9.** $\frac{8}{12} = \frac{\blacksquare}{3}$

**10.** $\frac{4}{12} = \frac{\blacksquare}{3}$

**11.** $\frac{4}{16} = \frac{\blacksquare}{4}$

# PRACTICE

Is the fraction in lowest terms? Write *yes* or *no*.

**12.** $\frac{12}{24}$    **13.** $\frac{6}{12}$    **14.** $\frac{4}{8}$    **15.** $\frac{3}{6}$    **16.** $\frac{2}{4}$    **17.** $\frac{1}{2}$

**18.** $\frac{8}{16}$    **19.** $\frac{7}{16}$    **20.** $\frac{6}{16}$    **21.** $\frac{5}{16}$    **22.** $\frac{16}{16}$    **23.** $\frac{3}{16}$

Write the fraction in lowest terms.

**24.** $\frac{5}{10}$    **25.** $\frac{3}{3}$    **26.** $\frac{4}{6}$    **27.** $\frac{2}{4}$    **28.** $\frac{2}{12}$    **29.** $\frac{2}{10}$

**30.** $\frac{2}{6}$    **31.** $\frac{9}{12}$    **32.** $\frac{10}{15}$    **33.** $\frac{9}{9}$    **34.** $\frac{6}{18}$    **35.** $\frac{12}{16}$

**36.** $\frac{3}{24}$    **37.** $\frac{4}{32}$    **38.** $\frac{7}{28}$    **39.** $\frac{8}{20}$    ★ **40.** $\frac{10}{100}$    ★ **41.** $\frac{30}{100}$

Complete. Remember, 0.01 is 1 hundredth and 0.1 is 1 tenth.

★ **42.** $0.5 = \frac{\blacksquare}{10} = \frac{1}{\blacksquare}$    ★ **43.** $0.25 = \frac{\blacksquare}{100} = \frac{\blacksquare}{4}$    ★ **44.** $0.2 = \frac{\blacksquare}{10} = \frac{\blacksquare}{5}$

★ **45.** $0.50 = \frac{\blacksquare}{100} = \frac{1}{\blacksquare}$    ★ **46.** $0.75 = \frac{\blacksquare}{100} = \frac{\blacksquare}{4}$    ★ **47.** $0.10 = \frac{\blacksquare}{100} = \frac{\blacksquare}{10}$

Divide mentally to find the lowest terms. Write only the answer.

**MENTAL MATH**

**48.** $\frac{2}{8}$    **49.** $\frac{3}{9}$    **50.** $\frac{4}{12}$    **51.** $\frac{12}{24}$    **52.** $\frac{18}{18}$    **53.** $\frac{9}{27}$

## PROBLEM SOLVING APPLICATIONS
### Using a Picture

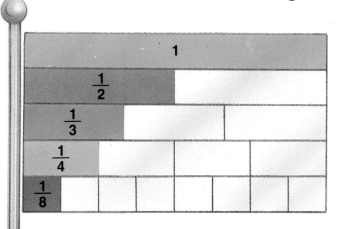

Use the picture at the left to solve the problem.

**54.** How many halves are in 1?

**55.** How many thirds are in 1?

**56.** How many fourths are in 1?

**57.** How many eighths are in 1?

★ **58.** $1 = \frac{2}{\blacksquare} = \frac{3}{\blacksquare} = \frac{\blacksquare}{4} = \frac{\blacksquare}{8}$

# MIXED NUMBERS

When the numerator of a fraction is greater than the denominator, the fraction is greater than 1. You can write a fraction greater than 1 as a **mixed number.**

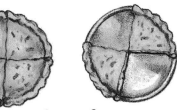

$$\text{fraction} \longrightarrow \frac{6}{4} = \frac{4}{4} + \frac{2}{4} = 1 + \frac{2}{4} = 1\frac{2}{4} \longleftarrow \text{mixed number}$$

$$\frac{4}{4} \quad + \quad \frac{2}{4}$$

Here's another way to write a fraction as a mixed number. Divide the numerator by the denominator to find the whole number. The remainder becomes the numerator of the fractional part. The divisor becomes the denominator of the fractional part.

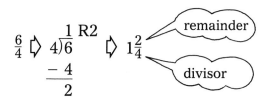

$$\frac{6}{4} \Rightarrow 4\overline{)6} \; \begin{array}{c} 1 \; R2 \\ -4 \\ \hline 2 \end{array} \Rightarrow 1\frac{2}{4}$$

remainder

divisor

To write a mixed number in lowest terms, you write the fractional part in lowest terms.

$$\frac{2}{4} = \frac{2 \div 2}{4 \div 2} = \frac{1}{2}, \text{ so } 1\frac{2}{4} = 1\frac{1}{2}$$

Sometimes a fraction names a whole number.

$$\frac{8}{4} \Rightarrow 4\overline{)8}\;^{2} \Rightarrow 2$$

To find which two whole numbers a fraction is between, you can estimate.

$\frac{6}{4}$ is between 1 and 2 because $\frac{4}{4} = 1$ and $\frac{8}{4} = 2$.

## CLASS EXERCISES

Write the mixed number for the shaded parts.

1.    2.    3.    4.

Is the fraction greater than 1? Answer *yes* or *no*. If *yes*, tell what the mixed number in lowest terms will be.

5. $\frac{8}{9}$     6. $\frac{7}{4}$     7. $\frac{12}{9}$     8. $\frac{15}{16}$     9. $\frac{19}{17}$     10. $\frac{6}{5}$

Solve. Write the answer in lowest terms.

7. A bag contains 5 red apples and 10 green apples. John picks a piece of fruit without looking. What is the probability that he gets a green apple?

8. Sheila buys 9 tickets for a class raffle. There are 81 tickets sold. What is the probability that she will win?

9. Jeremy and Jean are playing a game with a spinner. Jeremy needs to spin a 5 or a 6 to win. There are six different numbers on the spinner. What is the probability of Jeremy's winning?

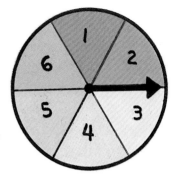

10. You have a group of pens. If you pick one pen, the probability of getting a red one is $\frac{1}{4}$. The probability of getting a blue one is $\frac{1}{2}$. One of the pens is green. How many pens of each color do you have?

★ 11. **Think:** If you flip a penny 100 times, about how many times should you get heads?

## CHECKPOINT 1

Write the fraction for the shaded part. *(pages 330–333)*

1.    2.

Write a number sentence to show equivalent fractions.
*(pages 334–335)*

3. 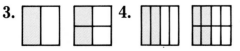   4.

Write in lowest terms.
*(pages 336–337)*

5. $\frac{4}{6}$   6. $\frac{3}{15}$   7. $\frac{9}{12}$

Write as a mixed number in lowest terms. *(pages 338–339)*

8. $\frac{6}{5}$   9. $\frac{10}{4}$   10. $\frac{8}{3}$

Solve. *(pages 342–343)*

11. A bag contains 4 blue marbles and 5 red marbles. Gary picks a marble without looking. What is the probability that he gets a red marble?

*Extra practice on page 424*

# ADDING FRACTIONS

Rose and Paul planted part of their garden. They planted $\frac{1}{3}$ of the garden with beans and $\frac{1}{3}$ with peas. How much of the garden has been planted?

To find out, you add the fractions.

one third + one third = two thirds

$$\frac{1}{3} + \frac{1}{3} = \frac{2}{3}$$

The picture shows that Rose and Paul planted $\frac{2}{3}$ of their garden.

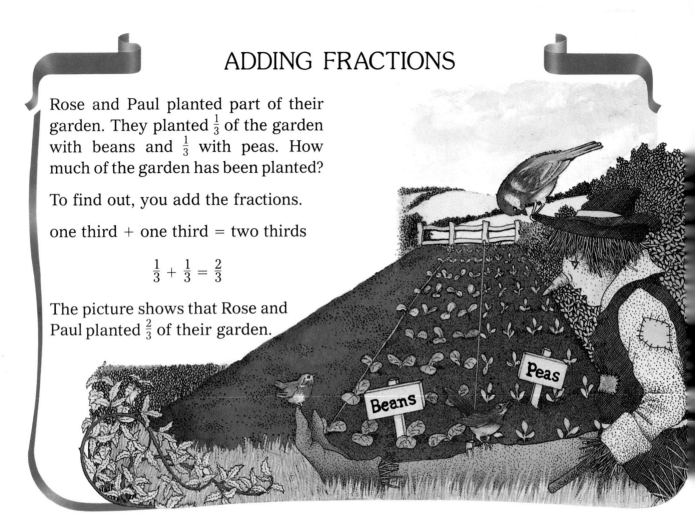

## CLASS EXERCISES

Complete.

**1.**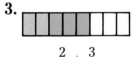

one fifth + two fifths = ▦ fifths

$$\frac{1}{5} + \frac{2}{5} = \frac{▦}{5}$$

**2.**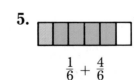

four sixths + one sixth = ▦ sixths

$$\frac{4}{6} + \frac{1}{6} = \frac{▦}{6}$$

## PRACTICE

Add.

**3.**

$$\frac{2}{8} + \frac{3}{8}$$

**4.**

$$\frac{1}{7} + \frac{1}{7}$$

**5.**

$$\frac{1}{6} + \frac{4}{6}$$

**6.**

$$\frac{2}{9} + \frac{3}{9}$$

**7.**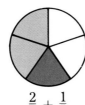
$\frac{1}{8} + \frac{2}{8}$

**8.**
$\frac{2}{5} + \frac{1}{5}$

**9.**
$\frac{2}{6} + \frac{3}{6}$

**10.**
$\frac{1}{4} + \frac{2}{4}$

**11.**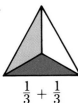
$\frac{1}{3} + \frac{1}{3}$

**12.**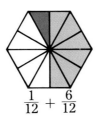
$\frac{1}{12} + \frac{6}{12}$

**13.**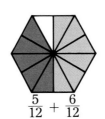
$\frac{5}{12} + \frac{6}{12}$

**14.**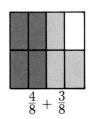
$\frac{4}{8} + \frac{3}{8}$

★ **15.**
$\frac{1}{2} + \frac{1}{2}$

★ **16.**
$\frac{1}{8} + \frac{1}{8} + \frac{1}{8}$

★ **17.**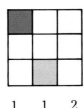
$\frac{1}{9} + \frac{1}{9} + \frac{2}{9}$

★ **18.**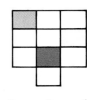
$\frac{1}{10} + \frac{1}{10} + \frac{1}{10}$

# PROBLEM SOLVING APPLICATIONS
## Drawing a Picture

Draw a picture to show the problem. Then solve.

**19.** Part of the school garden is planted. One third of the garden is corn and $\frac{1}{3}$ is beans. What part of the garden is planted?

**20.** Carmen planted part of a garden. She planted $\frac{3}{6}$ with tomatoes and $\frac{2}{6}$ with peppers. What part of the garden is planted?

★ **21.** A crate has 8 red apples for every 12 green apples. If the crate has 48 green apples, how many red apples are in the crate?

★ **22.** Jerod spent $\frac{1}{6}$ of the time digging up the ground, $\frac{3}{6}$ planting, and $\frac{1}{6}$ watering. The rest of the time he spent cleaning up. What part of the time did he clean up?

# ADDING FRACTIONS, SAME DENOMINATORS

James completed $\frac{1}{6}$ of his art project on Thursday and $\frac{2}{6}$ on Friday. What part of the art project had he completed by Friday night?

To find the answer, you add the fractions.

| Add the numerators. | Use the same denominator. | Write the sum in lowest terms. |
|---|---|---|
| $\begin{array}{r} \frac{2}{6} \\ + \frac{1}{6} \\ \hline 3 \end{array}$ | $\begin{array}{r} \frac{2}{6} \\ + \frac{1}{6} \\ \hline \frac{3}{6} \end{array}$ | $\begin{array}{r} \frac{2}{6} \\ + \frac{1}{6} \\ \hline \frac{3}{6} = \frac{1}{2} \end{array}$ |

James had completed $\frac{1}{2}$ of the project by Friday night.

When the sum of two fractions is greater than 1, you write the sum as a mixed number in lowest terms.

$$\frac{3}{4} + \frac{3}{4} = \frac{6}{4} = 1\frac{2}{4} = 1\frac{1}{2}$$

 You can use mental math to add some fractions with the same denominator.

$\frac{3}{8} + \frac{4}{8} = \frac{7}{8}$ — 3 + 4 = 7

## CLASS EXERCISES

Is the answer correct? Write *yes* or *no*. If the answer is not correct, explain why the answer is wrong.

**1.** $\frac{1}{5} + \frac{2}{5} = \frac{3}{5}$ **2.** $\frac{1}{4} + \frac{1}{4} = \frac{1}{8}$ **3.** $\frac{1}{6} + \frac{1}{6} = \frac{2}{12} = \frac{1}{6}$ **4.** $\frac{2}{3} + \frac{2}{3} = \frac{4}{3} = 1\frac{1}{3}$

## PRACTICE

Add. Write the sum in lowest terms.

**5.** $\frac{1}{9} + \frac{2}{9}$ **6.** $\frac{4}{7} + \frac{2}{7}$ **7.** $\frac{4}{9} + \frac{4}{9}$ **8.** $\frac{3}{10} + \frac{1}{10}$ **9.** $\frac{3}{12} + \frac{3}{12}$

10. $\frac{1}{8}$
$+\frac{1}{8}$

11. $\frac{2}{7}$
$+\frac{3}{7}$

12. $\frac{1}{8}$
$+\frac{3}{8}$

13. $\frac{3}{12}$
$+\frac{5}{12}$

14. $\frac{2}{10}$
$+\frac{4}{10}$

15. $\frac{2}{11}$
$+\frac{2}{11}$

16. $\frac{3}{10}$
$+\frac{6}{10}$

17. $\frac{2}{8}$
$+\frac{6}{8}$

18. $\frac{2}{9}$
$+\frac{3}{9}$

19. $\frac{1}{6}$
$+\frac{2}{6}$

Add. Write the sum as a mixed number in lowest terms.

20. $\frac{2}{4}$
$+\frac{3}{4}$

21. $\frac{3}{5}$
$+\frac{4}{5}$

22. $\frac{4}{8}$
$+\frac{5}{8}$

23. $\frac{2}{6}$
$+\frac{5}{6}$

24. $\frac{8}{9}$
$+\frac{5}{9}$

25. $\frac{7}{8}$
$+\frac{3}{8}$

26. $\frac{5}{8}$
$+\frac{7}{8}$

27. $\frac{5}{7}$
$+\frac{6}{7}$

★ 28. $\frac{1}{4}$
$\frac{3}{4}$
$+\frac{1}{4}$

★ 29. $\frac{5}{6}$
$\frac{5}{6}$
$+\frac{5}{6}$

Use mental math to solve. Write only the answer.

30. $\frac{5}{8} + \frac{2}{8}$

31. $\frac{3}{18} + \frac{8}{18}$

32. $\frac{5}{10} + \frac{4}{10}$

★ 33. $\frac{1}{8} + \frac{3}{8}$

MENTAL MATH

## PROBLEM SOLVING APPLICATIONS
### Mental Math or Pencil

Use mental math or paper and pencil to solve. Write *m* or *p* to tell which method you chose. Write fractions in lowest terms.

34. Dixie finished $\frac{1}{8}$ of her painting on Friday. She finished $\frac{5}{8}$ of her painting on Saturday. How much of the painting was finished by Saturday night?

35. Danny spends $\frac{1}{6}$ of his spare time reading. He spends $\frac{2}{12}$ doing his art project. Does he spend the same amount of time reading as he does on art?

★ 36. Miki finished $\frac{1}{4}$ of the project on Thursday and $\frac{1}{4}$ on Friday. She finished $\frac{1}{2}$ of the project on Saturday. Did she finish the project?

★ 37. Mike and Chris finished $\frac{2}{5}$ of the project on Friday, $\frac{1}{5}$ on Saturday, and the rest on Sunday. What part did they finish on Sunday?

# SUBTRACTING FRACTIONS, SAME DENOMINATORS

While on a bicycle trip, Steve and Janice see a sign that reads $\frac{7}{8}$ mi to a scenic view. They bike $\frac{5}{8}$ mi. How much farther must they bike to reach the scenic view?

Since you need to find the difference, subtract.

Here's how you subtract two fractions with the same denominator.

| Subtract the numerators. | Use the same denominator. | Write the difference in lowest terms. |
|---|---|---|
| $\begin{array}{r} \frac{7}{8} \\ -\frac{5}{8} \\ \hline 2 \end{array}$ | $\begin{array}{r} \frac{7}{8} \\ -\frac{5}{8} \\ \hline \frac{2}{8} \end{array}$ | $\begin{array}{r} \frac{7}{8} \\ -\frac{5}{8} \\ \hline \frac{2}{8} = \frac{1}{4} \end{array}$ |

Steve and Janice must bike another $\frac{1}{4}$ mi to reach the scenic view.

## CLASS EXERCISES

Subtract. Write the difference in lowest terms.

1. $\frac{6}{8} - \frac{1}{8}$
2. $\frac{6}{8} - \frac{2}{8}$
3. $\frac{6}{8} - \frac{3}{8}$
4. $\frac{6}{8} - \frac{4}{8}$
5. $\frac{6}{8} - \frac{5}{8}$

6. $\frac{5}{6} - \frac{1}{6}$
7. $\frac{5}{6} - \frac{2}{6}$
8. $\frac{5}{6} - \frac{3}{6}$
9. $\frac{5}{6} - \frac{4}{6}$
10. $\frac{5}{6} - \frac{5}{6}$

## PRACTICE

Subtract. Write the difference in lowest terms.

11. $\frac{3}{5} - \frac{1}{5}$
12. $\frac{3}{4} - \frac{2}{4}$
13. $\frac{4}{6} - \frac{3}{6}$
14. $\frac{4}{5} - \frac{1}{5}$
15. $\frac{4}{8} - \frac{3}{8}$

**16.** $\frac{7}{8}$ $-\frac{1}{8}$

**17.** $\frac{7}{10}$ $-\frac{2}{10}$

**18.** $\frac{3}{6}$ $-\frac{1}{6}$

**19.** $\frac{4}{10}$ $-\frac{2}{10}$

**20.** $\frac{7}{9}$ $-\frac{4}{9}$

**21.** $\frac{9}{10}$ $-\frac{1}{10}$

**22.** $\frac{8}{8}$ $-\frac{6}{8}$

**23.** $\frac{6}{10}$ $-\frac{1}{10}$

**24.** $\frac{7}{8}$ $-\frac{3}{8}$

**25.** $\frac{10}{10}$ $-\frac{2}{10}$

**26.** $\frac{3}{4}$ $-\frac{1}{4}$

**27.** $\frac{7}{8}$ $-\frac{2}{8}$

**28.** $\frac{9}{10}$ $-\frac{3}{10}$

**29.** $\frac{5}{6}$ $-\frac{1}{6}$

**30.** $\frac{5}{8}$ $-\frac{4}{8}$

**31.** $\frac{5}{9}$ $-\frac{2}{9}$

**32.** $\frac{4}{4}$ $-\frac{2}{4}$

**33.** $\frac{5}{8}$ $-\frac{1}{8}$

**34.** $\frac{6}{8}$ $-\frac{4}{8}$

**35.** $\frac{2}{6}$ $-\frac{2}{6}$

Write the answer.

**36.** $36 \div 6$  **37.** $8 \times 4$  **38.** $63 \div 7$  **39.** $9 \times 8$

**40.** $21 \times 342$  **41.** $525 \div 15$  **42.** $47 \times 298$

**MIXED REVIEW**

## PROBLEM SOLVING APPLICATIONS
### Choosing the Operation

Solve.

**43.** Janice bought $\frac{2}{8}$ yd of green twine and $\frac{5}{8}$ yd of blue twine for a key holder. How much more blue twine did she buy?

**44.** Steve ran $\frac{2}{5}$ mi on the first day of the trip and $\frac{1}{5}$ mi on the second day. How far did he run the first two days?

★ **45.** On the first 2 days of their trip, Steve and Janice biked $\frac{3}{10}$ of the distance. If the trip was 10 days long, how much farther did they have to bike in the last 8 days?

★ **46.** Steve and Janice walked two nature trails. The first trail was $1\frac{3}{5}$ mi and the second was $\frac{4}{5}$ mi. How much longer was the first trail than the second?
Hint: Change $1\frac{3}{5}$ to a fraction.

# EQUIVALENT FRACTIONS

You can write an equivalent fraction by multiplying the numerator and the denominator by the same number.

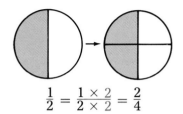

$$\frac{1}{2} = \frac{1 \times 2}{2 \times 2} = \frac{2}{4}$$

You can write other equivalent fractions for $\frac{1}{2}$.

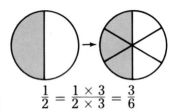 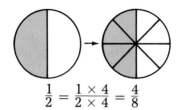 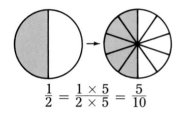

$$\frac{1}{2} = \frac{1 \times 3}{2 \times 3} = \frac{3}{6} \qquad \frac{1}{2} = \frac{1 \times 4}{2 \times 4} = \frac{4}{8} \qquad \frac{1}{2} = \frac{1 \times 5}{2 \times 5} = \frac{5}{10}$$

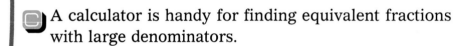 A calculator is handy for finding equivalent fractions with large denominators.

$$\frac{5}{9} = \frac{?}{261}$$

**Think:** How many nines are in 261?    26l ÷ 9 = 29

$$\frac{5}{9} = \frac{5 \times 29}{9 \times 29} = \frac{145}{261}$$

## CLASS EXERCISES

Complete.

**1.** $\frac{1}{2} = \frac{1 \times 2}{2 \times 2} = \frac{\blacksquare}{4}$

**2.** $\frac{1}{2} = \frac{1 \times 3}{2 \times 3} = \frac{\blacksquare}{6}$

**3.** $\frac{1}{2} = \frac{1 \times 4}{2 \times 4} = \frac{\blacksquare}{\blacksquare}$

By what number is the denominator multiplied? Complete the equivalent fraction.

**4.** $\frac{1}{3} = \frac{\blacksquare}{6}$

**5.** $\frac{1}{4} = \frac{\blacksquare}{12}$

**6.** $\frac{1}{5} = \frac{\blacksquare}{10}$

**7.** $\frac{2}{7} = \frac{\blacksquare}{21}$

**8.** $\frac{3}{4} = \frac{\blacksquare}{16}$

## PRACTICE

Complete.

**9.** $\frac{1}{8} = \frac{\blacksquare}{24}$

**10.** $\frac{1}{5} = \frac{\blacksquare}{20}$

**11.** $\frac{2}{4} = \frac{\blacksquare}{24}$

**12.** $\frac{1}{7} = \frac{\blacksquare}{21}$

**13.** $\frac{3}{8} = \frac{\blacksquare}{16}$

14. $\frac{3}{4} = \frac{}{8}$  15. $\frac{2}{3} = \frac{}{18}$  16. $\frac{4}{5} = \frac{}{25}$  17. $\frac{5}{6} = \frac{}{36}$  18. $\frac{7}{9} = \frac{}{27}$

19. $\frac{1}{2} = \frac{}{10}$  20. $\frac{3}{8} = \frac{}{24}$  21. $\frac{1}{6} = \frac{}{12}$  22. $\frac{1}{2} = \frac{}{12}$  23. $\frac{4}{5} = \frac{}{10}$

24. $\frac{3}{5} = \frac{}{10}$  25. $\frac{1}{7} = \frac{}{14}$  26. $\frac{3}{5} = \frac{}{20}$  27. $\frac{5}{8} = \frac{}{16}$  28. $\frac{1}{8} = \frac{}{16}$

29. $\frac{2}{3} = \frac{}{6}$  30. $\frac{1}{5} = \frac{}{15}$  31. $\frac{1}{3} = \frac{}{15}$  32. $\frac{5}{6} = \frac{}{18}$  33. $\frac{1}{6} = \frac{}{18}$

34. $\frac{1}{9} = \frac{}{27}$  35. $\frac{1}{4} = \frac{}{8}$  36. $\frac{5}{8} = \frac{}{24}$  37. $\frac{6}{6} = \frac{}{12}$  38. $\frac{3}{4} = \frac{}{12}$

39. $\frac{2}{7} = \frac{}{14}$  40. $\frac{1}{8} = \frac{}{32}$  41. $\frac{2}{5} = \frac{}{15}$  42. $\frac{1}{7} = \frac{}{28}$  43. $\frac{2}{3} = \frac{}{15}$

44. $\frac{1}{9} = \frac{}{36}$  45. $\frac{3}{4} = \frac{}{16}$  46. $\frac{2}{5} = \frac{}{10}$  47. $\frac{1}{6} = \frac{}{24}$  48. $\frac{3}{7} = \frac{}{21}$

Complete. Use a calculator if you have one.

49. $\frac{7}{8} = \frac{}{256}$  50. $\frac{1}{6} = \frac{}{318}$  51. $\frac{4}{7} = \frac{}{651}$  52. $\frac{7}{9} = \frac{}{531}$

CALCULATOR

# PROBLEM SOLVING APPLICATIONS
## Choosing the Operation

Solve. Write fractions in lowest terms.

53. In the travel club, $\frac{1}{2}$ of the students are girls and $\frac{2}{4}$ of the students are boys. Does the club have the same number of girls and boys?

54. At a club meeting $\frac{5}{7}$ of the members ask to see slides of Canada. One seventh ask to see slides of England. What fraction of the members ask to see slides?

55. On the first trip the club used $\frac{5}{8}$ of a tank of gas. On the second trip the club used $\frac{3}{8}$ of a tank of gas. How much more gas was used on the first trip than the second?

56. This year, $\frac{3}{5}$ of the new club members are boys and $\frac{4}{10}$ of the new club members are girls. Did the same number of boys and girls join the club this year?

★57. Look in this lesson for a 9-letter word in which $\frac{1}{3}$ of the letters are vowels. What is the word?

# COMPARING FRACTIONS

Is a fraction greater than, less than, or equal to another fraction? Find out by comparing the two fractions.

Compare $\frac{1}{6}$ and $\frac{4}{6}$. The denominators are the same, so you can compare the numerators.

$1 < 4$, so $\frac{1}{6} < \frac{4}{6}$

Compare $\frac{3}{4}$ and $\frac{7}{8}$. The denominators are not the same. You can write both fractions with the denominator 8. Just use equivalent fractions.

$$\frac{3}{4} = \frac{3 \times 2}{4 \times 2} = \frac{6}{8} \qquad \frac{7}{8}$$

The denominator 8 is called a **common denominator.**

Now compare. $\frac{6}{8} < \frac{7}{8}$, so $\frac{3}{4} < \frac{7}{8}$.

You can estimate that $\frac{7}{8}$ is about 1 because the numerator is close to the denominator. You can estimate that $\frac{5}{8}$ is about $\frac{1}{2}$ because the denominator is about twice the numerator. You can estimate that $\frac{1}{8}$ is about 0 because the numerator is much less than the denominator.

BRIDGE
ENDS
$\frac{1}{8}$ mi

## CLASS EXERCISES

Complete the list of equivalent fractions.

**1.** $\frac{1}{2}, \frac{\ }{4}, \frac{\ }{6}, \frac{\ }{8}, \frac{\ }{10}, \frac{\ }{12}$

**2.** $\frac{2}{3}, \frac{\ }{6}, \frac{\ }{9}, \frac{\ }{12}, \frac{\ }{15}$

**3.** $\frac{3}{4}, \frac{\ }{8}, \frac{\ }{12}, \frac{\ }{16}, \frac{\ }{20}$

Compare the fractions. Write $<$, $>$, or $=$. Use the number line to help you.

**4.** $\frac{1}{8} \ \blacksquare \ \frac{3}{8}$

**5.** $\frac{4}{8} \ \blacksquare \ \frac{2}{4}$

**6.** $\frac{4}{4} \ \blacksquare \ \frac{3}{4}$

**7.** $\frac{1}{4} \ \blacksquare \ \frac{1}{8}$

**8.** $\frac{3}{4} \ \blacksquare \ \frac{7}{8}$

**9.** $\frac{6}{8} \ \blacksquare \ \frac{2}{4}$

# PRACTICE

Compare the fractions. Write $<$, $>$, or $=$.

**10.** $\frac{3}{4}$ ▨ $\frac{2}{4}$
**11.** $\frac{4}{5}$ ▨ $\frac{2}{5}$
**12.** $\frac{3}{8}$ ▨ $\frac{5}{8}$
**13.** $\frac{1}{7}$ ▨ $\frac{2}{7}$
**14.** $\frac{6}{10}$ ▨ $\frac{1}{10}$

**15.** $\frac{2}{5}$ ▨ $\frac{4}{5}$
**16.** $\frac{5}{8}$ ▨ $\frac{2}{8}$
**17.** $\frac{9}{10}$ ▨ $\frac{7}{10}$
**18.** $\frac{0}{8}$ ▨ $\frac{7}{8}$
**19.** $\frac{3}{8}$ ▨ $\frac{7}{8}$

**20.** $\frac{1}{4}$ ▨ $\frac{1}{2}$
**21.** $\frac{1}{3}$ ▨ $\frac{2}{6}$
**22.** $\frac{1}{3}$ ▨ $\frac{1}{9}$
**23.** $\frac{1}{4}$ ▨ $\frac{1}{8}$
**24.** $\frac{1}{10}$ ▨ $\frac{1}{5}$

**25.** $\frac{1}{9}$ ▨ $\frac{2}{3}$
**26.** $\frac{3}{8}$ ▨ $\frac{1}{4}$
**27.** $\frac{3}{4}$ ▨ $\frac{1}{8}$
**28.** $\frac{2}{6}$ ▨ $\frac{1}{3}$
**29.** $\frac{3}{8}$ ▨ $\frac{3}{4}$

Write the fractions in order from least to greatest.

**30.** $\frac{3}{8}, \frac{1}{8}, \frac{5}{8}$
**31.** $\frac{4}{5}, \frac{2}{5}, \frac{1}{5}$
**32.** $\frac{2}{6}, \frac{5}{6}, \frac{3}{6}$
★ **33.** $\frac{1}{6}, \frac{1}{2}, \frac{1}{3}$
★ **34.** $\frac{2}{3}, \frac{3}{4}, \frac{5}{12}$

Estimate. Is the fraction about 1, about $\frac{1}{2}$, or about 0?

**35.** $\frac{9}{10}$
**36.** $\frac{3}{8}$
**37.** $\frac{1}{5}$
**38.** $\frac{4}{7}$
**39.** $\frac{2}{9}$

ESTIMATE

## PROBLEM SOLVING APPLICATIONS
### Fractions and Distance

Use the table to solve.

**40.** Which bridge is shorter, the George Washington or the Golden Gate?

**41.** Which bridge is longer, the Golden Gate or Walt Whitman?

**42.** Which bridges are less than 1 mi long?

★ **43.** Which bridges are longer than the Tacoma bridge?

| LENGTH OF BRIDGES | |
|---|---|
| NAME OF BRIDGE | LENGTH |
| George Washington | $\frac{13}{20}$ mi |
| Golden Gate | $\frac{4}{5}$ mi |
| Lion's Gate | $\frac{53}{100}$ mi |
| Tacoma | $\frac{1}{2}$ mi |
| Walt Whitman | $\frac{19}{50}$ mi |

# ADDING, DIFFERENT DENOMINATORS

Lauren has a paper route. She delivers $\frac{1}{3}$ of her newspapers on Pratt Street and $\frac{1}{6}$ of them on Grace Drive. What part of her newspapers is that altogether?

Adding the fractions will give you the total.

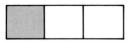  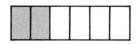

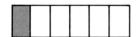  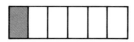

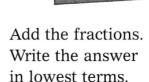

| Are the denominators different? Yes. | Write equivalent fractions with a common denominator. | Add the fractions. Write the answer in lowest terms. |
|---|---|---|

$$\begin{array}{r} \frac{1}{3} \\ + \frac{1}{6} \\ \hline \end{array}$$

$$\begin{array}{r} \frac{1}{3} = \frac{2}{6} \\ + \frac{1}{6} = + \frac{1}{6} \\ \hline \end{array}$$  $\boxed{2 \times 3 = 6}$

$$\begin{array}{r} \frac{1}{3} = \frac{2}{6} \\ + \frac{1}{6} = + \frac{1}{6} \\ \hline \frac{3}{6} = \frac{1}{2} \end{array}$$

That is $\frac{1}{2}$ of her newspapers.

Remember, when adding fractions you must have a common denominator.

 When both addends are less than $\frac{1}{2}$, you can estimate that the sum is less than 1. **Think:** If both addends are greater than $\frac{1}{2}$, what can you say about the sum?

## CLASS EXERCISES

Which fraction must you change? What is the common denominator? Add. Write the sum in lowest terms.

**1.** $\begin{array}{r} \frac{1}{2} \\ + \frac{1}{4} \\ \hline \end{array}$  **2.** $\begin{array}{r} \frac{3}{8} \\ + \frac{1}{2} \\ \hline \end{array}$  **3.** $\begin{array}{r} \frac{3}{4} \\ + \frac{5}{12} \\ \hline \end{array}$  **4.** $\begin{array}{r} \frac{1}{4} \\ + \frac{7}{8} \\ \hline \end{array}$  **5.** $\begin{array}{r} \frac{1}{3} \\ + \frac{5}{6} \\ \hline \end{array}$  **6.** $\begin{array}{r} \frac{7}{9} \\ + \frac{2}{3} \\ \hline \end{array}$

## PRACTICE

Add. Write the sum in lowest terms.

7. $\frac{1}{2}$ $+\frac{5}{8}$

8. $\frac{3}{5}$ $+\frac{1}{10}$

9. $\frac{1}{6}$ $+\frac{1}{3}$

10. $\frac{7}{12}$ $+\frac{1}{2}$

11. $\frac{3}{10}$ $+\frac{2}{5}$

12. $\frac{1}{4}$ $+\frac{1}{8}$

13. $\frac{1}{4}$ $+\frac{3}{8}$

14. $\frac{1}{12}$ $+\frac{1}{3}$

15. $\frac{1}{3}$ $+\frac{1}{9}$

16. $\frac{4}{5}$ $+\frac{7}{10}$

17. $\frac{2}{3}$ $+\frac{1}{6}$

18. $\frac{5}{12}$ $+\frac{5}{6}$

19. $\frac{2}{3} + \frac{1}{15}$

20. $\frac{2}{9} + \frac{1}{3}$

21. $\frac{2}{10} + \frac{3}{5}$

22. $\frac{1}{8} + \frac{1}{16}$

23. $\frac{1}{12} + \frac{1}{4}$

24. $\frac{5}{6} + \frac{7}{12}$

25. $\frac{3}{7} + \frac{1}{14}$

★ 26. $\frac{2}{8} + \frac{1}{4} + \frac{1}{2}$

★ 27. $\frac{3}{5} + \frac{1}{2} + \frac{7}{10}$

★ 28. $\frac{2}{3} + \frac{1}{4} + \frac{5}{12}$

Estimate. Is the sum *greater than 1* or *less than 1*?

29. $\frac{1}{3} + \frac{1}{6}$

30. $\frac{3}{4} + \frac{5}{8}$

31. $\frac{4}{5} + \frac{6}{10}$

32. $\frac{3}{7} + \frac{5}{14}$

ESTIMATE

## PROBLEM SOLVING APPLICATIONS
### Choosing the Operation

Solve. Write fractions in lowest terms.

33. Gerald works on his paper route records $\frac{3}{4}$ of an hour before dinner and $\frac{1}{4}$ of an hour after dinner. How much longer does he work before dinner than after dinner?

34. On Friday $\frac{3}{8}$ of Gerald's customers pay him. On Saturday $\frac{1}{2}$ pay him. What part of Gerald's customers pay him on these two days?

★ 35. Diana delivers $\frac{1}{3}$ of her Sunday newspapers on North Street and $\frac{4}{6}$ on Birch Road. Is this $\frac{1}{6}, \frac{2}{6}, \frac{3}{6}, \frac{5}{6}$, or all of her Sunday papers?

★ 36. Elizabeth delivers papers 5 days each week. How many days does Elizabeth deliver newspapers in 35 days?

# SUBTRACTING, DIFFERENT DENOMINATORS

Audrey bought $\frac{7}{8}$ yd of material. She uses $\frac{3}{4}$ yd to make a puppet. How much material does she have left?

To find out, you subtract $\frac{3}{4}$ from $\frac{7}{8}$.

 ⇨

 ⇨

| Are the denominators different? Yes. | Write equivalent fractions with a common denominator. | Subtract. Write the answer in lowest terms. |
|---|---|---|
| $\frac{7}{8}$ | $\frac{7}{8} = \quad \frac{7}{8}$ | $\frac{7}{8} = \quad \frac{7}{8}$ |
| $-\frac{3}{4}$ | $-\frac{3}{4} = -\frac{6}{8}$  $2 \times 4 = 8$ | $-\frac{3}{4} = -\frac{6}{8}$ |
| | | $\frac{1}{8}$ |

Audrey has $\frac{1}{8}$ yd of material left.

Remember, when subtracting fractions you must have a common denominator.

## CLASS EXERCISES

Which fraction must you change? What is the common denominator? Subtract. Write the difference in lowest terms.

1.  $\frac{1}{2}$       2.  $\frac{3}{4}$       3.  $\frac{2}{3}$       4.  $\frac{5}{6}$       5.  $\frac{1}{4}$       6.  $\frac{5}{8}$

   $-\frac{1}{4}$         $-\frac{1}{2}$         $-\frac{1}{6}$         $-\frac{1}{3}$         $-\frac{1}{8}$         $-\frac{1}{4}$

# PRACTICE

Subtract. Write the difference in lowest terms.

7.  $\frac{1}{2}$ $-\frac{3}{8}$

8.  $\frac{1}{5}$ $-\frac{1}{10}$

9.  $\frac{3}{4}$ $-\frac{1}{2}$

10. $\frac{1}{6}$ $-\frac{1}{12}$

11. $\frac{5}{6}$ $-\frac{1}{2}$

12. $\frac{7}{12}$ $-\frac{1}{3}$

13. $\frac{5}{8}$ $-\frac{1}{16}$

14. $\frac{1}{4}$ $-\frac{1}{12}$

15. $\frac{5}{12}$ $-\frac{1}{4}$

16. $\frac{3}{8}$ $-\frac{1}{4}$

17. $\frac{7}{8}$ $-\frac{5}{16}$

18. $\frac{5}{6}$ $-\frac{1}{3}$

19. $\frac{5}{8}$ $-\frac{5}{16}$

20. $\frac{3}{4}$ $-\frac{1}{16}$

21. $\frac{1}{2}$ $-\frac{3}{10}$

22. $\frac{2}{3}$ $-\frac{1}{9}$

23. $\frac{3}{5}$ $-\frac{2}{15}$

24. $\frac{3}{4}$ $-\frac{1}{24}$

25. $\frac{4}{7} - \frac{2}{14}$

26. $\frac{2}{3} - \frac{3}{9}$

27. $\frac{5}{6} - \frac{5}{12}$

28. $\frac{4}{9} - \frac{7}{18}$

29. $\frac{11}{16} - \frac{1}{4}$

30. $\frac{7}{9} - \frac{5}{18}$

31. $\frac{9}{24} - \frac{3}{8}$

32. $\frac{11}{21} - \frac{2}{7}$

33. $\frac{5}{12} - \frac{7}{36}$

34. $\frac{5}{6} - \frac{11}{18}$

Complete.

★ 35. $\frac{\blacksquare}{6} - \frac{1}{12} = \frac{1}{12}$

★ 36. $\frac{3}{4} + \frac{\blacksquare}{8} = \frac{7}{8}$

★ 37. $\frac{7}{9} - \frac{\blacksquare}{3} = \frac{1}{9}$

★ 38. $\frac{\blacksquare}{7} + \frac{9}{14} = \frac{11}{14}$

## PROBLEM SOLVING APPLICATIONS
### Choosing the Operation

Solve.

39. How much greater is $\frac{3}{4}$ yd of ribbon than $\frac{5}{8}$ yd of ribbon?

40. Martin needs $\frac{8}{9}$ yd of trim. He has $\frac{2}{3}$ yd of trim. Does he have enough? If not, how much more does he need?

★ 41. Audrey wants to make two puppets. She has $\frac{7}{8}$ yd of material. If she uses $\frac{1}{4}$ yd for each puppet, how much material will she have left?

★ 42. Dorothy needs $\frac{3}{8}$ yd of material for one part of a puppet theater and $\frac{1}{4}$ yd for another part. She has 1 yd of material. How much will she have left over?

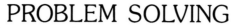

# PROBLEM SOLVING
## Strategy: Using a Circle Graph

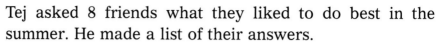

Tej asked 8 friends what they liked to do best in the summer. He made a list of their answers.

| Activity | Number | Fraction |
|---|---|---|
| Swimming | 3 | $\frac{3}{8}$ |
| Hiking | 2 | $\frac{2}{8} = \frac{1}{4}$ |
| Traveling | 2 | $\frac{2}{8} = \frac{1}{4}$ |
| Playing Soccer | 1 | $\frac{1}{8}$ |
| Total | 8 | $\frac{8}{8}$ |

FAVORITE ACTIVITY

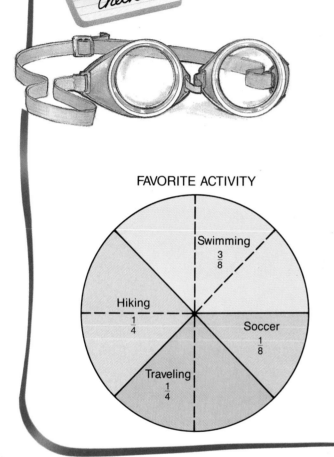

Tej uses the survey to make a **circle graph** that shows the results. He starts with a circle and divides it into 8 equal parts because the fractions are in eighths. Then he colors the circle graph to match the fractions in the table.

## CLASS EXERCISES

Use the circle graph at the right to answer.

FAVORITE SEASON

1. What fraction of the people like spring best?

2. Do more people like winter better than fall?

3. Which season is most popular?

4. What fraction of the people like winter best?

5. Do fewer people like summer or fall?

6. What fraction of the people like fall best?

# PRACTICE

Use the circle graph at the right to answer.

**7.** Which month do the fewest people like?

**8.** Which month do people like best?

**9.** Do more people like June or December?

**10.** What fraction of the people like November or December?

**11.** What is the difference between the fraction of people who chose December and the fraction of people who chose November?

**12.** Which is less, the fraction of the people who chose August or the sum of the people who chose the other months?

★ **13.** Look at the circle graph at the right. Write the fraction for each part.

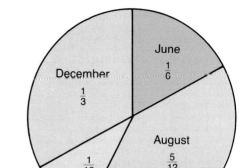

FAVORITE MONTH

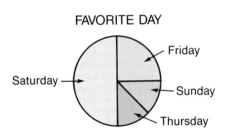

FAVORITE DAY

---

# CHECKPOINT 2

Add or subtract. Write the answer in lowest terms. *(pages 344–349, 354–357)*

**1.** $\frac{2}{10}$ $+\frac{3}{10}$

**2.** $\frac{2}{5}$ $+\frac{1}{5}$

**3.** $\frac{5}{8}$ $-\frac{3}{8}$

**4.** $\frac{1}{6}$ $+\frac{2}{3}$

**5.** $\frac{3}{4}$ $-\frac{1}{8}$

**6.** $\frac{3}{5}$ $-\frac{1}{10}$

Compare the fractions. Write < or >. *(pages 350–353)*

**7.** $\frac{2}{6}$ ▓ $\frac{5}{6}$

**8.** $\frac{4}{9}$ ▓ $\frac{1}{3}$

Use the graph to answer the questions. *(pages 358–359)*

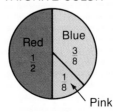

FAVORITE COLOR

**9.** What is the favorite color?

**10.** What is the least favorite color?

*Extra practice on page 424*

Write a number sentence to show the equivalent fractions. *(pages 330–335)*

1.

Write the fraction in lowest terms. *(pages 336–337)*

2. $\frac{12}{15}$   3. $\frac{5}{5}$   4. $\frac{8}{12}$   5. $\frac{14}{20}$

Write the fraction as a mixed number in lowest terms. *(pages 338–339)*

6. $\frac{26}{5}$   7. $\frac{18}{4}$

Measure to the nearest quarter inch. *(pages 340–341)*

8. _____

Solve. *(pages 342–343)*

9. A game has 7 green cubes and 6 yellow cubes. Megan picks a cube without looking. What is the probability that she picks a yellow cube?

Write the answer in lowest terms. *(pages 344–349)*

10. $\frac{2}{7} + \frac{3}{7}$   11. $\frac{3}{8} + \frac{7}{8}$   12. $\frac{9}{10} - \frac{5}{10}$   13. $\frac{3}{6} - \frac{1}{6}$

Compare the fractions. Write $<$, $>$, or $=$. *(pages 350–353)*

14. $\frac{5}{6}$ ▨ $\frac{4}{6}$   15. $\frac{1}{6}$ ▨ $\frac{1}{2}$   16. $\frac{2}{3}$ ▨ $\frac{3}{6}$   17. $\frac{7}{10}$ ▨ $\frac{3}{5}$

Write the answer in lowest terms. *(pages 354–357)*

18. $\frac{5}{6} + \frac{1}{12}$   19. $\frac{2}{5} + \frac{3}{10}$   20. $\frac{3}{4} - \frac{3}{16}$   21. $\frac{19}{21} - \frac{5}{7}$

**Favorite Subjects**

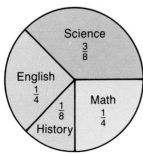

Use the circle graph to solve. *(pages 358–359)*

22. What fraction of students like math best?

23. What subject do the fewest students like?

*Extra practice on page 425*

# MATHEMATICS and MUSIC

Most musical pieces have a certain beat. This beat counts the time that each note takes.

The name of each note gives you a clue to how long or how short it is. The whole note is the longest note.

Two half notes equal one whole note.

You can write $\frac{1}{2} + \frac{1}{2} = \frac{2}{2} = 1$.

| NAME | BEAT | SYMBOL | | | |
|------|------|--------|--|--|--|
| whole note | 1 | 𝅝 | | | |
| half note | $\frac{1}{2}$ | 𝅗𝅥 | | 𝅗𝅥 | |
| quarter note | $\frac{1}{4}$ | ♩ | ♩ | ♩ | ♩ |
| eighth note | $\frac{1}{8}$ | ♪♪ | ♪♪ | ♪♪ | ♪♪ |

# DO YOU HAVE THE BEAT?

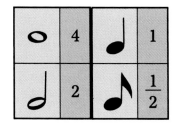

| | | | |
|---|---|---|---|
| 𝅝 | 4 | ♩ | 1 |
| 𝅗𝅥 | 2 | ♪ | $\frac{1}{2}$ |

Use the chart above to write the number sentence.

**1.** Two quarter notes equal a half note.

**2.** Four quarter notes equal a whole note.

**3.** Two eighth notes equal a quarter note.

The composer can change the beat. Suppose the quarter note will have one beat. The chart shows the number of beats the other notes will have.

Use the chart at left.

Write the total number of beats for the group of notes.

**4.** 𝅗𝅥𝅗𝅥    **5.** ♩♩♩    **6.** ♪♪𝅗𝅥    **7.** ♩♩♪𝅝♪

# Enrichment

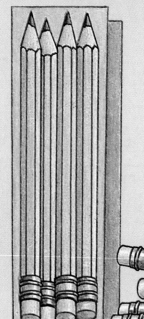

Remember that a multiple is a product of one whole number and another whole number.

Some multiples of 3 are 3, 6, 9, 12, 15, 18, 21, 24, 27.
Some multiples of 4 are 4, 8, 12, 16, 20, 24, 28, 32.

The numbers 12 and 24 are common multiples of 3 and 4. The number 12 is the **least common multiple** of 3 and 4.

There can be many common multiples of two numbers. There is only one least common multiple of two numbers.

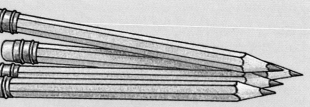
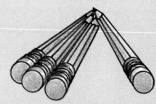

Write *a* or *b* to tell which is a list of common multiples of the two numbers. Then write the least common multiple.

1. 4 and 8      a. 4, 8, 12, 16      b. 8, 16, 24, 32

2. 3 and 6      a. 3, 6, 9, 12      b. 6, 12, 18, 24

3. 4 and 6      a. 12, 24, 36, 48      b. 6, 12, 18, 24

4. 3 and 5      a. 3, 5, 9, 10      b. 15, 30, 45, 60

5. 4 and 5      a. 10, 20, 30, 40      b. 20, 40, 60, 80

## LEAST COMMON MULTIPLE

Write the least common multiple.

6. 4 and 12      7. 3 and 8      8. 2 and 7

9. 5 and 8      10. 4 and 10      11. 8 and 12

12. 8 and 10      13. 2 and 16      14. 1 and 8

15. 6 and 8      16. 6 and 10      17. 6 and 16

18. 2, 4, and 8      19. 3, 4, and 12      20. 2, 3, and 7

You can write equivalent fractions by finding
the least common multiple of the denominators.

Write $\frac{1}{2}$ and $\frac{2}{3}$ as equivalent fractions with
the same denominator.

**Think:** The least common multiple of 2
and 3 is 6.

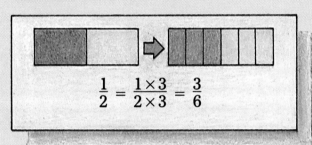

$$\frac{1}{2} = \frac{1 \times 3}{2 \times 3} = \frac{3}{6}$$

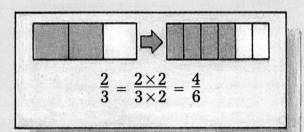

$$\frac{2}{3} = \frac{2 \times 2}{3 \times 2} = \frac{4}{6}$$

Write equivalent fractions by finding the least common
multiple of the denominators.

**21.** $\frac{1}{2}, \frac{1}{5}$   **22.** $\frac{1}{5}, \frac{2}{3}$   **23.** $\frac{1}{3}, \frac{1}{4}$   **24.** $\frac{3}{4}, \frac{3}{5}$   **25.** $\frac{1}{3}, \frac{3}{8}$

The least common multiple can help you add or subtract
fractions. To find the sum of $\frac{1}{2}$ and $\frac{2}{3}$, first think of the
least common multiple of the denominators. Then add.

$$\begin{array}{r} \frac{1}{2} = \quad \frac{3}{6} \\[4pt] + \frac{2}{3} = + \frac{4}{6} \\[2pt] \hline \frac{7}{6} = 1\frac{1}{6} \end{array}$$

Add or subtract. Write the answer in lowest terms.

**26.** $\frac{1}{2}$   **27.** $\frac{1}{5}$   **28.** $\frac{1}{3}$   **29.** $\frac{3}{4}$   **30.** $\frac{3}{8}$
$\quad +\frac{1}{5}$   $\quad +\frac{2}{3}$   $\quad +\frac{1}{4}$   $\quad -\frac{3}{5}$   $\quad -\frac{1}{3}$

**31.** $\frac{1}{2}$   **32.** $\frac{1}{3}$   **33.** $\frac{2}{5}$   **34.** $\frac{2}{6}$   **35.** $\frac{4}{5}$
$\quad +\frac{3}{8}$   $\quad +\frac{1}{8}$   $\quad +\frac{1}{3}$   $\quad -\frac{1}{5}$   $\quad -\frac{1}{4}$

# CUMULATIVE REVIEW

Choose the correct answer. Write *a*, *b*, *c*, or *d*.

Find the answer.

**1.**  38
$\times 40$

   a. 1220
   b. 1520
   c. 1620
   d. none of these

**2.**  85
$\times 17$

   a. 1445
   b. 1345
   c. 1335
   d. none of these

**3.**  29
$\times 86$

   a. 2484
   b. 2494
   c. 2394
   d. none of these

Find the answer.

**4.** 709
$\times 83$

   a. 58,747
   b. 57,847
   c. 57,747
   d. none of these

**5.** 564
$\times 19$

   a. 9716
   b. 10,706
   c. 10,716
   d. none of these

**6.** $8.62
$\times 47$

   a. $4051.40
   b. $405.14
   c. $415.14
   d. none of these

Find the answer.

**7.** $46\overline{)53}$

   a. 1 R6
   b. 1 R7
   c. 1 R8
   d. none of these

**8.** $83\overline{)616}$

   a. 7 R25
   b. 7 R35
   c. 7 R5
   d. none of these

**9.** $67\overline{)178}$

   a. 2
   b. 2 R44
   c. 2 R34
   d. none of these

Find the answer.

**10.** $38\overline{)946}$

   a. 24 R4
   b. 23 R23
   c. 24 R24
   d. none of these

**11.** $52\overline{)799}$

   a. 15
   b. 15 R19
   c. 15 R29
   d. none of these

**12.** $28\overline{)869}$

   a. 31 R1
   b. 30 R29
   c. 31
   d. none of these

Find the most likely answer.

**13.** Claire drove at 80 km per hour. How long did it take her to travel 480 km?

   **a.** 60 hours
   **b.** 6 hours
   **c.** 6 km
   **d.** 600 hours

**14.** Four friends made $25 raking leaves. They divided up the money equally. How much did each friend get?

   **a.** $62.50
   **b.** $.62
   **c.** $6.25
   **d.** $100

Estimate.

**15.** $19\overline{)448}$

   **a.** 20
   **b.** 30
   **c.** 400
   **d.** 200

**16.** $76\overline{)643}$

   **a.** 800
   **b.** 8
   **c.** 900
   **d.** 10

**17.** $53\overline{)468}$

   **a.** 100
   **b.** 90
   **c.** 800
   **d.** 9

# LANGUAGE and VOCABULARY REVIEW

Use the words below to complete the sentence. Write the word on your paper.

triangle   parallelogram   ray   numerator   denominator   vertexes
decimal   order property   grouping property   line

**1.** The __?__ of a fraction shows the total number of equal parts.

**2.** The points where the sides of a polygon meet are called __?__.

**3.** A polygon with three sides is a __?__.

**4.** A __?__ is a special kind of quadrilateral.

**5.** A __?__ has only one endpoint.

**6.** The number 0.53 is called a __?__.

**7.** $40 \times 15 = 15 \times 40$ is an example of the __?__.

# DEBUGGING

Kristen wrote a program that tells the computer to find the sum of 13, 27, and 22. Before she typed RUN, she estimated that the sum should be about 60.

```
RUN
ADD 3 NUMBERS
35
```

When the output was 35, Kristen knew it was wrong. There was a **bug,** or error, in her program. By **debugging** her program, Kristen would find and correct her mistakes.

Kristen typed the BASIC word **LIST** to tell the computer to show the program.

Kristen checked the spelling of the BASIC words. She checked numbers, signs, and line numbers. She found the mistake in line 50. Kristen entered this line to correct the program.

```
LIST
10 PRINT "ADD 3 NUMBERS"
20 LET A = 13
30 LET B = 22
40 LET C = 27
50 PRINT A + B
60 END
```

```
50 PRINT A + B + C
```

There is one mistake in the program. Debug the program to get the output shown at the right.

**1.** 
```
LIST
10 LET R = 40
20 LET T = 2
30 PRINNT R * T
40 END
```
Output
```
80
```

**2.** 
```
LIST
10 PRINT "MULTIPLY"
20 PRINT "12 * 5 IS"
30 PRINT 12 + 5
40 END
```
Output
```
MULTIPLY
12 * 5 IS
60
```

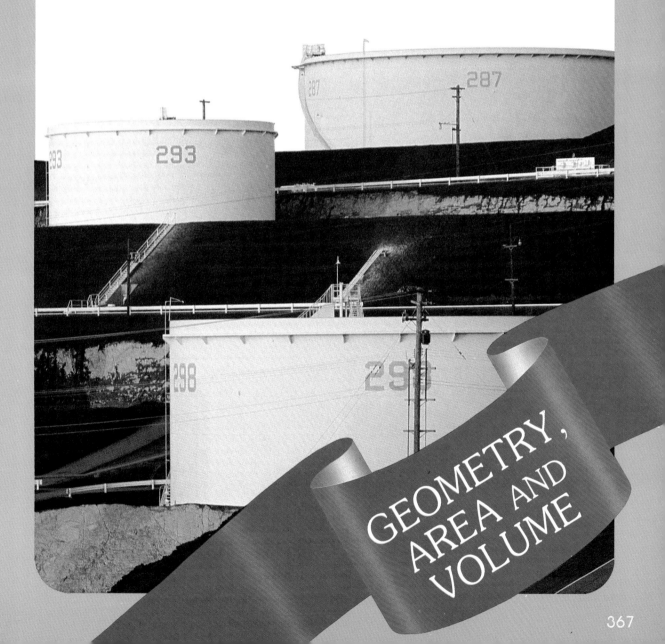

From the air, the top of this oil tank looks like a circle. This picture shows how the tank looks from the ground. What shape do you see?

13

GEOMETRY, AREA AND VOLUME

# SYMMETRY

If you fold a piece of paper once and cut out a figure, each half is the same size and shape. The line that divides the two matching halves is a **line of symmetry.**

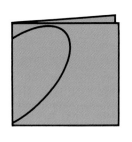 

Some shapes have more than one line of symmetry. This shape has two lines of symmetry.

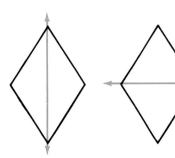  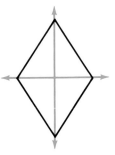

Some shapes, such as the one at the right, have no lines of symmetry.

 When you see only half of a shape that has symmetry, you can picture the whole shape in your mind.

## CLASS EXERCISES

Is the line a line of symmetry? Write *yes* or *no*.

1.

2.
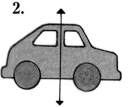

3.

4.

5.

6.

7.

8.

# PRACTICE

How many lines of symmetry does the figure have? Write
*0, 1,* or *2.*

**9.**

**10.**

**11.**

**12.**

**13.**

**14.**

**15.**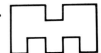

**16.**

**17.**

**18.**

★ **19.** $COB$

★ **20.** $BOB$

The line of symmetry divides the shape in half. Picture the
other half of the shape in your mind. Then draw the whole
shape.

**MENTAL MATH**

**21.**

**22.**

**23.**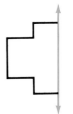

## PROBLEM SOLVING APPLICATIONS
### Drawing a Picture

Draw the shape.

**24.** Draw a geometric shape that has
only 1 line of symmetry. Check to
be sure there are no others.

**25.** Draw any shape that has only 2
lines of symmetry. Check to be
sure there are no others.

★ **26.** Draw any shape that has 4 lines
of symmetry.

★ **27.** Name and draw 5 different living
things that have at least 1 line of
symmetry.

# SLIDES, FLIPS, AND TURNS

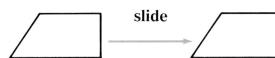

**slide**

When you move a figure along a straight line, you **slide** it.

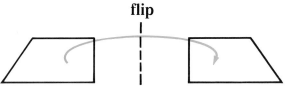

**flip**

When you turn a figure over, you **flip** it.

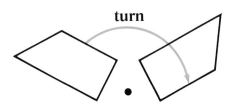

**turn**

When you move a figure around a point, you **turn** it.

## CLASS EXERCISES

Which shows a slide of the first figure? Choose *a*, *b*, or *c*.

**1.**    **a.**    **b.** 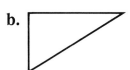   **c.**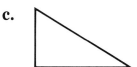

Which shows a flip of the first figure?

**2.**    **a.**    **b.**    **c.**

Which shows a turn of the first figure?

**3.**    **a.**    **b.**    **c.**

## PRACTICE

Tell whether the movement of the figure is a slide, a flip, or a turn. Write *s*, *f*, or *t*.

**4.**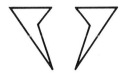

**5.**

**6.**

**7.**

**8.**

**9.**

Copy the figure. Then do the slide, flip, or turn and draw the new figure.

**10.** a flip

**11.** a slide

★ **12.** a turn

Write the answer.

**13.** 4572 + 8986

**14.** 63 ÷ 30

**15.** 5940 − 4963

**16.** 28 × 67

**17.** 358 × 42

**18.** 73,972 − 5095

**19.** 63,291 + 4786

**20.** 410 ÷ 13

**21.** 295 + 18

**MIXED REVIEW**

## PROBLEM SOLVING APPLICATIONS
### Mental Images

Picture yourself moving from one position to the other. Then answer.

**22.** You walk forward 10 ft. Did you slide, flip, or turn?

**23.** You look in a mirror. Is your reflection a slide, a flip, or a turn?

★ **24.** You are facing a tree. Then you move so your right side is facing the tree. Did you slide, flip, or turn?

# CONGRUENT FIGURES

The triangles are the same size and the same shape.

You can slide one triangle to fit over the other exactly.

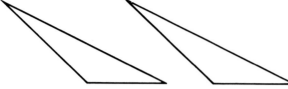

When two figures are the same size and shape, they are **congruent.**

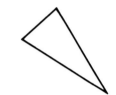

You can flip the triangle on the left to fit over the other exactly.

**Think:** Are the two triangles congruent?

## CLASS EXERCISES

Which figure is congruent to the first figure? Choose *a, b,* or *c.*

1.    a.    b.    c.

2.    a.    b.   c.

3.  a.   b.   c.

4.    a.    b.    c.

# PRACTICE

Match the congruent figures. Write the letter from the group of figures below.

5.

6.

7.

8.

9.

10.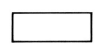

11.

12.

13.

14.

15.

16.

A.

B.

C.

D.

E.

F.

G.

H.

I.

J.

K.

L.

## PROBLEM SOLVING APPLICATIONS
### Using a Picture

Use the picture to solve.

17. Triangle 1 is $\frac{1}{4}$ of square *DEFG* and triangle 2 is $\frac{1}{4}$ of square *DEFG*. How much of square *DEFG* are triangles 1 and 2 together?

18. Name the lines of symmetry shown in square *DEFG*.

19. How many triangles in square *DEFG* are congruent to triangle *DHE*? Name them.

★ 20. How many triangles in square *DEFG* are congruent to triangle *DEF*? Name them.

# SIMILAR FIGURES

The triangles are the same shape but not the same size.

The rectangles are the same shape but not the same size.

Figures that are the same shape but not necessarily the same size are called **similar** figures.

## CLASS EXERCISES

Are the figures similar to each other? Explain why or why not.

**1.**     **2.** 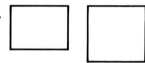    **3.**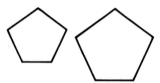

**4.**     **5.**     **6.**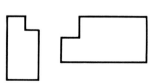

## PRACTICE

Choose the figure that is similar to the first. Write the letter.

**7.**     **a.**     **b.**     **c.**

**8.**     **a.**     **b.**     **c.**

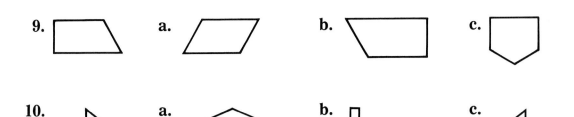

**9.**    **a.**    **b.**    **c.**

**10.**    **a.**    **b.**    **c.**

Choose the figures that are similar to each other. Write the letters.

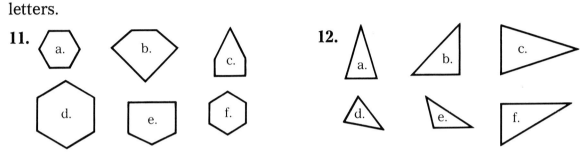

**11.**    a.   b.   c.   d.   e.   f.

**12.**    a.   b.   c.   d.   e.   f.

Use the pictures to solve.

**13. Think:** Why is book 1 similar to book 2?

★ **14. Think:** Why isn't book 1 similar to book 3?

## PROBLEM SOLVING APPLICATIONS
### Classifying Figures

Write *All, Some,* or *No.*

**15.** ___?___ rectangles are similar.

**16.** ___?___ squares are similar.

**17.** ___?___ circles are similar.

**18.** ___?___ triangles are similar.

★ **19.** ___?___ figures that are congruent are similar.

★ **20.** ___?___ figures that are similar are congruent.

# PROBLEM SOLVING
## Strategy: Logical Thinking

1. Understand
2. Plan
3. Work
4. Answer/Check

To solve some problems you need to decide how objects are alike or different.

Which shape is different from the other shapes?

The third shape is different because it is not similar to the other shapes.

For other problems you need to look for a pattern and then decide how the next object will look.

What comes next?

The shape has been turned to make this pattern. This shape will be next.

## CLASS EXERCISES

Which shape is different? Explain your answer.

1.

  a.     b.     c.     d.

2.

  a.     b.     c.     d.

3.

  a.     b.     c.     d.

4.
 J W H B
  a.     b.     c.     d.

# PRACTICE

What comes next? Write the letter.

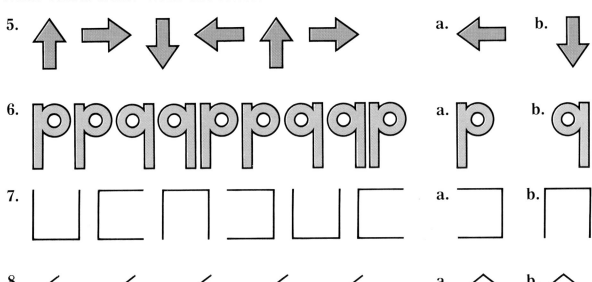

Draw the figure that comes next.

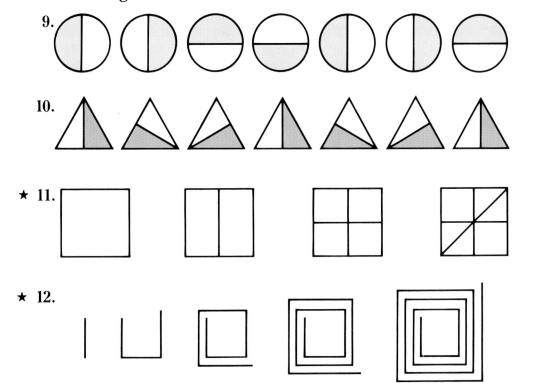

# AREA,
# COUNTING SQUARE UNITS

1 cm

1 cm

The picture at the right shows a **square centimeter.** It measures 1 cm on each side.

The **area** of a figure is the number of square units that fit inside it. A square centimeter is often used to measure area. Twelve square units fit inside the photo. Each unit is 1 square centimeter. The area of the photo is 12 square centimeters.

You can estimate the area of this figure. The area of the longer row is 3 square centimeters. The area of two rows of three would be 6 square centimeters. The area of the figure is between 3 and 6 square centimeters. The exact area is 5 square centimeters.

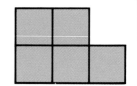

## CLASS EXERCISES

What is the area? Complete.

**1.**

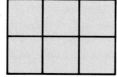

▓ square centimeters

**2.**

square centimeters

**3.**

▓ square centimeters

## PRACTICE

Write the area of the shaded part in square centimeters.

**4.**

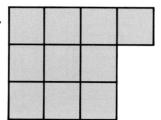

**5.**

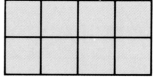

**6.**

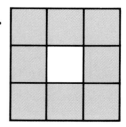

**7.**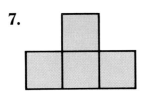

**8.**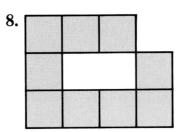

**9.**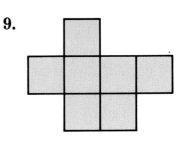

★ **10.** Draw a figure with an area of 12 square units.

Use estimation to match the figure with the correct description.

**11.**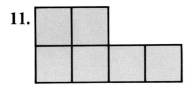

**12.**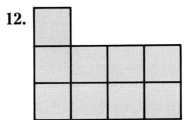

**ESTIMATE**

**A.** The area is greater than 8 square centimeters.

**B.** The area is between 4 square centimeters and 8 square centimeters.

# PROBLEM SOLVING APPLICATIONS
## Reading a Plan

Use the plan to solve.

**13.** What is the area of the bookcase?

**14.** What is the area of the desk?

**15.** What is the area of the bed?

**16.** Which item has the greatest area?

★ **17.** Which item has the greatest perimeter?

MY ROOM PLAN
Each ☐ = 1 square unit

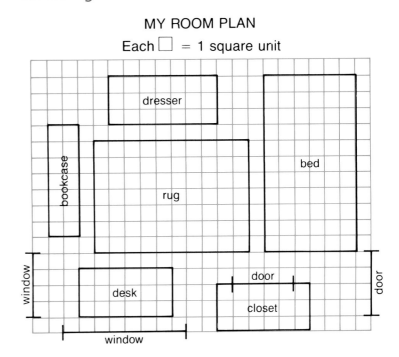

# AREA

Rebecca's family is putting in a new patio. The patio is 4 m long and 3 m wide. What is the area of the patio?

You can find the area of the patio by counting the number of square meters. You also can find the area by multiplying the length times the width.

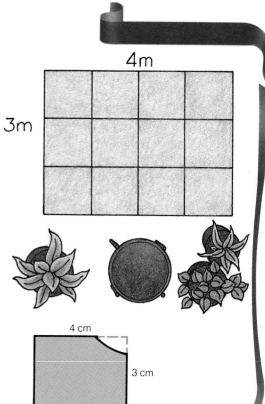

4m

3m

Area = length × width
Area = 4 × 3
Area = 12

The area of the patio is 12 square meters.

 The shaded part has about the same area as the rectangle. Its area is about 12 square centimeters.

4 cm

3 cm

## CLASS EXERCISES

What numbers do you multiply to find the area? What is the area?

**1.**
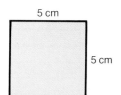
5 cm
5 cm

**2.**

6 km
2 km

## PRACTICE

Find the area. Be sure to write the correct units.

**3.**
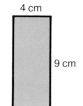
4 cm
9 cm

**4.**

2 m
2 m

**5.**
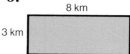
8 km
3 km

**6.**

3 mm
9 mm

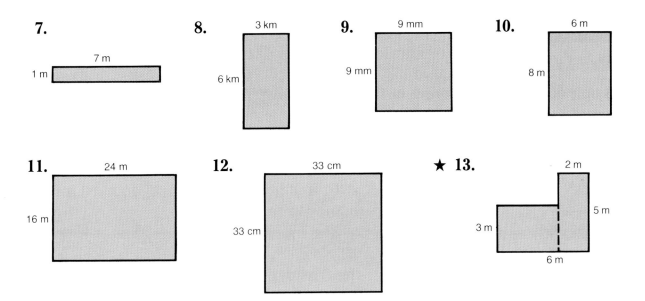

**7.**
7 m
1 m

**8.**
3 km
6 km

**9.**
9 mm
9 mm

**10.**
6 m
8 m

**11.**
24 m
16 m

**12.**
33 cm
33 cm

**★ 13.**
2 m
5 m
3 m
6 m

Estimate the area by finding the area of the rectangle.

**14.**
8 m
5 m

**15.**
6 km
6 km

**16.**
12 cm
6 cm

ESTIMATE

## PROBLEM SOLVING APPLICATIONS
### Using Pictures

The Greenway Company plants new lawns for people. The sizes of 4 lawns are shown at the right.

**17.** What is the area of lawn 2?

**18.** Which lawn has the largest area?

**19.** Which lawn has the smallest area?

**20.** Write a number sentence that you could use to figure out the number of meters of fence needed to go around lawn 4.

**★ 21.** Another lawn shaped like a rectangle has the same area as lawn 3. What could be the lengths of the sides?

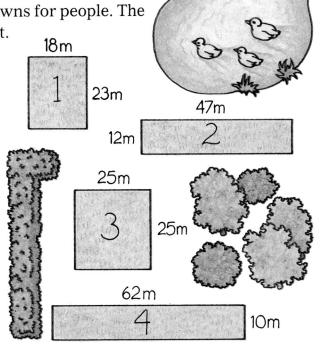

18m
1
23m

47m
2
12m

25m
3
25m

62m
4
10m

# PROBLEM SOLVING
## Strategy: Using a Picture

1. Understand
2. Plan
3. Work
4. Answer/Check

Look at the **scale drawing** of the room below. With a scale drawing you can find actual measurements. The **scale** tells you what each square in the drawing means.

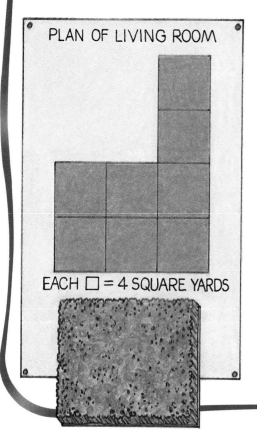

PLAN OF LIVING ROOM

EACH □ = 4 SQUARE YARDS

To find how much carpet you need for the room, you find the area.

First count the squares. There are 8 squares.

Then read the scale. It tells you that each square stands for 4 square yards.

To find the number of square yards in all, you multiply.

$$\begin{array}{r} 4 \text{ square yards} \\ \times 8 \\ \hline 32 \text{ square yards} \end{array}$$

You need 32 square yards of carpet.

**Think:** The room is not drawn to its actual size. Why?

# CLASS EXERCISES

Use the scale to find the area. Explain how you found your answer.

Scale: Each □ = 4 square inches

**1.**

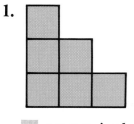

☐ square inches

**2.**

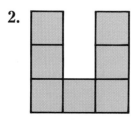

☐ square inches

**3.**

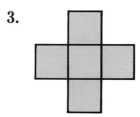

☐ square inches

# PRACTICE

Use the scale to find the area of the room.

Each □ = 9 square feet

**4.**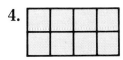

**5.**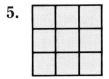

**6.**

**7.**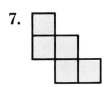

**8.**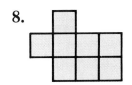

**9.**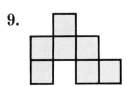

Use the scale to find the area of the patio. Count the whole squares and the half squares to find the total number of squares before you multiply.

Each □ = 4 square feet

★ **10.**

★ **11.**

★ **12.**

## CHECKPOINT 1

Match the congruent figures.
Write the letter. *(pages 370–373)*

**1.**   **2.**

**A.**   **B.**

Choose the figure that is similar.
Write the letter. *(pages 374–375)*

**3.** 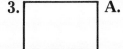 **A.**  **B.**

What is the area? *(pages 378–383)*

**4.** 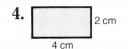  **5.**

Each □ is
4 square meters.

*Extra practice on page 426*

# CUBES, RECTANGULAR PRISMS, AND PYRAMIDS

The figures below all have flat sides, or **faces.** The part of the figure where the faces meet is an **edge.** The part of the figure where the edges meet is a **vertex.**

**cube**

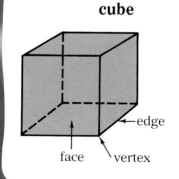

edge
face   vertex

**rectangular prism**

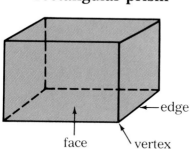

edge
face   vertex

**pyramid**

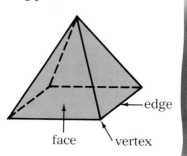

edge
face   vertex

## CLASS EXERCISES

Write *cube, rectangular prism,* or *pyramid* to name the figure.

1.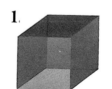

2.

3.

4.

5.

6.

7.

8.

## PRACTICE

How would the first figure look from the top? Write the letter.

9.

a.    b.    c.    d.

10.

a.    b.    c.    d.

How would the first figure look from the bottom?
Write the letter.

**11.**   a.   b. ▢  c.   d. ▯

**12.**   a.   b. ▢  c.   d. ▯

How would the first figure look from the side?
Write the letter.

**13.**   a.   b.   c. ▢  d.

**14.**   a.   b. ▱  c. △  d. ▯

---

Write the answer. Write fractions in lowest terms.

**15.** $\frac{1}{2} + \frac{1}{4}$ **16.** $\frac{5}{6} - \frac{2}{3}$ **17.** $\frac{5}{8} + \frac{3}{4}$ **18.** $\frac{7}{10} - \frac{3}{5}$

**19.** $0.62 - 0.48$ **20.** $0.72 + 0.29$ **21.** $0.83 - 0.5$

**MIXED REVIEW**

# PROBLEM SOLVING APPLICATIONS
## Logical Thinking

Some of these shapes can be folded to form a cube, a rectangular prism, or a pyramid. Some cannot. Name the shape that can be formed, or write *none of these*.

**22.** 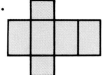  **23.**   **24.**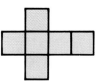

**★ 25.** 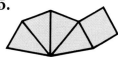  **★ 26.** 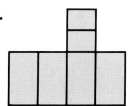  **★ 27.**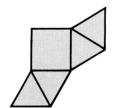

# CYLINDERS, CONES, SPHERES

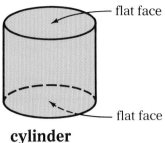 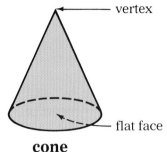 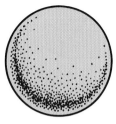

**cylinder**          **cone**          **sphere**

This is a **cylinder.** It has two flat **faces** and no vertexes. Each face is circular.

This **cone** has one flat circular face and one vertex.

A **sphere** has no flat faces and no vertexes.

 Picture a can of soup in your mind. You know it is a cylinder because it has two flat circular faces.

## CLASS EXERCISES

Write *cylinder, cone,* or *sphere* to name the figure.

1.
2.
3.
4.

5.
6.
7.
8.

## PRACTICE

How would the first figure look from the top? Write the letter.

9.    a.    b.    c.    d.

10.    a.    b.    c.    d.

How would the first figure look from the bottom? Write the letter.

11.   a.   b.   c.   d.

12.   a. ○  b. ⬭  c. △  d. ◻

How would the first figure look from the side? Write the letter.

13.   a.   b.   c.   d.

14.   a.   b.   c.   d.

Picture the object described. Name the object and its shape.

15. It has two flat faces and holds paint.

16. You can wear it on your head. It has one vertex.

17. It has no flat faces. It can be seen at a soccer game.

MENTAL MATH

## PROBLEM SOLVING APPLICATIONS
### Picturing an Answer

Picture the answer in your mind. Then draw it.

18. If you cut the cone in half along the line shown, what shape would the new faces be?

19. If you cut the sphere in half along the line shown, what shape would the new faces be?

20. If you cut a sphere along the line shown, what shape would the new faces be?

21. If you cut a cylinder in half, parallel to one of the flat faces, what would the shape of the new faces be?

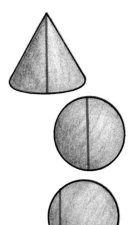

# VOLUME, COUNTING CUBIC UNITS

The **volume** of a figure is the number of cubic units it contains.

The picture at the right shows 1 **cubic centimeter.** One cubic centimeter measures 1 cm on each edge. A cubic centimeter is often used to measure volume.

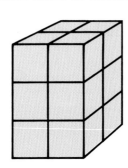

Look at the figure at the left. Twelve cubic units fit inside it. Each unit is 1 cubic centimeter. The volume of the figure is 12 cubic centimeters.

Sometimes you cannot see all of the cubic units. Picture the cubic units that are hidden behind the units you can see.

## CLASS EXERCISES

What is the volume? Complete.

**1.**

░ cubic centimeters

**2.**
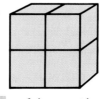
░ cubic centimeters

**3.**
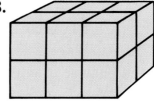
░ cubic centimeters

## PRACTICE

Write the volume in cubic centimeters.

**4.**
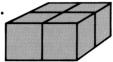

**5.**
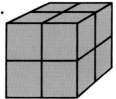

**6.**
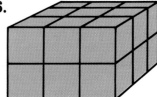

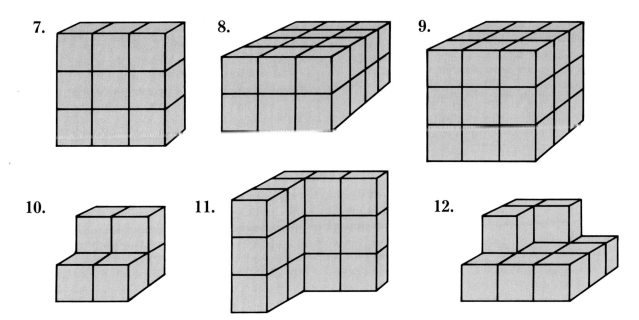

**7.** **8.** **9.**

**10.** **11.** **12.**

The figure has a hole just in the center. What is the greatest number of cubic units that could be missing?

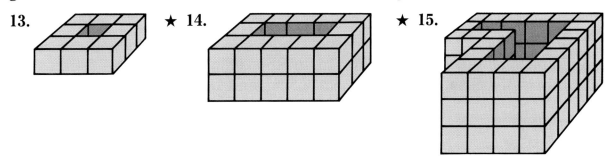

**13.** **★ 14.** **★ 15.**

## PROBLEM SOLVING APPLICATIONS
### Logical Thinking

Ray used cubic units for these buildings. Solve.

**16.** Which building has the greatest volume?

**17.** Which building covers the most ground?

**18.** Which building's roof has the greatest area?

**19.** Which building has the greatest distance around it?

**★ 20. Think:** Will a shape with a greater volume always have a greater distance around the bottom?

**A.**

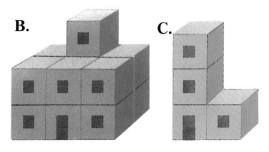

**B.** **C.**

# VOLUME

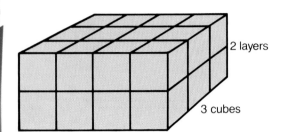

2 layers

3 cubes

4 cubes

You can find the volume of this box by counting. You also can find the volume by multiplying.

There are 2 layers of cubes. Each layer has $4 \times 3$, or 12 cubes. You can find the volume by multiplying the number of cubes in each layer by the number of layers.

$$4 \times 3 \times 2 = 24 \text{ cubes}$$

There are 2 layers in this rectangular prism. Each layer is 4 cm by 3 cm. You can find the volume by multiplying.

$$4 \times 3 \times 2 = 24$$

The volume of the rectangular prism is 24 cubic centimeters.

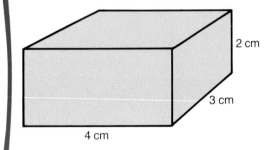

2 cm

3 cm

4 cm

 Explain how to use a calculator to find the volume of a box with measurements of 16 cm, 22 cm, and 18 cm.

## CLASS EXERCISES

What numbers do you multiply to find the volume? What is the volume?

**1.**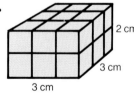

2 cm

3 cm

3 cm

**2.**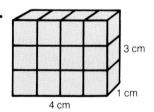

3 cm

1 cm

4 cm

**3.**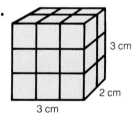

3 cm

2 cm

3 cm

**4.**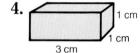

1 cm

1 cm

3 cm

**5.**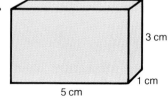

3 cm

1 cm

5 cm

**6.**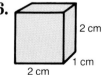

2 cm

1 cm

2 cm

# PRACTICE

What is the volume? Be sure to write the correct units.

**7.**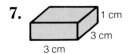
1 cm
3 cm
3 cm

**8.**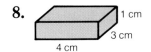
1 cm
3 cm
4 cm

**9.**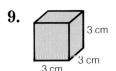
3 cm
3 cm
3 cm

**10.**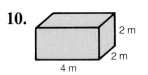
2 m
2 m
4 m

**11.**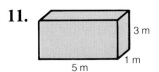
3 m
1 m
5 m

**12.**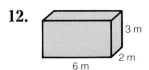
3 m
2 m
6 m

**13.**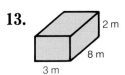
2 m
8 m
3 m

**14.**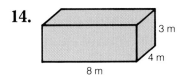
3 m
4 m
8 m

**15.**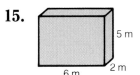
5 m
2 m
6 m

Write the volume of a box with the given measurements.

**16.** 13 cm, 15 cm, 24 cm

**17.** 11 cm, 21 cm, 26 cm

CALCULATOR

★ **18.** A box has a volume of 32 cubic cm. You know that two of the measurements are 4 cm and 4 cm. What is the third measurement?

## PROBLEM SOLVING APPLICATIONS
### Using Pictures

Use the pictures to solve.

**19.** What is the volume of Box A?

**20.** What is the volume of Box C?

**21.** Which box has the greatest volume?

**22.** You have 28 cubic centimeters of sand. Which box could you fill?

★ **23.** You have 60 cubic centimeters of sand. Which boxes could hold all of it?

★ **24.** Which box is a cube? Why?

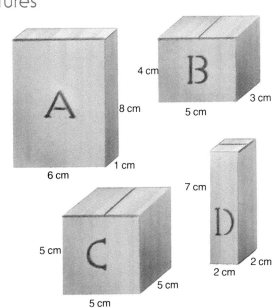

# PROBLEM SOLVING
## Strategy: Using a Picture

Mary Jane drew a picture of her garden. How much space does her garden cover?

**Think:** Are you looking for perimeter, area, or volume?

You want to measure the surface of Mary Jane's garden. Find the area.

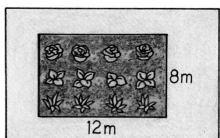

$$\text{Area} = 12 \times 8 = 96$$

The area of Mary Jane's garden is 96 square meters.

Mary Jane wants to fill her flower box with soil. How much soil does she need?

You are looking for the amount of soil the flower box will hold. Find the volume of the flower box.

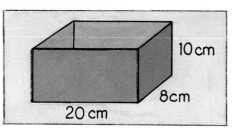

$$20 \times 8 \times 10 = 1600$$

Mary Jane needs 1600 cubic centimeters of soil for her flower box.

## CLASS EXERCISES

Does the problem ask you to find perimeter, area, or volume? Write *p*, *a*, or *v*. Use the pictures above to help you decide.

1. A dog ran around Mary Jane's garden 8 times. How far did the dog run?

2. How much water will the empty flower box hold?

3. How much space will be covered by soil in the garden?

4. Mary Jane wants to put a string fence around her garden. How many meters of string does she need?

# PRACTICE

Here is Jonah's picture of his patio and pool. Tell whether the problem asks you to find perimeter, area, or volume. Write *p*, *a*, or *v*. Then solve.

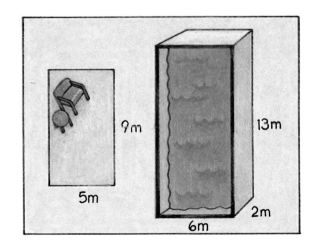

5. How much space does Jonah's patio cover?

6. What is the distance around Jonah's patio?

7. Jonah covers his patio with cement. How much space does the cement cover?

8. Jonah fills his pool with water. How much water does the pool hold?

★ 9. Jonah paints the rim of his pool. How many meters does he paint?

★ 10. A neighbor's patio is twice as long and twice as wide as Jonah's patio. How many times as great is the perimeter of the neighbor's patio? How many times as great is the area?

# CHECKPOINT 2

**Name the figure.** *(pages 384–387)*

1.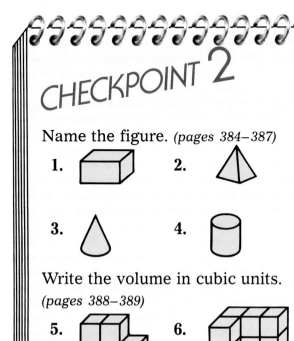

2.

3.

4.

**Write the volume in cubic units.** *(pages 388–389)*

5.

6.

**What is the volume?** *(pages 390–391)*

7.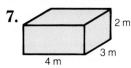

Write *p*, *a*, or *v* to tell whether the problem asks you to find perimeter, area, or volume. Then solve. *(pages 392–393)*

8. How much carpet would you need to cover the floor in the picture?

*Extra practice on page 426*

Write the correct letters. *(pages 370–375)*

**1.** Choose the figures that are congruent to each other.

a.       b.       c.       d.

**2.** Choose the figures that are similar to each other.

a.       b.       c.       d.

Draw the figure that comes next. *(pages 376–377)*

**3.**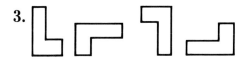

**4.**

Find the area. *(pages 380–381)*

**5.**
5 cm
7 cm

**6.**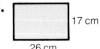
17 cm
26 cm

**7.**
44 m
44 m

Name the figure. *(pages 384–387)*

**8.**

**9.**

**10.**

**11.**

Find the volume. *(pages 390–391)*

**12.**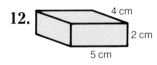
4 cm
2 cm
5 cm

**13.**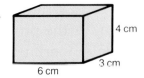
4 cm
6 cm
3 cm

**14.**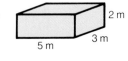
2 m
3 m
5 m

Write *p*, *a*, or *v* to tell whether the problem asks for perimeter, area, or volume. Then solve. *(pages 392–393)*

**15.** Rancher Rick covers the inside of the horse corral with grass seed. How much ground does the grass seed cover?

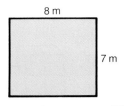
8 m
7 m

*Extra practice on page 427*

# MATHEMATICS and SCIENCE

To measure the height of a horse, you measure from the withers to the ground when the horse is standing. The height of a pony is less than 58 in.

WITHERS

Usually when talking about the height of a horse or pony, you use the term *hands*. A hand is 4 in.

To write 58 in. as hands, you divide by 4.

$$\begin{array}{r} 14 \text{ R2} \\ 4\overline{)\,58} \end{array}$$

You write this as 14–2 hands. You read 14–2 hands as *14 hands 2 in.* A pony has a height less than 14–2 hands.

## HOW MANY HANDS?

Answer these questions about horses.

1. The Shetland pony was 45 in. tall. How many hands is this?

2. The Standardbred horse ranges in height from 60 in. to 65 in. Write these heights in hands.

3. The farmers' workhorse weighed 1905 lb, and the riding horse weighed 917 lb. What is the difference in the weights of the two horses?

4. American Thoroughbreds descend from one of three types of horses that came from England in 1689, 1706, and 1724. Which of these years was longest ago? How many years ago was it?

5. The horse's hoofs touch ground in this order: right rear, left rear, right front, left front. What is the next hoof to touch the ground?

# Enrichment

Here's a puzzle. Divide the figure into two congruent parts.

It may take a few tries, but it can be done. Using tracing paper may help.

Trace the figure. Divide it into two congruent parts.

1. 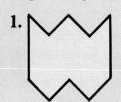  2.   3. 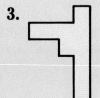  4.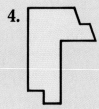

Here's one way to make your own puzzles.

Trace a figure.

Trace the figure again so that one side of it touches the first figure.

Erase the line between the two figures. Trace the new shape on another sheet of paper.

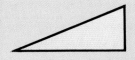

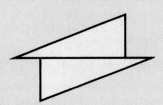

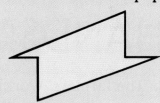

Use the figure to make a puzzle. Then see if a friend can solve it. Some puzzles have more than one answer. If your friend gets a different answer, check it. It might be correct!

5.   6.   7.   8.

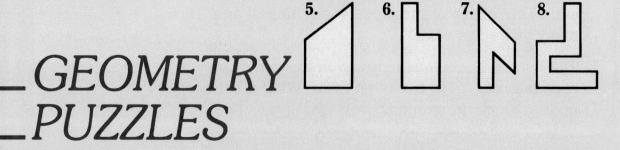

# GEOMETRY
# PUZZLES

These pictures show another type of puzzle. Divide the figure into four congruent parts that are similar to the large figure.

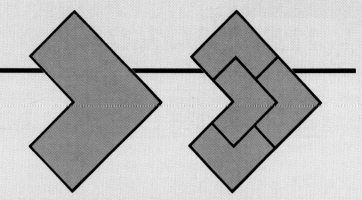

The small parts are called **reptiles**. Each part has the same shape as the whole.

9. Trace the figure. Draw the reptiles to complete the puzzle.

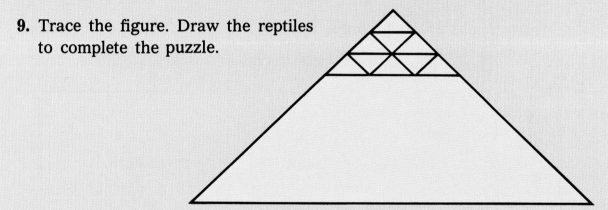

Trace the figure. Divide it into four reptiles.

10.    11.    12.    13.

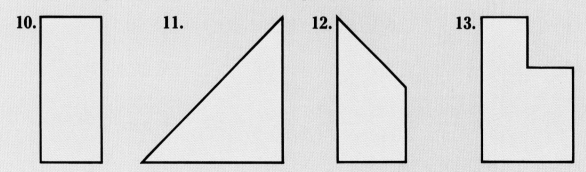

Make a reptile puzzle. Trace the figure four times. Make sure that the large figure is similar to the small reptile.

14.    15.    16.    17.

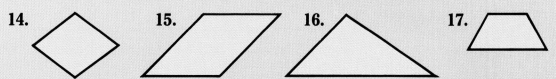

 # CUMULATIVE REVIEW

Choose the correct answer. Write *a*, *b*, *c*, or *d*.

**Find the equivalent fractions.**

**1.**

    **a.** $\frac{2}{5} = \frac{2}{15}$

    **b.** $\frac{2}{5} = \frac{6}{15}$

    **c.** $\frac{2}{5} = \frac{2}{10}$

    **d.** none of these

**Find the equivalent fraction in lowest terms.**

**2.** $\frac{8}{16}$

  **a.** $\frac{4}{8}$   **b.** $\frac{2}{4}$

  **c.** $\frac{1}{2}$

  **d.** none of these

**3.** $\frac{9}{24}$

  **a.** $\frac{3}{8}$   **b.** $\frac{1}{3}$

  **c.** $\frac{1}{4}$

  **d.** none of these

**Find the fraction as a mixed number in lowest terms.**

**4.** $\frac{14}{6}$

  **a.** $2\frac{1}{6}$   **b.** $2\frac{2}{6}$

  **c.** $2\frac{1}{3}$

  **d.** none of these

**5.** $\frac{26}{8}$

  **a.** $3\frac{2}{8}$   **b.** $3\frac{1}{4}$

  **c.** $2\frac{5}{4}$

  **d.** none of these

**Measure to the nearest quarter inch.**

**6.** _____

  **a.** $1\frac{1}{4}$ in.   **b.** $1\frac{3}{4}$ in.

  **c.** $2\frac{1}{4}$ in.

  **d.** none of these

**Find the answer in lowest terms.**

**7.** $\frac{3}{8} + \frac{7}{8}$

  **a.** $\frac{10}{8}$   **b.** $1\frac{2}{8}$

  **c.** $1\frac{1}{4}$

  **d.** none of these

**8.** $\frac{8}{9} - \frac{5}{9}$

  **a.** $\frac{1}{3}$   **b.** $\frac{3}{9}$

  **c.** $1\frac{4}{9}$

  **d.** none of these

**9.** $\frac{9}{10} - \frac{7}{10}$

  **a.** $\frac{2}{10}$   **b.** $\frac{1}{5}$

  **c.** $\frac{2}{5}$

  **d.** none of these

**Complete the equivalent fractions.**

**10.** $\frac{5}{9} = \frac{}{27}$

  **a.** 27   **b.** 15

  **c.** 14

  **d.** none of these

**11.** $\frac{5}{8} = \frac{}{16}$

  **a.** 32   **b.** 16

  **c.** 10

  **d.** none of these

**12.** $\frac{3}{4} = \frac{}{24}$

  **a.** 12   **b.** 18

  **c.** 7

  **d.** none of these

Find the answer in lowest terms.

**13.** $\frac{2}{5} + \frac{3}{10}$

    **a.** $\frac{1}{3}$

    **b.** $\frac{7}{10}$

    **c.** $\frac{5}{10}$

    **d.** none of these

**14.** $\frac{5}{12} + \frac{1}{4}$

    **a.** $\frac{2}{3}$

    **b.** $\frac{6}{16}$

    **c.** $\frac{8}{12}$

    **d.** none of these

**15.** $\frac{7}{9} - \frac{5}{18}$

    **a.** $\frac{2}{9}$

    **b.** $\frac{2}{18}$

    **c.** $\frac{1}{2}$

    **d.** none of these

Simplify the problem. Solve.

**16.** Amy's dinner cost $5.27, her mother's dinner cost $6.18, and her sister's dinner cost $3.89. How much change did Amy's mother receive from $20?

    **a.** $15.34    **b.** $35.34    **c.** $4.66    **d.** none of these

# LANGUAGE and VOCABULARY REVIEW

Copy the words on your paper. Write the letter of the matching definition next to each word.

**1.** in lowest terms

**2.** congruent figures

**3.** similar figures

**4.** volume

**5.** equivalent fractions

**6.** parallel lines

**7.** perpendicular lines

**A.** Number of cubic units in a figure

**B.** Figures that have the same shape but not necessarily the same size

**C.** Describes a fraction whose numerator and denominator cannot be divided by a factor greater than 1

**D.** Figures that have the same shape and the same size

**E.** Two fractions with different numerators and denominators that name the same amount

**F.** Lines that never meet

**G.** Lines that meet at right angles

# GRAPHICS

Some computers can draw designs. You can think of a computer screen as a grid. It is made up of many tiny squares that are numbered beginning with 0.

You can make a design by telling the computer which squares to light up. You need two numbers for each square.

3, 4 tells the computer to light up the square shown in yellow at the right. The first number is the number of squares *across* the grid. The second number is the number of squares *down* the grid.

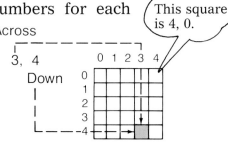

This square is 4, 0.

These steps tell the computer to make the design shown at the right.

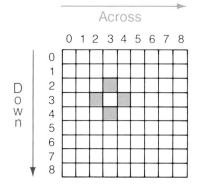

1. Go across to 3 and down to 2.
2. Go across to 2 and down to 3.
3. Go across to 4 and down to 3.
4. Go across to 3 and down to 4.

Use grid paper. Label across and down from 0 to 8. Draw the designs.

| 1. Across, Down | 2. Across, Down | 3. Across, Down |
|---|---|---|
| 2, 2 | 1, 1 | 1, 1 |
| 3, 2 | 2, 2 | 2, 1 |
| 4, 2 | 3, 3 | 3, 1 |
| 2, 3 | 4, 4 | 4, 1 |
| 4, 3 | 5, 5 | 5, 1 |
| 2, 4 | 6, 6 | 3, 2 |
| 3, 4 | 7, 7 | 3, 3 |
| 4, 4 |  | 3, 4 |
|  |  | 3, 5 |

FOR USE AFTER THE CHAPTER TEST

Add. *(pages 2–7)*

| | | | | | |
|---|---|---|---|---|---|
| **1.** 9<br>+ 6 | **2.** 7<br>+ 8 | **3.** 4<br>+ 6 | **4.** 8<br>+ 6 | **5.** 6<br>+ 9 | **6.** 8<br>+ 7 |
| **7.** 13<br>+ 8 | **8.** 52<br>+ 8 | **9.** 37<br>+ 7 | **10.** 5<br>3<br>+ 7 | **11.** 4<br>7<br>+ 6 | **12.** 8<br>9<br>+ 2 |

Subtract. *(pages 8–11)*

| | | | | | |
|---|---|---|---|---|---|
| **13.** 13<br>− 5 | **14.** 12<br>− 8 | **15.** 15<br>− 8 | **16.** 17<br>− 9 | **17.** 14<br>− 7 | **18.** 15<br>− 8 |
| **19.** 15<br>− 6 | **20.** 17<br>− 8 | **21.** 11<br>− 9 | **22.** 14<br>− 8 | **23.** 16<br>− 9 | **24.** 18<br>− 9 |

Write the standard form. *(pages 14–19)*

**25.** one hundred eighty-five

**26.** 5 hundreds 6 tens

**27.** 300 million, 4 thousand, 82

Compare the numbers. Write $<$, $>$, or $=$.
*(pages 20–21)*

**28.** 354 ▨ 345

**29.** 4454 ▨ 4554

**30.** 89,998 ▨ 90,001

Round to the place of the underlined digit.
*(pages 22–25)*

**31.** 4̲3    **32.** 7̲73    **33.** 42̲36    **34.** 54̲82    **35.** 53̲,841    **36.** 42̲,534

Use the graph to solve. *(pages 12–13, 26–27)*

**37.** Who waxed the greatest number of cars?

**38.** How many cars did Bert wax?

**39.** How many cars were waxed alto-gether?

**40.** How many more cars did Sal wax than Ted wax?

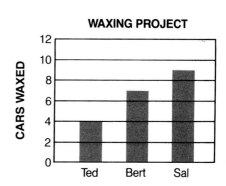

WAXING PROJECT

403

## CHAPTER 2

EXTRA PRACTICE

Estimate the sum.  *(pages 38–39)*

| 1. | 44<br>+ 25 | 2. | 36<br>+ 15 | 3. | 48<br>+ 24 | 4. | 57<br>+ 34 | 5. | 88<br>+ 13 | 6. | 29<br>+ 66 |
|---|---|---|---|---|---|---|---|---|---|---|---|

Add.  *(pages 36–37, 40–43)*

| 7. | 74<br>+ 16 | 8. | 52<br>+ 18 | 9. | 63<br>+ 29 | 10. | 644<br>+ 276 | 11. | 524<br>+ 188 | 12. | 897<br>+ 108 |
|---|---|---|---|---|---|---|---|---|---|---|---|

| 13. | 2765<br>+ 4117 | 14. | 5133<br>+ 1639 | 15. | 84,579<br>+ 39,076 | 16. | 61<br>17<br>+ 20 | 17. | 257<br>115<br>+ 578 | 18. | 4678<br>1119<br>+ 2238 |
|---|---|---|---|---|---|---|---|---|---|---|---|

Estimate. If the answer is reasonable, write *reasonable*. If the
answer is not reasonable, give the correct answer.  *(pages 44–45)*

**19.** The club needs $750 for the trip. It has $164. How
much money is needed? *Answer:* $914

Estimate the difference.  *(pages 48–49)*

| 1. | 32<br>– 17 | 2. | 57<br>– 38 | 3. | 73<br>– 59 | 4. | 44<br>– 19 | 5. | 70<br>– 34 | 6. | 56<br>– 28 |
|---|---|---|---|---|---|---|---|---|---|---|---|

Subtract.  *(pages 46–47, 50–55)*

| 7. | 68<br>– 32 | 8. | 54<br>– 26 | 9. | 65<br>– 48 | 10. | 324<br>– 143 | 11. | 852<br>– 528 | 12. | 534<br>– 226 |
|---|---|---|---|---|---|---|---|---|---|---|---|

| 13. | 600<br>– 584 | 14. | 704<br>– 239 | 15. | 908<br>– 683 | 16. | 6320<br>– 3175 | 17. | 81,602<br>– 19,847 | 18. | 26,831<br>– 21,746 |
|---|---|---|---|---|---|---|---|---|---|---|---|

Use a dollar sign and decimal point to write the value.  *(pages 56–57)*

**19.** 10 dollars 3 pennies     **20.** 4 dollars 1 nickel     **21.** 432¢     **22.** 6 dollars

Add or subtract.  *(pages 58–59)*

| 23. | $11.95<br>+ 16.43 | 24. | $14.82<br>– 6.48 | 25. | $67.14<br>– 21.56 | 26. | $72.97<br>+ 9.85 | 27. | $38.64<br>+ 10.23 |
|---|---|---|---|---|---|---|---|---|---|

Solve. Use the fewest coins and bills possible.  *(pages 60–61)*

**28.** You spend $15.98. What is your change from $20?

FOR USE AFTER THE CHAPTER TEST

**Estimate the sum.** *(pages 38–39)*

| | | | | | | | | | | | |
|---|---|---|---|---|---|---|---|---|---|---|---|
| **1.** 56 | **2.** 33 | **3.** 27 | **4.** 34 | **5.** 45 | **6.** 36 |
| + 25 | + 49 | + 15 | + 63 | + 28 | + 63 |

**Add.** *(pages 36–37, 40–43)*

| | | | | | |
|---|---|---|---|---|---|
| **7.** 23 | **8.** 58 | **9.** 43 | **10.** 626 | **11.** 365 | **12.** 770 |
| + 56 | + 46 | + 42 | + 270 | + 422 | + 229 |

| | | | | | |
|---|---|---|---|---|---|
| **13.** 5354 | **14.** 23,467 | **15.** 73,776 | **16.** 42 | **17.** 366 | **18.** 5261 |
| + 2678 | + 29,553 | + 8,175 | 76 | 142 | 3428 |
| | | | + 37 | + 328 | + 2534 |

**Estimate. If the answer is reasonable, write *reasonable*. If the answer is not reasonable, give the correct answer.** *(pages 44–45)*

**19.** There are 28 students in Carl's class, 19 in Peter's class, and 24 in Anna's class. How many students are there in all in the classes?   Answer: 71 students

**Estimate the difference.** *(pages 48–49)*

| | | | | | |
|---|---|---|---|---|---|
| **20.** 44 | **21.** 63 | **22.** 82 | **23.** 77 | **24.** 68 | **25.** 78 |
| − 25 | − 34 | − 56 | − 68 | − 19 | − 23 |

**Subtract.** *(pages 46–47, 50–55)*

| | | | | | |
|---|---|---|---|---|---|
| **26.** 52 | **27.** 82 | **28.** 75 | **29.** 381 | **30.** 868 | **31.** 526 |
| − 39 | − 23 | − 38 | − 194 | − 299 | − 479 |

| | | | | | |
|---|---|---|---|---|---|
| **32.** 604 | **33.** 770 | **34.** 830 | **35.** 9840 | **36.** 7480 | **37.** 64,083 |
| − 298 | − 394 | − 681 | − 8170 | − 5297 | − 41,897 |

**Use a dollar sign and decimal point to write the value.** *(pages 56–57)*

**38.** 4 dollars 6 dimes 7 pennies     **39.** 12 dollars and 7 dimes     **40.** 307¢

**Add or subtract.** *(pages 58–59)*

| | | | | |
|---|---|---|---|---|
| **41.** $23.77 | **42.** $43.22 | **43.** $25.52 | **44.** $15.25 | **45.** $52.83 |
| + 11.88 | + 32.68 | − 13.98 | − 14.59 | − 34.29 |

**Solve. Use the fewest coins and bills possible.** *(pages 60–61)*

**46.** Sarah gives the clerk $10 for a paint set that costs $3.87. What change does Sarah receive?

FOR USE AFTER CHECKPOINT 1
Complete. *(pages 70–73)*

1. The second month of the year is ▨.

2. The time is ▨ minutes before ▨.   | 6:42 |

Add or subtract. *(pages 74–75)*

3.     3 hours 21 minutes
   + 3 hours 45 minutes

4.     6 hours 29 minutes
   − 2 hours 35 minutes

Solve. *(pages 76–77)*

5. The meeting started at 7:00 P.M. It ended at 8:37 P.M. How long did the meeting last?

6. Tara started her chores at 3:25 P.M. She finished at 4:37 P.M. How long did she spend doing chores?

Measure to the nearest centimeter. *(pages 78–79)*

7. ───────────

8. ──────────────────

Choose the better estimate. Write *a* or *b*. *(pages 80–81)*

9. length of a shoe
   a. 20 cm    b. 20 m

10. distance to next town
   a. 40 m    b. 40 km

FOR USE AFTER CHECKPOINT 2
Choose the better estimate. Write *a* or *b*. *(pages 82–87)*

1. a tennis ball
   a. 15 g    b. 15 kg

2. a baseball bat
   a. 1 g    b. 1 kg

3. milk in a pitcher
   a. 1 mL    b. 1 L

4. gasoline in a full tank
   a. 70 ml    b. 70 L

5. the temperature on a very cold day
   a. 20°C    b. 20° below 0°C

Choose the better estimate. Write *a* or *b*. *(pages 88–91)*

6. height of a house
   a. 20 in.    b. 15 yd

7. width of an apple
   a. 3 in.    b. 3 ft

8. a glass of milk
   a. 1 c    b. 1 gal

9. a pail of water
   a. 5 c    b. 5 gal

10. weight of a baby
   a. 9 oz    b. 9 lb

11. weight of a letter
   a. 2 oz    b. 2 lb

Choose the fact you need. Write *a*, *b*, or *c*. Then solve. *(pages 92–93)*

12. The oven needs to be set 50°F higher for the potatoes than for the bread. What temperature is needed for the potatoes?

   a. The boiling point is 212°F.
   b. Bread bakes at 325°F.
   c. There are 6 potatoes to bake.

FOR USE AFTER THE CHAPTER TEST

**Complete.** *(pages 70–73)*

1. The eighth month is ▨.

2. The time is ▨ minutes after ▨.

| 10:12 |

**Add or subtract.** *(pages 74–75)*

3.　7 hours 18 minutes
　　− 3 hours 27 minutes

4.　　1 hour 30 minutes
　　+ 3 hours 58 minutes

**Measure to the nearest centimeter.** *(pages 78–79)*

5. ——————————————

6. ————————

**Choose the better estimate. Write *a* or *b*.**
*(pages 80–81, 82–87)*

7. length of a diving board
   **a.** 2 m      **b.** 2 km

8. length of swimming pool
   **a.** 20 m      **b.** 20 cm

9. mass of a safety pin
   **a.** 1 g      **b.** 1 kg

10. mass of a pumpkin
    **a.** 3 g      **b.** 3 kg

11. perfume in a bottle
    **a.** 50 mL      **b.** 50 L

12. a pitcher of juice
    **a.** 2 mL      **b.** 2 L

13. room temperature
    **a.** 40°C      **b.** 20°C

14. a hot bath
    **a.** 60°C      **b.** 10°C

**Choose the better estimate. Write *a* or *b*.**
*(pages 88–91)*

15. height of a friend
    **a.** 4 in.      **b.** 4 ft

16. length of a puddle
    **a.** 2 ft      **b.** 2 mi

17. water in a mug
    **a.** 1 c      **b.** 1 gal

18. milk in a thermos
    **a.** 10 gal      **b.** 1 pt

19. weight of a chair
    **a.** 7 oz      **b.** 7 lb

20. weight of a puppy
    **a.** 5 t      **b.** 5 lb

**Choose the fact you need. Write *a*, *b*, or *c*. Then solve.**
*(pages 76–77, 92–93)*

21. Kate needs to turn the oven up 50°F to bake muffins. What temperature is the oven set at now?

22. It takes 25 minutes to bake the muffins. What time will they be done?

a. The recipe makes 12 muffins.
b. Kate put the muffins in at 1:10 P.M.
c. The muffins bake at 375°F.

# CHAPTER 4 EXTRA PRACTICE

## FOR USE AFTER CHECKPOINT 1
Multiply. *(pages 102–111)*

| 1. | 2
×3 | 2. | 4
×3 | 3. | 2
×4 | 4. | 3
×4 | 5. | 4
×1 | 6. | 2
×5 | 7. | 3
×5 |

1. 2 ×3
2. 4 ×3
3. 2 ×4
4. 3 ×4
5. 4 ×1
6. 2 ×5
7. 3 ×5

8. 4 ×4
9. 4 ×6
10. 5 ×7
11. 4 ×8
12. 5 ×9
13. 5 ×6
14. 5 ×2

15. 1 ×5
16. 1 ×3
17. 0 ×6
18. 1 ×7
19. 0 ×4
20. 1 ×6
21. 0 ×8

22. $(3 \times 5) \times 2$     23. $4 \times (3 \times 6)$     24. $(5 \times 7) \times 2$     25. $3 \times (2 \times 6)$

Draw a tree diagram. Solve. *(pages 112–113)*

26. Adam has 3 different shirts and 3 different pairs of slacks. How many different outfits can he make?

27. Sarah is making sandwiches with tuna, egg salad, and ham. She has whole wheat and rye bread. How many different sandwiches can she make?

## FOR USE AFTER CHECKPOINT 2
Multiply. *(pages 114–119)*

1. 7 ×6
2. 6 ×8
3. 7 ×7
4. 7 ×4
5. 7 ×5
6. 6 ×6
7. 7 ×8

8. 8 ×6
9. 9 ×7
10. 8 ×7
11. 9 ×6
12. 9 ×8
13. 9 ×9
14. 8 ×8

Write the numbers. *(pages 120–121)*

15. five multiples of 4

16. six multiples of 3

17. two common multiples of 2 and 6

18. three common multiples of 4 and 8

Solve. *(pages 122–123)*

19. Abby bought 2 books for $4 each and a magazine for $1.25. How much did she spend in all?

20. Carlin has 3 flats of snapdragons and 1 flat of zinnias. There are 6 plants in each flat. How many plants does she have in all?

FOR USE AFTER THE CHAPTER TEST

Multiply.  *(pages 102–111, 114–119)*

| | | | | | | |
|---|---|---|---|---|---|---|
| **1.** 4 ×3 | **2.** 2 ×8 | **3.** 3 ×6 | **4.** 4 ×5 | **5.** 4 ×8 | **6.** 2 ×6 | **7.** 3 ×5 |
| **8.** 4 ×2 | **9.** 2 ×2 | **10.** 3 ×1 | **11.** 3 ×2 | **12.** 4 ×5 | **13.** 2 ×2 | **14.** 3 ×9 |
| **15.** 5 ×8 | **16.** 3 ×9 | **17.** 5 ×3 | **18.** 4 ×7 | **19.** 3 ×7 | **20.** 4 ×4 | **21.** 5 ×9 |
| **22.** 5 ×4 | **23.** 3 ×8 | **24.** 4 ×6 | **25.** 2 ×9 | **26.** 0 ×5 | **27.** 5 ×6 | **28.** 5 ×7 |
| **29.** 9 ×8 | **30.** 7 ×9 | **31.** 2 ×5 | **32.** 4 ×3 | **33.** 8 ×4 | **34.** 0 ×9 | **35.** 7 ×4 |
| **36.** 7 ×2 | **37.** 6 ×3 | **38.** 9 ×5 | **39.** 6 ×9 | **40.** 2 ×6 | **41.** 6 ×7 | **42.** 4 ×9 |
| **43.** 5 ×8 | **44.** 9 ×4 | **45.** 7 ×6 | **46.** 6 ×8 | **47.** 9 ×9 | **48.** 9 ×6 | **49.** 6 ×5 |

Draw a tree diagram. Solve.  *(pages 112–113)*

**50.** Mei Lee has 2 skirts and 3 blouses. How many different outfits does she have?

Write the numbers.  *(pages 120–121)*

**51.** five multiples of 5

**52.** six multiples of 9

**53.** two common multiples of 4 and 6

**54.** four common multiples of 2 and 4

Solve.  *(pages 122–123)*

**55.** Darby bought 2 blank tapes for $3 each and a record for $8.98. How much did he spend in all?

## CHAPTER 5    EXTRA PRACTICE

FOR USE AFTER CHECKPOINT 1
Divide. *(pages 132–137)*

1. $3\overline{)21}$    2. $4\overline{)28}$    3. $2\overline{)16}$    4. $4\overline{)20}$    5. $3\overline{)27}$    6. $5\overline{)35}$

7. $2\overline{)10}$    8. $3\overline{)6}$    9. $3\overline{)9}$    10. $2\overline{)14}$    11. $3\overline{)12}$    12. $4\overline{)8}$

13. $2\overline{)6}$    14. $3\overline{)3}$    15. $2\overline{)12}$    16. $4\overline{)4}$    17. $2\overline{)2}$    18. $5\overline{)0}$

Divide. Check by multiplying. *(pages 138–139)*

19. $5\overline{)30}$    20. $4\overline{)16}$    21. $5\overline{)45}$    22. $3\overline{)18}$    23. $4\overline{)32}$    24. $3\overline{)15}$

Write *add, subtract, multiply,* or *divide* for your plan.
Then solve. *(pages 140–141)*

25. Ted collected 9 bottles and Sarah collected 3. How many bottles did they collect in all?

26. Jimmie collected 4 bottles at each house. He went to 8 houses. How many bottles did he collect?

FOR USE AFTER CHECKPOINT 2
Divide. *(pages 142–149)*

1. $6\overline{)54}$    2. $7\overline{)14}$    3. $7\overline{)28}$    4. $6\overline{)30}$    5. $7\overline{)49}$    6. $9\overline{)18}$

7. $6\overline{)18}$    8. $7\overline{)63}$    9. $7\overline{)21}$    10. $6\overline{)24}$    11. $6\overline{)42}$    12. $9\overline{)54}$

13. $9\overline{)36}$    14. $8\overline{)8}$    15. $9\overline{)63}$    16. $8\overline{)40}$    17. $8\overline{)56}$    18. $8\overline{)72}$

19. $3\overline{)16}$    20. $4\overline{)26}$    21. $6\overline{)31}$    22. $8\overline{)42}$    23. $5\overline{)47}$    24. $9\overline{)51}$

List the common factors. *(pages 150–151)*

25. 6 and 8    26. 8 and 14    27. 12 and 6    28. 18 and 9    29. 24 and 6

Solve. *(pages 152–153)*

30. May bought a 262-page book for $2.95. She gave the clerk $10.00. How much change did she get?

31. There are 9 players on a baseball team and 11 players on a soccer team. There are 36 students. How many baseball teams can they have?

# EXTRA PRACTICE    CHAPTER 5

FOR USE AFTER THE CHAPTER TEST

## Divide. Check by multiplying.
*(pages 132–139)*

| | | | | | |
|---|---|---|---|---|---|
| **1.** $5\overline{)45}$ | **2.** $3\overline{)21}$ | **3.** $4\overline{)20}$ | **4.** $2\overline{)14}$ | **5.** $4\overline{)32}$ | **6.** $4\overline{)28}$ |
| **7.** $2\overline{)12}$ | **8.** $3\overline{)27}$ | **9.** $5\overline{)35}$ | **10.** $2\overline{)4}$ | **11.** $3\overline{)15}$ | **12.** $4\overline{)8}$ |
| **13.** $5\overline{)30}$ | **14.** $4\overline{)4}$ | **15.** $4\overline{)36}$ | **16.** $2\overline{)10}$ | **17.** $3\overline{)24}$ | **18.** $5\overline{)10}$ |
| **19.** $2\overline{)16}$ | **20.** $5\overline{)20}$ | **21.** $5\overline{)25}$ | **22.** $2\overline{)18}$ | **23.** $3\overline{)12}$ | **24.** $5\overline{)15}$ |
| **25.** $3\overline{)3}$ | **26.** $4\overline{)0}$ | **27.** $2\overline{)8}$ | **28.** $4\overline{)12}$ | **29.** $4\overline{)16}$ | **30.** $5\overline{)40}$ |

## Divide.  *(pages 142–149)*

| | | | | | |
|---|---|---|---|---|---|
| **31.** $8\overline{)40}$ | **32.** $5\overline{)25}$ | **33.** $4\overline{)32}$ | **34.** $3\overline{)18}$ | **35.** $2\overline{)16}$ | **36.** $8\overline{)56}$ |
| **37.** $6\overline{)48}$ | **38.** $7\overline{)42}$ | **39.** $6\overline{)36}$ | **40.** $7\overline{)56}$ | **41.** $6\overline{)42}$ | **42.** $9\overline{)54}$ |
| **43.** $6\overline{)54}$ | **44.** $5\overline{)30}$ | **45.** $7\overline{)35}$ | **46.** $2\overline{)12}$ | **47.** $4\overline{)24}$ | **48.** $9\overline{)72}$ |
| **49.** $5\overline{)19}$ | **50.** $7\overline{)68}$ | **51.** $9\overline{)80}$ | **52.** $8\overline{)49}$ | **53.** $4\overline{)36}$ | **54.** $8\overline{)48}$ |
| **55.** $5\overline{)12}$ | **56.** $7\overline{)24}$ | **57.** $3\overline{)14}$ | **58.** $6\overline{)25}$ | **59.** $8\overline{)36}$ | **60.** $4\overline{)23}$ |
| **61.** $6\overline{)33}$ | **62.** $5\overline{)42}$ | **63.** $9\overline{)57}$ | **64.** $6\overline{)47}$ | **65.** $8\overline{)52}$ | **66.** $7\overline{)30}$ |

## Write the common factors.
*(pages 150–151)*

| | | | | |
|---|---|---|---|---|
| **67.** 4 and 6 | **68.** 14 and 18 | **69.** 15 and 20 | **70.** 21 and 6 | **71.** 9 and 21 |
| **72.** 18 and 28 | **73.** 15 and 25 | **74.** 9 and 18 | **75.** 10 and 12 | **76.** 14 and 28 |

## Solve.  *(pages 140–141, 152–153)*

**77.** It cost Renee $24 to make 4 small tables. How much did each table cost?

**78.** Marcus bought 3 mirrors for $6 each. He needs 4 fasteners to hang each one. How many fasteners does he need in all?

## CHAPTER 6     EXTRA PRACTICE

FOR USE AFTER CHECKPOINT 1

Estimate the product. *(pages 164–165)*

| | | | | | |
|---|---|---|---|---|---|
| **1.** 38<br>×2 | **2.** 29<br>×3 | **3.** 496<br>×4 | **4.** 312<br>×6 | **5.** 449<br>×7 | **6.** 550<br>×5 |

Multiply. *(pages 162–163, 166–171)*

| | | | | | |
|---|---|---|---|---|---|
| **7.** 30<br>×8 | **8.** 600<br>×5 | **9.** 4000<br>×6 | **10.** 44<br>×2 | **11.** 31<br>×3 | **12.** 23<br>×3 |
| **13.** 17<br>×5 | **14.** 24<br>×3 | **15.** 19<br>×5 | **16.** 26<br>×5 | **17.** 34<br>×6 | **18.** 47<br>×7 |

Use the pictograph to solve. *(pages 172–173)*

**19.** How many pear trees does the nursery have?

**20.** How many more apple trees are there than cherry trees?

**TREES AT THE NURSERY**

| | |
|---|---|
| Apple | △ △ △ △ △ △ |
| Pear | △ △ |
| Cherry | △ △ △ △ |

Each △ means 4 trees.

FOR USE AFTER CHECKPOINT 2

Multiply. *(pages 174–181)*

| | | | | | |
|---|---|---|---|---|---|
| **1.** 125<br>×4 | **2.** 174<br>×3 | **3.** 378<br>×2 | **4.** 136<br>×6 | **5.** 324<br>×4 | **6.** 457<br>×5 |
| **7.** 642<br>×8 | **8.** 236<br>×7 | **9.** 5207<br>×3 | **10.** 3764<br>×6 | **11.** 4183<br>×7 | **12.** 6244<br>×4 |
| **13.** $.92<br>×3 | **14.** $1.75<br>×4 | **15.** $3.05<br>×9 | **16.** $11.49<br>×5 | **17.** $19.99<br>×6 | **18.** $70.28<br>×8 |

Estimate the answer. *(pages 182–183)*

**19.** Joe gave the clerk $20.00. The shirt cost $15.95. About how much change will Joe get back?

**20.** Maria bought 3 rolls of film for $2.98 each. About how much did she spend?

FOR USE AFTER THE CHAPTER TEST

Estimate the product.   *(pages 164–165)*

| | | | | | |
|---|---|---|---|---|---|
| **1.** 52 ×8 | **2.** 19 ×6 | **3.** 82 ×7 | **4.** 351 ×8 | **5.** 749 ×5 | **6.** 909 ×7 |

Multiply.   *(pages 162–163, 166–171, 174–181)*

| | | | | | |
|---|---|---|---|---|---|
| **7.** 40 ×8 | **8.** 600 ×6 | **9.** 4000 ×5 | **10.** 23 ×2 | **11.** 16 ×4 | **12.** 39 ×2 |
| **13.** 36 ×2 | **14.** 19 ×5 | **15.** 38 ×4 | **16.** 52 ×6 | **17.** 85 ×9 | **18.** 39 ×5 |
| **19.** 34 ×2 | **20.** 61 ×5 | **21.** 53 ×3 | **22.** 72 ×3 | **23.** 91 ×5 | **24.** 64 ×4 |
| **25.** 21 ×9 | **26.** 71 ×8 | **27.** 83 ×2 | **28.** 61 ×7 | **29.** 93 ×3 | **30.** 77 ×4 |
| **31.** 123 ×4 | **32.** 429 ×2 | **33.** 154 ×5 | **34.** 254 ×3 | **35.** 136 ×7 | **36.** 439 ×5 |
| **37.** 323 ×4 | **38.** 643 ×8 | **39.** 464 ×5 | **40.** 2152 ×6 | **41.** 6205 ×3 | **42.** 2033 ×8 |
| **43.** 9398 ×8 | **44.** 6868 ×3 | **45.** 9724 ×8 | **46.** 6035 ×7 | **47.** 5672 ×5 | **48.** 6564 ×2 |
| **49.** $6.80 ×5 | **50.** $49.21 ×3 | **51.** $.66 ×9 | **52.** $11.01 ×7 | **53.** $4.97 ×4 | **54.** $28.14 ×6 |

Use the pictograph to solve.
*(pages 172–173, 182–183)*

**55.** How many more red T-shirts are there than yellow T-shirts?

**56.** T-shirts sell for $7.98. About how much will the store receive if they sell all the purple T-shirts?

**T-SHIRTS FOR SALE**

| | |
|---|---|
| Red | ☐ ☐ ☐ ☐ |
| Yellow | ☐ ☐ |
| Purple | ☐ ☐ ☐ |

Each ☐ means 2 T-shirts.

413

FOR USE AFTER CHECKPOINT 1

Divide. *(pages 192–199)*

1. $2\overline{)24}$     2. $3\overline{)63}$     3. $2\overline{)64}$     4. $4\overline{)44}$     5. $2\overline{)82}$     6. $4\overline{)48}$

7. $2\overline{)45}$     8. $3\overline{)38}$     9. $2\overline{)83}$     10. $3\overline{)64}$     11. $5\overline{)59}$     12. $4\overline{)85}$

13. $3\overline{)51}$     14. $2\overline{)52}$     15. $4\overline{)68}$     16. $7\overline{)85}$     17. $5\overline{)79}$     18. $6\overline{)98}$

19. $5\overline{)265}$     20. $2\overline{)134}$     21. $4\overline{)346}$     22. $6\overline{)387}$     23. $3\overline{)289}$     24. $8\overline{)667}$

Solve. *(pages 200–201)*

25. Hinges are sold in packages of 4. The shop class needs 75 hinges. How many packages of hinges should they buy?

26. It takes 7 pieces of wood to build a bird house. There are 110 pieces of wood. How many bird houses can be built?

FOR USE AFTER CHECKPOINT 2

Divide. *(pages 202–209)*

1. $4\overline{)484}$     2. $3\overline{)693}$     3. $2\overline{)482}$     4. $4\overline{)844}$     5. $3\overline{)936}$

6. $2\overline{)408}$     7. $6\overline{)624}$     8. $7\overline{)721}$     9. $5\overline{)540}$     10. $2\overline{)408}$

11. $6\overline{)\$6.24}$     12. $4\overline{)\$4.32}$     13. $2\overline{)\$6.14}$     14. $4\overline{)\$7.32}$     15. $8\overline{)\$9.84}$

16. $3\overline{)652}$     17. $7\overline{)786}$     18. $6\overline{)686}$     19. $4\overline{)645}$     20. $5\overline{)758}$

Find the average. *(pages 210–211)*

21. 9, 7, 4, 6, 11, 5     22. 11, 15, 17, 9, 13     23. 14, 9, 23, 6

24. 15, 14, 21, 10     25. 9, 15, 13, 11, 17     26. 18, 12, 14, 13, 16, 11

Use the graph. *(pages 212–213)*

27. What is the normal temperature in Marquette, MI in April?

28. What is the difference between the normal temperatures in February and June?

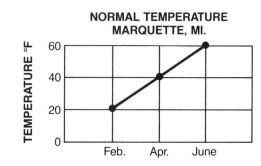

NORMAL TEMPERATURE
MARQUETTE, MI.

FOR USE AFTER THE CHAPTER TEST
Divide.    *(pages 192–199, 202–209)*

**1.** $3\overline{)33}$    **2.** $4\overline{)84}$    **3.** $2\overline{)84}$    **4.** $8\overline{)88}$    **5.** $3\overline{)63}$    **6.** $3\overline{)96}$

**7.** $2\overline{)28}$    **8.** $4\overline{)84}$    **9.** $3\overline{)96}$    **10.** $2\overline{)46}$    **11.** $9\overline{)99}$    **12.** $2\overline{)42}$

**13.** $3\overline{)34}$    **14.** $5\overline{)56}$    **15.** $7\overline{)79}$    **16.** $4\overline{)86}$    **17.** $3\overline{)64}$    **18.** $4\overline{)89}$

**19.** $2\overline{)87}$    **20.** $4\overline{)49}$    **21.** $5\overline{)59}$    **22.** $3\overline{)68}$    **23.** $6\overline{)69}$    **24.** $4\overline{)47}$

**25.** $4\overline{)68}$    **26.** $3\overline{)72}$    **27.** $5\overline{)80}$    **28.** $8\overline{)96}$    **29.** $7\overline{)84}$    **30.** $5\overline{)77}$

**31.** $2\overline{)57}$    **32.** $6\overline{)85}$    **33.** $4\overline{)79}$    **34.** $3\overline{)85}$    **35.** $7\overline{)94}$    **36.** $6\overline{)73}$

**37.** $5\overline{)425}$    **38.** $8\overline{)672}$    **39.** $6\overline{)276}$    **40.** $4\overline{)268}$    **41.** $3\overline{)207}$

**42.** $6\overline{)579}$    **43.** $4\overline{)394}$    **44.** $8\overline{)479}$    **45.** $5\overline{)376}$    **46.** $7\overline{)506}$

**47.** $4\overline{)448}$    **48.** $3\overline{)639}$    **49.** $2\overline{)864}$    **50.** $5\overline{)555}$    **51.** $3\overline{)993}$

**52.** $4\overline{)744}$    **53.** $8\overline{)968}$    **54.** $4\overline{)964}$    **55.** $7\overline{)917}$    **56.** $6\overline{)966}$

**57.** $3\overline{)315}$    **58.** $7\overline{)763}$    **59.** $6\overline{)624}$    **60.** $4\overline{)424}$    **61.** $4\overline{)804}$

**62.** $5\overline{)\$6.50}$    **63.** $8\overline{)\$9.52}$    **64.** $2\overline{)\$5.36}$    **65.** $7\overline{)\$9.52}$    **66.** $8\overline{)\$9.92}$

**67.** $4\overline{)465}$    **68.** $5\overline{)571}$    **69.** $6\overline{)698}$    **70.** $8\overline{)969}$    **71.** $3\overline{)875}$

**72.** $7\overline{)925}$    **73.** $3\overline{)797}$    **74.** $5\overline{)686}$    **75.** $8\overline{)997}$    **76.** $6\overline{)865}$

Solve.    *(pages 200–201)*

**77.** A ribbon is 276 cm long. It is cut into pieces 5 cm long
to make decorations. How many pieces are cut long
enough for decorations?

Find the average.    *(pages 210–211)*
**78.** 10, 8, 11, 7, 9    **79.** 16, 13, 12, 15    **80.** 8, 12, 10, 11, 9    **81.** 25, 20, 15, 20

Use the graph.    *(pages 212–213)*
**82.** How many people visited Acadia
National Park in July, 1984?

**83.** How many more people visited in
October than in April?

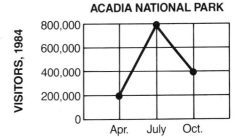

ATTENDANCE
ACADIA NATIONAL PARK

## CHAPTER 8      EXTRA PRACTICE

FOR USE AFTER CHECKPOINT 1

Write the decimal. *(pages 222–225)*

**1.** 2 tenths      **2.** 5 tenths      **3.** 7 tenths      **4.** 3 and 5 tenths

**5.** 46 and 8 tenths      **6.** 3 tenths      **7.** 9 tenths      **8.** 16 and 7 tenths

**9.** 62 hundredths      **10.** 41 hundredths      **11.** 50 hundredths

**12.** 2 and 36 hundredths      **13.** 8 and 5 hundredths      **14.** 39 and 72 hundredths

Complete. Write <, >, or = . *(pages 226–229)*

**15.** 3.42 ▦ 3.24    **16.** 0.9 ▦ 1.6    **17.** 6.08 ▦ 8.50    **18.** 13.46 ▦ 13.64

**19.** 0.06 ▦ 0.6    **20.** 5.62 ▦ 6.5    **21.** 3.4 ▦ 3.46    **22.** 27.09 ▦ 27.9

Round to the place of the underlined digit. *(pages 230–231)*

**23.** 3<u>6</u>.42      **24.** 52.<u>4</u>1      **25.** 8<u>5</u>.65      **26.** 41.<u>2</u>5      **27.** 3<u>6</u>.71      **28.** 21.<u>0</u>9

FOR USE AFTER CHECKPOINT 2

Estimate to solve. *(pages 232–233)*

**1.** Lorraine has $8.86 in her pocket and $6.12 in her bank. About how much money does she have?

**2.** Betty is 28.1 kg. Her father is 78.8 kg. About how much heavier is her father?

Add or subtract. *(pages 234–239)*

| | | | | | | | | | | | |
|---|---|---|---|---|---|---|---|---|---|---|---|
| **3.** | 2.3<br>+ 0.5 | **4.** | 5.3<br>+ 8.6 | **5.** | 7.83<br>+ 3.94 | **6.** | 4.56<br>+ 7.89 | **7.** | 18.42<br>+ 7.53 | **8.** | 26.35<br>+ 5.88 |
| **9.** | 7.6<br>+ 2.3 | **10.** | 8.7<br>+ 0.5 | **11.** | 5.62<br>+ 8.95 | **12.** | 7.48<br>+ 5.57 | **13.** | 2.87<br>+ 19.36 | **14.** | 8.02<br>+ 6.19 |
| **15.** | 9.6<br>− 7.3 | **16.** | 8.5<br>− 6.9 | **17.** | 13.6<br>− 9.7 | **18.** | 4.63<br>− 2.97 | **19.** | 53.72<br>− 9.48 | **20.** | 32.46<br>− 2.55 |
| **21.** | 6.7<br>+ 8 | **22.** | 8<br>− 3.2 | **23.** | 7.24<br>+ 6.3 | **24.** | 8.5<br>− 2.26 | **25.** | 19.5<br>− 8.75 | **26.** | 18.2<br>+ 2.96 |

Make a table to solve. *(pages 240–241)*

**27.** On Saturday, Erin delivered 36 papers and Sam delivered 29 papers. On Sunday, Erin delivered 78 papers and Sam delivered 85 papers. What was the total number of papers delivered by each person?

FOR USE AFTER THE CHAPTER TEST

Write the decimal.  *(pages 222–225)*

**1.** 3 tenths      **2.** 6 tenths      **3.** 2 and 7 tenths      **4.** 4 and 8 tenths

**5.** twenty-six and five tenths           **6.** twelve and two tenths

**7.** 21 hundredths        **8.** 3 hundredths        **9.** 5 and 62 hundredths

**10.** fifteen and eighty hundredths        **11.** twenty-eight and six hundredths

Complete. Write <, >, or = .  *(pages 226–229)*

**12.** 5.0 ▓ 3.6          **13.** 6.15 ▓ 6.51          **14.** 28.3 ▓ 28.45

Round to the place of the underlined digit.  *(pages 230–231)*

**15.** 4$\underline{2}$.63      **16.** 54.$\underline{5}$7      **17.** 5$\underline{0}$.63      **18.** 72.$\underline{1}$5      **19.** 2$\underline{9}$.46

**20.** 1$\underline{8}$.19      **21.** 8$\underline{4}$.65      **22.** 1$\underline{2}$.19      **23.** 45.$\underline{6}$2      **24.** 24.8$\underline{3}$

Write the answer.  *(pages 234–239)*

| **25.** | **26.** | **27.** | **28.** | **29.** | **30.** |
|---|---|---|---|---|---|
| 5.6 | 8.9 | 12.6 | 5.71 | 24.83 | 56.70 |
| + 0.7 | + 5.6 | + 3.5 | + 8.67 | + 19.76 | + 9.69 |

| **31.** | **32.** | **33.** | **34.** | **35.** | **36.** |
|---|---|---|---|---|---|
| 7.8 | 9.5 | 78.1 | 7.56 | 52.56 | 64.81 |
| − 1.9 | − 3.7 | − 39.5 | − 4.80 | − 13.58 | − 9.76 |

| **37.** | **38.** | **39.** | **40.** | **41.** | **42.** |
|---|---|---|---|---|---|
| 0.8 | 6 | 5.63 | 7.5 | 12.57 | 52.7 |
| + 7 | − 4.5 | − 2.7 | − 3.46 | + 24.7 | − 21.24 |

**43.** 7 − 3.6          **44.** 5 − 3.2          **45.** 2.5 + 9          **46.** 12.5 − 9.64

**47.** 9 + 4.7          **48.** 56.3 − 2.79          **49.** 23 − 2.6          **50.** 57 − 24.83

Estimate to solve.  *(pages 232–233)*

**51.** Troy rode 1.87 km on his bike in the morning. In the afternoon he rode 3.12 km. About how many kilometers did he ride in all?

Make a table to solve.  *(pages 240–241)*

**52.** Anita picked 6.5 kg of peaches on Monday and 7.2 kg on Tuesday. Patrick picked 7.8 kg of peaches on Monday and 8.2 kg on Tuesday. How many kilograms of peaches did they each pick on the two days?

FOR USE AFTER CHECKPOINT 1

Name the figure. *(pages 250–251)*

1.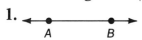

2.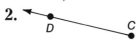

3.

Name the angles. Then write *R* for right, *A* for acute, or *O* for obtuse. *(pages 252–253)*

4.

5.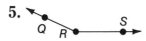

6.

Write *parallel* or *perpendicular* to describe the lines. *(pages 254–255)*

7.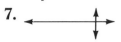

8.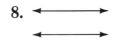

9.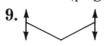

10.

Complete. *(pages 256–257)*

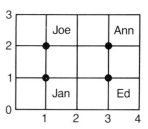

11. Ed is at (  ,   ).

12. Ann is at (  ,   ).

13. Joe is at (  ,   ).

14. Jan is at (  ,   ).

Write *All, Some,* or *No.* *(pages 258–259)*

15. ___?___ lines have endpoints.

16. ___?___ angles are obtuse angles.

FOR USE AFTER CHECKPOINT 2

Write the letter of the picture that matches the description. *(pages 260–263)*

1. square     2. triangle     3. pentagon     4. rectangle

A.    B.    C.    D.    E.

Name the center, a radius, and a diameter. *(pages 266–267)*

5.

6.

7.

8.

What is the perimeter? *(pages 264–265)*

9.

10.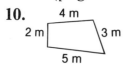

11.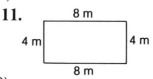

12.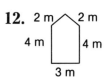

Draw a picture. Solve. *(pages 268–269)*

13. The playground is a rectangle measuring 70 ft by 120 ft. How many feet of fence are needed for the playground?

# EXTRA PRACTICE     CHAPTER 9

FOR USE AFTER THE CHAPTER TEST

Name the angle. Then write *R* for right, *A* for acute, and *O* for obtuse.  *(pages 250–253)*

**1.**      **2.**      **3.**      **4.**

Write *parallel* or *perpendicular* to describe the lines. *(pages 254–255)*

**5.**      **6.** 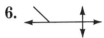     **7.**      **8.**

Complete.  *(pages 256–257)*

**9.** Bank is at (  ,   ).

**10.** Movie is at (  ,   ).

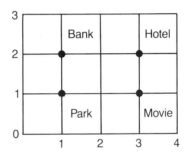

Write the letter of the picture that matches the name.  *(pages 260–263)*

**11.** pentagon     **12.** square     **13.** triangle     **14.** parallelogram

**A.**      **B.**      **C.** 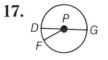     **D.**      **E.** (triangle)

Name the center, a radius, and a diameter.  *(pages 266–267)*

**15.** 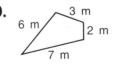     **16.** 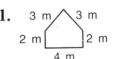     **17.** 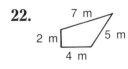     **18.** (circle)

What is the perimeter?  *(pages 264–265)*

**19.** 5 m, 4 m, 4 m, 5 m     **20.** 3 m, 6 m, 2 m, 7 m     **21.** 3 m, 3 m, 2 m, 2 m, 4 m     **22.** 7 m, 2 m, 5 m, 4 m

Write *All, Some,* or *No.*  *(pages 258–259)*

**23.** ___?___ rectangles are squares.     **24.** ___?___ circles have a center.

Draw a picture. Solve.  *(pages 268–269)*

**25.** One side of a rectangle is 3 m in length. Another side is 4 m in length. What is the perimeter of the rectangle?

419

FOR USE AFTER CHECKPOINT 1
Multiply.   (pages 278–281, 284–287)

| 1. 15 ×10 | 2. 24 ×10 | 3. 60 ×10 | 4. 248 ×10 | 5. 809 ×10 | 6. 710 ×10 |
|---|---|---|---|---|---|
| 7. 33 ×30 | 8. 54 ×20 | 9. 466 ×60 | 10. 184 ×80 | 11. 402 ×40 | 12. 563 ×50 |
| 13. 24 ×12 | 14. 41 ×16 | 15. 64 ×12 | 16. 92 ×13 | 17. 42 ×14 | 18. 72 ×13 |
| 19. 31 ×25 | 20. 62 ×44 | 21. 81 ×37 | 22. 84 ×49 | 23. 83 ×38 | 24. 53 ×64 |

Round to the greatest place value and estimate the product.   (pages 282–283)

| 25. 15 ×28 | 26. 68 ×19 | 27. 78 ×14 | 28. 20 ×24 | 29. 47 ×24 | 30. 18 ×32 |
|---|---|---|---|---|---|

Solve. Look for a pattern. Use a chart if needed.
(pages 288–289)

31. Mira plans to put 2¢ in her bank today, 5¢ tomorrow, 8¢ the next day, 11¢ on the fourth day, and 14¢ on the fifth day. If she continues this pattern, how much will she put in her bank on the twelfth day?

FOR USE AFTER CHECKPOINT 2
Multiply.   (pages 290–295)

| 1. 176 ×16 | 2. 842 ×17 | 3. 264 ×15 | 4. 426 ×18 | 5. 536 ×17 | 6. 642 ×19 |
|---|---|---|---|---|---|
| 7. 263 ×25 | 8. 671 ×34 | 9. 514 ×64 | 10. 696 ×37 | 11. 790 ×63 | 12. 362 ×41 |
| 13. $.89 ×53 | 14. $6.73 ×63 | 15. $.59 ×34 | 16. $9.98 ×84 | 17. $.46 ×39 | 18. $4.95 ×67 |

Solve. There is more than one answer.   (pages 296–297)

19. Melba runs 4 mi in 2 days. If she runs at least 1 mi at a time, in what order might she run the miles on those 2 days?

FOR USE AFTER THE CHAPTER TEST

Write the answer.   *(pages 278–281, 284–287)*

| 1. 49 ×10 | 2. 26 ×10 | 3. 42 ×10 | 4. 83 ×10 | 5. 37 ×10 | 6. 52 ×10 |
|---|---|---|---|---|---|
| 7. 48 ×30 | 8. 92 ×60 | 9. 65 ×70 | 10. 31 ×80 | 11. 40 ×40 | 12. 28 ×60 |
| 13. 52 ×13 | 14. 64 ×12 | 15. 81 ×18 | 16. 32 ×14 | 17. 43 ×13 | 18. 78 ×13 |
| 19. 27 ×68 | 20. 61 ×58 | 21. 77 ×33 | 22. 43 ×28 | 23. 82 ×74 | 24. 91 ×34 |

Estimate the product.   *(pages 282–283)*

| 25. 75 ×32 | 26. 19 ×68 | 27. 38 ×24 | 28. 99 ×65 | 29. 45 ×88 | 30. 47 ×56 |
|---|---|---|---|---|---|

Write the answer.   *(pages 290–295)*

| 31. 426 ×16 | 32. 534 ×14 | 33. 528 ×19 | 34. 826 ×17 | 35. 257 ×15 | 36. 475 ×15 |
|---|---|---|---|---|---|
| 37. 431 ×36 | 38. 537 ×49 | 39. 526 ×56 | 40. 862 ×27 | 41. 773 ×54 | 42. 719 ×24 |
| 43. 432 ×82 | 44. 257 ×53 | 45. 654 ×39 | 46. 736 ×46 | 47. 847 ×85 | 48. 303 ×98 |
| 49. $2.49 ×17 | 50. $6.98 ×46 | 51. $8.77 ×62 | 52. $7.65 ×48 | 53. $4.39 ×74 | 54. $3.59 ×25 |

Solve. Look for a pattern. Use a chart if needed.
*(pages 288–289)*

55. Andrew swam 4 laps the first day, 6 the second day, and 8 the third day. If this pattern continued, how many laps did he swim on the eighth day?

Solve. There is more than one answer.   *(pages 296–297)*

56. Libby received $.45 in change. None of the coins were pennies. What coins might she have received?

# CHAPTER 11     EXTRA PRACTICE

FOR USE AFTER CHECKPOINT 1

Divide. *(pages 306–307, 312–315)*

| | | | | |
|---|---|---|---|---|
| **1.** 20)‾63‾ | **2.** 40)‾86‾ | **3.** 50)‾53‾ | **4.** 30)‾94‾ | **5.** 40)‾48‾ |
| **6.** 40)‾360‾ | **7.** 30)‾183‾ | **8.** 70)‾486‾ | **9.** 50)‾375‾ | **10.** 60)‾540‾ |
| **11.** 36)‾93‾ | **12.** 17)‾67‾ | **13.** 61)‾88‾ | **14.** 31)‾82‾ | **15.** 19)‾63‾ |
| **16.** 82)‾367‾ | **17.** 74)‾527‾ | **18.** 49)‾238‾ | **19.** 83)‾384‾ | **20.** 81)‾174‾ |
| **21.** 30)‾628‾ | **22.** 50)‾773‾ | **23.** 20)‾436‾ | **24.** 40)‾897‾ | **25.** 30)‾627‾ |
| **26.** 19)‾634‾ | **27.** 34)‾489‾ | **28.** 48)‾634‾ | **29.** 52)‾719‾ | **30.** 47)‾798‾ |
| **31.** 22)‾903‾ | **32.** 39)‾964‾ | **33.** 41)‾876‾ | **34.** 65)‾725‾ | **35.** 36)‾823‾ |
| **36.** 32)‾658‾ | **37.** 69)‾874‾ | **38.** 19)‾436‾ | **39.** 52)‾628‾ | **40.** 39)‾326‾ |

If the answer makes sense, write *correct*. If not, give the correct answer. *(pages 310–311)*

**41.** There are 187 people on a bus tour. Each bus can hold 40 people. How many buses are on the tour?
*Answer:* 5 buses

FOR USE AFTER CHECKPOINT 2

Divide. *(pages 316–317)*

| | | | | |
|---|---|---|---|---|
| **1.** 16)‾398‾ | **2.** 36)‾756‾ | **3.** 23)‾417‾ | **4.** 21)‾834‾ | **5.** 48)‾972‾ |
| **6.** 35)‾782‾ | **7.** 24)‾837‾ | **8.** 43)‾843‾ | **9.** 36)‾785‾ | **10.** 42)‾905‾ |
| **11.** 24)‾537‾ | **12.** 38)‾897‾ | **13.** 29)‾854‾ | **14.** 43)‾957‾ | **15.** 32)‾989‾ |

Simplify the problem. Solve. *(pages 318–319)*

**16.** Inez sold 37 raffle tickets in one week. Each ticket cost $1.95. How much money did Inez collect in all?

Estimate the answer. *(pages 320–321)*

| | | | | |
|---|---|---|---|---|
| **17.** 7)‾517‾ | **18.** 4)‾279‾ | **19.** 6)‾385‾ | **20.** 8)‾154‾ | **21.** 6)‾435‾ |
| **22.** 4)‾238‾ | **23.** 7)‾488‾ | **24.** 4)‾197‾ | **25.** 23)‾417‾ | **26.** 18)‾623‾ |
| **27.** 36)‾238‾ | **28.** 52)‾358‾ | **29.** 23)‾195‾ | **30.** 38)‾314‾ | **31.** 17)‾118‾ |

# EXTRA PRACTICE     CHAPTER 11

FOR USE AFTER THE CHAPTER TEST
Divide. *(pages 306–309)*

1. $20\overline{)23}$  2. $30\overline{)62}$  3. $20\overline{)86}$  4. $40\overline{)85}$  5. $30\overline{)95}$

6. $50\overline{)79}$  7. $30\overline{)243}$  8. $20\overline{)165}$  9. $40\overline{)280}$  10. $80\overline{)666}$

11. $51\overline{)73}$  12. $48\overline{)53}$  13. $75\overline{)92}$  14. $61\overline{)84}$  15. $89\overline{)96}$

16. $51\overline{)235}$  17. $83\overline{)392}$  18. $94\overline{)412}$  19. $69\overline{)293}$  20. $97\overline{)381}$

If the answer makes sense, write *correct*. If not, give the correct answer. *(pages 310–311)*

21. A plane holds 360 people. There are 60 rows in the plane. How many people are in each row?
*Answer:* 60 people

Divide. *(pages 312–317)*

22. $20\overline{)480}$  23. $60\overline{)668}$  24. $40\overline{)860}$  25. $50\overline{)750}$  26. $30\overline{)659}$

27. $48\overline{)690}$  28. $37\overline{)953}$  29. $23\overline{)495}$  30. $18\overline{)627}$  31. $62\overline{)943}$

32. $63\overline{)789}$  33. $47\overline{)798}$  34. $28\overline{)612}$  35. $68\overline{)964}$  36. $38\overline{)491}$

37. $34\overline{)509}$  38. $37\overline{)943}$  39. $53\overline{)838}$  40. $27\overline{)888}$  41. $19\overline{)456}$

42. $46\overline{)987}$  43. $32\overline{)625}$  44. $41\overline{)817}$  45. $29\overline{)892}$  46. $37\overline{)798}$

47. $32\overline{)683}$  48. $18\overline{)424}$  49. $49\overline{)583}$  50. $38\overline{)856}$  51. $23\overline{)624}$

52. $38\overline{)786}$  53. $19\overline{)394}$  54. $22\overline{)406}$  55. $27\overline{)884}$  56. $14\overline{)511}$

Simplify the problem. Solve. *(pages 318–319)*

57. Nora sold 38 books at a book sale. Each book cost $3.25. How much money did Nora make selling books?

Estimate the answer. *(pages 320–321)*

58. $3\overline{)218}$  59. $6\overline{)550}$  60. $3\overline{)172}$  61. $8\overline{)322}$  62. $4\overline{)814}$

63. $7\overline{)199}$  64. $9\overline{)824}$  65. $7\overline{)621}$  66. $27\overline{)614}$  67. $38\overline{)740}$

68. $36\overline{)178}$  69. $42\overline{)232}$  70. $27\overline{)158}$  71. $19\overline{)177}$  72. $33\overline{)264}$

FOR USE AFTER CHECKPOINT 1

Write the fraction for the shaded part.  *(pages 330–333)*

1.      2.      3.      4.

Write a number sentence to show equivalent fractions.  *(pages 334–335)*

5.      6.

Write in lowest terms. *(pages 336–337)*

7. $\frac{4}{8}$     8. $\frac{3}{12}$     9. $\frac{6}{8}$     10. $\frac{4}{16}$

Write as a mixed number in lowest terms.  *(pages 338–339)*

11. $\frac{9}{7}$     12. $\frac{10}{6}$     13. $\frac{12}{8}$     14. $\frac{14}{6}$

Measure to the nearest quarter inch.  *(pages 340–341)*

15. _____

Solve.  *(pages 342–343)*

16. A game has 3 yellow cubes and 2 orange cubes. Mary picks a cube without looking. What is the probability that she gets an orange cube?

17. A bag contains 5 red marbles and 6 blue marbles. James picks a marble without looking. What is the probability that he gets a red marble?

FOR USE AFTER CHECKPOINT 2

Add or subtract. Write the answer in lowest terms.  *(pages 346–349, 354–357)*

1. $\frac{5}{8}$ $+\frac{1}{8}$
2. $\frac{3}{6}$ $+\frac{1}{6}$
3. $\frac{8}{10}$ $-\frac{4}{10}$
4. $\frac{9}{12}$ $-\frac{5}{12}$
5. $\frac{1}{3}$ $+\frac{1}{5}$
6. $\frac{2}{7}$ $+\frac{3}{14}$
7. $\frac{8}{9}$ $-\frac{2}{3}$

Compare the fractions. Write <, >, or = .  *(pages 350–353)*

8. $\frac{3}{5}$ ▨ $\frac{2}{5}$     9. $\frac{2}{7}$ ▨ $\frac{4}{7}$     10. $\frac{1}{3}$ ▨ $\frac{1}{4}$     11. $\frac{3}{5}$ ▨ $\frac{3}{10}$     12. $\frac{3}{7}$ ▨ $\frac{3}{14}$

Use the graph to answer the question. *(pages 358–359)*

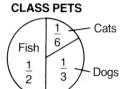

**CLASS PETS**

13. What is the most common pet?

14. What is the least common pet?

424

FOR USE AFTER THE CHAPTER TEST

Write the fraction for the shaded part.  *(pages 330–333)*

1.     2.     3.     4.

Write a number sentence to show equivalent fractions.  *(pages 334–335)*

5.

Write in lowest terms. *(pages 336–337)*

6. $\frac{6}{16}$    7. $\frac{6}{12}$    8. $\frac{9}{12}$    9. $\frac{4}{10}$

Write as a mixed number in lowest terms.  *(pages 338–339)*

10. $\frac{15}{9}$    11. $\frac{21}{6}$    12. $\frac{18}{10}$    13. $\frac{10}{8}$

Measure to the nearest quarter inch.  *(pages 340–341)*

14. _____

Add or subtract. Write the answer in lowest terms.  *(pages 346–349)*

15. $\frac{2}{8}$ $+\frac{4}{8}$    16. $\frac{3}{10}$ $+\frac{5}{10}$    17. $\frac{4}{12}$ $+\frac{6}{12}$    18. $\frac{5}{6}$ $-\frac{3}{6}$    19. $\frac{7}{9}$ $-\frac{4}{9}$    20. $\frac{9}{12}$ $-\frac{6}{12}$

Compare the fractions. Write $<$, $>$, or $=$ .  *(pages 350–353)*

21. $\frac{5}{8}$ ▨ $\frac{8}{8}$    22. $\frac{3}{8}$ ▨ $\frac{1}{4}$    23. $\frac{1}{2}$ ▨ $\frac{3}{5}$    24. $\frac{2}{3}$ ▨ $\frac{3}{4}$    25. $\frac{3}{8}$ ▨ $\frac{6}{16}$    26. $\frac{4}{5}$ ▨ $\frac{13}{15}$

Add or subtract. Write the answer in lowest terms.  *(pages 354–357)*

27. $\frac{2}{5}$ $+\frac{4}{10}$    28. $\frac{2}{8}$ $+\frac{1}{3}$    29. $\frac{3}{5}$ $+\frac{3}{10}$    30. $\frac{4}{5}$ $-\frac{3}{10}$    31. $\frac{6}{7}$ $-\frac{5}{14}$    32. $\frac{2}{3}$ $-\frac{1}{2}$

Solve.  *(pages 342–343)*

33. Diana has 5 blue pencils and 3 red pencils. She picks one without looking. What is the probability that she gets a blue pencil?

Use the graph to answer the question. *(pages 358–359)*

34. What is the most favored fruit?

35. What is the least favored fruit?

**FAVORITE FRUIT**

FOR USE AFTER CHECKPOINT 1
Match the congruent figures. Write the letter.   *(pages 370–373)*

1.    2.    3. 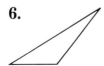        A.    B.   C.

Choose the figure that is similar. Write the letter.   *(pages 374–377)*

4.    5.   6.         A.   B.   C.

What is the area?   *(pages 378–383)*

7.        8.            9. 5 m  6 m          10. 8 m  9 m

Each ☐ = 3 square meters

FOR USE AFTER CHECKPOINT 2
Name the figure.   *(pages 384–387)*

1.   2.   3.   4.   5.   6.

What is the volume in cubic
centimeters?   *(pages 388–389)*

7. 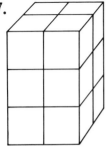       8.

What is the volume?
*(pages 390–391)*

9. 3 m  2 m  7 m       10. 2 m  4 m  6 m

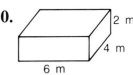

Write *p*, *a*, or *v* to indicate
whether the problem
asks you to find perimeter, area, or volume.
Then solve.   *(pages 392–393)*

11. How much soil does the box hold?

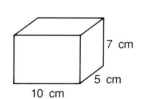

7 cm  5 cm  10 cm

2

FOR USE AFTER THE CHAPTER TEST

Match the congruent figures. Write the letter.
*(pages 370–373)*

**1.**    **2.**    **3.**         **A.**    **B.**    **C.**

Choose the figure that is similar. Write the letter.
*(pages 374–375)*

**4.**    **5.**    **6.**         **A.**    **B.**   **C.**

What is the area?  *(pages 378–383)*

**7.**    **8.** 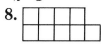   **9.**  2 m
4 m   **10.** 5 m
8 m

Each ☐ = 5 square meters.

Name the figure.  *(pages 384–387)*

**11.**    **12.**    **13.** 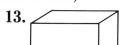   **14.**    **15.**   **16.**

What is the volume in cubic
centimeters?  *(pages 388–389)*

**17.** 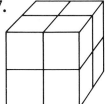   **18.**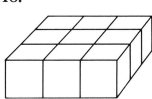

What is the volume?
*(pages 390–391)*

**19.**  2 m
4 m
5 m   **20.**  7 m
2 m  4 m

Write *p*, *a*, or *v* to indicate whether
the problem asks you to find perimeter,
area, or volume. Then solve.  *(pages 392–393)*

**21.** How much fence is needed for this garden?

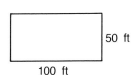 50 ft
100 ft

# USING MENTAL MATH STRATEGIES

Sometimes you can use mental mathematics to solve problems. You may be doubling a recipe in cooking, building a birdhouse, or counting change in a store. You use mental math to find an exact answer without using pencil and paper or a calculator. In this book strategies for mental math are used that will help you improve your skills. Here are some examples.

**Counting On and Back**

The change from a five dollar bill for $3.65 is counted on as:

| 1 dime | 1 quarter | 1 dollar |
|--------|-----------|----------|
| $3.75 | $4.00 | $5.00 |

**Using Facts**

If you forget $9 \times 8$, you can think that $8 \times 8 = 64$. Then, one more 8 gives $9 \times 8$, or 72.

**Comparing and Ordering**

To compare the numbers 3497 and 3274, mentally compare the thousands to see if they are the same. Then, compare the hundreds. Since 4 hundreds > 2 hundreds, 3497 > 3274.

**Using Properties**

To multiply $5 \times 7 \times 2$, you can think $5 \times 2 = 10$ and $10 \times 7 = 70$. The product is 70.

**Using Patterns**

$3 \times 5 = 15$      This pattern helps us know that
$3 \times 50 = 150$     $3 \times 5000 = 15,000$.
$3 \times 500 = 1500$

**Using Visual Images**

You can think of $\frac{7}{8}$ as a pizza divided into 8 pieces of the same size with one piece missing.

**Changing Numbers and Operations**

To subtract 250 from 589, you can think $500 - 200 = 300$, $89 - 50 = 39$. So, the difference is 339.

To divide 640 by 8, you can think that $8 \times 80 = 640$, so $640 \div 8 = 80$.

To add 36 and 48, you can think of 48 as $50 - 2$. Then, $36 + 50 = 86$. Subtract 2 to get 84. The sum is 84.

To change 4 ft to inches, multiply 12 by 4.

$4 \times 12 = 48$, so 4 ft = 48 in.

# USING ESTIMATION STRATEGIES

Sometimes you may not need an exact answer, and an estimate will do. Each person develops a personal style of estimation to use in practical situations such as shopping, figuring the time needed to complete a job, or walking to a friend's house. In this book, strategies for estimation are used that should help you in using math in everyday life. Here are some examples.

**Rounding**  The teacher said that there were exactly 78 days on which it snowed this year. Jane rounded 78 to the greatest place value as 80.

The two problems at the right show the exact and estimated differences between 763 and 250. The estimate shows that the exact answer is reasonable.

| | *exact* | *estimate* |
|---|---|---|
| | 763 | 800 |
| | − 250 | − 300 |
| | 513 | 500 |

**Comparing**  $9 \times 16$ is less than 160 because $10 \times 16 = 160$ and 9 is less than 10.

To estimate $4735 + 2893$, you can round to $5000 + 3000$. The answer is less than 8000, because you rounded up.

**Using Compatible Numbers**  To estimate $126 \div 6$, you can think $120 \div 6$, or 20. You found this estimate by thinking of the fact $12 \div 6$.

**Using Clustering**  To estimate the average of the scores 22, 21, and 18, notice that all three scores are about 20. The average is about 20.

**Using Measurement**  The key measures about $2\frac{1}{2}$ in. to the nearest half inch.

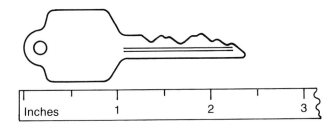

Of the following, the best estimate for the weight of a loaf of bread is 1 lb.

1 oz      1 lb      20 lb

You can estimate what part of the paper is colored. Think of dividing the paper into parts of about the same size. There would be six parts in all. Five parts are colored. That's $\frac{5}{6}$ of the paper.

**Sampling and Predicting**

There are about 50 marbles in section A. Sections B and C are about the same size. So, there are about $3 \times 50 = 150$ marbles in the jar.

# USING A CALCULATOR

Every calculator is different. You should read the instructions for your calculator to learn how to use it. Most calculators have the keys (buttons) pictured below, but they may be in different places.

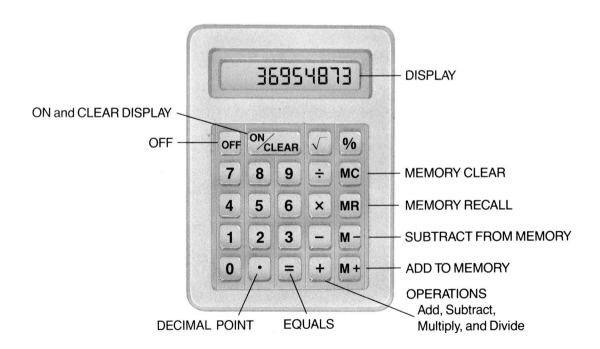

The Display    A calculator display usually does not show commas. Usually 8 digits is the most the display will show. A display never shows a dollar sign. You must press the decimal point key to show a decimal number. You press the clear key to remove the display.

The Memory    You can add the same number to several other numbers by using
Feature    the memory keys.

Add 36 to each of these numbers:    9, 29, 58.

| Press | Display |
|-------|---------|
| ③ ⑥ | 36 |
| Ⓜ₊ | 36$^M$ |
| ⑨ ⊞ | 9$^M$ |
| MR | 36$^M$ |
| ⊜ | 45$^M$ |
| ② ⑨ ⊞ | 29$^M$ |
| MR | 36$^M$ |
| ⊜ | 65$^M$ |
| ⑤ ⑧ ⊞ | 58$^M$ |
| MR | 36$^M$ |
| ⊜ | 94$^M$ |

So, 9 + 36 = 45, 29 + 36 = 65, 58 + 36 = 94

The Constant    On many calculators the equals key is also a constant key. This
Feature    means you can press the equals key to perform an operation with the same numbers over and over again. For example, you can count by twos on the calculator.

| Press | Display |
|-------|---------|
| ② | 2 |
| ⊞ | 2 |
| ⊜ | 4 |
| ⊜ | 6 |
| ⊜ | 8 |
| ⊜ | 10 |

The calculator is adding 2 each time you press the equals key.

431

For each problem, choose the method you think is best: calculator, mental math, or estimation. Write C, M, or E. Then solve the problem using that method.

**Chapter 1**

**1.** $9 + 4 + 1 + 6 = $

**2.** Order the numbers from least to greatest.

36,825    36,285    36,528

**3.** Will the difference be greater than, less than, or the same as the number with which you started?    $13 - 4$

**4.** Myra sold 48 tickets to the Jazz Jamboree. Leo sold 38 tickets. Who sold about 50 tickets?

**Chapter 2**

**1.** Rounded to the greatest place value, $26,278 + 10,469$ is about

**2.** $66,428 - 28,769 = $

**3.** Nancy bought a sweater for $11.95, a purse for $10.80, and a pair of shoes for $13.15. Did she pay more than $30.00 for the three items?

**4.** Len paid $4.78 for a bicycle tire. He gave the clerk $10.00. How much change did he receive?

**Chapter 3**

**1.** The length of your shoe is about      cm.

**2.** $7 \text{ kg} = $      g

**3.** Today is Wednesday, June 2. Two weeks and two days from now is graduation day. When is graduation?

**4.** Barry ran 4800 m on Monday, 5500 m on Wednesday, and 3250 m on Friday. What was the total distance that Barry ran?

**Chapter 4**

1. Complete the pattern.

    7, 14, 21, 28, 35, ▦ , ▦ , ▦ , ▦ , ▦

2. Is the product of 7 and 9 greater than, less than, or equal to 50?

3. Ray plans to wear a jacket and a hat when he goes to school. He has 2 jackets and 3 hats. How many different outfits can Ray have?

4. Lenora walks 8 dogs for 7 minutes each the first day. The second day she walks 9 dogs for 8 minutes each. On the second day does she walk more, less, or the same amount as on the first day?

**Chapter 5**

1. Is $56 \div 9$ between 5 and 6 or between 6 and 7?

2. Write $<$ , $>$ , or $=$ .

    $8 \div 8$ ▦ $4 \div 4$

3. Helen bought 67 plants for her garden. Each row is to have 7 plants. Does she have enough plants for 10 rows?

4. A canoe trip up a river took 4 hours and 26 minutes. The trip back down took 3 hours and 10 minutes. How long did the trip take altogether?

**Chapter 6**

1. Is $9 \times 3173$ greater than, less than, or equal to 27,000?

2. What is the product of $8 \times 7856$?

3. During her trip to Los Angeles, Ellen Carter spent $26.72 for gasoline, $38.85 for food, and $28.92 for a room. About how much did she spend on the trip?

4. The produce truck to Yosemite is carrying 2650 cartons of fruit drink. Each carton contains 8 cans. How many cans will be delivered to Yosemite?

**Chapter 7**

1. $148 \div 4 =$ ▦

2. Is $85 \div 9$ between 8 and 9 or between 9 and 10?

3. Joe spent $8.34 on 6 qt of oil. How much did each quart cost?

4. Miguel spent $9.85 for 5 model airplanes. About how much did each airplane cost?

433

For each problem, choose the method you think is best: calculator, mental math, or estimation. Write C, M, or E. Then solve the problem using that method.

**Chapter 8**

**1.** Is 38.95 − 16.82 < 20?

**2.** Order the decimals from greatest to least.

7.6, 0.8, 8.2, 6.8

**3.** Lila has a ten dollar bill and a five dollar bill. She wants to buy two cans of paint for $6.95 each. Does she have enough money?

**4.** Peter had a ten dollar bill and a five dollar bill. He bought two shirts for $6.95 each. How much money did he get back?

**Chapter 9**

**1.** Is a right angle always greater than an obtuse angle?

**2.** The diameter of a circle is 18 cm. Is the radius less than 18 cm?

**3.** What is the perimeter of the rectangle at the right?

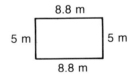

8.8 m
5 m    5 m
8.8 m

**4.** Is the perimeter of the square at the right greater than, less than, or equal to 25 cm?

4.5 cm
4.5 cm    4.5 cm
4.5 cm

**Chapter 10**

**1.** Is 2 × 250 less than, greater than, or equal to 20 × 25?

**2.** 48 × 879 =

**3.** A baseball costs $2.79. An average of 70 baseballs are used in a major league game. About how much is spent on baseballs in each game?

**4.** Rodolfo bought 8 tennis rackets for $39.95 each. He gave two to each of the school's tennis teams. How much did Rodolfo spend for the rackets?

**Chapter 11**

1. $630 \div 30 = $ ▓

2. Is $820 \div 90$ closer to 9 or to 10?

3. Manny packs 26 oranges in each box. If he has a pile of 728 oranges, how many boxes does he pack?

4. Heidi packs 28 apples in each box. She has 1000 apples to pack. Will she need more than 30 boxes?

**Chapter 12**

1. Write the fraction in lowest terms.　$\frac{416}{832}$

2. Which is closer to 2, $\frac{17}{8}$ or $\frac{18}{8}$?

3. Donna takes 3 jumps in a row. She jumps a distance of $4\frac{1}{3}$ ft each time. Does she jump more than 12 ft in all?

4. What is the difference between $\frac{7}{9}$ and $\frac{2}{9}$?

**Chapter 13**

1. Turn a square. Has its area changed?

2. Do either of the squares at the right have an area that is less than 20 square centimeters?

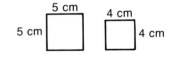

3. Think of a square. How many lines of symmetry does it have?

4. Look at the square and the rectangle below. Which has the greater area?

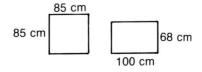

# TABLE OF NUMBERS

|    | A    | B    | C    | D    | E    | F    | G              | H              |
|----|------|------|------|------|------|------|----------------|----------------|
| 1  | 7    | 7    | 75   | 69   | 0.3  | 0.5  | $\frac{1}{4}$  | $\frac{3}{4}$  |
| 2  | 7    | 8    | 98   | 84   | 0.8  | 0.9  | $\frac{1}{2}$  | $\frac{3}{8}$  |
| 3  | 7    | 9    | 36   | 42   | 2.5  | 1.7  | $\frac{5}{6}$  | $\frac{1}{3}$  |
| 4  | 8    | 8    | 73   | 66   | 4.2  | 8.0  | $1\frac{1}{2}$ | $4\frac{1}{2}$ |
| 5  | 8    | 9    | 52   | 79   | 3.8  | 2.9  | 4              | $2\frac{1}{2}$ |
| 6  | 18   | 17   | 69   | 213  | 2847 | 1001 | 88¢            | 79¢            |
| 7  | 2    | 9    | 447  | 598  | 1562 | 1065 | 45¢            | 36¢            |
| 8  | 39   | 13   | 78   | 203  | 3851 | 4013 | 19¢            | 64¢            |
| 9  | 15   | 74   | 365  | 287  | 5101 | 5011 | $7.00          | $8.25          |
| 10 | 11   | 16   | 608  | 496  | 8913 | 9400 | $4.80          | $5.90          |
| 11 | 45   | 8    | 340  | 701  | 1415 | 908  | $7.60          | $3.90          |
| 12 | 55   | 65   | 75   | 85   | 95   | 105  | $5.20          | $.69           |
| 13 | 900  | 1000 | 1100 | 1200 | 1300 | 1400 | $2.35          | $.85           |
| 14 | 2100 | 3100 | 4100 | 5100 | 6100 | 7100 | $1.02          | $.89           |

Ideas for using this table for mental math, estimation, and calculator activities are found under *Computation Strategies* on the Cumulative Review pages at the end of each chapter of the Teacher's Edition.

# PROBLEM SOLVING ACTIVITIES

## CHAPTER 1

Keep a record for one school week. Write the number of hours spent daily on each of the activities shown in the chart below. At the end of the week, study your results.

| ACTIVITY | HOURS SPENT EACH DAY | | | | |
|---|---|---|---|---|---|
| | M | T | W | T | F |
| School | | | | | |
| Homework | | | | | |
| Play | | | | | |
| Television | | | | | |
| Sleep | | | | | |

- At which activity do you spend the most time?

- Are the number of hours spent for each activity the same or different each day?

- Work with a partner and compare charts. Describe how they are alike or different.

## CHAPTER 2

Do you know what the number printed on a light bulb means? It shows the number of watts, or power, of the bulb. A 100-watt bulb gives a brighter light than a 60-watt bulb. It also uses more electricity.

Try this activity to see how many watts of power are in the light bulbs used in your home.

- Make a list of all the light bulbs and the number of watts for each. Don't forget the refrigerator bulb!

- How many watts of electricity would be in use if all the lights were on at once?

- List some ways to help lower the electric bill. Discuss your list with a partner.

Work with a partner. Take turns. Use the information from the map and train schedule to write two word problems.

Ask your partner to solve your word problems. Be sure to check the answers!

| TRAIN SCHEDULE | |
|---|---|
| Stanton | Lv. 6:25 A.M. |
| Danvers | Arr. 7:32 A.M. |
| Philipstown | Arr. 8:51 A.M. |
| Ashton | Arr. 9:49 A.M. |
| Elden | Arr. 10:53 A.M. |
| Stanton | Arr. 11:59 A.M. |

CHAPTER 4

The insurance company wants to know how many miles your family's car is driven each year.

- Design a chart that you could use to figure out your mileage for one week.

- How can you use this information to estimate the yearly mileage for the car?

- What changes in the weekly schedule should you think about when you are estimating yearly mileage?

# CHAPTER 5

You have been collecting pennies in a huge glass jar for a year. The jar is completely full. You want to wrap the pennies in rolls of 100 to take them to the bank.

How would you count the pennies? How would you decide how many paper wraps you need?

- Decide on a plan. Write out your plan.

- Work with a partner. Compare your plans. Which do you think will help you count the pennies faster? Why?

# CHAPTER 6

You and your partner are planning how to cover the three windows in your new room. You can spend up to $100 on window coverings. Use the information in the picture below to help you decide what to do.

- Decide how you would like to cover your windows. Draw a picture to show what you would do.

- What would the total cost be? Do you have enough money? Adjust your plan if you don't.

- Compare your plan with another group's. Discuss how you planned your rooms.

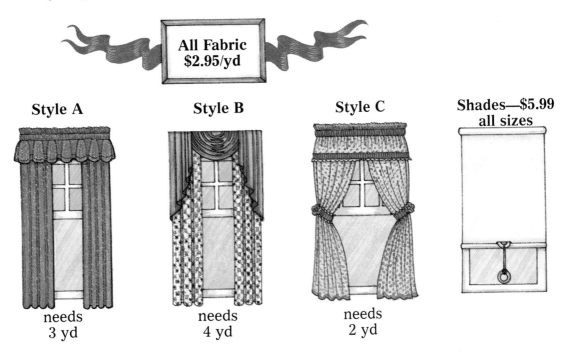

**All Fabric $2.95/yd**

Style A — needs 3 yd

Style B — needs 4 yd

Style C — needs 2 yd

Shades—$5.99 all sizes

Your class is going on a picnic. Work with a group to discuss these questions about the food for the picnic.

- How many sandwiches can you make from one can of tuna? How many sandwiches will you need to make?

- How much of each of the other items on the menu do you think each person will eat or drink?

- You are in charge of buying the food for the picnic. Make a shopping list. What food items will you need to buy? How many or how much of each item will you buy?

Louis's older sister earns $15 each week. She uses the money for things she needs, such as school lunches, and for fun things, such as seeing a movie. She'd like to save some money each week to buy a new radio.

Suppose you were Louis's older sister. Make a plan, or *budget*, for using your money.

- Decide how much you would like to save each week. Then figure out how much of your allowance is left.

- Make a list of how you plan to spend the rest of your allowance. Do you have enough money to cover these expenses? How can you adjust your list if you do not?

## CHAPTER 9

A new boy in your class lives on your street. He asks you to draw a map that shows how to get to school from your street.

Use graph paper to draw the map. Draw lines to show the streets. Write the names of the streets that he will need to know.

Ask a partner to write out directions from your street to your school, using your map. Do the map and directions match?

## CHAPTER 10

A friend is going to take care of your cat during your vacation this summer. You need to buy a month's supply of cat food and litter at FIFI's.

- Ask someone who owns a cat how much food and litter you will need for a week. Take notes to keep track of what you need.

- Use the prices shown on FIFI's sign. Plan how you will find the amount of food and litter you will need for a month.

- Find the total cost for the food and litter.

## CHAPTER 11

Your school puts on a play every year. The principal took photographs at the play.

There are about 150 photographs. The principal of your school wants you to put the photos in albums. She needs to know how many albums to buy.

Work with a partner. What kind of research will you need to do to find out the number of albums she should buy?

Write down your plan. Then find the number of albums the principal should buy.

# CHAPTER 12

You can use your feet to help you measure!

• By placing one foot in front of the other over and over again, measure the length and width of your classroom. Try to measure to the nearest half foot.

• Now measure the actual length and width in feet and inches.

• Compare the results. How close are they? Can you think of a reason why some are closer than others?

# CHAPTER 13

If you flattened out a cube, you might get one of several different shapes. Two are shown below.

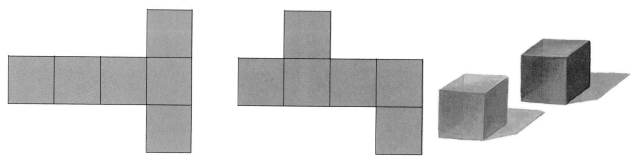

Work with a partner. Collect several boxes that have different shapes and sizes.

• Try to imagine what each box would look like if it were flattened out. Each of you draw a picture of your own to show this.

• Compare your drawings with your partner's. Are they always the same? Should they be?

• Now work together and actually cut the boxes to flatten them. Do they have the same shape as your drawings? If not could you have cut the boxes differently to make their flattened shapes match your drawings? How?

# GLOSSARY

## A

**acute angle** (p. 252) An angle less than a right angle.

**addend** (p. 2) A number added to another number. In the problem $5 + 4 = 9$, 5 and 4 are addends.

**angle** (p. 252) A figure formed by two rays that have a common endpoint. The picture shows angle *CAB* or angle *BAC*.

**area** (p. 378) The number of square units that fit inside a figure.

**average** (p. 210) The quotient found by dividing the sum of a group of numbers by the number of addends.

## B

**bar graph** (p. 26) A picture that uses bars to show information.

## C

**Celsius** (p. 86) The metric temperature scale that measures the freezing point as 0 degrees and the boiling point as 100 degrees.

**center of a circle** (p. 266) The point that is the same distance from all points on the circle.

**centimeter** (cm) (p. 78) A metric unit of length. 100 cm = 1 m

**circle** (p. 266) A figure, such as this one, made up of points that are all the same distance from the center point.

**circle graph** (p. 358) A circle divided into parts to show numbers.

**closed figure** (p. 272) A figure with an inside and an outside.

**common denominator** (p. 352) A common multiple of two or more denominators.

**common factor** (p. 150) A number that is a factor of two or more numbers. 4 is a common factor of 12 and 16.

**common multiple** (p. 120) A number that is a multiple of two or more numbers. 12 is a common multiple of 2, 3, 4, and 6.

**concave** (p. 273) These are concave figures.

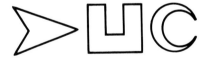

**cone** (p. 386) A figure in space with one flat circular face and one vertex.

**congruent** (p. 372) Having the same size and shape.

**convex** (p. 273) These are convex figures.

**cube** (p. 384) A figure in space with six square faces, all the same size.

**cubic centimeter** (p. 388) A metric unit used to measure volume.

**cup** (c) (p. 90) A U.S. Customary unit of capacity. 2 c = 1 pt

**cylinder** (p. 386) A figure in space with two flat circular faces and no vertexes.

## D

**decimal** (p. 222) A number that uses a decimal point to show tenths and hundredths. The numbers 0.2 and 1.76 are decimals.

**degree** (°) (p. 86) A standard unit for measuring temperature.

**denominator** (p. 330) The denominator in the fraction $\frac{2}{3}$ is 3.

**diameter** (p. 266) The distance across a circle through its center. Segment $AB$ is a diameter of the circle.

**difference** (p. 8) The answer in subtraction. In the number sentence 15 − 6 = 9, 9 is the difference.

**digit** (p. 14) The symbol 0, 1, 2, 3, 4, 5, 6, 7, 8, or 9.

**dividend** (p. 132) The number that is divided by another number. In the number sentence 18 ÷ 2 = 9, 18 is the dividend.

**divisor** (p. 132) A number that is divided into another number. In the number sentence 18 ÷ 2 = 9, 2 is the divisor.

## E

**edge** (p. 384) The segment formed when two faces of a figure in space meet.

**equivalent fractions** (p. 334) Fractions that have the same value. $\frac{2}{4}$ and $\frac{1}{2}$ are equivalent fractions.

**estimate** (p. 38) An answer that is not exact.

**even number** (p. 120) A number that is a multiple of 2. The number 0 is even.

**expanded form** (p. 14) The expanded form of 378 is 300 + 70 + 8.

## F

**face** (p. 384) A flat side of a figure in space.

**fact family** (p. 10) Related facts such as 3 + 4 = 7, 7 − 3 = 4, 4 + 3 = 7, and 7 − 4 = 3.

**factor** (p. 102) A number to be multiplied. In the number sentence 2 × 6 = 12, 2 and 6 are factors.

**Fahrenheit** (p. 92) The U.S. Customary temperature scale that measures the freezing point as 32 degrees and the boiling point as 212 degrees.

**flip** (p. 370) The second figure is a flip of the first figure.

**foot** (ft) (p. 88) A U.S. Customary unit of length. 1 ft = 12 in.

**fraction** (p. 330) A number that shows part of a whole or part of a group. $\frac{1}{2}$, $\frac{6}{10}$, $\frac{1}{3}$ are fractions.

## G

**gallon** (gal) (p. 90) A U.S. Customary unit of capacity. 1 gal = 4 qt

**gram** (g) (p. 82) A metric unit of mass. 1000 g = 1 kg

**greatest common factor** (p. 156) The greatest number that is a factor of two or more numbers. The greatest common factor of 8 and 12 is 4.

**grid** (p. 256) Parallel and perpendicular line segments on which points are plotted.

**Grouping Property of Addition** (p. 4) Changing the grouping of the addends does not change the sum.
Example: (3 + 6) + 2 = 11,
3 + (6 + 2) = 11
so (3 + 6) + 2 = 3 + (6 + 2)

**Grouping Property of Multiplication** (p. 110) Changing the grouping of the factors does not change the product.

Example: $(3 \times 2) \times 4 = 24$
$3 \times (2 \times 4) = 24$
so $(3 \times 2) \times 4 = 3 \times (2 \times 4)$

## I

**inch** (in.) (p. 88) A U.S. Customary unit of length. 12 in. = 1 ft

## K

**kilogram** (kg) (p. 82) A metric unit of mass. 1 kg = 1000g

**kilometer** (km) (p. 80) A metric unit of length. 1 km = 1000 m

## L

**least common multiple** (p. 362) The least multiple of two or more numbers. The least common multiple of 6 and 10 is 30.

**line** (p. 250) A straight path that goes on and on in both directions.

**line graph** (p. 212) A picture that uses a line to show changes in data.

**line of symmetry** (p. 368) A line that divides a figure into two matching parts.

**liter** (L) (p. 84) A metric unit of capacity. 1 L = 1000 mL

**lowest terms** (p. 336) When the numerator and the denominator cannot be divided by a factor greater than 1. You write $\frac{3}{6}$ in lowest terms as $\frac{1}{2}$.

## M

**meter** (m) (p. 80) A metric unit used to measure length. 1 m = 100 cm

**mile** (mi) (p. 88) A U.S. Customary unit of length. 1 mi = 5280 ft

**milliliter** (mL) (p. 84) A metric unit of capacity. 1000 mL = 1 L

**mixed number** (p. 338) A whole number and a fraction. $2\frac{1}{2}$ is a mixed number.

**multiple** (p. 120) The product of a number and any other whole number. A multiple of 4 is 12.

## N

**number sentence** (p. 2) A statement that shows how numbers are related. $7 \times 2 = 14$ and $8 - 5 = 3$ are number sentences.

**numerator** (p. 330) The numerator in the fraction $\frac{2}{3}$ is 2.

## O

**obtuse angle** (p. 252) An angle greater than a right angle.

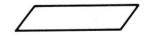

**odd number** (p. 120) A number that is not a multiple of 2.

**Order Property of Addition** (p. 4) Changing the order of the addends does not change the sum.

Example: $3 + 4 = 7$     $4 + 3 = 7$
so $3 + 4 = 4 + 3$

**Order Property of Multiplication** (p. 110) Changing the order of the factors does not change the product.

Example: $5 \times 3 = 15$     $3 \times 5 = 15$
so $5 \times 3 = 3 \times 5$

**ordered pair** (p. 256) A pair of numbers in which the order shows the location of a point on a grid. (4, 3) is an ordered pair.

**ordinal numbers** (p. 70) Numbers like first, second, third, and fourth that show the order of a set of things.

**ounce** (oz) (p. 90) A U.S. Customary unit of weight. 16 oz = 1 lb

## P

**parallel lines** (p. 254) Lines that never meet.

**parallelogram** (p. 262) A quadrilateral whose opposite sides are parallel.

**pentagon** (p. 260) A polygon with five sides.

**percent** (p. 244) Hundredths written with a % sign. Example: $83\% = \frac{83}{100} = 0.83$

**perimeter** (p. 264) The distance around a figure.

**perpendicular lines** (p. 254) Lines that form right angles.

**pictograph** (p. 172) A graph that uses pictures to show information.

**pint** (pt) (p. 90) A U.S. Customary unit of capacity. 1 pt = 2 c

**point** (p. 250) The figure below is called point A.

• A

**polygon** (p. 260) A figure whose sides are formed by three or more line segments.

**pound** (lb) (p. 90) A U.S. Customary unit of weight. 1 lb = 16 oz

**probability** (p. 342) The chance that something will happen.

**product** (p. 102) The answer in multiplication. In the number sentence 2 × 6 = 12, 12 is the product.

**Property of One** (p. 108) The product of one and any number is that number. Example: 1 × 9 = 9

**pyramid** (p. 384) A figure in space with one face that is a polygon and three or more faces that are triangles.

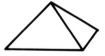

# Q

**quadrilateral** (p. 260) A polygon with four sides.

**quart** (qt) (p. 90) A U.S. Customary unit of capacity. 1 qt = 4 c

**quotient** (p. 132) The answer in division. In the number sentence 18 ÷ 2 = 9, 9 is the quotient.

# R

**radius** (p. 266) The distance from the center of a circle to a point on the circle. Segment OA is a radius of the circle.

**ray** (p. 250) Part of a line that starts at an endpoint and goes on and on in one direction. The picture shows ray AB.

**rectangle** (p. 262) A parallelogram with four right angles.

**rectangular prism** (p. 384) A figure in space with six faces whose opposite faces are congruent.

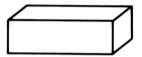

**remainder** (p. 148) The number left over when a division is complete.

**reptile** (p. 397) Small parts of a puzzle that have the same shape as the whole puzzle.

**right angle** (p. 252) An angle that looks like the corner of a page.

**Roman numerals** (p. 30) Symbols such as I, V, X, L, D, C, and M that the Romans used for numbers many years ago.

**round** (p. 22) To write a number to the nearest ten, hundred, thousand, and so on. 762 rounded to the nearest hundred is 800.

# S

**sample** (p. 324) Part of a group that is used for a survey.

**scale** (p. 382) The meaning of each unit in a scale drawing.

**scale drawing** (p. 382) A drawing of an object that is not actual size with a scale showing what each unit in the drawing means.

**segment** (p. 250) A straight path between two points. The picture shows segment *AB*.

A         B

**sides** (p. 260) The segments that make up a polygon.

**similar figures** (p. 374) Figures that are the same shape but are not necessarily the same size.

**slide** (p. 370) The second figure is a slide of the first figure.

**sphere** (p. 386) A figure in space, such as the one below, that has no flat faces and no vertexes.

**square** (p. 262) A rectangle with four sides the same length.

**square centimeter** (p. 378) A metric unit used to measure area.

**standard form** (p. 14) The usual, short form of a number. 573 is the standard form for 5 hundreds, 7 tens, and 3 ones.

**sum** (p. 2) The answer in addition. In the number sentence 5 + 4 = 9, 9 is the sum.

**survey** (p. 300) Information gathered by asking questions and recording answers.

## T

**temperature** (p. 86) A measure of heat.

**ton** (t) (p. 90) A U.S. Customary unit of weight. 1 t = 2000 lb

**tree diagram** (p. 112) A picture used to count the ways things can be combined.

**triangle** (p. 260) A polygon with three sides.

**turn** (p. 370) The second figure is a turn of the first figure.

## V

**variable** (p. 127) A letter that takes the place of a number.

**vertex** (pp. 252, 260, 384) The point at which two rays meet. The point at which two sides of a polygon or three or more edges of a figure in space meet.

**volume** (p. 388) The number of cubic units a figure contains.

## Y

**yard** (yd) (p. 88) A U.S. Customary unit of length. 1 yd = 3 ft

## Z

**Zero Property of Addition** (p. 2) The sum of zero and any number is that number. Example: 0 + 8 = 8

**Zero Property of Multiplication** (p. 108) The product of zero and any number is 0. Example: $0 \times 4 = 0$

**Zero Property of Subtraction** (p. 8) The difference of any number and zero is that number. The difference between any number and itself is zero. Example: 8 − 0 = 8   8 − 8 = 0

# INDEX

# CREDITS

er concept and photography by Lehman Millet Incorporated.

Cove page photography by Lehman Millet Incorporated.

Title mon Art Elements by Linda Phinney.

Com

## ILLUSTᴿATION

Lisa Adam ᴉs  108, 109, 136, 148, 149, 176, 177,
196, 1ᵁ ᵣ7, 200, 201, 208, 209, 230, 231, 234,
235, 28ᵗ ᵌ, 287, 310, 311, 318, 319, 338, 339,
346, 347, 348, 349, 370, 371

ANCO/BOST ON  27, 28, 86, 92, 112, 135, 160,
212, 213, 21ᵣ 4, 303, 330, 331, 334, 335, 338,
344, 345, 348ᵣ 350, 352, 354, 356, 358, 359,
360, 379

Alan Baker  17, 4ᵗ ᵌ, 47, 90, 91, 114, 115, 164, 165,
168, 169, 206, 20ᵣ 7, 212, 236, 237, 238, 239,
264, 265, 332, 333, 344, 345, 354, 355

Michael Blaser  126, 1ᵣ 127, 156, 157

Paul Breeden  395

Mindy Brooks  244 (bla ᵣk line art), 245 (black
line art), 361

Simon Galkin  29, 63, 155, 2ᵣ 43, 300, 301

Bob Giuliani  215

Deirdre Griffin  271, 272, 273

Judith Griffith  244 (4/c art), 245 (4/ᵣ ᶜ art), 324,
325

Diane Jaquith  210, 211

Meg Kelleher  185, 299

David Lindroth  323

Linda Phinney  20, 21, 26, 68, 100, 120, 121,
130, 202, 203, 225, 227, 229, 334, 335, 337,
384, 389, 391

Claudia Karabaic Sargent  233, 250, 251, 254,
256, 257, 437, 438, 439

Margaret Sanfilippo  96, 97

Carol Schwartz  4, 5, 8, 9, 10, 11, 14, 15, 18, 19,
22, 23, 25, 30, 31, 70, 71, 74, 76, 77, 78, 79, 80,
81, 82, 83, 84, 85, 86, 87, 88, 89, 92, 93, 132,
133, 134, 135, 138, 139, 140, 141, 142, 143,
146, 198, 199, 216, 217, 252, 253, 260,
262, 267, 268, 306, 307, 312, 313, 320,
321, 362, 363, 368, 372, 374, 375, 380, 381,
382, 383, 386, 387, 392, 393

Michael Paul Smith  40, 41, 42, 50, 51, 55, 122,
123, 144, 145, 172, 173, 174, 180, 181, 195,
240, 278, 279, 284, 285, 288, 295, 308, 309,
315, 352, 353, 358

Ruth Brunner-Strosser  38, 39, 44, 52, 53, 56,
57, 58, 102, 103, 104, 105, 110, 111, 113, 118,
125, 150, 151, 162, 166, 167, 170, 171, 182,
183, 222, 223, 282, 292, 293, 296, 297, 330,
331, 340, 341, 342, 343, 351, 356, 357, 440, 442

Sue Tsang  396, 397

Anne Sargent Walker  64, 65, 95, 186, 187

Cherie Wyman  2, 6, 12, 13, 36, 37, 48, 49, 106,
107, 116, 152, 290, 291

## PHOTOGRAPHY

ED BISHOP PHOTOGRAPHY  56, 60, 72, 136,
342

BLACK STAR  Christopher Henning  34;
Charles Moore  224;  James A. Sugar  305

FOCUS ON SPORTS
© 1983 David  Madison  294

Michal Heron  54, 204, 205, © 266

IMAGE BANK  © Andy Caufield  35;
Al Satterwhite  131

INDEX STONE  75, © 119, © 175

Susan Lapides  © 232

MAGNUM  © Burt Glinn  277

PHOTO RESEARCHERS  281, 317;
© Marie Breton  1;  Jack Fields  367;
ᴳ B. Grunzweig  117 (left);
ᵣ ᵁusan McCartney  161;  Hank Morgan  34

ᴾᶦCTURE CUBE  © Eric Roth  193;
THE Pᶦ ve Schaeffer  191
© Daᵣ NIAN INSTITUTION

SMITHSOᵣ pace Museum  314
© Aero Sᵣ ON  Bill E. Barnes  117 (top);

STOCK BOSTᵣ din  249;  John Lei  147;
Frederik Boᵣ chi  69;
Mike Mazzasᵣ 101, © 1981  221;
© Peter Menzeᵣ 78
George Riley  3ᵗ ᵣlfred Owczarzak  163

TAURUS PHOTOS  Aᵣ Dᵣon Mason  179

WEST STOCK  137ᵣ

WOODFIN CAMP ᵣ ASSOᵣCIATES
© Mike Yamaᵣhita  280

Gale Zucker  © ᵣ25

# TABLE OF NUMBERS

| | A | B | C | D | E | F | G | H |
|---|---|---|---|---|---|---|---|---|
| 1 | 7 | 7 | 75 | 69 | 0.3 | 0.5 | $\frac{1}{4}$ | $\frac{3}{4}$ |
| 2 | 7 | 8 | 98 | 84 | 0.8 | 0.9 | $\frac{1}{2}$ | $\frac{3}{8}$ |
| 3 | 7 | 9 | 36 | 42 | 2.5 | 1.7 | $\frac{5}{6}$ | $\frac{1}{3}$ |
| 4 | 8 | 8 | 73 | 66 | 4.2 | 8.0 | $1\frac{1}{2}$ | $4\frac{1}{2}$ |
| 5 | 8 | 9 | 52 | 79 | 3.8 | 2.9 | 4 | $2\frac{1}{2}$ |
| 6 | 18 | 17 | 69 | 213 | 2847 | 1001 | 88¢ | 79¢ |
| 7 | 2 | 9 | 447 | 598 | 1562 | 1065 | 45¢ | 36¢ |
| 8 | 39 | 13 | 78 | 203 | 3851 | 4013 | 19¢ | 64¢ |
| 9 | 15 | 74 | 365 | 287 | 5101 | 5011 | $7.00 | $8.25 |
| 10 | 11 | 16 | 608 | 496 | 8913 | 9400 | $4.80 | $5.90 |
| 11 | 45 | 8 | 340 | 701 | 1415 | 908 | $7.60 | $3.90 |
| 12 | 55 | 65 | 75 | 85 | 95 | 105 | $5.20 | $.69 |
| 13 | 900 | 1000 | 1100 | 1200 | 1300 | 1400 | $2.35 | $.85 |
| 14 | 2100 | 3100 | 4100 | 5100 | 6100 | 7100 | $1.02 | $.89 |

Ideas for using this table for mental math, estimation, and calculator activities are found under *Computation Strategies* on the Cumulative Review pages at the end of each chapter of the Teacher's Edition.